AIR FORCE BASE
1957–2017

ROCKETS
& MISSILES
OF VANDENBERG AFB

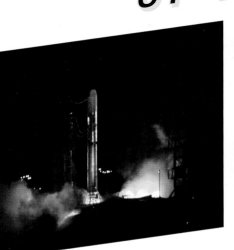

Joseph T. Page II

SCHIFFER MILITARY

4880 Lower Valley Road   Atglen, PA 19310

Copyright © 2019 by Joseph T. Page II

Library of Congress Control Number: 2018959397

Cover design by Molly Shields
Type set in Minion & Univers

ISBN: 978-0-7643-5679-7
Printed in China

Published by Schiffer Publishing, Ltd.
4880 Lower Valley Road
Atglen, PA 19310
Phone: (610) 593-1777; Fax: (610) 593-2002
E-mail: Info@schifferbooks.com
Web: www.schifferbooks.com

For our complete selection of fine books on this and related subjects, please
visit our website at www.schifferbooks.com. You may also write for
a free catalog.

Schiffer Publishing's titles are available at special discounts for bulk purchases
for sales promotions or premiums. Special editions, including personalized
covers, corporate imprints, and excerpts, can be created in large quantities for
special needs. For more information, contact the publisher.

We are always looking for people to write books on new and related subjects.
If you have an idea for a book, please contact us at
proposals@schifferbooks.com.

This book is dedicated to the men and women of the United States who have persevered to keep the hope of freedom alive from 1775 to the present day.

CONTENTS

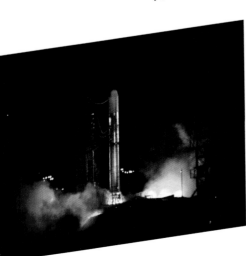

Acknowledgments

This book is a compilation of many documents created by the United States Air Force throughout the last sixty years, since Vandenberg Air Force Base was renamed and given the mission of developing and testing rockets and guided missiles. I would like to acknowledge the hard work of amateur, Air Force, and intelligence community historians over the last six decades in cataloging the information about these magnificent systems.

I would like to highlight the hard work of Air Force historians. Thanks to Ms. Shawn Riem, 30th Space Wing historian, for assisting me on the project. A warm "shout out" to Air Force Historical Research Agency personnel, especially Ms. Lynn Gamma, Ms. Cathy Cox, Ms. Marcie Green, Mr. Archie DiFante, Mr. Samuel Shearin, Mr. Carl Bailey, and Dr. Daniel Haulman. Through their tireless efforts over the last half decade, I was able to piece together this amazing historical story.

Also critical to the creation of this book was the "behind-the-scenes" hard work accomplished by the National Reconnaissance Office's Information Review and Release Group. Headed by Ms. Patricia Cameresi, her team has handled the brunt of my FOIA and MDR requests. To them, I can only say, "You've done your job protecting America's secrets." My thanks and appreciation on what you *have* declassified is sincere.

I would also like to give special recognition to Mr. Donald "Jay" Prichard, director of the Vandenberg Space and Missile Technology Center, SLC-10 "Pad Daddy," and all-around amazing guy. Through many hours of conversation, driving, and wandering around Vandenberg, he helped pull back and examine the layers of historical strata surrounding the base. Though the full story of Vandenberg may never be known, Jay Prichard has most volumes of that tale memorized. His constant companion Sage deserves fair mention here too, as SLC-10's resident guard dog and Mu-Q mooch. May she rest in peace.

Eternal thanks to the Air Force Office of Public Affairs Security and Policy Review Team, notably Ms. Devalee Gattison and her cadre of anonymous reviewers. Their diligent work helped me stay on the right side of the law with the book's focus area.

A virtual "high five" to the baristas who kept me in caffeine during the writing of this book: the Albuquerque team of Marcus, Avery, Sam, Daniel, Benji, Celestina, Charlotte, and Jarius at Satellite Coffee; Jacob, Jack, Jordan, and Cassandra at Starbucks Coffee; and Regina and Jessica at Jitters Coffee.

Special thanks to my reviewers: Esther Kenner, TSgt Stefan Mckinley, Jim Widlar, Jerry Little, Lt Col Douglas Carmean, Dr. Dwayne Day, Steve Cooke, Ben Wash, Shadow, Trace Lawrence, Peter Merlin, Dr. Jonathan McDowell, Michael Cassutt, Julius Sanks, Valkyrie, John Boyes, Jim Behling, Ted Morris, Lt Col Joe Iungerman, Paula Taylor, Scott Murdock, and Ian Robertson.

Finally, I would like to thank my family: My wife, Kim, my amazing children, and one fuzzy puppy dog. The numerous trips to Seal Beach and Abalone Beach with them were enough to imbue an indefatigable sense of wonder and love for the ocean.

CHAPTER 1:
A Brief History of Vandenberg Air Force Base

Author's Note: This is not an in-depth history of Vandenberg Air Force Base, Camp Cooke, Naval Missile Facility Point Arguello (NMFPA), or the surrounding area. Hundreds of military organizations have existed at this location over the last seven decades—too many to chronicle here. Readers are encouraged to contact the Air Force Historical Research Agency, Headquarters Air Force Space Command history office, or 30th Space Wing for more-broad-ranging historical information on the base and surrounding area.

During the 1930s, the central coast area that now defines Vandenberg Air Force Base was a quiet, agricultural area and ancestral homeland of the native Chumash people.[1] The nearby towns of Lompoc ("Lom-poke") and Santa Maria were country towns of a few thousand people, known for their agricultural prowess and stunning fields of flowers.[2] Along with the river valley, and spreading along the coastal plain to the ocean, Burton Mesa provided room for cattle and sheep grazing along the dry and windswept plateau.[3] Nearly ten years later, the specter of war would rouse these American communities into supporting the Allied effort against Nazi Germany and the Axis powers.[4]

Visitors to Vandenberg Air Force Base are greeted with "Welcome to Space Country" as they approach the garrison. Vandenberg's space and missile activities have supported the United States' national defense since the first launch in December 1958. *Author*

7

The area began its military association in 1941, when it was selected by the US Army for a $17 million construction project, building a training site for infantry and armored divisions.[5] Named Camp Cooke after Union Gen. Philip St. George Cooke, the camp trained three armored divisions, two infantry regiments, and thousands of men and women to take on the scourge of Nazism in Europe.[6] Camp Cooke remained in operation until 1946, when it was placed in caretaker status. Facilities were emptied, troops were demobilized and sent home, and the grounds were used by cattle and sheep farmers once more. When the Communist threat in Korea approached, the camp was reactivated briefly during the Korean War (1950–1953) to train infantry troops once more.[7] Soldiers stationed at Camp Cooke also participated in the early atomic atmospheric tests in Nevada

during Operation Buster-Jangle / Exercise DESERT ROCK in 1951.[8]

Inactivation of the camp and demobilization occurred yet again after the Korean War.[9] This time, the inactivation would be brief. The Soviet Union's burgeoning nuclear threat forced US military planners to seek the "high ground" for creating the defenses of the United States. Camp Cooke's geographic position along California's central coast allowed for the operational testing of intermediate-range ballistic missiles (IRBMs) and intercontinental ballistic missiles (ICBMs). Geographic advantages included year-round calm weather and access to an ocean for use as a test range, and the base also had the advantage of having an existing military infrastructure.[10] Missiles could be test-fired into the Pacific Ocean with no danger of falling on populated areas. Other

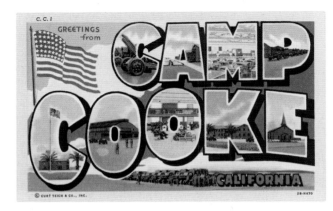

Printer Curt Teich created stylized postcards for many military installations during World War II. His company's unique designs used pronounced oversized letters and vivid colors. *Courtesy of Dianne Welch*

Camp Cooke was used by the US Army as an infantry and armor training center during World War II and the Korean War. The coastal hills provided a good location for weapons training, ranging from small arms to artillery. *Courtesy of the Lompoc Valley Historical Society*

Another Camp Cooke postcard highlights features of the installation, such as California Boulevard and the division headquarters building. Few if any buildings or infrastructure from the World War II era exist at Vandenberg today. *Courtesy of Dianne Welch*

Capt. Hoyt S. Vandenberg Jr. and his mother, Ms. Gladys Rose Vandenberg, inspect the main gate sign at the newly renamed Vandenberg Air Force Base. On 4 October 1958, Cooke AFB was renamed in honor of Gen. Hoyt S. Vandenberg, the Air Force's second chief of staff. *Courtesy of the United States Air Force*

Gen. Thomas D. White, United States Air Force chief of staff, gives the dedication address during the renaming ceremony of Vandenberg Air Force Base, California. *Courtesy of the United States Air Force*

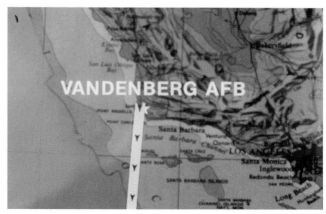

The southern launch direction from Vandenberg AFB was ideal for launch into polar orbit because the direction afforded the best possible downrange safety potential. This orbital track does not pass over any populated areas and does not overfly a landmass until Antarctica. *Courtesy of the National Reconnaissance Office*

factors that favored Camp Cooke were the isolation—providing an excellent safety buffer zone—and the proximity (via Highway 101) to ballistic missile manufacturers in Southern California.[11]

Additionally, by unique geographic quirk, the jut of land known as Point Arguello offered a launch site that could fire a rocket southward without crossing any land mass until Antarctica. This specific orbit, called a "polar orbit," gave complete worldwide coverage to a space vehicle flying along it, and originated an interesting offshoot of the space age: the advent of the photographic reconnaissance ("spy") satellite.[12]

In 1956, Secretary of Defense Charles Wilson directed that the northern portion of Camp Cooke be transferred to the USAF for missile development, specifically IRBMs and ICBMs. The southern portion of the base was transferred to the US Navy and renamed Naval Missile Facility, Point Arguello (NMFPA).[13] The US Army retained administration over the US Disciplinary Barracks near Lompoc.[14]

Groundbreaking activities for the future missile base began in May 1957, with the renaming of the facility as Cooke Air Force Base.[15] The installation was initially assigned to the Air Research and Development Command (ARDC), the major command overseeing the US ballistic missile effort. In April 1957, ARDC established the 392d Air Base Group at Cooke AFB, followed three months later by the activation of the 704th Strategic Missile Wing and the 1st Missile Division.[16] The $100 million buildup included a significant increase in the number of buildings, personnel, and equipment on base.[17] Aboveground missile launch complexes began appearing as construction equipment used tons of concrete and steel to remold the landscape.[18]

In his welcome letter to new personnel, Col. William Rader set the stage for Cooke AFB's critical mission:

Welcome to your new assignment to Cooke Air Force Base, the Nation's first Ballistic Missile Training Base. We are all aware that we stand on the threshold of an age of unusual military capabilities and here at Cooke we are pioneers in the creation of an operational capability with a weapons system which will contribute to the might of U. S. military strength.

Cooke Air Force Base is still in its infancy and, though it is developing rapidly, much work remains to be done. We are still faced with the many problems inherent in the rapid build-up of· a new type installation. The attainment of our goal presents many challenges, and we need the wholehearted enthusiasm and support of every member of our team for its ultimate achievement. We look to you for this kind of support.[19]

On 1 January 1958, management responsibilities for Cooke AFB were transferred from ARDC to the Strategic Air Command (SAC).[20] SAC also acquired three ARDC organizations responsible for reaching initial operational capability (IOC) for the operational nuclear missile force. In addition, SAC was directed to conduct training for missile launch crews, the men (and later women) in direct control of the missile complexes around the US.[21] Site activation tasks and research and development testing of ballistic missiles remained with ARDC. Space launches were to be conducted

A British Handley Page Victor flies over a Thor IRBM. As part of a US-UK agreement, Royal Air Force crews were trained on the Thor weapon system at Vandenberg. *Courtesy of the United States Air Force*

On the Strategic Air Command emblem, the mailed fist signifies strength and mastery of the art of war, while gripping both an olive branch, representing peace, and lightning bolts, signifying the power and speed of its forces. Vandenberg remained a SAC base from 1958 until 1991. *Courtesy of the Air Force Historical Research Agency*

jointly by both commands, utilizing the Cooke AFB and NMFPA launch and range facilities. Although the mission was now divided between the two commands, both SAC and ARDC maintained an integral relationship that was to blossom at Vandenberg over the next thirty-five years. Early assumptions about the base were that the missile mission would take priority:

It is expected there will be some space vehicle firings at the Pacific range. But the greater part of the operation will involve testing and training of crews using weapons.[22]

After only eighteen months as Cooke AFB, the base was renamed Vandenberg AFB on 4 October 1958[23] in honor of late Gen. Hoyt S. Vandenberg, second Air Force Chief of Staff.[24] Two months later, the first missile was launched from Vandenberg: a Thor IRBM on 16 December 1958.[25] This significant achievement was promptly followed by the successful launch of the world's first polar-orbiting satellite (Discoverer I) lifted into space by a Thor/Agena booster combination from Vandenberg on 28 February 1959.[26]

On 9 September 1959, the first Atlas ICBM launched by a SAC missile crew[27] marked the attainment of initial operational capability for the Atlas ICBM program. The

following month, America's first ICBM was placed on strategic alert at Vandenberg by the 576th Strategic Missile Squadron (576 SMS).[28]

While the Air Force and other agencies were launching space vehicles and missiles from Vandenberg, it became difficult to hide details of some classified missions, such as the time and day of the launch and booster vehicle. Newspaper articles would routinely mention the secret nature of the launches:

A secret satellite employing a Thor/Agena booster combination was launched from this west coast missile base yesterday, the Air Force said. Officials gave no other details.[29]

Launch failure notices would provide just as little information:

A piggyback satellite vehicle fired from here Thursday aboard an Atlas missile failed to go into orbit, an Air Force spokesman said today.[30]

And in rare cases, news sources would misidentify Vandenberg as the launch location:

President John F. Kennedy and CINCSAC Thomas Power watch the launch of Atlas 134D on 23 March 1962. This was the first time a president watched a live missile launch. *Courtesy of the United States Air Force*

The 392d Missile Training Squadron was activated on 15 September 1957 and later renamed the 392d Missile Training Squadron (IRBM). The unit was responsible for Thor IRBM training for Royal Air Force missile personnel until 1963. *Courtesy of the Air Force Historical Research Agency*

The first ICBM unit in the free world, the 576th Strategic Missile Squadron, placed the first ICBMs on alert at Vandenberg AFB on 31 October 1959. Their motto, "DUCIMUS," is Latin for "We Lead." *Courtesy of the Air Force Historical Research Agency*

The sprawling expanse of Sudden Ranch was added to the base in 1966 to provide a larger buffer zone for rocket launches from South Vandenberg. The land was acquired from the Sudden family through condemnation proceedings and a legal dispute. *Author*

A companion sentry satellite was expected to be fired into a 60,000–72,000-mile-high orbit today to join another Watchdog moonlet [Vela satellite] sent aloft to detect any nuclear explosions in space. The second space spy was expected to shoot into orbit on signal from scientists at this Pacific missile range base.[31]

Increasing shifts in the geopolitical environment and perceived advances in Soviet military capability gave rise to Vandenberg's importance not only as a missile test and launch site, but as a space launch complex. In 1964, the installation

The first Missile Combat Crew Competition, appropriately named CURTAIN RAISER, was held in 1967. Designed to mirror the Strategic Air Command's bombing competition, the competition pitted wings and crews of the Minuteman and Titan II (and later Peacekeeper) weapon systems against each other. The competition utilized facilities and missile procedure trainers (MPTs) at Vandenberg. *Courtesy of the United States Air Force*

The Air Force's missile inventory in the 1970s included three variants of the Minuteman missile and the behemoth Titan II ICBM. *Courtesy of the United States Air Force*

increased in size by 20,000 acres, when the Department of Defense transferred Naval Missile Facility at Point Arguello (NMFPA) from the Navy to the Air Force in an effort to consolidate duplicate range functions, and to meet rapidly expanding and complex mission requirements at Vandenberg.[32] The Navy had originally established the NMFPA and the Pacific Missile Range (PMR) in 1958, after receiving the southern portion of Camp Cooke.[33] The PMR, planned as the nation's largest test range, included an ocean test strip 500 miles long, paralleling the California coast and extending 250 miles out to sea. Later changes to PMR after annexation included expansion of the coastal boundaries westward across the Pacific to the middle of the Indian Ocean. The Naval Air Missile Test Center at Point Mugu controlled both the range and the NMFPA.

Although administered independently, the NMFPA and Vandenberg were closely linked. The Air Force conducted extensive space launch programs at Point Arguello Launch Complexes (PALC-A, B, C, and D), while NMFPA personnel had access to the facilities at Vandenberg, including its housing resources and commissary. Additionally, the Navy provided command and control for all launches from Vandenberg and the NMFPA until 1964. The Air Force developed an intricate network of range equipment—from electronic to optical tracking systems—to monitor and control the various ballistic and space vehicles inside the Western Test Range.

After the consolidation, this location became known by locals as South Vandenberg (or South Base). The final increase in acreage occurred in March 1966, when the base acquired nearly 15,000 acres of Sudden Ranch, at the southern end of

Vandenberg. The additional land increased the size of the base to its current 98,400 acres.[34]

By late 1979, the host organization was SAC's 1st Strategic Aerospace Division (1 STRAD)—formerly the 1st Missile Division—with the Western Space and Missile Center (WSMC) as the primary tenant organization.[35] This organizational structure remained static during the 1980s. The 1990s and the end of the Cold War brought many changes to the base. The first of several major organizational name changes and realignments involving the base occurred on 31 July 1990, when 1 STRAD was renamed the Strategic Missile Center (SMC). In addition to the realignments of SAC organizations at Vandenberg, changes during this time were also occurring at WSMC. After being reassigned to Air Force Space Command (AFSPC) on 1 October 1990, host base responsibilities for Vandenberg also transferred from SAC to AFSPC. As a result, WSMC picked up the 4392d Aerospace Support Wing, the 392d Communications Group, the hospital, and various staff functions. This increased the size of WSMC from about 500 people before the realignment to approximately 3,300 after the change. The remaining SAC organizations at Vandenberg continued their missions, launching Peacekeeper and Minuteman III ICBMs as part of the Follow-On Test and Evaluation (FOT&E) program and providing missile combat crew training.

On 19 November 1991, WSMC was renamed the 30th Space Wing (30 SW).[36] The new organization assumed the lineage and history of the 30th Bombardment Group (Heavy), which was activated in January 1941 and flew combat missions in the Pacific theater during World War II.[37] Simultaneously, the 2d Space Launch Squadron (2 SLS) was activated together with the Western Range and a support staff. Other former WSMC units involved in research and development programs remained as separate organizations.

group, and it provided space forces for the National Military Command System.[40]

On 15 April 1994, the 4th Space Launch Squadron (4 SLS) was activated to manage Titan II, Titan IV, and Delta II space launches.[41] On 18 May 1998, the 2 SLS and 4 SLS merged into one squadron: the 2 SLS. The consolidated squadron was responsible for overseeing launch operations due to the similarity in missions previously performed by both units. This organizational change would be reversed in 2003. The 4 SLS was reactivated on 1 December 2003 to manage operations for the Evolved Expendable Launch Vehicle (EELV) program, including Atlas V and Delta IV boosters. The 2 SLS was inactivated after the final legacy Titan IV launch in 2005.[42] Also in 2003, another launch squadron, the 1st Air and Space Test Squadron (1 ASTS), was activated to provide expertise for test launches of the Minotaur I and IV and the Pegasus space launch boosters.[43]

By September 2016, 1,948 vehicles had been launched from Vandenberg, ranging from ICBMs to space launch boosters, ground-to-air interceptor missiles, IRBMs, suborbital rockets, and a ground-launched cruise missile.[44]

576th Flight Test Squadron ("TOP HAND")

As America's only dedicated ICBM test squadron, the 576th Flight Test Squadron (576 FLTS) executes tests to accurately measure the current capability of the ICBM force.[45] In

In 1971, the Air Force began launching Titan IIID rockets from Space Launch Complex 4. The size and lift capacity of the rocket could lift the largest national-security payloads, such as the KH-9 HEXAGON satellite. *Courtesy of the United States Air Force*

In a separate action, HQ SAC reactivated the Twentieth Air Force (20 AF) at Vandenberg AFB.[38] The six SAC missile wings, composing the nation's land-based ICBM force, were reassigned from two other numbered Air Forces and consolidated under 20 AF. Then, on 1 June 1992, as part of an Air Force–wide restructuring program, SAC was inactivated and replaced by the newly established Air Combat Command (ACC).[39]

The higher headquarters changes rippled down through base-level organizations like wildfire. On 1 July 1993, 20 AF was reassigned from ACC to AFSPC. Simultaneously, its 310th Training and Test Wing (TRTW) was inactivated. The 310 TRTW Peacekeeper and Minuteman launch elements, along with its missile maintenance and support squadrons and helicopter rescue flight, were realigned under the newly established 30th Space Wing. Only the 4315th Combat Crew Training Squadron (CCTS) did not realign under the 30 SW, instead transferring missile training to the reestablished 392d Space and Missile Training Squadron. Also occurring on 1 July 1993 was the activation of Fourteenth Air Force (14 AF) to exercise operational control of four space wings and a space

As part of President Ronald Reagan's Strategic Modernization Program in the 1980s, the MX missile was proposed in a number of basing modes. One of the basing methods was the Rail Garrison, placing ICBMs on trains. The Peacekeeper Rail Garrison test site at Vandenberg had a small railroad loop to test the operational system but was canceled before the first test. *Courtesy of the United States Air Force*

The 30th Space Wing manages the Department of Defense space and missile testing and places satellites into polar orbit from the West Coast. *Courtesy of the Air Force Historical Research Agency*

Twentieth Air Force was reactivated at Vandenberg on 1 September 1991 to oversee the responsibility for all land-based ICBMs. It moved to F. E. Warren AFB, Wyoming, in 1993. *Courtesy of the Air Force Historical Research Agency*

Air Force Space Command (AFSPC) is a major command of the United States Air Force headquartered at Peterson Air Force Base, Colorado. AFSPC supports US military operations worldwide through the use of many different types of satellites and launches. *Courtesy of the Air Force Historical Research Agency*

Missile Combat Crew Members, or Missileers, are known for creating patch designs featuring their job responsibilities with a macabre sense of humor. In the patch design "Death Wears Bunny Slippers" by Joe Iungerman, a hooded Death figure sits at his control console ready to launch. *Courtesy of the artist*

On north Vandenberg, at the base of the Casmalia foothills, lies the Ronald Reagan Observation site. The plaque recognizes President Reagan's vision of making the United States more safe and secure through a missile defense program. *Author*

A 576th Flight Test Squadron maintenance airman is photographed in front of his "weapon system," the Minuteman III transporter-erector (TE). The vehicle transports the first, second, and third stages of the missile and assists in lowering it into the underground silo. *Courtesy of the United States Air Force*

The command staff of the 14th Air Force commemorate the space operator's distinct uniform, the "blue bag," on its last official wear date in 2000. Officially known as the Space and Missile Crew Uniform, the blue flight suit was replaced with the olive-green flight suit worn by the Air Force flying community until flight suit wear by space operators was eliminated in 2012. *Courtesy of the United States Air Force*

Visitors to Space Launch Complex 10 (SLC-10) are photographed inside the West Pad shelter, otherwise known as SLC-10W. This particular group are aficionados of the Thor weapon system and traveled from the United Kingdom to view the world's only remaining Thor protective shelter and booster—both at Vandenberg. *Courtesy of the United States Air Force*

executing the ICBM Initial Operational Test and Evaluation (IOT&E) and Force Development Evaluation (FDE) programs, the 576th conducts missile flight tests to analyze the ICBM force's performance, accuracy, and reliability to the Joint Staff, United States Strategic Command (USSTRATCOM), Air Staff, and Air Force Global Strike Command (AFGSC).[46] The squadron identifies missile system requirements, demonstrates current and future war-fighting capabilities, and validates missile system improvements and upgrades.[47]

The 576 FLTS was first activated as the 576th Bombardment Squadron (Heavy) at Davis-Monthan Field, Arizona, on 26 January 1943. The unit participated in the Eighth Air Force strategic bombardment campaigns over Europe and Germany,[48] assisting during the Normandy invasion and the Battle of the Bulge. The actions by 576 BS during combat resulted in seven European–African–Middle Eastern Theater campaign streamers and one Distinguished Unit Citation.[49]

With the close of World War II, the 576th was deactivated on 13 September 1945. It was reactivated on 24 September 1947 as a very heavy bombardment squadron at Barksdale Field, Louisiana. With the unit's adoption of the B-26 bomber in 1947, the designation was changed to a light jet bomb squadron in June 1949; this lasted until November 1949, when the 576th was again deactivated. During the rapid buildup of missile capabilities across the nation, the squadron was reactivated at Cooke AFB on 6 March 1958 as the 576th Strategic Missile Squadron (576 SMS). On 1 April 1958, the

The remnants of SLC-1E sit by the ocean, crumbling. While the Vandenberg Space and Missile Technology Center captures the history of the base, parts of the National Reconnaissance Program and the early spy satellites are being lost to time, climate, and neglect. SLC-1E was home to many CORONA launches before the program ended in 1972. *Author*

A newly minted second lieutenant smiles as he tours an underground launch control center. Every year, hundreds of new officers are trained to become missile combat crew members for the US nuclear alert force. *Courtesy of the United States Air Force*

A Minuteman III missile is inspected by members of the 576th Flight Test Squadron prior to emplacement in an underground silo. *Courtesy of the United States Air Force*

Members of the 576th Flight Test Squadron inspect a portion of the "raceway," the cabling that runs along the Minuteman III. *Courtesy of the United States Air Force*

576th was directed to operate the SM-65 Atlas as the nation's first ICBM unit. On 2 April 1966, the 576th was once again inactivated.[50]

Reactivated in the 1990s, first as a test squadron and later as a flight test squadron, the designation "576th" was chosen to ensure that the history and lineage of the squadron would continue with the critical task of testing the nation's ICBMs. The 576 FLTS was reassigned to AFGSC on 1 December 2009.

CHAPTER 2:
Alphabetical Listing of Rockets and Missiles

AMROC/IRR[1]

Established in 1985, the American Rocket Company (AMROC) of Camarillo, California, had designed and developed its own hybrid rocket motor in the hopes of grabbing part of the market share for commercial space launches.[2] AMROC's initial design was called the Industrial Launch Vehicle (ILV), but by 1989, three additional variants were under development:

- a single-module suborbital vehicle (SMSV), also known as the Industrial Research Rocket (IRR)

- a slightly larger suborbital rocket called the AMROC Explorer, consisting of the IRR fitted with an upper stage, such as a Morton Thiokol Star 48 motor
- Industrial Launch Vehicle (ILV-100) Series, consisting of two and a half stages with seven or ten 75,000 lb. thrust motors, depending on the particular payload requirements

In late 1985, the company had negotiated with Air Force Systems Command for the use of a rocket engine test stand

AMROC tests their hybrid rocket motor at Edwards Air Force Base, California, in the mid-1980s. *Courtesy of the United States Air Force*

Aerial view of ABRES A-3, formerly known as 576A-3, shows the launch site for AMROC SET. *Courtesy of the United States Air Force*

at Edwards Air Force Base, California. The search for a suitable polar launch site for AMROC at Vandenberg began in early 1987.[3] By mid-1988, the company had decided to develop its interim launch site and pursue a permanent launch site at a later date.[4] Agreements with the Air Force allowed AMROC use of the abandoned Advanced Ballistic Reentry Systems (ABRES) A-3 complex (also known as Ballistic Missile Reentry Systems [BMRS] A-3) as their temporary launch location.[5]

AMROC's main selling point was its hybrid rocket motors, marrying the benefits both of solid- and liquid-fueled technologies, such as high specific impulse and throttling, respectively.[6] Liquid oxygen is sprayed on a solid-rubber binder and ignited as the rocket launches. Since the solid fuel and oxidizer are kept separate until launch, there is less danger of explosion.[7]

A few months after its founding, AMROC began their first engine development test firings, using subscale, half-scale, and full-scale engines. Their unique engines used a nontoxic solid-hydrocarbon fuel (polybutadiene) and liquid oxygen as an oxidizer. This allowed the hybrid motors to produce clean, safe, nonexplosive propulsion that could be manufactured and fueled in a light-industry facility due to the advantages of low cost, reliability, and safety.[8]

The IRR would serve as a prototype for the industrial launch vehicles. The IRR consisted of a single 75,000 lb. thrust section measuring 58 ft. long and 51 inches in diameter, and weighing 32,000 lbs. The ILV-100 would be capable of boosting about 3,000 lbs. into a 150-mile circular orbit. The first and second stages shared a common liquid oxygen (LOX) oxidizer tank, while the third carried its own LOX supply. In the ILV-107 version, six motor units were clustered around a common LOX tank. The ILV-110 model had nine clustered motors.[9]

An illustration of the proposed AMROC Industrial Launch Vehicle shows it lifting off from an undesignated launchpad. Note the two rocket motors attached to the main body core, similar to a Titan 34D or Titan IV. *Courtesy of the United States Air Force*

The first of two suborbital demonstration flights (155 to 218 statute miles) using the IRR was planned from Vandenberg. On 5 October 1989, the Single Engine Test-1 (SET-1) failed to produce enough thrust, with controllers shutting down the engines after fifteen seconds.[10] Flames followed up the rocket body before the airframe tipped over and put a hole in the liquid oxygen tank.[11] The cause was determined to be insufficient liquid oxygen flow, likely due to icing. Reports state that while AMROC had done adequate engine testing prior to the launch, the test climate was the dry desert of Edwards AFB, not the humid atmosphere of Vandenberg.[12] The two payloads—Massachusetts Institute of Technology Space Systems Laboratory "ParaShield" (Project Skidbladnir) and a Strategic Defense Initiative passive experiment[13]—survived and the accident caused roughly $1,000 of damage to the launchpad. The failed SET-1 launch attempt at BMRS A-3 was the last launch operation at that complex. Modifications made to the gantry and launch stand,

as well as the AMROC sign on the access road, were still present as of 2016.

Following the death of AMROC founder George A. Koopman in July 1989,[14] and the failure of the SET-1 rocket on 5 October 1989, AMROC cut staff members,[15] was renamed, and finally declared bankruptcy in 1995.[16] Jim Benson, CEO of SpaceDev, purchased AMROC's intellectual property from the defunct company in 1997, including multiple patents[17] on hybrid rocket engine technology.[18]

AMROC/IRR Launches[19]

SEQUENCE	DATE	SITE	VEHICLE	CODENAME	NOTES
1639	5 OCT 89	BMRS A-3	AMROC/IRR	------	FAILURE DUE TO LACK OF THRUST. FIRST HYBRID ROCKET LAUNCH ATTEMPT.

ARGO D-8 (Journeyman)[20]

The Argo-D8 (Journeyman) was a four-stage solid-propellant[21] sounding rocket developed by Aerolab Development Company. Argo was the name of the ship in the ancient Greek myth of Jason's travels in search of the Golden Fleece. Jason named the ship after the builder, Argus.[22] Subsequent names in the Argo series started with the letter "J." (e.g., "Jason," "Javelin," and "Journeyman"). The alphanumeric designator stated the number of stages and design revision (e.g., "D" represented four stages, and "4" was the fourth design revision, while "8" was the eighth).[23]

The Argo rocket development was sponsored by NACA, Air Force Special Weapons Center, Naval Bureau of Ordnance, and the Allegany Ballistics Laboratory.[24] When NASA was created in 1958, the organization inherited a number of

sounding-rocket programs—such as the Javelin and Journeyman—as part of the Argo series.

The Journeyman rocket's first stage was a motor from the MGM-29 Sergeant battlefield missile. Stages 2 and 3 used motors from the MGM-52 Lance battlefield missile. The fourth stage was an Altair solid-fuel rocket engine (X-248). The rated lift capacity for the Argo D-8 Journeyman was 150 lbs. (68 kg) to 1,000 miles (1,600 km).[25]

The 19 September 1960 launch was scheduled as part of the "International Rocket Interval," as a follow-up to the International Geophysical Year (IGY) in 1958.[26] The scheduled payload was NERV (Nuclear Emulsion Recovery Vehicle), an emulsion experiment consisting of plates covered with special material to record streaks from radioactive particles as the payload traversed the Van Allen belts.[27] The launch was

Workers attach the upper stage to an Argo D-8 Journeyman. The initials "PMR" (Pacific Missile Range) are stenciled on the launch rail at Point Arguello Launch Complex-A (PALC-A). *Courtesy of the United States Navy*

An erected Argo D-8 Journeyman at PALC-A. The four stages are distinctly shown while looking along the launch rail. *Courtesy of the United States Navy*

successful, shooting the 83.6 lb. NERV capsule over 1,200 miles in altitude and 1,300 miles downrange before being picked up by US Navy ships.[28] This launch was the first NASA use of the Argo D-8 Journeyman sounding rocket. The NERV payload reached the highest known altitude for a man-made object to be recovered successfully from space.

On 15 November 1961, an Argo D-8 launched from PALC-A, carrying a Biological Investigations of Space (BIOS) capsule. The 86 lb. payload included biological samples such as sea urchin eggs, bacteria, mold, and human blood samples to be lifted into the Van Allen radiation belt.[29] The launch failed due to aerodynamic forces ripping the rocket apart. A subsequent attempt three days later, on 18 November, would result in the rocket and BIOS capsule being lost in the Pacific Ocean.[30] The launch was successful, but the telemetry was sporadic and recovery forces could not find the homing beacon.

The next launch of a Journeyman sounding rocket was on 9 July 1962, in support of the STARFISH PRIME exoatmospheric nuclear test conducted in the Johnston Island area.[31] The Journeyman rocket failed, as did another PALC launch (Astrobee 1500 magnetosphere mission from PALC-B),[32] and no data were obtained prior to the nuclear test.[33]

The Argo launch on 11 February 1963 saw a successful mission into the Van Allen belts, carrying a 104 lb. radiation detector from the University of Minnesota.[34] The electron spectrometry sensors also characterized the radiation field from the exoatmospheric nuclear test STARFISH PRIME conducted seven months prior. The flight lasted twenty-seven minutes, and the payload landed in the ocean 1,250 miles away from Point Arguello.

The early Journeyman launches were designed to assist NASA in gathering data on radiation prior to the manned Mercury flights. Due to the vehicle's excessive size and use of government off-the-shelf (GOTS) components—namely, military rocket motors—NASA use of the Argo D-8 was limited.[35]

All five launches of the Argo D-8 Journeyman took place at Point Arguello Launch Complex-A (PALC-A) during the period from September 1960 to February 1963.[36]

ARGO D-8 (Journeyman) Launches[37]

SEQUENCE	DATE	SITE	VEHICLE	CODENAME	NOTES
56	19 SEP 60	PALC-A	ARGO D-8	--	SUCCESS. FIRST ARGO D-8 LAUNCH. FIRST NASA LAUNCH FROM PALC/VANDENBERG. NERV PAYLOAD.
106	15 NOV 61	PALC-A	ARGO D-8	--	FAILURE. BIOS CAPSULE
107	18 NOV 61	PALC-A	ARGO D-8	--	FAILURE. BIOS CAPSULE
150	9 JUL 62	PALC-A	ARGO D-8	--	FAILURE. DATA COLLECTION FROM STARFISH PRIME TEST
201	11 FEB 63	PALC-A	ARGO D-8	--	SUCCESS. VAN ALLEN BELT RESEARCH. LAST FLIGHT OF ARGO D-8 AT PALC/VANDENBERG

ASTRID

The Advanced, Single-Stage Technology, Rapid-Insertion Demonstration (ASTRID) rocket was a technology testbed developed by Lawrence Livermore National Laboratory (LLNL) engineers for the Ballistic Missile Defense Organization's BRILLIANT PEBBLES space-based antimissile program.[38] As stated in a 1994 GAO report, the BRILLIANT PEBBLES project had its origins in President Reagan's "Star Wars" ballistic missile defense research program:

In 1983, the President directed the establishment of the Strategic Defense Initiative to eliminate the threat of first strike strategic nuclear ballistic missiles. The Secretary of Defense established the SDIO to manage the Strategic Defense Initiative. Space-based interceptors became a vital part of the SDIO missile defense architecture because space-based interceptors could meet the requirement to intercept missiles during the boost and post-boost phases of intercontinental ballistic missile flight. In 1990, BRILLIANT PEBBLES was chosen to fulfill SDIO's space-based interceptor requirement.[39]

The concept of BRILLIANT PEBBLES was to deploy a large constellation (around 4,000 small satellites) of nonnuclear, boost-phase intercept antimissile interceptor platforms.[40] The satellites would then fire tungsten projectiles to intercept targets. The linkage of BRILLIANT PEBBLES to ASTRID was through the development of propulsion components for orbital insertion and on-orbit maneuvering of the small-sat interceptors. Changes in the geopolitical landscape resulting in the end of the Cold War forced the Department of Defense to change the scope of the interceptor program from a pre-engineering and manufacturing development program to a technology demonstration program in early 1993.

The ASTRID rocket was designed as a small, high-velocity interceptor vehicle equipped with a navigation system and side-mounted steering thrusters utilizing the world's smallest pump-fed rocket motor.[41] Typical propulsion thrusters were constrained by a balance of pressure within the tanks and engine chambers. Engineers would settle on a median pressure value, between the high pressure required for thrust and a pressure low enough for the fuel tank to remain thin and lightweight. Rocket engines use turbopumps to increase

John C. Whitehead, developer of ASTRID's unique pump-fed propulsion system, stands next to the prototype rocket at Vandenberg. *Courtesy of Lawrence Livermore National Laboratories*

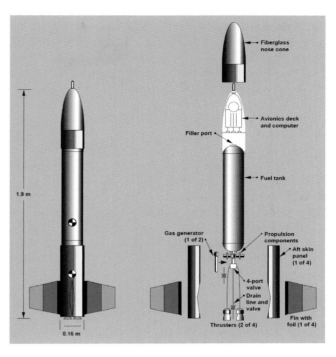

An illustrated cutaway of ASTRID shows the simple design for the planned interceptor. *Courtesy of Lawrence Livermore National Laboratories*

the pressure of fuel through the combustion chamber. These pumps are usually large and are discarded during rocket staging. Smaller systems use inert gasses to raise fuel tank to a pressure value. ASTRID was designed around pairs of small reciprocating pumps that stroke alternately to provide a high thrust-to-weight ratio, roughly equal to 50:1.

The ASTRID flight test article was launched on 4 February 1994 from an ad hoc launch site near Launch Facility 08 (LF-08).[42] The launch occurred during windless conditions from a 60-ft. (18.3 m) launcher rail set at an angle of 80° from horizontal. After the rocket left the rail, roll was induced immediately to provide aerodynamic stability from fixed fins on the aft section.

The flight lasted approximately one minute and took the rocket velocity to nearly Mach 1, while obtaining an altitude of 1.2 miles (2 km) and a downrange distance of 5 miles (8

km). The attained speed was limited because ASTRID was launched from sea level; the densest part of the atmosphere is subjected to severe aerodynamic drag. When igniting the engine in the planned environment of the upper atmosphere, the rocket engine would have performed in excess of 2 kilometers per second.

The test was successful in demonstrating the small pump-fed rocket's ability to maneuver fast enough (within milliseconds) to intercept ballistic missiles in flight through thrust-on-demand, pumped-propulsion technology for spacecraft.

Restructuring of the space-based segment of missile defense in 1991 and 1993 occurred because of the increasingly remote possibility of a massive Soviet missile attack. The reformulated program—the Global Protection against Limited Strikes (GPALS) system—reduced the requirement of 4,000 interceptors to about 1,000. The BRILLIANT PEBBLES program was eventually canceled in December 1993.[43]

ASTRID Launches[44]

SEQUENCE	DATE	SITE	VEHICLE	CODENAME	NOTES
1697	4 FEB 94	LF-08	ASTRID	-----	SUCCESS. SDIO TESTBED FOR PROPULSION. ONLY FLIGHT OF ASTRID.

ASTROBEE 1500

The Astrobee 1500 was a two-stage, solid-propellant sounding rocket used by NASA for geodetic missions. The Astrobee 1500 was a replacement for the Argo D-8 (Journeyman) rocket due to the increasing scarcity of Sergeant rocket motors that powered the Journeyman.[45] Support for the Astrobee 1500 program at NMFPA/Vandenberg was provided by the Air Force Cambridge Research Laboratory as an extension of their space probe and Project Cambridge programs.

The first stage consisted of an Aerobee 100 / Aerobee Junior motor augmented by two XM19 Recruit motors.[46] The second stage consisted of an Alcor motor inside a clamshell payload fairing. The first-stage rockets would fire inside the atmosphere, while the second stage would ignite outside of the atmosphere. This combination could lift a 75 lb. payload to a 1,000-mile altitude, or a 50 lb. payload to 1,400 miles[47] (conflicting resources stated a 50 lb. payload to 2,000 miles or 160 lb. payload to 1,200 miles).[48] Aerodynamic stability was provided by cruciform fins on the aft section inducing a stabilizing spin.

The first Astrobee 1500 flight took place at PALC-A on 1 August 1961 and was a failure due to first-stage nozzle burn-through.[49] The second Astrobee 1500 launch took place at PALC-A on 8 December 1961.[50] The vehicle carried a payload of three sets of seven (21 total) 62-million-candlepower flares. The flares were ejected at 920 miles, 1,400 miles, and 900 miles (returning down).[51] Prior to the flight, Air Force Cambridge Research Laboratory scientists placed geodetic stellar cameras at Sitka, Alaska; Spokane, Washington; Lincoln and El Centro, California; and two sites in Hawaii (Mauna Loa and Kaena Point), as well as on Johnston Island.[52] The experiment was designed to help ground-based cameras use triangulation to precisely determine distances between land masses.[53]

The final launch of an Astrobee 1500 at NMFPA/Vandenberg took place on 9 July 1962. A pair of sounding rockets—Astrobee 1500 at PALC-B and an Argo D-8 Journeyman at PALC-A—were prepared to support the Joint Task Force 8 (JTF-8) STARFISH PRIME nuclear test with rocket-borne scintillation X-ray experiments and photoelectric X-ray experiments developed by Los Alamos Scientific Laboratory. The dual launch was synchronized with the JTF-8 count at minus 780 seconds, and both vehicles were fired at the proper time. However, no data were obtained, due to the failure of both vehicles. Telemetry contact with the Astrobee was lost about fifteen seconds after launch, apparently due to disintegration in the early phase of powered flight.[54]

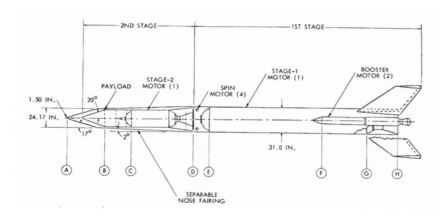

TOP: Cutaway illustration of an Astrobee 1500 shows the two stages, the interstage with spin motors, and the nose payload fairing. Note the inclusion of two strap-on booster motors near the tail fins. *Courtesy of National Aeronautics and Space Administration*

LEFT: An Astrobee 1500 stands erect prior to launch. While the launch rail provided some stability, the spin motors between the first and second stages kept the rocket flying true. *Courtesy of National Aeronautics and Space Administration*

ASTROBEE 1500 Launches[55]

SEQUENCE	DATE	SITE	VEHICLE	CODENAME	NOTES
92	1 AUG 61	PALC-A	ASTROBEE 1500	--	FAILURE. FIRST LAUNCH OF ASTROBEE 1500.
113	8 DEC 61	PALC-A	ASTROBEE 1500	--	SUCCESS. GEODETIC FLARE EXPERIMENT.
151	9 JUL 62	PALC-B	ASTROBEE 1500	--	FAILURE. DATA COLLECTION FROM STARFISH PRIME TEST.

ATHENA I

Athena I—also known as Lockheed Launch Vehicle (LLV) and, later, Lockheed Martin Launch Vehicle (LMLV)—was a two-stage launcher for low-earth orbiting (LEO) payload around 1,750 lbs. into a 100-mile orbit.[56] LLV was the United States' first privately funded launcher, starting its program in January 1993.[57] The rocket first stage is a Castor 120 solid-rocket motor burning hydroxyl-terminated polybutadiene (HTPB). The second stage is a Pratt & Whitney Orbus 21D motor.

The LLV/LMLV/Athena rocket family had a short stint at Vandenberg AFB, with only two launches. In the early 1990s, Lockheed entered the small-launcher market with the creation of the LLV to compete against Orbital Sciences' Pegasus, Pegasus XL, and Taurus family of launchers. The vehicle was launched at Space Launch Complex 6 (SLC-6), sitting atop a mount originally built for the solid-rocket boosters of the space shuttle, SLC-6's originally planned inhabitant.[58] While looking for a polar-orbit launch site, Lockheed engineers toured the then-mothballed site at South Vandenberg. SLC-6's mobile service tower had sat dormant for so long, Lockheed officials noted, "there were actually indentations in the rails."[59] The company built a "footstool" launchpad over a solid-rocket booster exhaust vent.

On 15 August 1995, the first launch of LLV-1 carried the GEMstar-1 small satellite, alternately known as VITASAT 1.[60] A catastrophic failure occurred after the first-stage firing, with the rocket pitching to nearly a 90° angle. The range safety officer, Capt. Richard Boltz,[61] destroyed the rocket after 160 seconds of flight, stating "The angles were wrong and high rates were a major concern. We weren't going to allow ourselves to get into a position of not being able to destroy it."[62] The launch was the first use of the Castor 120 solid-rocket motor. Accident investigation revealed that the loss was caused by the failure of the first-stage thrust-vectoring system and the inertial measurement unit (IMU).[63]

The second launch attempt of the newly renamed Lockheed-Martin Launch Vehicle 1 (LMLV-1)[64] took place on 22 August 1997 at SLC-6. The flight was successful, placing NASA's Lewis satellite into its initial orbit. Problems with the spacecraft developed in subsequent days, but these were ruled independent of the booster system.[65] This was the final flight of LLV-1/LMLV-1/Athena-1 at Vandenberg.

ATHENA I Launches[66]

SEQUENCE	DATE	SITE	VEHICLE	CODENAME	NOTES
1715	15 AUG 95	SLC-6	LLV-1	--	FAILURE. GEMSTAR 1. FIRST LAUNCH OF LLV-1/LMLV-1.
1746	22 AUG 97	SLC-6	LMLV-1	--	NASA LEWIS SPACECRAFT. LAST LAUNCH OF LLV-1/LMLV-1.

ATHENA II

Athena II is a three-stage, expendable solid-rocket system for launching small payloads into low-earth orbit. Derived from the Athena I (LLV-1/LMLV-1) design, the Athena II includes an additional stage with a second Castor 120 solid-rocket motor burning hydroxyl-terminated polybutadiene (HTPB).[67] The third stage is an Orbus 21D, able to place 4,390 lbs. into low-earth orbit.

The Athena II used the same launch facilities at SLC-6 as the previous Athena I, including the solid-rocket booster mount built for the space shuttle.[68]

On 27 April 1999, the Athena launch failed to place the IKONOS 1 imaging satellite into orbit. The payload shroud did not separate from the satellite bus, preventing the satellite from achieving orbital velocity.[69] The payload shroud was constructed of aluminum-lithium and weighed nearly 1,400 lbs. Separation of the shroud should have occurred approximately four minutes after launch, but no telemetry was received either at the McMurdo Tracking Station, Antarctica, or the Melindi, Kenya, downlink site. Accident investigation revealed that the fourth stage and shroud took the payload back into the atmosphere until crashing into the South Pacific.[70]

The second Athena II launch attempt took place at SLC-6 on 24 September 1999. The mission was a redux of the previous launch, complete with another LM900-based 1-meter resolution imagery satellite dubbed IKONOS-2—later renamed to the singular IKONOS. The 1,600 lb. satellite was successfully lofted into a 422-mile sun-synchronous orbit.[71]

During the first decade of the twenty-first century, a glut of launch capabilities from commercial providers made Athena booster sales difficult. No additional launches of Athena have taken place at Vandenberg since 1999. Facilities at SLC-6 were modified in late 1999 for the Evolved Expendable Launch Vehicle (EELV) program, eliminating the pad as a future Athena launch site.[72] An effort to revive the Athena line took place in 2010.[73]

ATHENA II Launches[74]

SEQUENCE	DATE	SITE	VEHICLE	CODENAME	NOTES
1777	27 APR 99	SLC-6	ATHENA II	-----	FAILURE. FIRST USE OF ATHENA II BOOSTER. PAYLOAD WAS IKONOS-1.
1783	24 SEP 99	SLC-6	ATHENA II	-----	SUCCESS. LAST USE OF ATHENA II. PAYLOAD WAS IKONOS-2.

ATLAS-D (ICBM)

The Atlas-D ICBM (SM-65D, CGM-16D, WS 107A-1) was a first-generation, liquid-fueled, nuclear-tipped missile with intercontinental range. Its mission was to deliver a thermonuclear warhead more than a quarter of the way around the world to destroy top-priority enemy targets within minutes of launch. The USAF built six variations of the Atlas missile.[75] Three variants saw service at Vandenberg: Atlas-D (PGM-16D/CGM-16D), Atlas-E (CGM-16E), and Atlas-F (HGM-16F).[76] Atlas incorporated two unique features. The first was its "stage and a half" propulsion system, consisting of two large booster engines flanking a smaller sustainer engine. All engines on Atlas were ignited at liftoff, with the boosters dropping away, unlike the staging concept of later ICBMs.

In 1946, Army Air Forces' Air Material Command awarded a contract to Consolidated Vultee Aircraft Corporation (Convair) for a study for a long-range missile. Originally designated Project MX-774, the program suffered from limited funds and was canceled in 1947. Derived from the nascent rocket design were new techniques on nose cone separation, integral fuel tanks, and swiveling (gimbaled) rocket engine exhaust responding to in-flight commands from a rudimentary guidance system.[77] Using remaining funds, Convair engineers performed static tests at Point Loma and three test launches at White Sands Proving Ground in 1948.

The origin of the name "Atlas" is captured in the volume *Origins of NASA Names*:

> Early in 1951 Karel J. Bossart, head of the design team at Convair (Consolidated Vultee Aircraft Corporation) that was working on the missile project for the Air Force, decided the project (officially listed as MX-1593) should have a popular name. He asked some of his staff for ideas and they considered several possibilities before agreeing upon "Atlas"—Bossart's own suggestion. The missile they were designing would be the biggest and most powerful yet devised.

Bossart recalled that Atlas was the mighty god of ancient Greek mythology who supported the world on his powerful shoulders. The appropriateness of the name seemed confirmed by the fact that the parent company of Convair was the Atlas Corporation. The suggestion was submitted to the Air Force and was approved by the Department of Defense Research and Development Board's Committee on Guided Missiles in August 1951.[78]

The project for a long-range missile remained almost nonexistent until 1951. Convair continued work on a low-priority project designated MX-1593 for a long-range missile.[79] Intelligence reports stated that the Soviet Union was also researching long-range rockets, with the German V-2 design. Actions in Korea and the development of a thermonuclear bomb, with subsequent reductions in warhead weight, provided enough impetus to develop a long-range missile. In 1954, Project Atlas was renamed from Strategic Missile 65 (SM-65) to Weapon System 107A-1 (WS 107A-1). The WS 107A-1 designation refers to all components of the system, including the missile airframe with high-yield thermonuclear warhead, the associated ground equipment to transport and maintain the missile, trained personnel for operations and maintenance, and a logistics support system to make repairs.

As early as 1956, plans were being formulated for the use of Atlas missiles to launch reconnaissance satellites into orbit.[80]

With this new manufacturing endeavor, Convair developed revolutionary techniques for Atlas airframe construction.[81] The airframe of the Atlas consisted of sheets of thin, type 301 stainless steel, requiring internal pressurization for stability.[82] Fusion welding allowed for a continuous seam without introducing additional weld material. Early techniques in forming the curved forward bulkheads used dry ice to cool the material to −600°F, since the steel hardened rapidly and was not heat treatable afterward. A quality control ratio of thirty to forty "good"

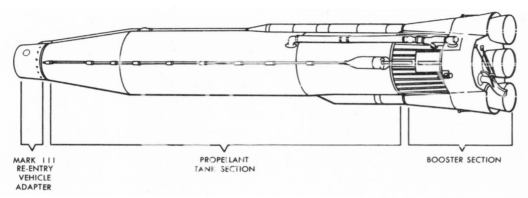

MARK III
RE-ENTRY
VEHICLE
ADAPTER

PROPELLANT
TANK SECTION

BOOSTER SECTION

The simple Atlas design as a pressurized metal "balloon" belies its ingenuity as an effective vehicle airframe. Fuel and oxidizer tanks, guidance system, booster and sustainer engines, and the nuclear warhead were the main subsystems of the Atlas missile. *Courtesy of the United States Air Force*

pieces out of one hundred was deemed acceptable.[83] Developmental testing of Atlas by Convair used Edwards AFB, California, and Patrick AFB, Florida (overseer of Cape Canaveral AFS), as well as contractor-run facilities in San Diego.[84] Logistic concepts such as concurrency were new to the Air Force; Vandenberg automatically became a proving ground for solutions.

Another feature unique to Atlas was the pressurized integral fuel tanks. The designers adopted this technique to save weight. The tanks and airframe were built from thin sheets of stainless steel, ranging from 0.1 inches (2.54 mm) to 0.4 inches (10.16 mm) thick. When empty, the tanks were filled with nitrogen gas at 5 psi to maintain positive internal pressure. Without positive pressure or mechanical stretching, the airframe would collapse on itself.

The sustainer engine provides 57,000 lbs. of thrust. The two booster engines, set next to the sustainer engine, are MA-2 engines, providing a combined 368,000 lbs. of thrust. After the initial liftoff command, the sustainer and boosters fire and continue for the next 140 seconds. Once the boosters are no longer required, they are jettisoned, providing a decrease in mass. The flight profile continues until the sustainer engine has completed its run (for another 130 seconds), and the nose cone is separated from the airframe and continues on a ballistic path toward its target.[85]

Since early Atlas designs used a radio command guidance system developed by General Electric, the Vandenberg complex consisted of two discrete parts: a launch location and a guidance control station.[86] Limits on the number of missiles controlled with radio guidance prevented the Atlas force from being used as mass salvos toward the enemy. Radio-commanded guidance also had suspected vulnerabilities to enemy jamming. Later upgrades used inertial guidance, which is not susceptible to radio frequency jamming. Complex 65-1, later known as 576A, used MOD-1 radio guidance. Complex 65-2, later known as 576B, also used command guidance from the MOD-2 and upgraded MOD-3 system.

The Atlas-D warhead was a W49 thermonuclear bomb encased in a General Electric Mark 3 ablative reentry vehicle (RV), weighing approximately 2,400 lbs. The Los Alamos National Laboratories–designed W49 warhead could provide a megaton-range yield with either an airburst or ground burst.[87]

Construction of Atlas facilities at Vandenberg began in 1957, distinguishing the location both as an ICBM operational test location and an on-alert military launch site.[88] Atlas Complex 65-1, consisting of a control center and launches 576A-1, 576A-2, and 576A-3, were turned over to SAC on 31 August 1959.[89] Launches made at gantry sites required a seventeen-person team, combining operations (launch) and maintenance personnel.[90]

The first operational static test firing of an Atlas-D at Vandenberg took place on 22 August 1959.[91] A Convair crew,

Atlas 6D sits inside the horizontal gantry at Complex 576A-3. The gantry launch configuration was present at only two locations—Vandenberg and Cape Canaveral—and only Vandenberg's missiles were put on nuclear alert in late 1959. *Courtesy of the United States Air Force*

under the supervision of SAC 1STRAD and ARDC, completed the operation. The first Atlas-D ICBM launch took place on 9 September 1959 from Complex 576A-2 under the code name DESERT HEAT.[92] Initially the launch was designed to be closed to the press, but the decision to allow the media was reversed only two hours before the launch. The launch was successful and took the warhead mockup 4,480 miles toward Wake Island after reaching an apogee of 500 miles.[93]

Three Atlas-Ds were place on operational alert at Vandenberg AFB in late 1959. Atlas missiles were included in SAC's Emergency War Order starting on 10 October 1959.[94] While the Atlas-D was originally designed for a horizontal aboveground (a.k.a. "coffin") launchpad, under emergency measures the first Atlas-Ds deployed at Vandenberg were on open-gantry launchpads (Complex 576A). These missiles were completely exposed to the elements and were serviced by a gantry crane. One missile was kept on operational alert at all times.

Four squadrons nationwide operated the Atlas-D ICBM:[95]
- 549th Strategic Missile Squadron—Offutt AFB, NE—3 complexes (9 missiles)
- 564th Strategic Missile Squadron—F.E. Warren AFB, WY—2 complexes (6 missiles)

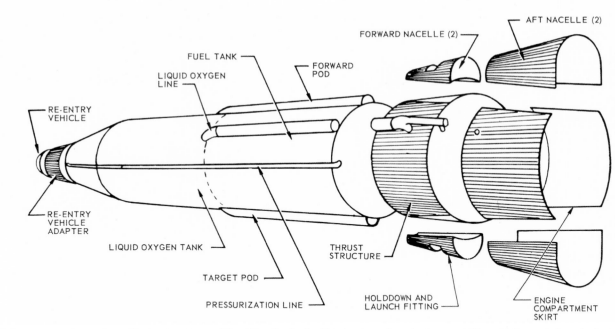

Side cutaway shows the critical subsystems of the Atlas-D missile. This basic system design would fly until the early twenty-first century. *Courtesy of the United States Air Force*

- 565th Strategic Missile Squadron—F.E. Warren AFB, WY—3 complexes (9 missiles)
- 576th Strategic Missile Squadron—Vandenberg AFB, CA—2 complexes (6 missiles)

The 576th Strategic Missile Squadron commanded a full Atlas military configuration at Vandenberg AFB. An evolutionary number of missile launch complexes were constructed for each squadron, the whole being the manageable complement of missiles that a squadron could be expected to launch effectively during a time of attack. The first US Atlas squadrons commanded nine missiles or fewer, the second squadrons had ten missiles, and the final, fully developed squadrons had twelve missiles.

The 576 SMS controlled nine launch sites, with two complexes used initially for the Atlas-D missile and, later, the Atlas-D space launch booster configuration:
- 576A complex, with 3 launchpads with gantries (A-1, A-2, A-3)[96] (1959–1967)
- 576B complex with 3 coffin launchers (B-1, B-2, B-3) (1960–1967)

The first Atlas launch complex under design and construction was 576A (a.k.a. SM 65-1, ABRES-A), a soft site comprising three unprotected missiles maintained on alert in a vertical position with servicing mobile gantries. The second complex designed and built was 576B (SM 65-2, ABRES-B, BMRS), with construction timelines overlapping 576A. 576B was also considered a soft site, consisting of three missiles maintained in a horizontal position in aboveground concrete coffins.

The first successful coffin launch took place on 6 May 1960, with a crew from the 564th Strategic Missile Squadron at F. E. Warren AFB, Wyoming. The launch also debuted the MOD III radio inertial guidance for the Atlas coffin complexes in the Midwest.[97]

Operation GOLDEN RAM—a training and reliability program—was initiated at Vandenberg to refine operational launch procedures to eliminate the problems that led to five partially successful launches during 1960.[98] Military launches prior to GOLDEN RAM did not have the precision of the contractor-led launches. SAC, the Ballistic Missile Division, and the major contractors for Atlas were involved. The first GOLDEN RAM launch on 16 December 1960 successfully delivered the Mark 3 reentry vehicle 4,384 miles into Eniwetok Atoll.[99] 576B was the complex for use during GOLDEN RAM testing, in addition to SAC operational readiness and Category III testing.[100] Procedural changes were incorporated into Atlas-E and Atlas-F variants. During summer and fall 1963, the Air Force saw thirteen consecutive launch failures from Atlas-D, E, and F missiles.[101]

In the early 1960s, Secretary of Defense Robert McNamara ordered the phasing out of first-generation ICBM systems Atlas and Titan I due to numerous accidents at operational sites. After the Atlas-D ICBMs went off-alert in December 1964, the inventory of missiles was used in a variety of ways.[102] Starting in 1962, Atlas-Ds were used as target vehicles in the Nike-Zeus Anti-Ballistic Missile (ABM) program until 1966.[103] Missiles launched by SAC crews for combat-training launches were used as targets for Nike-Zeus.[104] Other uses of Atlas ICBMs were in the Advanced Ballistic Reentry Systems

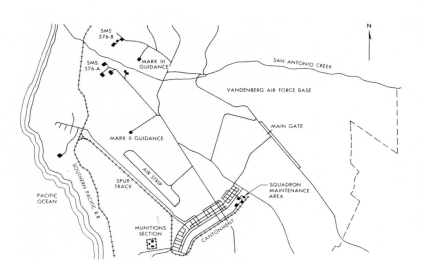

This map of North Vandenberg shows Complex 576's tight clustering. A mixture of gantry and coffin launchers housed the Atlas-D ICBM fleet until later variants were housed in underground silos. *Courtesy of the United States Air Force*

Atlas 23D is readied for launch from Complex 576B-1. This "coffin" configuration gave minimal protection against overpressure after a nuclear blast but kept the missile safe from the elements until launch. *Courtesy of the United States Air Force*

(ABRES) program.[105] ABRES research covered all phases of ballistic missile reentry, as well as materials, terminal guidance, and techniques, tactics, and procedures.[106] RVs flown during ABRES were of new design, rather than the stock Atlas warhead RVs. The last Atlas-D ABRES flight took place on 7 November 1967, carrying a Mark 11 reentry vehicle to Kwajalein Atoll.

The entire on-alert Atlas-D force stood at twenty-seven missiles, plus potentially a maximum of three additional sorties at Vandenberg.[107] A total of ninety-one Atlas-D ICBM launches took place at Vandenberg from 1959 to 1967.

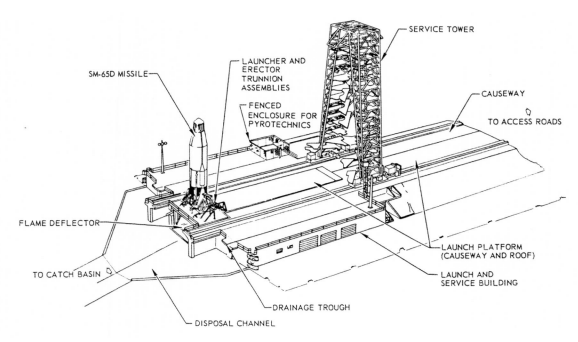

An illustrated view of Complex 576A launchpads. The service tower, a.k.a. "gantry," rolled along tracks away from the launch platform and missile prior to launch. Required pressurization tanks and other industrial components were held in the launch and service building beneath the pad. *Courtesy of the United States Air Force*

ATLAS-D ICBM Launches[108]

SEQUENCE	DATE	SITE	VEHICLE	CODENAME	NOTES
24	9 SEP 59	576A-2	ATLAS-D	DESERT HEAT	
34	26 JAN 60	576A-3	ATLAS-D	DUAL EXHAUST	
40	22 APR 60	576B-2	ATLAS-D	QUICK START	
42	6 MAY 60	576B-1	ATLAS-D	LUCKY DRAGON	
50	22 JUL 60	576B-1	ATLAS-D	TIGER SKIN	
54	12 SEP 60	576B-3	ATLAS-D	GOLDEN JOURNEY	
57	29 SEP 60	576B-2	ATLAS-D	HIGH ARROW	
61	12 OCT 60	576B-1	ATLAS-D	DIAMOND JUBILEE	
73	16 DEC 60	576B-3	ATLAS-D	HOT SHOT	
84	24 MAY 61	576B-2	ATLAS-D	LITTLE SATIN	
94	22 AUG 61	576B-3	ATLAS-D	NEW NICKLE	
109	29 NOV 61	576B-2	ATLAS-D	BIG PUSH	
112	7 DEC 61	576B-3	ATLAS-D	BIG CHIEF	
117	17 JAN 62	576B-2	ATLAS-D	BLUE FIN	
119	23 JAN 62	576B-3	ATLAS-D	BLUE MOSS	
120	16 FEB 62	576B-2	ATLAS-D	BIG JOHN	
121	21 FEB 62	576B-3	ATLAS-D	CHAIN SMOKE	
129	23 MAR 62	576B-2	ATLAS-D	CURRY COMB I	
131	11 APR 62	576B-2	ATLAS-D	CURRY COMB II	
135	27 APR 62	576B-2	ATLAS-D	BLUE BALL	
138	11 MAY 62	576B-3	ATLAS-D	CANNONBALL FLYER	
148	26 JUN 62	576B-3	ATLAS-D	ALL JAZZ	
152	12 JUL 62	576B-2	ATLAS-D	LONG LADY	
155	19 JUL 62	576B-1	ATLAS-D	FIRST TRY	
163	9 AUG 62	576B-3	ATLAS-D	PEG BOARD	
164	9 AUG 62	576B-2	ATLAS-D	PEG BOARD II	
173	2 OCT 62	576B-2	ATLAS-D	BRIAR STREET	
177	26 OCT 62	576A-1	ATLAS-D	CLOSED CIRCUITS	
186	12 DEC 62	576A-3	ATLAS-D	DEER PARK	
194	22 DEC 62	576A-1	ATLAS-D	FLY HIGH	
197	25 JAN 63	576B-2	ATLAS-D	BIG SUE	
199	31 JAN 63	576A-3	ATLAS-D	FAINT CLICK	
202	13 FEB 63	576A-1	ATLAS-D	FLAG RACE	
205	28 FEB 63	576A-3	ATLAS-D	PITCH PINE	
207	9 MAR 63	576B-3	ATLAS-D	TALL TREE 3	
208	11 MAR 63	576B-2	ATLAS-D	TALL TREE 2	
210	15 MAR 63	576B-1	ATLAS-D	TALL TREE 1	
212	16 MAR 63	576A-1	ATLAS-D	LEADING EDGE	
238	12 JUN 63	576A-3	ATLAS-D	HARPOON GUN	
260	31 JUL 63	576B-1	ATLAS-D	COOL WATER I	
265	28 AUG 63	576B-3	ATLAS-D	COOL WATER II	
269	6 SEP 63	576B-2	ATLAS-D	COOL WATER III	
271	11 SEP 63	576B-1	ATLAS-D	COOL WATER IV	
281	7 OCT 63	576B-3	ATLAS-D	COOL WATER V	
288	4 NOV 63	4300A-1	ATLAS-D	HICKORY HOLLOW	
292	13 NOV 63	576B-2	ATLAS-D	COOL WATER VI	
304	18 DEC 63	4300A-1	ATLAS-D	LENS COVER	
358	18 JUN 64	4300A-1	ATLAS-D	IRON LUNG	
371	29 JUL 64	4300A-3	ATLAS-D	KNOCK WOOD	
392	15 SEP 64	4300A-1	ATLAS-D	BUTTERFLY NET	
395	22 SEP 64	4300A-3	ATLAS-D	BUZZING BEE	

SEQUENCE	DATE	SITE	VEHICLE	CODENAME	NOTES
418	1 DEC 64	576A-1	ATLAS-D	BROOK TROUT	
419	4 DEC 64	576A-3	ATLAS-D	OPERA GLASS	
431	12 JAN 65	576B-1	ATLAS-D	PENSIL SET	
436	21 JAN 65	576B-3	ATLAS-D	BEAVERS DAM	
442	27 FEB 65	576A-1	ATLAS-D	DRAG BAR	
444	2 MAR 65	576A-3	ATLAS-D	PORK BARREL	
450	12 MAR 65	576B-3	ATLAS-D	ANGEL CAMP	
456	26 MAR 65	576A-1	ATLAS-D	FRESH FROG	
458	6 APR 65	576B-1	ATLAS-D	FLIP SIDE	
473	27 MAY 65	576B-3	ATLAS-D	TENNIS MATCH	
475	3 JUN 65	576B-2	ATLAS-D	OLD FOGEY	
477	8 JUN 65	576A-1	ATLAS-D	LEA RING	
479	10 JUN 65	576A-3	ATLAS-D	STOCK BOY	
487	1 JUL 65	576B-1	ATLAS-D	BLIND SPOT	
495	4 AUG 65	576B-1	ATLAS-D	PIANO WIRE	
504	26 AUG 65	576B-2	ATLAS-D	TONTO RIM	
509	29 SEP 65	576B-1	ATLAS-D	WATER SNAKE	
511	5 OCT 65	576B-3	ATLAS-D	SEETHING CITY	
521	29 NOV 65	576A-1	ATLAS-D	WILD GOAT	
527	20 DEC 65	576B-2	ATLAS-D	TAG DAY	
540	10 FEB 66	576A-1	ATLAS-D	YEAST CAKE	
541	11 FEB 66	576B-2	ATLAS-D	LONELY MOUNTAIN	
546	19 FEB 66	576B-1	ATLAS-D	SYCAMORE RIDGE	
549	4 MAR 66	576A-1	ATLAS-D	ETERNAL CAMP	
555	19 MAR 66	576A-1	ATLAS-D	WHITE BEAR	
562	30 MAR 66	576B-3	ATLAS-D	BRONZE BELL	
574	3 MAY 66	576A-1	ATLAS-D	CRAB CLAW	
576	13 MAY 66	576B-1	ATLAS-D	SUPPLY ROOM	
585	26 MAY 66	576B-2	ATLAS-D	SAND SHARK	
591	10 JUN 66	576B-1	ATLAS-D	VENEER PANEL	
596	26 JUN 66	576B-2	ATLAS-D	GOLDEN MOUNTAIN	
597	30 JUN 66	576A-1	ATLAS-D	HEAVY ARTILLERY	
602	13 JUL 66	576B-3	ATLAS-D	STONY ISLAND	
646	11 DEC 66	576B-3	ATLAS-D	BUSY PANAMA	
658	22 JAN 67	576B-2	ATLAS-D	BUSY NIECE	
679	7 APR 67	576B-2	ATLAS-D	BUSY SUNRISE	
717	6 JUL 67	576B-2	ATLAS-D	--	
726	27 JUL 67	576B-3	ATLAS-D	--	
741	11 OCT 67	576B-3	ATLAS-D	--	
748	7 NOV 67	576B-2	ATLAS-D	--	

ATLAS-E (ICBM)

The Atlas-E ICBM (SM-65E, CGM-16E, WS 107A-1) was a first-generation, liquid-fueled, nuclear-tipped missile with intercontinental range. Its mission was to deliver a thermonuclear warhead more than a quarter of the way around the world to destroy top-priority enemy targets within minutes of launch.

The Atlas-E ICBM was an upgrade from its Atlas-D predecessor, with internal changes along with a different basing scheme. The launch sequence was the same as the Atlas-D, but the Atlas-E used a hypergolic "start." In comparison, the Atlas-D performed a hold-down as the engines were ignited to ensure that ignition was successful. This new method caused a few early failures due to instability inside the combustion chamber. The Atlas-E replaced the D-model General Electric MOD 3 radio guidance with an all-inertial system produced by American Bosch Arma. This inertial system could detect preprogrammed flight path deviations and provide midcourse corrections without human intervention.[109] Checkout equipment called Mobile Automatic Programmed Checkout Equipment (MAPCE) used punch card–based computer systems to check all major systems and

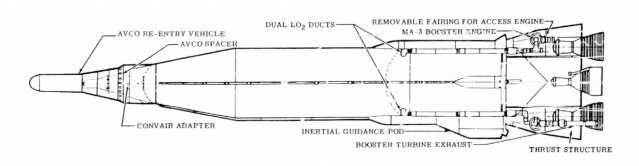

AVCO RE-ENTRY VEHICLE — AVCO SPACER — DUAL LO$_2$ DUCTS — REMOVABLE FAIRING FOR ACCESS ENGINE — MA-3 BOOSTER ENGINE — CONVAIR ADAPTER — INERTIAL GUIDANCE POD — BOOSTER TURBINE EXHAUST — THRUST STRUCTURE

The Atlas-E had minor differences from the D variant, including a larger warhead and an inertial guidance system. *Courtesy of the United States Air Force*

Atlas 27E sits upright at Complex 576F before its launch on 7 June 1961. Note the short distance to the parking lot in the background. *Courtesy of the United States Air Force*

An Atlas lifts off from Complex 576B-2 on 6 September 1963. As part of the ABRES program, this missile was configured with a prototype Mark 11 reentry vehicle. *Courtesy of the United States Air Force*

What is left of 576F after Atlas 27E exploded on 7 June 1961. *Courtesy of the United States Air Force*

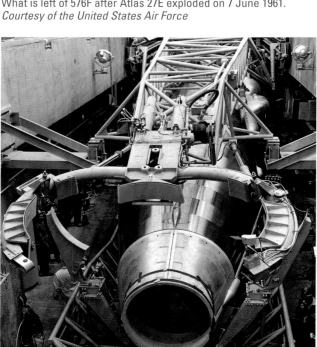

The cradle at 576F holds Atlas 24E sans warhead before its launch on 26 July 1963. *Courtesy of the United States Air Force*

subsystems.[110] The E-model also used an improved MA-3 propulsion system.

The first Atlas-E launch attempt (ironically code-named SURE SHOT) from a coffin launcher failed when the missile exploded on the pad on 7 June 1961.[111] The research-and-development (R&D) launch was the first attempt from a semihard "coffin," a hardened structure that was neither fully belowground nor completely aboveground. The attempt took place at Operational Suitability Test Facility 1 (OSTF-1)—also known as 576F—under the control of a mixed Ballistic Missile Division and Convair launch team.

In the first few months of 1961, a string of failures (seven of ten launches)[112] caused the Atlas-E program to undergo review.[113] Vandenberg's Atlas-E training complexes were fully turned over to SAC in June 1961.[114] Modifications to the missile-basing configuration took the aboveground "coffin" launcher and moved it underground. These "semihardened" sites allowed protection from overpressure from a nearby nuclear blast.[115] Due to the inertial guidance, no external control facilities were needed. The concrete Launch and Service Building and Launch Operations Building (located 150 ft. away) were partially buried, with only the roof penetrating ground level.

Four squadrons nationwide operated the Atlas-E ICBM, with one missile per complex.[116] Only one site at Vandenberg was fully configured for Atlas-E (576C), while OSTF-1 (576F) was for R&D tests.

- 567th Strategic Missile Squadron—Fairchild AFB, WA—9 complexes (9 missiles)
- 548th Strategic Missile Squadron—Forbes AFB, KS—9 complexes (9 missiles)
- 549th Strategic Missile Squadron—F.E. Warren AFB, WY—9 complexes (9 missiles)
- 576th Strategic Missile Squadron—Vandenberg AFB, CA—1 complex (1 missile)

The phaseout of Atlas-E took place soon after the Atlas-D phaseout. Secretary of Defense Robert S. McNamara estimated that the cost of operations and maintenance for *each* Atlas and Titan I missile was upward of $1 million per year, contrasted with $100,000 per Minuteman missile.

By June 1965, all Atlas-E missiles were taken off alert concurrently with the Atlas-F and Titan I ICBM force.[117] The sale of Atlas and Titan sites around the US was quoted as earning "over $5.5 billion, and represented probably the largest real estate disposal in U.S. military history."[118]

A total of 135 E/F boosters were used by the Air Force for the Ballistic Missile Reentry Systems (BMRS) program and launched from the ABRES/BMRS launch sites (also known as Complex 576A).[119]

Seconds before its fiery death, Atlas 27E tips over. *Courtesy of the United States Air Force*

ATLAS-E ICBM Launches[120]

SEQUENCE	DATE	SITE	VEHICLE	CODENAME	NOTES
85	7 JUN 61	576F	ATLAS-E	SURE SHOT	
125	28 FEB 62	OSTF-1	ATLAS-E	SILVER SPUR	
153	13 JUL 62	OSTF-1	ATLAS-E	EXTRA BONUS	
193	18 DEC 62	OSTF-1	ATLAS-E	OAK TREE	
224	24 APR 63	OSTF-1	ATLAS-E	BLACK BUCK	
237	4 JUN 63	OSTF-1	ATLAS-E	DOCK HAND	
249	3 JUL 63	576C	ATLAS-E	GO BOY	
256	26 JUL 63	576F	ATLAS-E	SILVER DOLL	
258	30 JUL 63	576C	ATLAS-E	BIG FLIGHT	
264	24 AUG 63	576F	ATLAS-E	PIPE DREAM	
275	25 SEP 63	576C	ATLAS-E	FILTER TIP	
321	12 FEB 64	576F	ATLAS-E	BLUE BAY	
384	27 AUG 64	576F	ATLAS-E	GALLANT GAL	
781	6 MAR 68	576A-3	ATLAS-E	--	
790	18 APR 68	576A-1	ATLAS-E	--	
792	27 APR 68	576A-3	ATLAS-E	--	

ATLAS-F ICBM

The Atlas-F ICBM (SM-65F, HGM-16F, WS 107A-1) was a first-generation, liquid-fueled, nuclear-tipped missile with intercontinental range. Its mission was to deliver a thermonuclear warhead more than a quarter of the way around the world to destroy top-priority enemy targets within minutes of launch.

The Atlas-F ICBM was an upgrade from its Atlas-E predecessor, with a different basing scheme. The F-model had an improved fuel-loading system and was stored inside underground silos in a vertical position for more rapid launch. Like Atlas-E, the F-model used the Bosch Arma all-inertial guidance system to guide its Mark 4 warhead—with its megaton-range yield—to its target. The first successful Atlas-F launch from Vandenberg was on 1 August 1962 from 576E.

Seven squadrons nationwide operated the Atlas-F ICBM, with one missile per silo/complex: Two sites at Vandenberg were fully configured for Atlas-F (576D and 576E), while OSTF-2 (576G) was used for R&D tests.

- 550th Strategic Missile Squadron—Schilling AFB, KS—12 complexes (12 missiles)
- 551st Strategic Missile Squadron—Lincoln AFB, NE—12 complexes (12 missiles)
- 556th Strategic Missile Squadron—Plattsburgh AFB, NY—12 complexes (12 missiles)
- 577th Strategic Missile Squadron—Altus AFB, OK—12 complexes (12 missiles)
- 578th Strategic Missile Squadron—Dyess AFB, TX—12 complexes (12 missiles)
- 579th Strategic Missile Squadron—Walker AFB, NM—12 complexes (12 missiles)
- 576th Strategic Missile Squadron—Vandenberg AFB, CA—3 complexes

The Atlas-F force had a maximum of seventy-two missiles on alert, plus potentially two additional sorties at Vandenberg (less four destroyed silos at Altus and Walker) before its stand-down.[121] After the stand-down, remaining Atlas

Lifting off its launch elevator at "E by the Sea" (576E), Atlas 15F reaches skyward. The concrete silo doors are noticeable near the bottom of the photo. *Courtesy of the United States Air Force*

A little over two weeks after the Cuban Missile Crisis ended, Atlas 13F lifts off from OSTF-2 (576G) on 14 November 1962. *Courtesy of the United States Air Force*

Atlas 3F collapses atop its silo-lift elevator at 576G during its launch on 3 April 1964. *Courtesy of the United States Air Force*

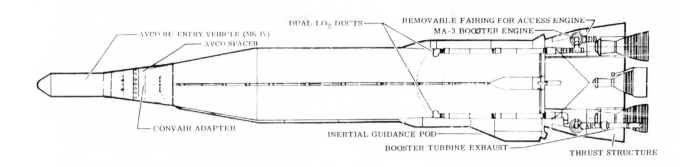

A cutaway of the Atlas-F ICBM. *Courtesy of the United States Air Force*

missiles were used during the ABRES program or were refitted as space launch vehicles.

The ABRES program objective was to validate, with full-scale testing, the theoretical investigations toward an understanding of reentry physics phenomena.[122] ABRES used Atlas missiles to test new designs for reentry vehicles and the effectiveness of penetration aids ("chaff" and active decoys) to spoof hostile radars.[123] A total of 135 E and F boosters were used by the Air Force for the Ballistic Missile Reentry Systems (BMRS) program and were launched from the ABRES/BMRS launch sites (also known as Complex 576A).[124]

Other programs included Reduced Exoatmospheric Cross Section (REX), which investigated slender reentry vehicles with lower radar cross sections; SLEIGH RIDE, which looked at the reentry vehicle's vulnerability to a nuclear blast; Optical Particle Decoy (OPADEC); and Low Observable Reentry Vehicle (LORV). Once the inventory of Atlas missiles was exhausted, the ABRES program used older-model Minuteman I missiles as target vehicles.

Another ABRES launch (Atlas 54F) with a prototype warhead takes off from the renamed BMRS A-1 (formerly 576A-1) on 1 May 1974. *Courtesy of the United States Air Force*

ATLAS-F ICBM Launches[125]

SEQUENCE	DATE	SITE	VEHICLE	CODENAME	NOTES
159	1 AUG 62	576E	ATLAS-F	HIS NIBS	
165	10 AUG 62	OSTF-2	ATLAS-F	CRASH TRUCK	
180	14 NOV 62	OSTF-2	ATLAS-F	ACTION TIME	
211	15 MAR 63	576D	ATLAS-F	TALL TREE 5	
214	21 MAR 63	OSTF-2	ATLAS-F	KENDALL GREEN	
215	23 MAR 63	576E	ATLAS-F	TALL TREE 4	
279	3 OCT 63	576G	ATLAS-F	HOT RUM	
306	18 DEC 63	576G	ATLAS-F	DAY BOOK	
339	3 APR 64	576G	ATLAS-F	HIGH BALL	
374	7 AUG 64	576E	ATLAS-F	LARGE CHARGE	
387	31 AUG 64	576D	ATLAS-F	BIG DEAL	

SEQUENCE	DATE	SITE	VEHICLE	CODENAME	NOTES
429	22 DEC 64	576E	ATLAS-F	STEP OVER	
430	8 JAN 65	576G	ATLAS-F	PILOT LIGHT	
496	5 AUG 65	576A-2	ATLAS-F	SEA TRAMP	
610	8 AUG 66	576A-2	ATLAS-F	BUSY RAMROD	
632	11 OCT 66	576A-2	ATLAS-F	LOW HILL	
657	17 JAN 67	576A-2	ATLAS-F	BUSY STEPSON	
668	13 FEB 67	576A-3	ATLAS-F	BUSY BOXER	
675	16 MAR 67	576A-2	ATLAS-F	LITTLE CHURCH	
698	19 MAY 67	576A-1	ATLAS-F	BUSY PIGSKIN	
709	9 JUN 67	576A-3	ATLAS-F	--	
724	22 JUL 67	576A-3	ATLAS-F	--	
728	29 JUL 67	576A-2	ATLAS-F	BREAD HOOK	
742	14 OCT 67	576A-2	ATLAS-F	--	
745	27 OCT 67	576A-3	ATLAS-F	--	
749	10 NOV 67	576A-1	ATLAS-F	--	
762	21 DEC 67	576A-3	ATLAS-F	--	
774	31 JAN 68	576A-3	ATLAS-F	--	
778	26 FEB 68	576A-1	ATLAS-F	--	
787	6 APR 68	576A-2	ATLAS-F	--	
795	3 MAY 68	576A-2	ATLAS-F	--	
802	1 JUN 68	576A-2	ATLAS-F	--	
806	22 JUN 68	576A-3	ATLAS-F	--	
808	29 JUN 68	576A-1	ATLAS-F	--	
811	11 JUL 68	576A-2	ATLAS-F	--	
823	25 SEP 68	576A-3	ATLAS-F	--	
824	27 SEP 68	576A-1	ATLAS-F	--	
835	16 NOV 68	576A-3	ATLAS-F	--	
838	24 NOV 68	576A-1	ATLAS-F	--	
846	16 JAN 69	576A-3	ATLAS-F	--	
862	17 MAR 69	576A-2	ATLAS-F	--	
902	20 AUG 69	576A-1	ATLAS-F	--	
912	16 SEP 69	576A-3	ATLAS-F	--	
922	10 OCT 69	576A-3	ATLAS-F	--	
935	3 DEC 69	576A-1	ATLAS-F	--	
938	12 DEC 69	576A-3	ATLAS-F	--	
944	8 FEB 70	576A-3	ATLAS-F	--	
953	13 MAR 70	576A-3	ATLAS-F	--	
969	30 MAY 70	576A-3	ATLAS-F	--	
971	9 JUN 70	576A-1	ATLAS-F	--	
1023	22 DEC 70	576A-3	ATLAS-F	--	
1047	5 APR 71	576A-1	ATLAS-F	--	
1067	29 JUN 71	576A-3	ATLAS-F	--	
1077	6 AUG 71	576A-2	ATLAS-F	--	
1081	1 SEP 71	576A-1	ATLAS-F	--	
1197	29 AUG 73	576A-3	ATLAS-F	--	
1204	30 SEP 73	576A-1	ATLAS-F	--	
1222	6 MAR 74	576A-1	ATLAS-F	--	
1227	23 MAR 74	576A-3	ATLAS-F	--	
1235	1 MAY 74	576A-1	ATLAS-F	--	
1240	28 JUN 74	576A-1	ATLAS-F	--	
1251	8 SEP 74	576A-1	ATLAS-F	--	
1258	12 OCT 74	576A-3	ATLAS-F	--	

ATLAS-E/F SLV

The Atlas-E/F was a stage-and-a-half, liquid-fueled, medium-lift space launch vehicle (SLV) derived from the Atlas ICBM. These Atlas—similar to previous variants—had a thin-walled, fully monocoque, corrosion-resistant stainless-steel outer body. The fuel/oxidizer system was RP-1 and liquid oxygen.[126] Major modifications for the Atlas-E/F SLV included replacing the inertial guidance system with a radio-controlled one—reversing the evolution of Atlas ICBM guidance (e.g., radio controlled to inertial guidance). This allowed the Atlas-E/F SLV to use the GE MOD III guidance system already in place at Vandenberg.[127]

The Atlas-E/F space booster was modified from Atlas-E and Atlas-F ICBMs by using parts from both programs after they were taken off alert in 1965.[128] Convair received a contract in 1966 to convert the two ICBM variants.[129] The Vandenberg Atlas Modification Program (VAMP) allowed refurbishment of the airframes at the base, instead of at Convair's Kearny Mesa plant.

The Atlas-E/F airframe was similar to previous Atlases, with a stainless-steel and aluminum structure 10 ft. in diameter and over 70 ft. in length. The airframe consisted of three sections: the booster section, containing the sustainer engine and two booster engines; the tank section, containing the stainless-steel, monocoque shell, which provides structural support for the payload and space for approximately 30,000 gallons of propellant; and the adapter section, which contains the payload. The empty airframe weighs about seven tons. Additionally, there are two electronic equipment pods attached to the tank skin.

Both SLC-3W and SLC-3E were modified for the Atlas-E/F. SLC-3W was modified in 1974, after the Thor/Agena program at SLC-3 ended.[130] SLC-3E was modified to launch Atlas-E/F in 1976.

While the E/F series flew a variety of payloads, one of the most notable was the series of global positioning system (GPS) Block 1 satellites. The early missions began launching in 1978 and were designated Navigation Technology Satellite (NTS) and, later, the NAVSTAR Global Positioning System.[131,132] Out of eleven launches, there was only one failure.[133] The later NAVSTAR GPS satellite blocks were launched aboard Delta II rockets at Cape Canaveral. Early

A new era in navigation begins with the launch of Navstar I (GPS Block 1) on 22 February 1978 aboard Atlas 64F. The first eleven GPS Block 1 satellites were launched from Vandenberg. *Courtesy of the United States Air Force*

Navstar III awaits launch aboard Atlas 47F from SLC-3E on 7 October 1978. *Courtesy of the United States Air Force*

A modified Atlas-E/F lifts off from SLC-3W on 8 December 1977. *Courtesy of the United States Air Force*

Air Force Space Test Program payload P72-2 is launched aboard Atlas 71F on 13 April 1975. *Courtesy of the United States Air Force*

control of the Block 1s was done at the GPS ground station at North Vandenberg.

NASA's NOAA series of polar-orbiting weather satellites and the Air Force's Defense Meteorological Support Program (DMSP) satellites also flew aboard Atlas-E/F boosters.[134] Just as the heavier DMSP Block 5D satellites necessitated a move from the Thor/Burner launcher, the later generation of DMSP Block 5Ds moved to the Titan II SLV and, later, to the Delta IV and Atlas V.[135]

ATLAS-E/F SLV Launches[136]

SEQUENCE	DATE	SITE	VEHICLE	CODENAME	NOTES
1243	13 JUL 74	SLC-3W	ATLAS-F	--	
1277	12 APR 75	SLC-3W	ATLAS-F	--	
1325	30 APR 76	SLC-3W	ATLAS-F	--	
1369	23 JUN 77	SLC-3W	ATLAS-F	--	
1385	8 DEC 77	SLC-3W	ATLAS-F	--	
1390	22 FEB 78	SLC-3E	ATLAS-F	--	NAVSTAR-1
1399	13 MAY 78	SLC-3E	ATLAS-F	--	NAVSTAR-2
1411	6 OCT 78	SLC-3E	ATLAS-F	--	NAVSTAR-3
1412	13 OCT 78	SLC-3W	ATLAS-F	--	
1418	10 DEC 78	SLC-3E	ATLAS-F	--	NAVSTAR-4
1424	24 FEB 79	SLC-3W	ATLAS-F	--	
1432	27 JUN 79	SLC-3W	ATLAS-F	--	
1449	9 FEB 80	SLC-3E	ATLAS-F	--	NAVSTAR-5
1453	3 MAR 80	SLC-3W	ATLAS-F	--	
1457	26 APR 80	SLC-3E	ATLAS-F	--	NAVSTAR-6
1458	29 MAY 80	SLC-3W	ATLAS-F	--	
1469	8 DEC 80	SLC-3W	ATLAS-E	--	
1484	23 JUN 81	SLC-3W	ATLAS-F	--	
1493	18 DEC 81	SLC-3E	ATLAS-E	--	NAVSTAR-7; LAUNCH FAILURE
1510	20 DEC 82	SLC-3W	ATLAS-E	--	
1518	28 MAR 83	SLC-3W	ATLAS-E	--	
1529	14 JUL 83	SLC-3W	ATLAS-E	--	NAVSTAR-8
1535	17 NOV 83	SLC-3W	ATLAS-E	--	
1549	13 JUN 84	SLC-3W	ATLAS-E	--	NAVSTAR-9
1553	8 SEP 84	SLC-3W	ATLAS-E	--	NAVSTAR-10
1561	12 DEC 84	SLC-3W	ATLAS-E	--	
1566	12 MAR 85	SLC-3W	ATLAS-E	--	
1576	8 OCT 85	SLC-3W	ATLAS-E	--	NAVSTAR-11
1591	17 SEP 86	SLC-3W	ATLAS-E	--	
1605	19 JUN 87	SLC-3W	ATLAS-E	--	
1618	2 FEB 88	SLC-3W	ATLAS-E	--	
1626	24 SEP 88	SLC-3W	ATLAS-E	--	
1647	11 APR 90	SLC-3W	ATLAS-E	--	
1654	1 DEC 90	SLC-3W	ATLAS-E	--	
1660	14 MAY 91	SLC-3W	ATLAS-E	--	
1670	28 NOV 91	SLC-3W	ATLAS-E	--	
1691	9 AUG 93	SLC-3W	ATLAS-E	--	
1704	29 AUG 94	SLC-3W	ATLAS-E	--	
1707	30 DEC 94	SLC-3W	ATLAS-E	--	
1711	24 MAR 95	SLC-3W	ATLAS-E	--	

ATLAS-H

The Atlas-H was a stage-and-a-half, liquid-fueled, medium-lift space launch vehicle derived from the Atlas ICBM. This Atlas, similar to previous variants, had a thin-walled, fully monocoque, corrosion-resistant stainless-steel outer body. The fuel/oxidizer system was RP-1 and liquid oxygen.[137] The Atlas-H used modifications developed for the Atlas-G rocket, which was never flown at Vandenberg.[138] These modifications included an improved Atlas core, stretched propellant tanks, and modernized electronics. Space Launch Complex 3 East (SLC-3E) was modified to Atlas-H configuration in 1982 and was used until 1987, with the final Atlas-H launch.

Stated succinctly in the Historic American Engineering Record (HAER) for SLC-3E, the Atlas-H

> was designed in response to a military payload sponsor's concern about reliability of the Atlas E/F. Several E/F missions had been aborted in flight due to the failure of one or more engines to ignite prior to free launch. The Atlas H was designed to combine desirable features of the E/F model with the reliability of the hold-down system.[139]

The rocket had much in common with previous Atlas vehicles. Guidance for the Atlas-H launches was performed with the General Electric Radio Tracking System (GERTS), similar to the guidance on the Atlas-D ICBM. Advantages to using GERTS for Atlas-H missions were twofold: first, it was the cheapest guidance around; second, it was the most reliable.[140]

Common launch equipment was also a boon for Atlas-H operations. This commonality allowed for reuse of equipment during modifications at SLC-3E. In one instance, an Atlas SLV launcher was relocated from Cape Canaveral's Launch Complex 13 to SLC-3E. The hold-down system allowed the three engines to generate 90 percent thrust before releasing the rocket.[141] Payload fairing diameters remained relatively constant at 7 ft. or less.

The primary customer(s) for the Atlas-H have not been officially stated in open or declassified literature, nor have the payloads been definitively identified.[142] All five Atlas-H launches were successful, with zero launch failures.[143]

RIGHT: The Atlas-H was derived from the SLV-3D, also known as the Atlas/Centaur, with the listed modifications. *Courtesy of the United States Air Force*

Atlas 6004H lifts off from SLC-3E on 9 February 1986 during a nighttime launch. *Courtesy of the United States Air Force*

Five launches of Atlas-H culminated in the final one on 15 May 1987 (Atlas 6005H). The payload fairing configuration was identical for all launches, but as of 2016, the payloads have not been officially identified. *Courtesy of the United States Air Force*

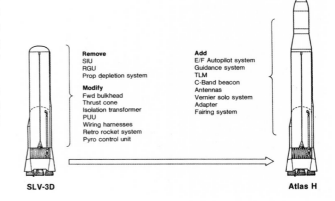

ATLAS-H Launches[144]

SEQUENCE	DATE	SITE	VEHICLE	CODENAME	NOTES
1514	9 FEB 83	SLC-3E	ATLAS-H	--	
1523	9 JUN 83	SLC-3E	ATLAS-H	--	
1541	5 FEB 84	SLC-3E	ATLAS-H	--	
1579	9 FEB 86	SLC-3E	ATLAS-H	--	
1604	15 MAY 87	SLC-3E	ATLAS-H	--	

ATLAS IIAS

The Atlas IIAS was a stage-and-a-half, liquid-fueled, medium-lift space launch vehicle derived from the Atlas ICBM. This Atlas, similar to previous variants, had a thin-walled, fully monocoque, corrosion-resistant stainless-steel outer body. The fuel/oxidizer system was RP-1 and liquid oxygen.[145] The structural integrity of the system is maintained through pressurization (on pad) or mechanical stretching (in storage). The booster engine is a Rocketdyne MA-5A engine system, with the sustainer motor and two Vernier engines consisting of 1.5 stages, using propellants from the same tanks. The core vehicle uses 108,000 lbs. of rocket propellant 1 (RP-1) as fuel and 242,000 lbs. of liquid oxygen as oxidizer (RP-1 is a kerosene hydrocarbon). Hydrazine-fueled thrusters provide roll control for aerodynamic stability.

The Atlas IIAS contains modification to the original Atlas SLV configuration to provide additional performance through increased booster thrust, lengthening of propellant tanks, and upgraded navigation avionics.[146] Additional thrust is provided by four Castor IVA solid rocket motors,[147] containing 22,300 lbs. of hydroxyl-terminated polybutadiene (HTPB) each as propellant, with the casing constructed of steel. HTPB propellant contains aluminum as fuel and ammonium perchlorate as oxidizer, with HTPB as a bonding material.

The Centaur booster was the world's first high-impulse, liquid-fueled upper stage. The version on the Atlas IIAS (Centaur II) contains an upgraded Pratt & Whitney dual RL10A-4 propulsion system and remote-control unit.[148] The upper stage is fueled by 5,692 lbs. of liquid hydrogen and 31,308 lbs. of liquid oxygen as oxidizer.

The first launch of an Atlas IIAS booster took place on 18 December 1999 from SLC-3E. The booster carried a $1.3 billion Terra satellite, the first of NASA's Earth Observing System (EOS) program.[149] The satellite carried five instrument packages to monitor interaction of solar radiation with Earth

The Terra EOS satellite is launched aboard Atlas IIAS AC-141 from SLC-3 on 18 December 1999. Note the four strap-on solid boosters. *Courtesy of the United States Air Force*

features, such as oceans, land, and atmosphere. The launch was controlled and monitored at Vandenberg's Remote Launch Control Center, since the SLC-3E blockhouse became a computer data complex during the pad upgrade in the mid-1990s.

The 8 September 2001 launch was the first Atlas IIAS to carry a NRO payload.[150] The use of a Centaur II upper stage on the launch stack gave indications of a new variant of

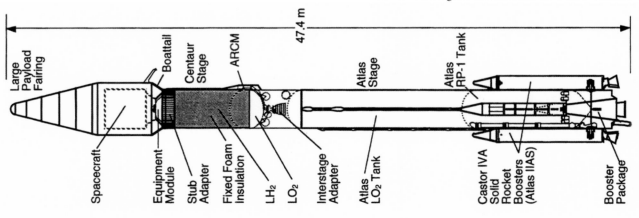

The Atlas IIAS schematic illustrates the placement of the LOX and RP-1 fuel tank, a configuration little changed from the original Atlas ICBM. *Courtesy of the United States Air Force*

spacecraft being launched.[151] Development of a medium-lift capability into a high-inclination orbit was indicated by a massive spending effort (estimated at $200–$330 million) to refurbish SLC-3E.[152] The flight marked another achievement as the heaviest Atlas-Centaur payload launched at the time.[153]

The final Atlas IIAS launch took place on 2 December 2003, with a similar booster configuration and launch profile as the September 2001 NRO mission.[154]

ATLAS IIAS Launches[155]

SEQUENCE	DATE	SITE	VEHICLE	CODENAME	NOTES
1787	18 DEC 99	SLC-3E	ATLAS IIAS	--	FIRST LAUNCH OF ATLAS IIAS.
1809	8 SEP 01	SLC-3E	ATLAS IIAS	--	NRO PAYLOAD
1841	2 DEC 03	SLC-3E	ATLAS IIAS	--	NRO PAYLOAD. FINAL LAUNCH OF ATLAS IIAS.

ATLAS V

The Atlas V is a two-stage, liquid-fueled, medium- to heavy-lift space launch vehicle. While the Atlas name is used for the vehicle and is included in the Atlas launch family, there are major design differences compared to previous Atlas rockets:

- There is only one first stage, unlike the previous "stage and a half" design.
- The main diameter of the core booster was enlarged from 10 ft. to 12.5 ft.

- The airframe is made of aluminum and is internally supported, unlike the stainless-steel body, requiring pressurization.
- The Atlas engines—booster, sustainer, and Vernier—have been replaced with one RD-180 Russian-made engine.

Changes in Atlas evolution are evident here. Note the two-chambered engines instead of the stage-and-a-half booster and sustainer engines on previous versions. *Courtesy of the United States Air Force*

An Atlas V lifts off from Vandenberg's Space Launch Complex 3. The two RD-180 exhaust chambers are visible at the first-stage rear. *Courtesy of the United States Air Force*

NROL-28 sits at SLC-3, awaiting launch aboard the inaugural Atlas V launch from Vandenberg on 13 March 2008. *Courtesy of the United States Air Force*

The Atlas V payload fairing containing the WorldView 4 satellite is moved into position into the SLC-3 mobile service tower. *Courtesy of the United States Air Force*

The Atlas V is the name for a system of configurable designs for a variety of space launch missions. The primary piece of the Atlas V is the common core booster (CCB) with a single RD-180 engine. The Centaur second stage (when utilized) uses an RL-10 engine. Modifications to the CCB and upper-stage pairing are given configuration numbers. These three-digit numbers indicate the size of payload fairing (4 m vs. 5 m), number of solid rocket boosters, and number of Centaur engines.[156]

For example, the 15 April 2011 launch from SLC-3 was designated an Atlas V 411. This flight used a 4-meter payload fairing, had one solid rocket booster, and used a Centaur upper stage with one engine. The 13 December 2014 launch from SLC-3 was designated an Atlas V 541, with the 5-meter fairing, four solid-rocket boosters, and one Centaur upper stage / engine.

Up to five solid rocket boosters encased in monolithic filament-wound carbon composite can be attached to the

A Centaur upper stage is lifted into position. The RL-10 liquid-fuel cryogenic rocket engine is visible at the bottom. *Courtesy of the United States Air Force*

Atlas V airframe.[157] The Centaur upper stage can have either one or two engines, depending on configuration requirements.

The first launch of an Atlas V at Vandenberg took place on 13 March 2008.[158]

ATLAS V Launches[159]

SEQUENCE	DATE	SITE	VEHICLE	CODENAME	NOTES
1878	13 MAR 08	SLC-3E	ATLAS V	--	NROL-28; FIRST ATLAS V LAUNCH
1894	18 OCT 09	SLC-3E	ATLAS V	--	DMSP F18
1902	20 SEP 10	SLC-3E	ATLAS V	--	NROL-41
1909	14 APR 11	SLC-3E	ATLAS V	--	NROL-34
1917	13 SEP 12	SLC-3E	ATLAS V	--	NROL-36
1920	11 FEB 13	SLC-3E	ATLAS V	--	LANDSAT 8
1928	6 DEC 13	SLC-3E	ATLAS V	--	NROL-39
1930	3 APR 14	SLC-3E	ATLAS V	--	DMSP F19
1933	13 AUG 14	SLC-3E	ATLAS V	--	WORLDVIEW-3
1935	12 DEC 14	SLC-3E	ATLAS V	--	NROL-35
1941	8 OCT 15	SLC-3E	ATLAS V	--	NROL-55

ATLAS/AGENA-A

The Atlas/Agena-A had a stage-and-a-half, liquid-fueled, medium-lift space launch vehicle derived from the Atlas ICBM, with an upper stage (Agena-A) for orbital insertion. The Atlas component, similar to previous variants, consisted of a thin-walled, fully monocoque, corrosion-resistant stainless-steel outer body. The fuel/oxidizer system was RP-1 and liquid oxygen. The Agena upper stage consisted of an airframe with propulsion, auxiliary power, guidance and control, and space-ground communication systems.[160] As a semistandardized "shell" for payloads, the Agena-A became the world's first general-purpose satellite.

The Agena upper stage (XLR-81, RM-81) was derived from a project to develop a powered pod for the B-58 Hustler bomber aircraft. The XLR-81 engine, also known as the "Bell Hustler," was built under contract with Convair and Bell Aircraft Corporation. After contract termination in 1957, the surplus inventory of engines was given to Lockheed Aircraft Corporation and given the new name of Agena:

> The Department of Defense's Advanced Research Projects Agency (ARPA) proposed to name the stage in 1958 for the star Agena in the constellation Centaurus because the rocket was an upper stage "igniting in the sky."[161]

The name "Agena" was originally published in *Geography of the Heavens*, a collection of celestial names by astronomer Elija H. Burritt.[162] This name followed the pattern set by Lockheed to name aircraft and missiles after stellar phenomena and was approved by ARPA in June 1959.[163]

The Agena-A primary systems include many subsystems.[164] The airframe included the main fuselage to protect the payload, booster adapter to mate the upper stage to the booster, explosive destruct package (if the launch goes awry), and pyrotechnics for upper stage (or payload) separation. The propulsion system included feed and load equipment to route fuel to the main engine, pressurization equipment, the main rocket engine, a smaller ullage motor to ensure propellant flowed to the main engine,[165] retarding rockets to slow acceleration, and backup (secondary) propulsion systems.

The propulsion power plant used a conventional turbopump-fed, gimbal-mounted, storable liquid propellant of unsymmetrical dimethylhydrazine (UDMH) and inhibited red fuming nitric acid (IRFNA). The electrical power subsystem included primary power sources, electrical distribution wiring, and solar power arrays (not present on all Agena-A missions).

Guidance and Control included flight control electronics, hydraulic and pneumatic attitude-control equipment, sensors to maintain inertial and stellar guidance orientation, and a velocity meter. The command and control system contained tracking and command control equipment, data links, antenna and RF transmit/receive devices, and special telemetry channels.

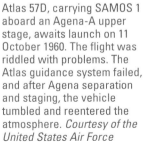

Atlas 57D, carrying SAMOS 1 aboard an Agena-A upper stage, awaits launch on 11 October 1960. The flight was riddled with problems. The Atlas guidance system failed, and after Agena separation and staging, the vehicle tumbled and reentered the atmosphere. *Courtesy of the United States Air Force*

SAMOS 2 is launched aboard Atlas 70D on 31 January 1961. The black-and-white paint scheme on the Agena upper stage mirrored those in the Discoverer/CORONA series. *Courtesy of the United States Air Force*

After the Atlas engines shut down, the Agena-A would separate from the Atlas and coast for approximately four minutes as the vehicle oriented itself for orbital injection.[166] Following proper orientation, the Agena-A's engine would burn for around two minutes up to a speed of 17,000 miles per hour to obtain proper orbit of around 300 miles in altitude, with an orbital period of ninety-four minutes. The Agena-A for the Atlas booster weighed around 4,100 lbs, compared to the Thor's Agena-A's weight of 1,700 lbs.

In 1960, the director of Defense Research and Engineering requested that the secretary of the Air Force build a new blockhouse and three additional launchpads for Atlas/Agena vehicles. These new pads were to be adjacent to PALC-1.[167]

PREVIOUS DESIGNATION	CURRENT DESIGNATION
PALC-1-1	SLC-3W
PALC-1-2	SLC-3E
PALC-2-3	SLC-4W
PALC-2-4	SLC-4E

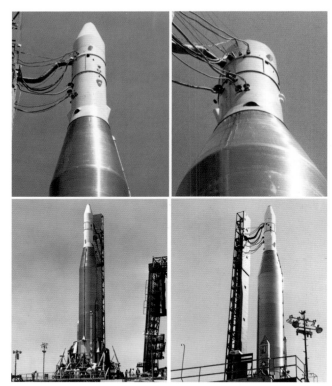

Four frames of SAMOS 1 aboard Atlas 57D show the umbilical connections from the gantry to the payload. Onboard electrical power from batteries is preserved until right before launch. *Courtesy of the United States Air Force*

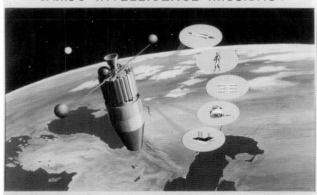

The missions for the SAMOS surveillance series: technical intelligence, troop and armament numbers, transportation, and infrastructure. *Courtesy of the National Reconnaissance Office*

The Atlas/Agena-A combination performed only two launches from Vandenberg, launching the first two SAMOS satellites. SAMOS was designed in the mid-1950s to be a photoreconnaissance satellite providing a near-real-time film readout system. At the time the SAMOS program's cover story was the following:

> Project SAMOS is a research and development program to determine the capabilities for making observations of space, the atmosphere and the nature of the globe from satellites.[168]

The priorities for the photographic SAMOS system were[169]

- location of Operational ICBM sites,
- descriptive information on high-priority target list items (indications/warning intelligence), and
- technical characteristics of high-priority list items (technical intelligence).

The design used analog film run through a line scanner, which would transmit the frequency-modulated signal down to earth.[170] The ill-fated SAMOS system had drawbacks, such as a small supply of film aboard, no storage or recall capability, lack of encoding or encryption on the downlinked images, and, finally, short downlink time when over a ground station.

The first launch on 11 October 1960 failed due to problems within the Agena-A upper stage. On 31 January 1961 the second launch of SAMOS was the final use of the Atlas/Agena-A combination. While the Agena-A worked satisfactorily, the intelligence "take" from the mission was poor: the radio-relayed images were of low quality and thus useless for intelligence purposes.

The Agena-A upper stage would be supplanted by the Agena-B, which had a larger fuel capacity and engines that could restart in space.

ATLAS/AGENA-A Launches[171]

SEQUENCE	DATE	SITE	VEHICLE	CODENAME	NOTES
60	11 OCT 60	PALC-1-1	ATLAS/AGENA-A	GIBSON GIRL	SAMOS 1; 698BK ELINT PACKAGE
76	31 JAN 61	PALC-1-1	ATLAS/AGENA-A	JAYHAWK JAMBOREE	SAMOS 2; 698BK ELINT PACKAGE

ATLAS/AGENA-B

The Atlas/Agena-B is a stage-and-a-half, liquid-fueled, medium-lift space launch vehicle derived from the Atlas ICBM, with an upper stage (Agena-B) for orbital insertion. The Atlas, similar to previous variants, consisted of a thin-walled, fully monocoque, corrosion-resistant stainless-steel outer body. The fuel/oxidizer system was RP-1 and liquid oxygen. The Agena-B upper stage consisted of an airframe with propulsion, auxiliary power, guidance and control, and space-ground communication systems.[172]

The Agena-B, mirroring the development of the Agena-A, was designed, engineered, and manufactured on an experimental basis for military satellite systems. As originally used by NASA and the Air Force, the Agena line was produced in twenty-three different configurations in pseudo "block" releases.[173]

The "advanced Agena," as it was briefly called, provided an on-orbit engine with restart capability, double the Agena-A burn time, increased power (specific impulse), greater payload capacity, and the ability to adjust orbital altitude.[174] The Atlas/Agena-B combination provided the transportation for two of the legacy programs separated from the WS-117L program effort: the film-based near-real-time transmission satellite and the infrared detection satellite (SAMOS and MIDAS, respectively). While the earth-centered pointing requirements for the photographic and infrared payloads rivaled the needs of the CORONA program, the Agena-B's combination of horizon sensor, inertial reference unit, and gas jet controls gave the vehicle a plus/minus of 2° of pointing accuracy.

The Agena-B contained a XLR81-BA-7 engine—improved over the previous model—to allow multiple restarts in space. The amount of propellant carried was also increased to double what the Agena-A carried. While the improvements were welcome, the Atlas/Agena-B combination still required a different configuration control from other Agena/booster

Atlas 106D carrying SAMOS 3 awaits launch at SLC-3W. The launch ended in failure when the Atlas engines shut down immediately after liftoff. The rocket fell back onto the pad and exploded. Postmortem on the launch determined that a pad umbilical detached milliseconds too late, causing the launch vehicle to switch from internal to external power. *Courtesy of the United States Air Force*

MIDAS 5 was launched aboard Atlas 110D on 9 April 1962. The satellite reached orbit successfully but suffered a power failure during its sixth orbit. *Courtesy of the United States Air Force*

The nose of the Atlas/Agena-B carrying a SAMOS payload looked similar to the CORONA capsules, but a little wider. *Courtesy of the United States Air Force*

SAMOS 7 takes off from Vandenberg carrying infrared sensors for measuring both thermal emissions and reflected solar radiation from the earth and its atmosphere. *Courtesy of the United States Air Force*

pairings. This disparity in standardization led directly to the development of the Agena-D upper stage.

The Vandenberg flight history of the Atlas/Agena-B focused solely on two satellite programs: MIDAS and SAMOS. SAMOS was composed of the E-1, E-2, and E-5 photographic systems. The primary mission of E-1 and E-2 was to obtain photography from a satellite 270 miles above the surface of the earth.[175] MIDAS was designed to detect infrared emissions from rocket and missile launches. While the MIDAS series was not the overwhelming success hoped for by its designers, its initial development helped pave the way for the Defense Support Program series of missile-warning satellites.

ATLAS/AGENA-B Launches[176]

SEQUENCE	DATE	SITE	VEHICLE	CODENAME	NOTES
90	12 JUL 61	PALC-1-2	ATLAS/AGENA-B	POLAR ORBIT	MIDAS 3
97	9 SEP 61	PALC-1-1	ATLAS/AGENA-B	FIRST MOTION	SAMOS 3
102	21 OCT 61	PALC-1-2	ATLAS/AGENA-B	BIG TOWN	MIDAS 4/WEST FORD
108	22 NOV 61	PALC-1-1	ATLAS/AGENA-B	ROUND TRIP	SAMOS 4
115	22 DEC 61	PALC-1-2	ATLAS/AGENA-B	OCEAN WAY	SAMOS 5
126	7 MAR 62	PALC-1-2	ATLAS/AGENA-B	LOOSE TOOTH	SAMOS 6
130	9 APR 62	PALC-1-2	ATLAS/AGENA-B	NIGHT HUNT	MIDAS 5
133	26 APR 62	PALC-1-1	ATLAS/AGENA-B	DAINTY DOLL	SAMOS 7
144	17 JUN 62	PALC-1-1	ATLAS/AGENA-B	RUBBER GUN	SAMOS 8
154	18 JUL 62	PALC-1-1	ATLAS/AGENA-B	ARMORED CAR	SAMOS 9
161	5 AUG 62	PALC-1-1	ATLAS/AGENA-B	AIR SCOUT	SAMOS 10
179	11 NOV 62	PALC-1-1	ATLAS/AGENA-B	AFTER DECK	SAMOS 11
190	17 DEC 62	PALC-1-2	ATLAS/AGENA-B	BARGIN COUNTER	MIDAS 6
231	9 MAY 63	PALC-1-2	ATLAS/AGENA-B	DAMP CLAY	MIDAS 7
240	12 JUN 63	PALC-1-2	ATLAS/AGENA-B	BIG FOUR	MIDAS 8
255	18 JUL 63	PALC-1-2	ATLAS/AGENA-B	DAMP DUCK	MIDAS 9

ATLAS/AGENA-D

The Atlas/Agena-D is a stage-and-a-half, liquid-fueled, medium-lift space launch vehicle derived from the Atlas ICBM, with an upper stage (Agena-D) for orbital insertion. The Atlas, similar to previous variants, consisted of a thin-walled, fully monocoque, corrosion-resistant stainless-steel outer body. The fuel/oxidizer system was RP-1 and liquid oxygen. The Agena-D upper stage consisted of an airframe with propulsion, auxiliary power, guidance and control, and space-ground communication systems.[177] After the experiences with the Agena-A and Agena-B variants, there was a great interest in "standardizing" the Agena upper stage for payloads. Propulsion system standardization was predetermined, since there was little variation in the Agena-B "blocks."[178] The power system allowed for choices: batteries, solar panels, or even nuclear generators (e.g., SNAP reactors).

The primary "user" for the Atlas/Agena-D combination was the National Reconnaissance Office for its GAMBIT program. GAMBIT was the first photographic satellite project to produce reconnaissance photographs with 2 to 3 ft. resolution.[179] The first Atlas/Agena-D flight was launched on 12 July 1963. The final Atlas GAMBIT (Project 206) flight, and thirty-eighth overall, was launched on 4 June 1967. The first three flights in the program kept the Agena-D attached to the orbital control vehicle in a so-called hitch-up mode. The remaining flights had the Agena-D separate from the OCV and payload.

The GAMBIT program was a phenomenal success, assisting the US intelligence community with assessing the Soviet strategic threat, monitoring arms control treaty compliance, and providing scientific and technical weapons analysis.[180]

A second series of satellites that used the Atlas/Agena-D pairing was the RTS-1 series, otherwise known as Program 461. These satellites used detectors and an optics system to detect and track infrared (heat) emissions from rocket and missile launches. Originally part of the WS-117L program, as Subsystem G, the infrared detection system went through a maturation period within the MIDAS program, and later the Research Test Series (RTS).[181] These missions led directly to the development of the Defense Support Program (DSP) missile-warning satellites.

The first launch of RTS took place on 9 June 1966 at SLC-3E. The Agena-D upper stage failed and the satellite reentered the atmosphere on 3 December 1966.[182] The remaining two flights (RTS-1 Flight 2 and Flight 3) were successful and lasted nearly a year and over a year, respectively.[183] The satellites successfully detected *all* US and Soviet missile and rocket tests during the time period—139 in all.

The final Atlas/Agena-D launch from Vandenberg was the Seasat-1 oceanographic satellite for NASA on 26 June 1978.[184]

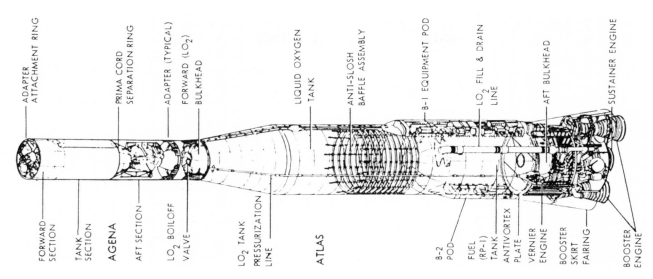

A cutaway shows the connectivity between the Atlas booster and Agena upper stage. *Courtesy of the United States Air Force*

Atlas 212D lifts the second GAMBIT flight (Mission 4002) from PALC 2-3 on 6 September 1963. *Courtesy of the United States Air Force*

The fifth GAMBIT flight (Mission 4005) lifts off from PALC 2-3 on 25 February 1964. *Courtesy of the United States Air Force*

First GAMBIT flight (Mission 4001) takes off aboard an Atlas/Agena-D on 12 July 1963. *Courtesy of the United States Air Force*

ATLAS/AGENA-D Launches[185]

SEQUENCE	DATE	SITE	VEHICLE	CODENAME	NOTES
252	12 JUL 63	PALC-2-3	ATLAS/AGENA-D	FISH POOL	GAMBIT MSN 4001 (KH-7)
270	6 SEP 63	PALC-2-3	ATLAS/AGENA-D	FIXED FEE	GAMBIT MSN 4002 (KH-7)
284	25 OCT 63	PALC-2-3	ATLAS/AGENA-D	HAY BAILER	GAMBIT MSN 4003 (KH-7)

SEQUENCE	DATE	SITE	VEHICLE	CODENAME	NOTES
305	18 DEC 63	PALC-2-3	ATLAS/AGENA-D	REST EASY	GAMBIT MSN 4004 (KH-7)
326	25 FEB 64	PALC-2-3	ATLAS/AGENA-D	UPPER OCTANE	GAMBIT MSN 4005 (KH-7)
332	11 MAR 64	PALC-2-3	ATLAS/AGENA-D	INK BLOTTER	GAMBIT MSN 4006 (KH-7)
343	23 APR 64	PALC-2-3	ATLAS/AGENA-D	ANCHOR DAN	GAMBIT MSN 4007 (KH-7)
349	19 MAY 64	PALC-2-3	ATLAS/AGENA-D	BIG FRED	GAMBIT MSN 4008 (KH-7)
364	6 JUL 64	PALC-2-3	ATLAS/AGENA-D	QUARTER ROUND	GAMBIT MSN 4009 (KH-7)
378	14 AUG 64	PALC-2-4	ATLAS/AGENA-D	BIG SICKLE	GAMBIT MSN 4010 (KH-7)
396	23 SEP 64	PALC-2-4	ATLAS/AGENA-D	SLOW PACE	GAMBIT MSN 4011 (KH-7)
402	8 OCT 64	PALC-2-4	ATLAS/AGENA-D	BUSY LINE	GAMBIT MSN 4012 (KH-7)
405	23 OCT 64	PALC-2-3	ATLAS/AGENA-D	BOON DECKER	GAMBIT MSN 4013 (KH-7)
420	4 DEC 64	PALC-2-4	ATLAS/AGENA-D	BATTLE ROYAL	GAMBIT MSN 4014 (KH-7)
437	23 JAN 65	PALC-2-3	ATLAS/AGENA-D	SAND LARK	GAMBIT MSN 4015 (KH-7)
449	12 MAR 65	PALC-2-3	ATLAS/AGENA-D	SHIP RAIL	GAMBIT MSN 4016 (KH-7)
457	3 APR 65	PALC-2-4	ATLAS/AGENA-D	AIR PUMP	SNAPSHOT/SECOR 4
463	28 APR 65	PALC-2-4	ATLAS/AGENA-D	DWARF TREE	GAMBIT MSN 4017 (KH-7)
472	27 MAY 65	PALC-2-4	ATLAS/AGENA-D	BOTTOM LAND	GAMBIT MSN 4018 (KH-7)
484	25 JUN 65	PALC-2-4	ATLAS/AGENA-D	WORN FACE	GAMBIT MSN 4019 (KH-7)
490	12 JUL 65	PALC-2-4	ATLAS/AGENA-D	WHITE PINE	GAMBIT MSN 4020 (KH-7)
494	3 AUG 65	PALC-2-4	ATLAS/AGENA-D	WATER TOWER	GAMBIT MSN 4021 (KH-7)
510	30 SEP 65	PALC-2-4	ATLAS/AGENA-D	LOG FOG	GAMBIT MSN 4022 (KH-7)
517	8 NOV 65	PALC-2-4	ATLAS/AGENA-D	SHOP DEGREE	GAMBIT MSN 4023 (KH-7)
533	19 JAN 66	PALC-2-4	ATLAS/AGENA-D	BLANKET PARTY	GAMBIT MSN 4024 (KH-7)
543	15 FEB 66	PALC-2-4	ATLAS/AGENA-D	MUCHO GRANDE	GAMBIT MSN 4025 (KH-7)
554	18 MAR 66	PALC-2-4	ATLAS/AGENA-D	DUMB DORA	GAMBIT MSN 4026 (KH-7)
569	19 APR 66	PALC-2-4	ATLAS/AGENA-D	SHALLOW STREAM	GAMBIT MSN 4027 (KH-7)
577	14 MAY 66	PALC-2-4	ATLAS/AGENA-D	PUMP HANDLE	GAMBIT MSN 4028 (KH-7)
589	3 JUN 66	PALC-2-4	ATLAS/AGENA-D	POWER DRILL	GAMBIT MSN 4029 (KH-7)
590	9 JUN 66	PALC-1-2	ATLAS/AGENA-D	MAMAS BOY	RTS-1 F1
600	12 JUL 66	SLC-4E	ATLAS/AGENA-D	SNAKE CREEK	GAMBIT MSN 4030 (KH-7)
612	16 AUG 66	SLC-4E	ATLAS/AGENA-D	SILVER DOLL	GAMBIT MSN 4031 (KH-7)
616	19 AUG 66	SLC-3E	ATLAS/AGENA-D	HAPPY MOUNTAIN	RTS-1 F2
623	16 SEP 66	SLC-4E	ATLAS/AGENA-D	TAXI DRIVER	GAMBIT MSN 4032 (KH-7)
631	5 OCT 66	SLC-3E	ATLAS/AGENA-D	DWARF KILLER	RTS-1 F3
633	12 OCT 66	SLC-4E	ATLAS/AGENA-D	GLEAMING STAR	GAMBIT MSN 4033 (KH-7)
640	2 NOV 66	SLC-4E	ATLAS/AGENA-D	RED CABOOSE	GAMBIT MSN 4034 (KH-7)
645	5 DEC 66	SLC-4E	ATLAS/AGENA-D	BUSY MERMAID	GAMBIT MSN 4035 (KH-7)
663	2 FEB 67	SLC-4E	ATLAS/AGENA-D	BUSY PARTY	GAMBIT MSN 4036 (KH-7)
699	22 MAY 67	SLC-4E	ATLAS/AGENA-D	BUSY CAMPER	GAMBIT MSN 4037 (KH-7)
708	4 JUN 67	SLC-4E	ATLAS/AGENA-D		GAMBIT MSN 4038 (KH-7)
1405	26 JUN 78	SLC-3W	ATLAS/AGENA-D		SEASAT-1

ATLAS/BURNER II

The Atlas/Burner II was a two-stage vehicle with an Atlas booster and a Burner II (or IIA) upper stage.

The Atlas/Burner II is a stage-and-a-half, liquid-fueled, medium-lift space launch vehicle derived from the Atlas ICBM, with an upper stage (Burner II or IIA) for orbital insertion. The Atlas, similar to previous variants, consisted of a thin-walled, fully monocoque, corrosion-resistant stainless-steel outer body. The fuel/oxidizer system was RP-1 and liquid oxygen. The Burner II (and IIA) upper stage used a Thiokol Star 37B solid-rocket motor mounted with electronics and an attitude control system.[186] The Burner II (and IIA) was traditionally used atop a Thor or Delta booster.

The Atlas/Burner II combination had only two launches from Vandenberg. The first one was an Atlas/Burner II on 16 August 1968. The vehicle carried a number of experiments aboard, which all failed to separate due to a malfunction in the heat shield shroud.[187]

The second flight was an Atlas/Burner IIA modified from the original Burner II specifications, which took place on 2 October 1972. This flight launched a payload for the Air Force's Space Test Program and a calibration satellite for the Army Ballistic Missile Defense Agency.

ATLAS/BURNER II Launches[188]

SEQUENCE	DATE	SITE	VEHICLE	CODENAME	NOTES	
817	16 AUG 68	SLC-3E	ATLAS/BURNER II	--	LCS 3/EGRS 12	ONLY USE OF ATLAS/BURNER II
1148	2 OCT 72	BMRS A-1	ATLAS/BURNER IIA	--	RADCAT/RADSAT	ONLY USE OF ATLAS/BURNER IIA

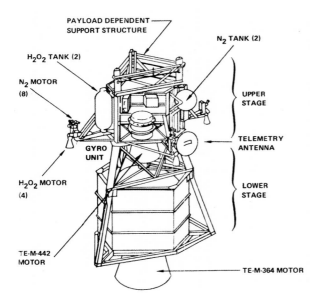

The long upper stage with distinctive yellow payload "nose" signifies a Burner II launch aboard Atlas 7004 on 16 August 1968. *Courtesy of the United States Air Force*

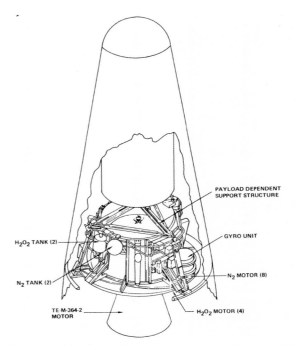

The internals of the Burner II upper-stage engine. *Courtesy of the United States Air Force*

A cutaway schematic shows the upper and lower stages of the Burner IIA. *Courtesy of the United States Air Force*

A Radcat satellite and Air Force Space Test Program P72-1 lifts off aboard the sole Atlas / Burner IIA launch on 2 October 1972. *Courtesy of the United States Air Force*

ATLAS/PRIME

The Atlas/PRIME series of three launches took place in late 1966 to early 1967. In the 1960s, NASA and the Air Force conducted a joint program called Aerothermodynamic/ Elastic Structural Systems Environmental Tests (ASSET). The designs, lifted aboard Thor, Thor-Delta, and Atlas rockets from Cape Canaveral, concentrated on aerothermodynamics, structural concepts and materials, reentry aerodynamics, and aeroperformance.[189]

A second series of tests by the Air Force used lifting bodies for a project named Precision Recovery Including Maneuvering Entry (PRIME). The lifting body shape was lofted into space and came back down to earth as a maneuvering reentry vehicle with cross-range capabilities. Again, research tests focused on thermodynamics through

an atmosphere, reentry aerodynamics, and cross-range problems.[190] The vehicle would travel through the atmosphere on its return flight and terminate the test at Mach 2 by deploying a drogue ballute (a large parachute-like braking device). After slowing, a parachute would deploy and the craft would be retrieved midair over the ocean by a JC-130B Hercules aircraft (similar to reentering CORONA and GAMBIT film capsules).[191]

Three flights of Atlas/PRIME were flown from SLC-3E, taking the vehicle from a low-earth orbit to recovery. Only the third, and last, flight followed a successful flight path—it is now on display at the National Museum of the US Air Force in Dayton, Ohio.[192] This research program provided critical data to the future atmospheric reentering vehicle known as the space shuttle orbiter.

Atlas 7001 with PRIME 1 payload lifts off from SLC-3E on 21 December 1966. *Courtesy of the United States Air Force*

The second PRIME mission launches from SLC-3E on 5 March 1967 aboard Atlas 7002. *Courtesy of the United States Air Force*

The third and final PRIME mission departs SLC-3E atop Atlas 7003 on 20 April 1967. *Courtesy of the United States Air Force*

ATLAS/PRIME Launches[193]

SEQUENCE	DATE	SITE	VEHICLE	CODENAME	NOTES
650	21 DEC 66	SLC-3E	ATLAS/PRIME	BUSY PEACOCK	PRIME-1
673	5 MAR 67	SLC-3E	ATLAS/PRIME	GIANT CHIEF	PRIME-2
684	19 APR 67	SLC-3E	ATLAS/PRIME	BUSY TOURNAMENT	PRIME-3

BLACK BRANT III

The Black Brant[194] was a family of sounding rockets designed and developed in Canada. In 1958, the Canadian Armament Research and Development Establishment created a new solid-rocket propellant and a test vehicle named "Black Brant."

The Black Brant III first flew in June 1962, but because of initial problems with stability and control, it took until April 1964 before the rocket was declared ready for operations. It was a spin-stabilized vehicle that could lift a 40 lb. payload to 110 miles.

The US Navy tested the Black Brant III twice at Point Arguello Launch Complex in 1963 but did not adopt it for regular use.

BLACK BRANT III Launches[195]

SEQUENCE	DATE	SITE	VEHICLE	CODENAME	NOTES
248	1 JUL 63	PALC-A	BLACK BRANT III	--	
289	7 NOV 63	PALC-A	BLACK BRANT III	--	

BOMARC-A

The IM-99/CIM-10A BOMARC-A was a nuclear-capable surface-to-air defensive interceptor missile in the 1950s and 1960s.[196] Early plans for BOMARC system deployment included an air defense squadron at Vandenberg, activating in October 1960 and being operational by October 1961.[197] This requirement was eventually eliminated, because when BOMARC completed its deployment in 1962, no West Coast interceptor sites had been built.[198] As the need for nuclear-tipped surface-to-air missiles waned, the remaining BOMARC missiles were retooled as supersonic target drones for US Air Force and US Navy aircrews.

The BOMARC was launched vertically and would climb to an altitude of 50,000-ft. before rotating to a horizontal flight path.[199] When the missile was within 10 miles of the target, internal guidance would control the missile until interception.

During the late 1940s, the Air Force contracted Boeing to design an antiaircraft missile. Partnering with the University of Michigan's Aeronautical Research Center, the missile was named IM-99A (later CIM-10A) BOMARC (Boeing/Michigan Aeronautical Research Center).[200] The BOMARC concept went into head-to-head competition with the Army's Nike surface-to-air missile.[201] While the Nike missile's low sustained fire rate allowed for point defense of ground targets, Air Force planners attempted to bridge the gap between point defense and long-range fighter interception with "area defense." This concept required a longer-range missile with a wide-dispersal warhead (e.g., nuclear) able to outright destroy or severely damage aircraft formations with overpressure (shockwaves). The BOMARC force was integrated into the Semi-Automatic Ground Environment (SAGE) system to forward early-warning and tracking data directly into the missile's guidance computer.

The BOMARC was described as a "pilot-less, stubby-winged fighter plane with an atom bomb in the nose."[202] The airframe looked like a fighter aircraft, with swept wings and

Once a mainstay of continental United States air defense, surplus BOMARCs were relegated to the target drone role in the 1970s and 1980s. *Courtesy of the United States Air Force*

two ramjet engines that provided a top speed of Mach 4 and a range of 230 miles. Initial tests took place in 1952 at Patrick AFB, Florida. The BOMARC-A used a booster powered by liquid fuel (kerosene and nitric acid) and guided by an electron tube–based guidance radar and computer.

The BOMARC-A system was phased out of air defense operations during 1964. After retirement, many of the missiles saw service as target drones.[203] The first target drone launch from Vandenberg took place on 25 August 1966 from BOMARC pad 2 (BOM-2). The target drone was code-named "AUGUST CORN." The final BOMARC-A launch from Vandenberg took place on 29 December 1972 from BOM-2.

A total of fifty-six CIM-10A BOMARC-A launches took place at Vandenberg from 1966 to 1972.

The sleek BOMARC was unrivaled for its speed during the 1960s. However, it was a dangerous weapon to yield, with one notorious accident involving its nuclear warhead at Fort Dix, New Jersey, on 7 June 1960. *Author*

BOMARC-A Launches[204]

SEQUENCE	DATE	SITE	VEHICLE	CODENAME	NOTES
618	25 AUG 66	BOM-2	BOMARC-A	AUGUST CORN	FIRST BOMARC-A LAUNCH
635	14 OCT 66	BOM-1	BOMARC-A	FALL HARVEST	
638	1 NOV 66	BOM-2	BOMARC-A	BLUE HAWK	
667	8 FEB 67	BOM-1	BOMARC-A	BUSY NEEDLE	
702	25 MAY 67	BOM-2	BOMARC-A	BUSY SPOTTER	
703	25 MAY 67	BOM-1	BOMARC-A	--	
718	6 JUL 67	BOM-1	BOMARC-A	BUCKBOARD SEAT	
756	1 DEC 67	BOM-1	BOMARC-A	--	
786	4 APR 68	BOM-1	BOMARC-A	--	
799	22 MAY 68	BOM-1	BOMARC-A	--	
807	27 JUN 68	BOM-1	BOMARC-A	--	
818	19 AUG 68	BOM-2	BOMARC-A	--	
827	7 OCT 68	BOM-1	BOMARC-A	--	
834	13 NOV 68	BOM-2	BOMARC-A	--	
845	8 JAN 69	BOM-2	BOMARC-A	--	
851	29 JAN 69	BOM-1	BOMARC-A	--	
857	21 FEB 69	BOM-2	BOMARC-A	--	
861	15 MAR 69	BOM-1	BOMARC-A	--	
871	17 APR 69	BOM-2	BOMARC-A	--	
875	30 APR 69	BOM-1	BOMARC-A	--	
880	21 MAY 69	BOM-2	BOMARC-A	--	
887	19 JUN 69	BOM-1	BOMARC-A	--	
892	3 JUL 69	BOM-1	BOMARC-A	--	
894	12 JUL 69	BOM-2	BOMARC-A	--	
905	24 AUG 69	BOM-1	BOMARC-A	--	
909	3 SEP 69	BOM-2	BOMARC-A	--	
914	20 SEP 69	BOM-1	BOMARC-A	--	
930	13 NOV 69	BOM-2	BOMARC-A	--	SALVO LAUNCH
931	13 NOV 69	BOM-1	BOMARC-A	--	SALVO LAUNCH
932	18 NOV 69	BOM-1	BOMARC-A	--	
941	15 JAN 70	BOM-1	BOMARC-A	--	
949	7 MAR 70	BOM-1	BOMARC-A	--	SALVO LAUNCH
950	7 MAR 70	BOM-2	BOMARC-A	--	SALVO LAUNCH
960	18 APR 70	BOM-1	BOMARC-A	--	
979	2 JUL 70	BOM-1	BOMARC-A	--	

986	29 JUL 70	BOM-2	BOMARC-A	--	
1004	26 SEP 70	BOM-1	BOMARC-A	--	SALVO LAUNCH
1005	26 SEP 70	BOM-2	BOMARC-A	--	SALVO LAUNCH
1037	27 FEB 71	BOM-1	BOMARC-A	--	SALVO LAUNCH
1038	27 FEB 71	BOM-2	BOMARC-A	--	SALVO LAUNCH
1049	14 APR 71	BOM-1	BOMARC-A	--	SALVO LAUNCH
1050	14 APR 71	BOM-2	BOMARC-A	--	SALVO LAUNCH
1069	29 JUN 71	BOM-1	BOMARC-A	--	SALVO LAUNCH
1070	29 JUN 71	BOM-2	BOMARC-A	--	SALVO LAUNCH
1087	16 SEP 71	BOM-2	BOMARC-A	--	SALVO LAUNCH
1088	16 SEP 71	BOM-1	BOMARC-A	--	SALVO LAUNCH
1109	19 JAN 72	BOM-1	BOMARC-A	--	
1122	14 APR 72	BOM-1	BOMARC-A	--	
1124	21 APR 72	BOM-2	BOMARC-A	--	
1141	27 JUL 72	BOM-1	BOMARC-A	--	SALVO LAUNCH
1142	27 JUL 72	BOM-2	BOMARC-A	--	SALVO LAUNCH
1160	29 NOV 72	BOM-1	BOMARC-A	--	
1161	1 DEC 72	BOM-2	BOMARC-A	--	
1168	18 DEC 72	BOM-1	BOMARC-A	--	
1172	27 DEC 72	BOM-1	BOMARC-A	--	
1173	29 DEC 72	BOM-2	BOMARC-A	--	LAST BOMARC-A LAUNCH

BOMARC-B

The IM-99B/CIM-10B BOMARC-B was a nuclear-capable surface-to-air defensive interceptor missile in the 1960s and 1970s.[205] It was a follow-on to the IM-99A/CIM-10A BOMARC-A model with ramjet engines, an M51 solid-fuel booster, pulse-Doppler radar, and a range of 440 miles.

The BOMARC-B used solid-rocket boosters to provide 50,000 lbs. of thrust. Just like its predecessor, the missile would launch vertically, reach the intended intercept altitude, and then continue horizontally to target engagement. After the booster fired, it would be jettisoned to decrease system weight. This, along with additional fuel for the improved ramjet engines, nearly doubled the range of the missile to 440 miles. The missile was the world's first active homing missile system, since the Westinghouse DPN-53 onboard radar would compute the final intercept parameters. This radar also gave the B-model the ability to track and destroy low-altitude targets.

BOMARC was able to carry either a nuclear or conventional warhead. The conventional warhead had a kill radius of 70 ft. with its proximity fuse.[206] In 1961, a BOMARC-B was tested against two US Navy Regulus II missiles. The BOMARC successfully engaged the targets at Mach 2 at nearly 375 miles downrange.

Boeing delivered 349 BOMARC-B missiles to the Air Force between 1961 and 1965.[207] The last squadron of air defense missiles was deactivated in 1972. Soon thereafter, missiles began launching from Vandenberg as target drones. A total of thirty-one IM-99B/CIM-10B BOMARC-B launches took place at Vandenberg from 1973 to 1982.

A BOMARC surface-to-air missile is readied for launch amid an overcast California sky. *Courtesy of the United States Air Force*

A rear three-quarter shot of the BOMARC at SLC-10. Two BOMARC airframes reside here, this being the better preserved of the two. *Author*

BOMARC-B Launches[208]

SEQUENCE	DATE	SITE	VEHICLE	CODENAME	NOTES
1200	11 SEP 73	BOM-1	BOMARC-B	--	FIRST BOMARC-B LAUNCH
1216	17 DEC 73	BOM-1	BOMARC-B	--	
1226	20 MAR 74	BOM-1	BOMARC-B	--	
1232	10 APR 74	BOM-2	BOMARC-B	--	
1237	30 MAY 74	BOM-1	BOMARC-B	--	
1253	1 OCT 74	BOM-1	BOMARC-B	--	
1259	16 OCT 74	BOM-2	BOMARC-B	--	
1274	20 MAR 75	BOM-1	BOMARC-B	--	
1276	10 APR 75	BOM-2	BOMARC-B	--	
1282	22 MAY 75	BOM-1	BOMARC-B	--	
1290	23 JUL 75	BOM-2	BOMARC-B	--	
1312	16 DEC 75	BOM-1	BOMARC-B	--	
1327	5 MAY 76	BOM-2	BOMARC-B	--	
1330	3 JUN 76	BOM-1	BOMARC-B	--	
1337	13 JUL 76	BOM-2	BOMARC-B	--	
1346	23 SEP 76	BOM-2	BOMARC-B	--	
1348	28 OCT 76	BOM-1	BOMARC-B	--	SALVO LAUNCH
1349	28 OCT 76	BOM-2	BOMARC-B	--	SALVO LAUNCH
1358	4 FEB 77	BOM-2	BOMARC-B	--	
1362	31 MAR 77	BOM-2	BOMARC-B	--	
1363	11 MAY 77	BOM-1	BOMARC-B	--	
1372	13 JUL 77	BOM-2	BOMARC-B	--	
1373	14 JUL 77	BOM-1	BOMARC-B	--	
1386	9 DEC 77	BOM-1	BOMARC-B	--	
1395	24 MAR 78	BOM-2	BOMARC-B	--	
1425	27 FEB 79	BOM-1	BOMARC-B	--	
1462	1 AUG 80	BOM-2	BOMARC-B	--	
1468	17 NOV 80	BOM-1	BOMARC-B	--	
1472	19 DEC 80	BOM-2	BOMARC-B	--	
1500	14 JUL 82	BOM-2	BOMARC-B	--	SALVO LAUNCH
1501	14 JUL 82	BOM-1	BOMARC-B	--	LAST BOMARC-B LAUNCH; SALVO LAUNCH

GROUND-BASED INTERCEPTOR

Vandenberg contains the West Coast launch activities for the Ballistic Missile Defense System. The purpose of the system is to intercept missile-transported threats during all phases of flight (i.e., boost, midcourse, and terminal). Development, testing, and deployment of missile defense system components are the responsibility of the Missile Defense Agency (MDA). The mission area addressing the midcourse phase of hostile missile flight—while the missile is in a ballistic trajectory—is the Ground-Based Midcourse Defense (GMD) program.

The objective of GMD is to develop and implement a ground-based missile system to intercept and destroy long-range missiles during the ballistic phase of flight before reentry into the atmosphere, where system speeds can reach Mach 23.

GMD employs integrated communications networks, fire control systems, and globally deployed sensors and missile interceptors that are capable of detecting, tracking, and destroying ballistic missile threats. The exoatmospheric kill vehicle (EKV) is a sensor/propulsion package that uses the kinetic energy from a direct hit to destroy the incoming target vehicle. This hit-to-kill technology has been proven in a number of successful flight tests using ground-based interceptor (GBI) missiles.

The GBI is a multistage, solid-fuel booster with an EKV payload. When launched, the booster carries the EKV toward the target's predicted location in space. Once released from the booster, the EKV uses guidance data transmitted from Ground Support & Fire Control System components and onboard sensors to close with and destroy the target warhead. The impact is outside the earth's atmosphere, using only the kinetic force of the direct collision to destroy the target warhead.

In fiscal year (FY) 2003, President George W. Bush directed that four GBI missiles be emplaced at Vandenberg.

This portion of the GBI program and related programs for test flights have used refurbished LGM-30 Minuteman and LGM-118A Peacekeeper facilities.

The GBI element of the Ballistic Missile Defense System provides combatant commanders the capability to engage and destroy limited intermediate- and long-range ballistic missile threats in space to protect the continental United States. GBIs are emplaced in Alaska and California.

A Ground-Based Interceptor (GBI) sits in its silo at Vandenberg. *Courtesy of the United States Air Force*

The smoke plume from the GBI launch on 24 June 2014 towers above its underground silo. *Courtesy of the United States Air Force*

Another angle of the 24 June 2014 test of the GBI from Vandenberg. *Courtesy of the United States Air Force*

The logo of the Ground-Based Midcourse Defense system. Note the inclusion of the Roman centurion silhouette as a historical nod to the US Army's SAFEGUARD antiballistic missile system from the 1960s and 1970s. *Courtesy of the United States Air Force*

GROUND BASED INTERCEPTOR Launches[209]

SEQUENCE	DATE	SITE	VEHICLE	CODENAME	NOTES
1808	31 AUG 01	LF-21	BOOST VEHICLE	--	BVT-2
1816	13 DEC 01	LF-21	BOOST VEHICLE	--	BVT-3
1832	6 FEB 03	576E	BOOST VEHICLE	--	GBI PROTOTYPE (BV-6) BASED ON TAURUS ROCKET
1838	16 AUG 03	LF-23	BOOST VEHICLE	--	BV-6
1842	9 JAN 04	LF-21	BOOST VEHICLE	--	BV-5+
1867	1 SEP 06	LF-23	BOOST VEHICLE (INTCPT)	--	(OBV)FTG-02
1871	20 MAR 07	LF-06	TLV-5 (MINUTEMAN F)	--	FTX-02
1874	23 AUG 07	LF-06	TLV-7 (MINUTEMAN F/G)	--	CHIMERA
1876	28 SEP 07	LF-23	BOOST VEHICLE (INTCPT)	--	(OBV) FTG-03A
1884	23 SEP 08	LF-06	TLV-8 (MINUTEMAN F/G)	--	CHIMERA
1887	5 DEC 08	LF-23	BOOST VEHICLE (INTCPT)	--	(OBV) FTG-05
1896	31 JAN 10	LF-23	BOOST VEHICLE (INTCPT)	--	(OBV) FTG-06

SEQUENCE	DATE	SITE	VEHICLE	CODENAME	NOTES
1898	6 JUN 10	LF-24	BOOST VEHICLE (INTCPT)	--	BVT-01
1905	15 DEC 10	LF-23	BOOST VEHICLE (INTCPT)	--	FTG-06A
1919	26 JAN 13	LF-23	BOOST VEHICLE (INTCPT)	--	GM/CTV-01
1923	5 JUL 13	LF-24	BOOST VEHICLE (INTCPT)	--	FTG-07
1931	22 JUN 14	LF-23	OBV INTERCEPTOR	--	FTG-06B
1944	28 JAN 16	LF-23	BOOST VEHICLE (INTCPT)	--	GM/CTV-02+

CASTOR/SCRAMJET

The Castor/Scramjet was a technology demonstration of ramjet technology. The lone test of the Castor/Scramjet occurred at Vandenberg on 11 January 1967 from complex 4300C. This singular test was part of the Air Force's Scramjet Incremental Flight Test Program, under the direction of the USAF Aero-Propulsion Laboratory, with the objective of demonstrating useful thrust from a supersonic combustion ramjet (Scramjet) in flight. Scramjet technology had its origins at the Applied Physics Laboratory (APL) at Johns Hopkins University and was attractive as an alternative propulsion for tactical missiles.[210] The name "Scramjet" stood for "supersonic combustion ramjet" and was coined by APL's Gordon Dugger and Frederick Billig.

The USAF Scramjet program began in October 1964 and had planned for flight tests of dummy (nonactive) scramjets, followed by three "hot" scramjet launches. The January 1967 flight was of the dummy Scramjet test vehicle for aerodynamic and instrumentation evaluation. The program attempted to achieve positive thrust from a scramjet in flight for follow-on research. Program goals sought to reach speeds of 6,000 ft. per second and an engine burn time of five seconds (or greater). Marquardt Corporation, one of the leaders in ramjet technology, was the lead contractor for the USAF scramjet.[211]

The Marquardt design had four axisymmetric hydrogen-fueled scramjet modules accelerated to separation and scramjet ignition speeds by a Castor solid-propellant rocket booster.[212] Developmental testing had the engines perform at Mach 5.73 at a simulated altitude of 79,000 ft. Modifications to the design caused drag to become a major concern. Countermeasures to drag caused the weight to increase from 400 lbs. to the flight article's 680 lbs.

On 11 January 1967, a test firing of the dummy vehicle at Complex 4300C revealed continued drag problems, causing a lower separation speed from Mach 5.4 down to 5.18, while simultaneously lowering the separation altitude by nearly 1,000 ft. Flight test objectives were aimed at demonstration of the launch vehicle and the data acquisition system in the hypersonic environment.

Confusion in technical publications listed the January 1967 launch vehicle as a Blue Scout Junior launch due to the use of the Castor engine as part of the first-stage motor.[213] The launch occurred from 4300C, which also supported the Blue Scout Junior/ERCS launch (Project Beanstalk). At the time of the Castor/Scramjet launch, Complex 4300C consisted of the launcher building (Bldg. 1681) and the blockhouse (Bldg. 1680), with an underground cable tunnel between them. The launcher and blockhouse were modified from the Blue Scout Junior configuration to be compatible with the Scramjet test. In addition, a 52-ft. wind (anemometer) tower was built next to the blockhouse before the test.

Despite the (potential) value of hypersonic technology, the Air Force canceled any remaining flight tests.

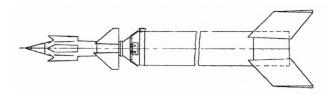

This side-view diagram shows the placement of the Scramjet (left side) atop the Castor rocket motor (center and right side). *Courtesy of the United States Air Force*

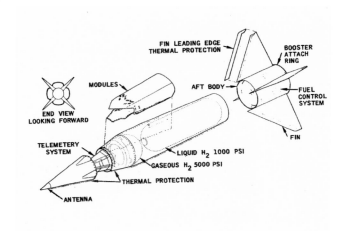

The cutaway diagram of the Scramjet shows the placement of the tanks containing gaseous and liquid hydrogen for the engine, along with the placement of the four scramjet modules aside the fuselage airframe. *Courtesy of the United States Air Force*

CASTOR/SCRAMJET Launches[214]

SEQUENCE	DATE	SITE	VEHICLE	CODENAME	NOTES
655	11 JAN 67	4300C	CASTOR/SCRAMJET	TREE MOSS	ONLY LAUNCH OF CASTOR/SCRAMJET

DAC ROC

Very little has been published on the Douglas Aircraft Company's Dac Roc series (also stated as Dac roc, DACroc, or DAC roc).[215] Official sources state that the US Navy fired two small, single-stage sounding rockets from PALC-A on 24 October 1963 and 10 December 1963.[216] Secondary sources state that both missions were dedicated to high-altitude study (known as aeronomy) and reached an estimated altitude of around 30 miles.[217]

DAC ROC Launches[218]

SEQUENCE	DATE	SITE	VEHICLE	CODENAME	NOTES
283	24 OCT 63	PALC-A	DAC ROC	--	FIRST DAC ROC LAUNCH
299	10 DEC 63	PALC-A	DAC ROC	--	LAST DAC ROC LAUNCH

DEACON/ARROW II

Deacon-Arrow II was a solid-rocket sounding rocket built by Sandia Research Laboratories (now Sandia National Laboratories), Albuquerque, New Mexico. The rockets were used to study the effects of high-altitude nuclear blasts on radio and radar transmissions during nuclear atmospheric testing of the early 1960s.[219] The first stage consisted of an Allegany Ballistic Laboratory Deacon first stage. The second stage was a Grand Central Arrow rocket motor.[220]

Unlike other launches in the Deacon Arrow II series, the launches from Vandenberg were not during nuclear test efforts, since a test moratorium had gone into effect on 31 October 1958.[221] The missions from PALC-B were for unidentified high-altitude studies.

DEACON/ARROW II Launches[222]

SEQUENCE	DATE	SITE	VEHICLE	CODENAME	NOTES
46	1 JUL 60	PALC-B	DEACON ARROW II	--	FIRST LAUNCH
47	8 JUL 60	PALC-B	DEACON ARROW II	--	
48	14 JUL 60	PALC-B	DEACON ARROW II	--	
79	27 MAR 61	PALC-B	DEACON ARROW II	--	LAST LAUNCH

DELTA

Delta was a three-stage, expendable liquid-fueled space launch system for launching small to medium payloads into low and medium earth orbit.[223] The Delta was created for NASA—using Thor components—to launch a 600 lb. payload into a 100-nautical-mile orbit. The original Delta design used three stages: a first-stage Thor, and two upper stages from the Vanguard rocket. Both the Thor first stage and Vanguard upper stages were modified to increase thrust.

When NASA was formed in 1958, it inherited from the Department of Defense's Advanced Research Projects Agency (ARPA) the booster programs using combinations of Thor or Atlas boosters with Vanguard upper stages. The first of these upper-stage configurations was designated "Able." The Delta was similar to the previous Thor-based combinations and was a fourth, or "D," version. Milton W. Rosen of NASA was responsible for the name. He had been referring to the combination as "Delta," which became the firm choice in January 1959, when a name was required because NASA was signing a contract for the booster. The vehicle was variously called "Delta" and "Thor-Delta."[224]

The Delta launch vehicle family used a coding scheme to designate its multiple configurations. The first digit represented basic vehicle configuration:

0: Castor 2 solid propellant strap-ons, Long Tank Thor core with MB-3 engine

1: Castor 2 strap-ons, Extended Long Tank core with MB-3 engine

2: Castor 2 strap-ons, Extended Long Tank core with RS-27 engine (derived from surplus H-1 engines of the Saturn IB)

3: Castor 4 solid propellant strap-ons, Extended Long Tank core with RS-27 engine

4: Castor 4A strap-ons, Extended Long Tank core with MB-3 engine

5: Castor 4A strap-ons, Extended Long Tank core with RS-27 engine

6: Castor 4A strap-ons, Extra Extended Long Tank core with RS-27 engine

7: GEM-40 solid propellant strap-ons, Extra Extended Long Tank core with RS-27A engine

8: GEM-46 solid propellant strap-ons, Delta-3 strengthened Extra Extended Long Tank core with RS-27A engine

9: GEM-60 solid propellant strap-ons, Delta-4 Lox/LH2 cryogenic core with RS-68 engine

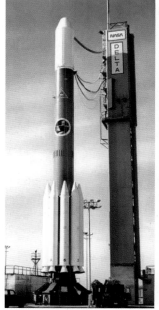

Delta number 155 launches from SLC-2W on 3 August 1981, carrying two Dynamics Explorer satellites. The pair was designed to investigate interactions between the magnetosphere and ionosphere relating to plasma dynamics. The second stage consisted of the "straight eight" 8 ft. diameter payload fairing. *Courtesy of the United States Air Force*

The earth observation satellite Landsat 4 was launched from SLC-2W on 16 July 1982 aboard Delta 163. The triangle logo adorning the side of the rocket represented the Greek symbol delta and contained the rocket number within. *Courtesy of the United States Air Force*

NASA's Infrared Astronomical Satellite (IRAS) sits on the launch mount at SLC-2W prior to its 26 January 1983 launch. IRAS's mission was to systematically survey the sky in the infrared spectrum. After ten months of operations the telescope exhausted its cryogen and ceased operations on 21 November 1983. *Courtesy of the United States Air Force*

The final Delta launch (Delta 189) at Vandenberg lifted NASA's Cosmic Background Explorer (COBE) into polar orbit on 18 November 1989. *Courtesy of the United States Air Force*

The second digit represented the number of solid propellant strap-on rockets (0, 3, or 9). The third digit represented the second-stage and engine configuration:

0: Delta storable propellant stage with AJ10-118 series engines
1: Delta storable propellant stage with TR-201 engines
2: Delta K storable propellant stage with AJ10-118K engine
3: Delta-3 Lox/LH2 cryogenic upper stage with RL10B-2 engine
4: Delta-4 Lox/LH2 cryogenic upper stage with 4 m diameter
5: Delta-4 Lox/LH2 cryogenic upper stage with 5 m diameter

Finally, the fourth digit represented the third-stage configuration and which engine was used to boost the payload into its final orbit:

0: No third stage
1: Not used

2: Not used
3: Star 37D / TE-364-3 solid propellant kick stage
4: Star 37E / TE-364-4 solid propellant kick stage
5: Star-48B / PAM-D solid propellant kick stage (often listed as "0" upper stage with a PAM-D due to the modular nature of the PAM configuration)
6: Star 37FM solid propellant kick stage

Note: Not all of these configurations were flown at Vandenberg. They are listed only for continuity and completeness.

The Delta launch vehicle was America's longest-lived, most reliable, and lowest-cost space launch vehicle. Delta had direct lineage to the Thor intermediate-range ballistic missile program, which began in 1955. Thirteen months after the contract signature, the first Thor missile flew, and fifteen months after that milestone, a space-launch version took flight. Changes in the Thor core and the Delta upper stages and the addition of strap-on solid-rocket motors allowed for unheard-of vehicle versatility in the aerospace industry.

A typical mission profile had the first-stage RS-27 main engine and six of the nine strap-on solid-rocket motors ignite at liftoff. After the six solids are exhausted, the remaining three solid-rocket motors are ignited, while the six spent motor casings are jettisoned. After the remaining three motors are exhausted, they are jettisoned around three seconds later. The main engine continues to fire until main engine cutoff.[225]

After a short coasting period the first stage is jettisoned, with the second-stage engine firing five seconds later. The payload fairing separates, exposing the satellite(s) carried aboard. The second-stage engine burns for anywhere from 340 to 420 seconds into a Hohmann transfer orbit. A second burn circularizes the orbit for payload orbital insertion. Once the payload is away from the rocket body, the remaining fuel is burned to limit any reentry hazards.

On 3 August 1981, the first Delta (3913) rocket took off from SLC-2W carrying two payloads for NASA: Dynamics Explorer 1 and 2. The rocket was configured as an Extended Long Tank core with RS-27 engine, nine strap-on booster rockets, second stage with TR-201 engines, and an RL10B-2 cryogenic upper stage.[226]

All launches of the Delta booster took place at SLC-2W. After the launch of COBE in November 1989, SLC-2W was taken out of service for refurbishment to the Delta II configuration.

The Delta 3920 configuration consisted of a Delta 3000 rocket with nine solid-propellant strap-on rockets, an AJ10-118K second-stage engine, and no third stage. *Courtesy of the United States Air Force*

DELTA Launches[227]

SEQUENCE	DATE	SITE	VEHICLE	CODENAME	NOTES
1486	3 AUG 81	SLC-2W	DELTA	--	DYNAMICS EXPLORER; DELTA 3913
1490	6 OCT 81	SLC-2W	DELTA	--	SOLAR MESOSPHERE EXPLORER/OSCAR 9; DELTA 2310
1502	16 JUL 82	SLC-2W	DELTA	--	LANDSAT 4; DELTA 3920
1512	25 JAN 83	SLC-2W	DELTA	--	IRAS/PIX 2; DELTA 3910
1521	26 MAY 83	SLC-2W	DELTA	--	EXOSAT; DELTA 3914
1543	1 MAR 84	SLC-2W	DELTA	--	LANDSAT 5/OSCAR 11; DELTA 3920
1641	18 NOV 89	SLC-2W	DELTA	--	COSMIC BACKGROUND EXPLORER (COBE); DELTA 5920-8

DELTA II

The Delta II is a two-stage, liquid-fueled, medium-lift space launch booster. Delta II is used to place payloads into low-earth orbit. The Delta II was the thirteenth version of medium-lift-class vehicles in the Delta family.

The Delta II was conceived as a medium-lift replacement for the space shuttle after the 1986 space shuttle *Challenger* disaster. McDonnell Douglas signed a $316.5 million contract for seven Delta IIs on 21 January 1987.[228] The need for a medium-lift vehicle was known before the *Challenger* disaster as a launcher for the Navstar Global Positioning Satellite constellation, since the shuttle's early manifest became convoluted and could not meet the GPS satellite deployment schedule. Months after *Challenger*, the loss of a Titan 34D on 18 April 1986 and its HEXAGON satellite payload further reinforced the US government's ill-conceived launch plans concentrating primarily on the space shuttle.[229] Before McDonnell Douglas signed the contract in early 1987, the company was about to permanently shut down the Delta production line.

With minor differences and uprated components, the Delta II airframe concept has changed little from the Thor's original design. The first stage contains a Rocketdyne RS-27 main engine burning RP-1 fuel (kerosene) and liquid oxygen propellants. The engine has a combined turbine and turbopump with a regeneratively cooled thrust chamber and a gimbaled nozzle for pitch and yaw control. Two Rocketdyne LR101-NA-11 Vernier engines provide roll control. The first stage also contains avionics, separation ordnance, and telemetry equipment.

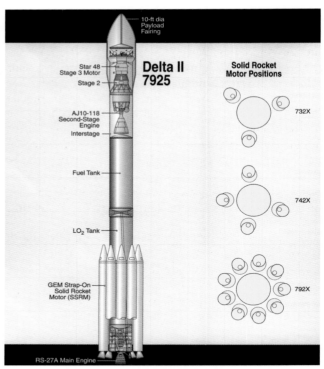

The first Delta II launch from Vandenberg aboard Delta 229 placed the Canadian Space Agency's RADARSAT 1 into orbit on 4 November 1995. The satellite used synthetic aperture radar (SAR) to obtain imagery of the earth's surface. The satellite was declared "end of life" in March 2013. *Courtesy of the United States Air Force*

The first Iridium launch took place on 5 May 1997 from SLC-2W. The telecommunications system was revolutionary, created as a way of reaching high latitudes with reliable satellite communication services. Each Delta II launch carried five satellites. *Courtesy of the United States Air Force*

This cutaway shows the three solid-rocket motor configurations on the Delta II series. Note the offset placing with four-rocket motors compared to the 120° spacing for three motors. *Courtesy of the United States Air Force*

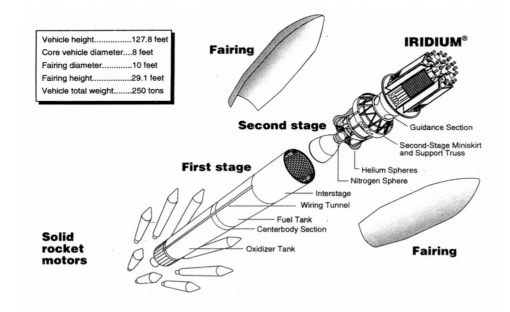

Vehicle height	127.8 feet
Core vehicle diameter	8 feet
Fairing diameter	10 feet
Fairing height	29.1 feet
Vehicle total weight	250 tons

The placement of five IRIDIUM satellites atop the second-stage support truss nestled inside the Delta II payload fairing. *Courtesy of the United States Air Force*

An outstanding view of the Pacific Ocean creates a beautiful backdrop to Delta 248's launch of four IRIDIUM satellites on 26 September 1997. *Courtesy of the United States Air Force*

Up to nine solid-rocket motors are attached to the first stage; six are ignited at liftoff, and the other three are ignited later on. An isogrid interstage between the first and second stages carries the loads from the upper stages, complete with six spring-driven separation rods.

The second stage contains a restartable Aerojet engine, along with its own hypergolic fuel and oxidizer tanks.

The moniker "SLC-2W" became superfluous after SLC-2E was inactivated in the early 1970s. Documents detailing the site state plainly "SLC-2." The East/West pad distinction remains in the launch manifest below. Orbital inclinations available at Vandenberg are between 63° and 145°, offering a variety of Molniya, polar, and retrograde inclination options.[230]

As with previous Delta boosters, a four-digit number explains the configuration:

- The first digit is either 6 or 7, denoting the 6000 or 7000 series.
- The second digit indicates the number of boosters (3, 4, or 9).

- The third digit is 2, denoting a second stage with an Aerojet AJ10 engine.
- The last digit denotes the third stage; 0 denotes no third stage, 5 indicates a Payload Assist Module (PAM) with Star 48B motor, and 6 indicates a Star 37FM motor.

The Delta II launch vehicle family includes the 7300, 7400, and 7900 series, with the first stage, with its graphite-epoxy motor (GEM) solid strap-on rocket motors; the second stage; and an optional third stage with spin table and the payload fairing. The graphite-epoxy motor cases are built by Hercules Aerospace and are lighter than the steel cases they replaced. The new motors are 6 ft. longer than and just as strong as their predecessors, providing greater thrust. The first-stage main engine nozzle was enlarged to give a greater expansion ratio for improved performance.

Forty-three Delta II boosters have launched from Vandenberg. As of the end of 2016, two Delta IIs remain for launching in 2017 and 2018.[231]

DELTA II Launches[232]

SEQUENCE	DATE	SITE	VEHICLE	CODENAME	NOTES
1717	4 NOV 95	SLC-2W	DELTA II	--	RADARSAT/SURFSAT; DELTA 7920-10
1719	24 FEB 96	SLC-2W	DELTA II	--	POLAR; DELTA 7925-10
1722	24 APR 96	SLC-2W	DELTA II	--	MSX; DELTA 7920-10
1738	5 MAY 97	SLC-2W	DELTA II	--	IRIDIUM 04/05/06/07/08; DELTA 7920-10C
1743	9 JUL 97	SLC-2W	DELTA II	--	IRIDIUM 15/17/18/20/21; DELTA 7920-10C
1745	20 AUG 97	SLC-2W	DELTA II	--	IRIDIUM 22/23/24/25/26; DELTA 7920-10C
1749	26 SEP 97	SLC-2W	DELTA II	--	IRIDIUM 19/34/35/36/37; DELTA 7920-10C
1752	8 NOV 97	SLC-2W	DELTA II	--	IRIDIUM 38/39/40/41/43; DELTA 7920-10C
1753	20 DEC 97	SLC-2W	DELTA II	--	IRIDIUM 45/46/47/48/49; DELTA 7920-10C
1756	18 FEB 98	SLC-2W	DELTA II	--	IRIDIUM 50/52/53/54/56; DELTA 7920-10C
1759	29 MAR 98	SLC-2W	DELTA II	--	IRIDIUM 55/57/58/59/60; DELTA 7920-10C
1763	17 MAY 98	SLC-2W	DELTA II	--	IRIDIUM 70/72/73/74/75; DELTA 7920-10C
1767	8 SEP 98	SLC-2W	DELTA II	--	IRIDIUM 77/79/80/81/82; DELTA 7920-10C
1770	6 NOV 98	SLC-2W	DELTA II	--	IRIDIUM 02/83/84/85/86; DELTA 7920-10C
1773	23 FEB 99	SLC-2W	DELTA II	--	ARGOS/ORSTED/SUNSAT; DELTA 7920-10
1776	15 APR 99	SLC-2W	DELTA II	--	LANDSAT 7; DELTA 7920-10
1793	25 MAR 00	SLC-2W	DELTA II	--	IMAGER FOR MAGNETOPAUSE TO AURORA GLOBAL EXPLORATION (IMAGE); DELTA 7326-9.5
1804	21 NOV 00	SLC-2W	DELTA II	--	EARTH ORBITER-1/SAC-C/MUNIN; DELTA 7320-10
1812	18 OCT 01	SLC-2W	DELTA II	--	QUICKBIRD 2; DELTA 7320-10
1815	7 DEC 01	SLC-2W	DELTA II	--	JASON-1/TIMED; DELTA 7920-10
1817	11 FEB 02	SLC-2W	DELTA II	--	IRIDIUM 90/91/94/95/96; DELTA 7920-10C
1820	4 MAY 02	SLC-2W	DELTA II	--	AQUA; DELTA 7920-10L
1831	12 JAN 03	SLC-2W	DELTA II	--	ICESAT/CHIPSAT; DELTA 7320-10
1843	20 APR 04	SLC-2W	DELTA II	--	GRAVITY PROBE B; DELTA 7920-10C
1846	15 JUL 04	SLC-2W	DELTA II	--	AURA; DELTA 7920-10L
1852	20 MAY 05	SLC-2W	DELTA II	--	NOAA 18; DELTA 7320-10C
1863	28 APR 06	SLC-2W	DELTA II	--	CLOUDSAT/CALIPSO; DELTA 7420-10C
1869	14 DEC 06	SLC-2W	DELTA II	--	USA 193; DELTA 7420-10C
1873	7 JUN 07	SLC-2W	DELTA II	--	COSMO-SKYMED 1; DELTA 7420-10C
1875	18 SEP 07	SLC-2W	DELTA II	--	WORLDVIEW 1; DELTA 7920-10C

SEQUENCE	DATE	SITE	VEHICLE	CODENAME	NOTES
1877	8 DEC 07	SLC-2W	DELTA II	--	COSMO-SKYMED 2; DELTA 7420-10C
1881	20 JUN 08	SLC-2W	DELTA II	--	JASON 2; DELTA 7320-10C
1883	6 SEP 08	SLC-2W	DELTA II	--	GEOEYE-1; DELTA 7420-10C
1885	24 OCT 08	SLC-2W	DELTA II	--	COSMO 3; DELTA 7420-10C
1888	6 FEB 09	SLC-2W	DELTA II	--	NOAA 19; DELTA 7320-10C
1890	5 MAY 09	SLC-2W	DELTA II	--	STSS; DELTA 7920-10C
1893	8 OCT 09	SLC-2W	DELTA II	--	WORLDVIEW 2; DELTA 7920-10C
1895	14 DEC 09	SLC-2W	DELTA II	--	WIDE FIELD INFRARED EXPLORER (WISE); DELTA 7320-10C
1904	5 NOV 10	SLC-2W	DELTA II	--	COSMO-4; DELTA 7420-10C
1910	10 JUN 11	SLC-2W	DELTA II	--	SAC-D/AQUARIUS; DELTA 7320-10C
1914	28 OCT 11	SLC-2W	DELTA II	--	NPP; DELTA 7920-10C
1932	2 JUL 14	SLC-2W	DELTA II	--	OCO-II; DELTA 7320-10C
1936	31 JAN 15	SLC-2W	DELTA II	--	SMAP; DELTA 7320-10C
1932	2 JUL 14	SLC-2W	DELTA II	--	OCO-II; DELTA 7320-10C
1936	31 JAN 15	SLC-2W	DELTA II	--	SMAP; DELTA 7320-10C

DELTA IV

The Delta IV is a liquid-fueled, medium- to heavy-lift space launch vehicle. The Delta family of launchers was derived from the Thor IRBM. In the 1990s, the need to lower the cost of space launches and make space access reliable drove the Air Force to develop requirements for the Evolved Expendable Launch Vehicle (EELV) program. After intense competition between Lockheed Martin's Atlas V and Boeing's Delta IV, the government selected both to represent future launch systems.

The EELV competition was aimed at reducing costs by phasing out the Delta, Atlas, and Titan legacy launch systems and increasing standardization with expensive launch hardware.

The Delta IV launch system is centered on a common booster core (CBC) with an upper stage and payload fairing. The system is available in five configurations:

- Delta IV Medium (Delta IV M): single CBC
- Delta IV M+ (4,2): two strap-on solid-rocket motors and 4 m fairing
- Delta IV M+ (5,2): two strap-on solid-rocket motors and 5 m fairing
- Delta IV M+ (5,4): four strap-on solid-rocket motors and a 5 m fairing
- Delta IV Heavy (Delta IV H): one main CBC, two additional CBCs (no solid-rocket motors)

One CBC uses a single RS-68 engine running on a liquid hydrogen and liquid oxygen blend to produce over 660,000 lbs. of thrust. The booster, with its payload fairing, stands around 200 to 225 ft. tall. With additional CBCs, the Delta Heavy configuration can lift up to 45,200 lbs. to low-earth orbit (LEO).

While the Delta IV has launched from Cape Canaveral since 2002, the first Delta IV launch from Vandenberg took place on 27 June 2006. The launch lifted a national-security payload designated NROL-22. To date, five of the six launches of Delta IV boosters have been for the National Reconnaissance Office. The remaining launch, on 4 November 2006, lifted a DMSP weather satellite into LEO.

The Boat Dock at South Vandenberg receives Delta IV components. The dock was originally constructed during the space shuttle era to receive the external tank and solid-rocket boosters by sea. *Courtesy of the United States Air Force*

The *Delta Mariner* cargo ship unloads a booster for the United Launch Alliance Delta IV at the boat dock near Space Launch Complex 6. *Courtesy of the United States Air Force*

A Delta IV-Heavy lifts off from Space Launch Complex 6 (SLC-6). This is the second Delta IV-Heavy launch from Vandenberg, and the largest rocket ever to launch from the West Coast of the United States. *Courtesy of the United States Air Force*

A Delta IV Medium+ (5,2) lifts off from Space Launch Complex 6 on 3 April 2012. This launch was the Department of Defense's first-ever Delta IV Medium launch vehicle configured with a 5-meter payload fairing and two solid-rocket motors. *Courtesy of the United States Air Force*

A singular common booster core makes up the majority of the Delta IV Medium launch vehicle, seen here during a night launch at SLC-6. *Courtesy of the United States Air Force*

DELTA IV Launches[233]

SEQUENCE	DATE	SITE	VEHICLE	CODENAME	NOTES
1865	27 JUN 06	SLC-6	DELTA IV	--	NROL-22
1868	4 NOV 06	SLC-6	DELTA IV	--	DMSP BLOCK 5D3 F17
1906	20 JAN 11	SLC-6	DELTA IV	--	NROL-49
1916	3 APR 12	SLC-6	DELTA IV	--	NROL-25
1924	28 AUG 13	SLC-6	DELTA IV	--	NROL-65
1945	10 FEB 16	SLC-6	DELTA IV	--	NROL-45

FALCON 9

The Falcon 9 is a two-stage, liquid-fueled medium- to heavy-lift launch vehicle. The Falcon 9 family has flown numerous times from Cape Canaveral Air Force Station; however, as of December 2016, the Falcon 9 has flown from Vandenberg twice. Falcon 9 is a two-stage booster that uses the industry standard LOX as oxidizer and RP-1 (kerosene) as propellant. [234] The first stage uses nine Merlin-1C engines, providing thrust ranging from 1.7 million lbs. at sea level to 1.8 million lbs. in space. The second stage uses only one Merlin-1C engine, providing restart capability and 210,000 lbs. of thrust. [235]

The Falcon 9 interstage, fixed to the forward end of the first-stage tank, connects the first and second stages and contains the stage separation system. The rocket is assembled horizontally and then erected vertically during preparation and prelaunch operations.

The Falcon 9 is configurable depending on payload size. A variant called the Falcon 9 Heavy uses a standard Falcon 9 core and two additional first stages as strap-on boosters.

The three cores contain twenty-seven engines producing around 5.5 million lbs. of thrust.[236]

Falcon 9 operations at Vandenberg AFB take place at SLC-4E, the previous home of Titan booster launches. The site has been heavily modified from the Titan years to accommodate SpaceX's Falcon 9 and Falcon Heavy rockets. Launch azimuths from SLC-4E allow high-inclination low-earth orbits, including polar and sun-synchronous orbits.[237]

As of the publication cutoff date, only two Falcon 9 boosters have launched from Vandenberg.[238] The first, launched on 29 September 2013 from SLC-4E, carried the Cascade, Smallsat, and Ionospheric Polar Explorer (CASSIOPE) for the Canadian Space Agency (CSA).[239] It was placed in an elliptical, polar orbit to maximize its mission objectives of space weather research and telecommunications technology development.

The second Falcon 9 launch from Vandenberg took place on 18 January 2016. The payload was the Joint Altimetry Satellite Oceanography Network (JASON-3) satellite, an international earth observation satellite partnering NASA, NOAA, CNES, and EUMETSAT.[240] This launch was unique in that the booster manufacturer SpaceX attempted to land the booster upright on a floating platform in the Pacific Ocean.[241] Video postmortem showed one of the four booster landing legs collapsing during landing, causing a fiery explosion on the unmanned floating platform.

A Falcon 9 lifts off from SLC-4 on 29 September 2013, carrying the Canadian-built CASSIOPE satellite. *Courtesy of the United States Air Force*

The Falcon 9 v1.1 is about 60 percent heavier than the previous Falcon 9 rocket, providing 60 percent more thrust. *Courtesy of the United States Air Force*

FALCON 9 Launches[242]

SEQUENCE	DATE	SITE	VEHICLE	CODENAME	NOTES
1927	29 SEP 13	SLC-4E	FALCON 9	--	CASSIOPE
1943	18 JAN 16	SLC-4E	FALCON-9	--	JASON-3

GROUND-LAUNCHED CRUISE MISSILE (BGM-109G Gryphon)

The BGM-109G Gryphon, better known as the Ground-Launched Cruise Missile (GLCM, pronounced "Glick-em"), was an intermediate-range, nuclear-capable cruise missile. GLCM was designed to penetrate hostile Warsaw Pact airspace at low altitude to deliver a tactical nuclear payload. The missile traveled 500 mph, with a range of around 1,500 miles.[243]

The BGM-109G Gryphon was a modification to the BGM-109 series of sea-launched cruise missiles used by the US Navy. Unlike the naval variants, the Gryphon was designed to carry only a nuclear warhead; no conventional capability existed.

The weapon system consisted of a flight of four transporter-erector launchers (TEL) and two launch control centers (LCC). Each TEL housed four BGM-109 nuclear cruise missiles (for a total of sixteen per flight), with the LCC providing command and control of the missiles.

Due to the short range of the GLCM, the missiles were inside western European countries at six locations, with deployment starting in 1982:[244]

- 38th Tactical Missile Wing—Wueschheim AB, Germany

- 303d Tactical Missile Wing—RAF Molesworth, UK
- 485th Tactical Missile Wing—Florennes AB, Belgium
- 486th Tactical Missile Wing—Woensdrecht AB, Netherlands
- 487th Tactical Missile Wing—Comiso AB, Italy
- 501st Tactical Missile Wing—RAF Greenham Common, UK

Due to the signing of the Intermediate-Range Nuclear Forces treaty, GLCMs were removed from Europe by 1991. There was only one launch of the GLCM from Vandenberg, which took place on 22 October 1985 from a site designated "HP-06," near the Peacekeeper Rail Garrison Loop at North Vandenberg.

GROUND-LAUNCHED CRUISE MISSILE Launches[245]

SEQUENCE	DATE	SITE	VEHICLE	CODENAME	NOTES
1577	22 OCT 85	HP-06	GLCM	--	ONLY LAUNCH OF BGM-109G

HONEST JOHN / NIKE / NIKE

The Honest John / Nike / Nike was a three-stage sounding rocket using an Honest John first stage and two upper stages from Nike-Ajax boosters. The Douglas Aircraft Company developed the Honest John as an unguided tactical battlefield rocket for the US Army in the 1950s. The solid-rocket motors served as the booster stage for a variety of sounding rockets.

Three Honest John / Nike / Nike rockets were launched from Point Arguello Launch Complex-A (PALC-A). Lawrence Radiation Laboratories developed the HAD test series launched aboard the rocket combination.

HONEST JOHN/NIKE/NIKE Launches[246]

SEQUENCE	DATE	SITE	VEHICLE	CODENAME	NOTES
294	18 NOV 63	PALC-A	HONEST JOHN / NIKE / NIKE	--	HAD-1
319	6 FEB 64	PALC-A	HONEST JOHN / NIKE / NIKE	--	HAD-2
330	3 MAR 64	PALC-A	HONEST JOHN / NIKE / NIKE	--	HAD-3

KIVA/HOPI

The Kiva/Hopi was a two-stage, solid-propellant sounding rocket. In 1959,[247] the Air Force Cambridge Research Lab (AFCRL) had a requirement for a two-stage solid-propellant sounding rocket to loft a 4.5 kg (10 lb.) payload to an altitude of 300 km (1 million ft.). It contracted the University of Michigan, which turned to the newly formed company Rocket Power Inc. (RPI) to build the rocket.

With a 10 lb. payload, the vehicle could reach a maximum altitude of about 365 km (225 miles).

The Phoenix sounding rocket consisted of two stages (named Kiva and Hopi) built by RPI, each of which was fitted with four tail fins. The first flight of the vehicle occurred on 21 June 1960 at the Naval Missile Test Center at Point Mugu. Within the next three years, at least nine Phoenix rockets launched from Point Arguello.

KIVA/HOPI Launches[248]

SEQUENCE	DATE	SITE	VEHICLE	CODENAME	NOTES
52	12 AUG 60	PALC-B	KIVA/HOPI	--	FIRST KIVA/HOPI LAUNCH
62	12 OCT 60	PALC-B	KIVA/HOPI	--	
64	27 OCT 60	PALC-B	KIVA/HOPI	--	
69	7 DEC 60	PALC-B	KIVA/HOPI	--	
71	14 DEC 60	PALC-B	KIVA/HOPI	--	
72	14 DEC 60	PALC-B	KIVA/HOPI	--	
74	16 DEC 60	PALC-B	KIVA/HOPI	--	
162	5 AUG 62	PALC-B	KIVA/HOPI	--	
232	11 MAY 63	PALC-B	KIVA/HOPI	--	FINAL KIVA/HOPI LAUNCH

MINOTAUR

The Minotaur is a four-stage, solid-propellant space launch vehicle used to launch small satellites into low-earth orbit. The rocket series uses a combination of government-supplied surplus Minuteman II ICBM motors and proven upper stages from the Pegasus family of launchers. Later versions of Minotaur (IV and IV Lite) use surplus Peacekeeper motor stages. Minuteman motors are the first and second stages of the Minotaur I and II, while the third and fourth stages are taken directly from Orbital's existing Pegasus XL rocket. The Minotaur I can loft 1,778 lbs. into low-earth orbit.[249]

Three variants of the Minotaur family have launched from Vandenberg.

- Minotaur I—LEO launcher, surplus Minuteman II downstages, Pegasus upper stage
- Minotaur II—suborbital target vehicle (a.k.a. Chimera)
- Minotaur IV—suborbital/LEO launcher, surplus Peacekeeper downstages

The Minotaur I is a small booster system. The Minotaur II is a target launch vehicle—also known as Chimera—used as a target for tracking and antiballistic missile tests. The Minotaur IV is a small booster system but can reach higher orbits or carry heavier payloads. The Minotaur I and II are derived from the Minuteman II missile, while the Minotaur IV (and IV Lite) are derived from the Peacekeeper ICBM.

Two locations at Vandenberg have hosted Minotaur launches: Launch Facility 06 when in its Chimera configuration, and Space Launch Complex 8 (SLC-8), also known as the California Spaceport.[250]

The first launch of the Minotaur, under the then-named Orbital Suborbital Program (OSP), was on 26 January 2000. The payloads included the Air Force Academy's FalconSat, Arizona State University's ASUSAT, Stanford University's Opal satellite, and an Air Force Research Laboratory experiment.[251]

While not a launcher with a storied rocket family name, Minotaur has launched an impressive list of national-security payloads. The Space-Based Space Surveillance (SBSS) satellite was launched aboard a Minotaur IV on 25 September 2010. SBSS was designed to survey orbital objects and determine whether they pose a hazard to US space systems.[252] The satellite was based on Ball Aerospace's BCP 2000 bus and featured a two-axis, high-angle gimbal mount with a telescope that could aim at 75 percent of the sky without repositioning the satellite's attitude.[253] The Air Force's Experimental Small Satellite 11 (XSS-11) was launched on 11 April 2005 from SLC-8. The mission of XSS-11 was to fly rendezvous and proximity operations (RPO) around other orbital objects—such as spent rocket bodies and dead satellites—for inspection.[254]

Minotaur-C

Due to a dismal launch record of three losses out of four launches between 2001 and 2011, the Taurus booster was rebranded the "Minotaur-C" (Minotaur Commercial) in late 2013 / early 2014. The new design uses Minotaur avionics and solid-fuel downstages purchased from ATK, not government-furnished missile motors as in previous models.[255] Launch listings for this variant are under "Taurus" for historical reference.

Minotaur IV launches occur at Space Launch Complex 8 (SLC-8), also known as the California Space Port. *Courtesy of the United States Air Force*

A Minotaur I rocket carried a national-security payload (NROL-66) for the National Reconnaissance Office during its launch on 6 February 2011. *Courtesy of the United States Air Force*

Minotaur IV is an expendable launch system derived from LGM-118 Peacekeeper ICBM technology. *Courtesy of the United States Air Force*

MINOTAUR Launches[256]

SEQUENCE	DATE	SITE	VEHICLE	CODENAME	NOTES
1790	26 JAN 00	SLC-8	MINOTAUR I	--	JAWSAT, FALCONSAT1
1795	28 MAY 00	LF-06	MINOTAUR II	--	OSP-TLV

SEQUENCE	DATE	SITE	VEHICLE	CODENAME	NOTES
1799	19 JUL 00	SLC-8	MINOTAUR I	--	MIGHTYSAT II
1814	4 DEC 01	LF-06	MINOTAUR II	--	TLV-1 IFT-7
1818	15 MAR 02	LF-06	MINOTAUR II	--	TLV-2 IFT-8
1826	14 OCT 02	LF-06	MINOTAUR II	--	TLV-3 GMDS
1829	11 DEC 02	LF-06	MINOTAUR II	--	TLV-4 GMDS
1850	11 APR 05	SLC-8	MINOTAUR I	--	XSS-11
1857	22 SEP 05	SLC-8	MINOTAUR I	--	STREAK
1862	14 APR 06	SLC-8	MINOTAUR I	--	FORMOSAT-3
1871	20 MAR 07	LF-06	MINOTAUR II	--	TLV-5 FTX-02 SBR
1874	23 AUG 07	LF-06	MINOTAUR II	--	TLV-7 NFIRE TARGET
1884	23 SEP 08	LF-06	MINOTAUR II	--	TLV-8 NFIRE TARGET
1897	22 APR 10	SLC-8	MINOTAUR IV (LITE)	--	HTV-2A
1903	25 SEP 10	SLC-8	MINOTAUR IV	--	SBSS
1907	6 FEB 11	SLC-8	MINOTAUR I	--	NROL-66
1913	11 AUG 11	SLC-8	MINOTAUR IV (LITE)	--	HTV-2B

MINUTEMAN (LGM-30A/B/F/G)

The Minuteman ICBM family (SM-80, LGM-30A/B/F/G) is a three-stage, solid-fueled, nuclear-capable missile with intercontinental range. Its mission is to deliver thermonuclear warheads against strategic targets from hardened underground launchers in the continental United States.[257] The US built four variants of the Minuteman: two Minuteman I (SM-80A/B, LGM-30A/B), the Minuteman II (LGM-30F), and the Minuteman III (LGM-30G). All variants have been retired except for the Minuteman III.

In 1954, the Von Neumann Committee gave approval to initial ICBM feasibility studies. In February 1958, the Air Force received approval for the development of an advanced solid-propellant ICBM. Originally designated "SENTINEL," Gen. Bernard Schriever recommended renaming the system "Minuteman" to reflect the system's rapid response time, as well as the allusion to the American Revolutionary War soldier.[258]

As the Air Force's only operational missile-testing center, Vandenberg was critical to the Minuteman program. While early R&D launches took place at Cape Canaveral (starting in February 1961), these tests were designed to establish missile parameters. The testing at Vandenberg allowed blue-suit and contractor personnel to identify and troubleshoot problems holistically throughout the entire weapons system (including ground support equipment). Additionally, performance data from operational test launches provided critical information to strategic planners for formulating the US nuclear war plan, also known as the Single Integrated Operational Plan (SIOP).[259] Finally, Vandenberg's unique expertise with operating and maintaining the Minuteman force segued nicely into incorporating missile launch officer training. Since the early 1960s, Minuteman personnel have trained at Vandenberg in preparation for their operational assignments at the six Minuteman wings.

The first Minuteman facilities at Vandenberg were six launch facilities (LF-02 through LF-07) and one launch

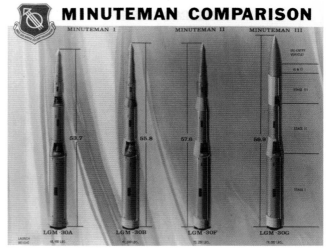

The Minuteman family of ICBMs, the backbone of the strategic nuclear alert force for over five decades. *Courtesy of the United States Air Force*

The steel "egg" of a Minuteman launch control center is shown during construction at North Vandenberg in the early 1960s. *Courtesy of the United States Air Force*

Project officers inspect a mockup of a Minuteman launch facility at Boeing Airplane Company facilities. Used launch facilities, such as the ones at Vandenberg, are never this pristine. *Courtesy of the United States Air Force*

control center (LCF-01A) constructed in the Casmalia Hills of north base in 1961. These LFs were used for testing of the Minuteman IA and IB ICBMs (LGM-30A and LGM-30B).[260] Two additional silos (LF-08 and LF-09) were completed by the Army Corps of Engineers in 1965. In July 1960, the 394th Missile Training Squadron (394 MTS) was activated to manage Minuteman training. During construction of the Vandenberg facilities, 394 MTS cadre received initial weapons system training at Cape Canaveral and at contractor plants around the country.[261] Minuteman maintenance training began in July 1962 for Malmstrom AFB personnel scheduled to receive the first Minuteman IA missiles. Maintenance training at Vandenberg did not last long, with the movement of the schoolhouse to Chanute AFB, Illinois, in March 1963. Training for missile launch officers remained at Vandenberg; the 394 MTS continued training throughout June 1963, until the 4315th Combat Crew Training Squadron (4315 CCTS) assumed all Minuteman training responsibilities. The 394 MTS was redesignated the 394th Strategic Missile Squadron (394 SMS) and continued supporting Minuteman operational test launches from the base.

In the 1980s, the 394 was again redesignated to a missile maintenance squadron and was finally inactivated on 1 July 1994.[262] Operational test launches for the Minuteman continued under the 6595th Aerospace Test Group, 310th Test and Training Wing, 595th Space Group, and, currently, the 576th Flight Test Squadron. Missile combat crew training responsibilities were transferred to the revived 392d Training Squadron[263] on 1 July 1993 and later to the 532d Training Squadron on 2 July 2012.[264]

The first operational Minuteman launch, code-named "AIR CRUSADE," took place on 28 September 1962.[265] The launch was a failure due to instability in the flight profile. It was destroyed in-flight by the range safety officer seconds after launch. The first successful Minuteman launch, code-named "AFGAN RUG," took place on 11 April 1963. The successor to the LGM-30A and B models, dubbed the Minuteman II (LGM-30F), influenced the construction of six new LFs[266] and three new LCFs[267] at North Vandenberg.

Strategic Triad

The Minuteman ICBM force is the land-based "leg" of the nation's strategic force, the "Triad." The Triad consists of the Air Force bomber fleet, the land-based ballistic missile fleet, and the Navy's sea-launched ballistic missile fleet:

> Each element [of the Triad] complements the other two. For example, each element depends on a different mode for prelaunch survival: the land-based missiles, upon dispersion and hardness; the sea-launched missiles, upon uncertainty of location; and the bomber force, upon tactical warning coupled with quick reaction. The diversified concept of the Triad provides a reasonable assurance of depriving an enemy of the ability to "knock out" more than one of the elements in a surprise attack.[268]

The basic characteristics of the Minuteman weapon system have not changed significantly since Minuteman I missiles were deployed in 1962. The 800 Minuteman I missiles stood guard and were later replaced by the more capable Minuteman II (LGM-30F) and Minuteman III (LGM-30G) missiles. In September 1992, after direction from President George H. W. Bush, the Air Force began taking the Minuteman II force off-alert and retiring them, leaving the LGM-30G missile as the only version of Minuteman fielded by 1995.

As conceived in the late 1950s, the Minuteman system differed from other first-generation ICBMs with the concept of basing and propellant used. The Minuteman missile was presented to the Air Force as a "new dimension in weaponry," with widely dispersed missiles in underground nuclear-hardened facilities.[269]

Due to increasing nuclear yields on Soviet ICBMs, the basing methods of early ICBMs were proven to be inadequate. The gantry and coffin launchers for the Atlas-D and E missiles did not provide protection from nuclear overpressure in excess of 5 lbs. per square inch (5 psi). To survive a shockwave after a nuclear blast, a target requires a hardness to withstand the overpressure, which drops off rapidly with distance from ground zero. Early missiles required shared equipment or facilities to guide and maintain the systems, so the missiles and launchers were within close proximity of each other.

During the nuclear tests of the 1950s and early 1960s, survivability tests showed that there is a choice between

President John F. Kennedy inspects a Minuteman launch facility at Vandenberg during his tour in 1962. Note the empty transporter-erector vehicle to the right-hand side. *Courtesy of the United States Air Force*

hardening the target (e.g., concrete and rebar), moving them some distance away, or a mixture of both.[270] The Minuteman basing concept defines the basic tactical unit as the missile squadron, consisting of five flights, with each flight containing one missile alert facility (MAF)—formerly called launch control facility (LCFs)—and ten launch facilities (LFs). This design ensured that one Soviet ICBM warhead could not destroy or disable an entire flight or squadron of missiles.

The Minuteman missile consists of three stages, each with a solid-propellant booster. Early versions of Minuteman were "topped off" with their respective reentry vehicles. The Minuteman III radically changed the design by including a "fourth stage"—a liquid-propellant postboost propulsion system—to assist in aiming and guiding the missile's multiple independently targeted reentry vehicles (MIRVs).[271, 272]

During its daily strategic alert status, ground equipment and the onboard missile computer run automatic status checks and tests and continually maintain spatial orientation for navigation.

After a commanded launch, the missile is boosted for approximately three minutes, with each of the three solid-propellant rocket motors burning in sequence and being jettisoned on command. The postboost vehicle provides maneuvering and guidance, releasing the warheads according to its preprogrammed targeting.

The Minuteman force was operational at seven bases, and at its peak had 1,000 missiles deployed:

WING	UNIT	BASE	MISSILES DEPLOYED
WING 0	394TH STRATEGIC MISSILE SQUADRON	VANDENBERG AFB, CA	0
WING I	341ST STRATEGIC MISSILE WING	MALMSTROM AFB, MT	200
WING II	44TH STRATEGIC MISSILE WING	ELLSWORTH AFB, SD	150
WING III	455TH STRATEGIC MISSILE WING	MINOT AFB, ND	150

The emblem of the 394th Strategic Missile Squadron contains a Minuteman-like missile taking center stage while the silhouette of a Revolutionary War Minuteman soldier looks on. *Courtesy of the United States Air Force*

WING	UNIT	BASE	MISSILES DEPLOYED
WING IV	351ST STRATEGIC MISSILE WING	WHITEMAN AFB, MO	150
WING V	90TH STRATEGIC MISSILE WING	F. E. WARREN AFB, WY	200
WING IV	321ST STRATEGIC MISSILE WING	GRAND FORKS AFB, ND	150

Cuban Missile Crisis

Vandenberg was unique among Minuteman bases as the location for operational test and development, not operationally deployed missiles. The moniker "Wing 0" (Wing Zero) denoted Vandenberg as the origination for technical order changes or equipment modifications from the manufacturer. The sole exception to Vandenberg's status with nonoperationally deployed missiles was during the Cuban Missile Crisis in October 1962. Gen. Thomas S. Power, commander in chief, Strategic Air Command (CINCSAC), relayed this message over the Primary Alerting System on 24 October 1962:

This is General Power speaking. I am addressing you for the purpose of re-emphasizing the seriousness of the situation this nation faces. We are in an advanced state of readiness to meet any emergencies and I feel that we are well prepared. I expect each of you to maintain strict security and use calm judgment during this tense period. Our plans are well prepared and are being executed smoothly. If there are any questions concerning instructions which by nature of the situation deviate from the normal, use the telephone for clarification. Review your plans for further action to insure that there will be no mistakes or confusion. I expect you to cut out all non-essentials and put yourself in a maximum readiness condition. If you are not sure of what you should do in any situation, and if time permits, get in touch with us here.[273]

During the crisis, the United States' nascent ICBM force was brought to the highest alert status in its history. On 19 October 1962, SAC had 112 ICBMs on alert; by 22 October—the date of President Kennedy's address to the nation—SAC had increased the number to 132 Atlas and Titan I missiles on operational status.

The urgency SAC attached to placing missiles on alert was reflected on 21 October in an order to deviate from normal technical data procedures in bringing ICBMs to rapid readiness configuration. Units would not check out systems or verify readiness, except when needed for personnel or equipment safety. This guidance was short lived, however; primarily because of safety considerations, it was rescinded three days later.[274]

After President Kennedy's speech on 22 October, SAC began Emergency Combat Capability of ballistic missile launch complexes on 24 October. SAC would assume operational control of all Air Force Systems Command launch complexes (ones being built or operationally checked-out prior to normal handover to SAC units). The ECC status meant that a missile could be launched on an Emergency War Order (EWO) mission in the event of strategic warning.[275]

Air Force Systems Command immediately began converting Vandenberg's missile force to ECC configuration:

- Atlas-E × 1
- Atlas-F × 1
- Titan I × 1
- Minuteman × 6

Additionally, Malmstrom AFB's Minuteman complex also became ECC configured. A critical fact to note was that the first operational test launch of the Minuteman I missile (code-named "AIR CRUSADE") had been launched on 28 September 1962—less than a month prior to the crisis.[276]

October 27 saw the first two Minuteman missiles at Malmstrom AFB go on alert. Two hours later, one 394th Strategic Missile Squadron Minuteman followed at Vandenberg.[277] As the crisis reached its peak, the number of Minuteman missiles also peaked at nine readied in ECC configuration on 30 October 1962. Since the Minuteman missile cadre had not been formed, contractor personnel remained in place assisting in the missile force readiness.

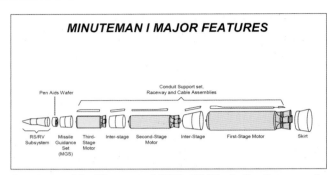

A cutaway of the Minuteman I (LGM-30A/B) missile. *Courtesy of the United States Air Force*

The prolonged nature of the crisis, and keeping Vandenberg's Minuteman force on twenty-four-hour alert, delayed the testing program that was "vital to the activation of the [WS-133A] weapon system at operational sites."[278]

Minuteman launch facilities 394A-1 through 394A-5 were released from ECC configuration to resume testing on 3 November 1962. The next Minuteman launch at Vandenberg proceeded a little over a month later, on 10 December 1962.[279]

As this vignette shows, early nuclear retaliatory systems, including the Minuteman, were rushed into operational service before their technical development had matured. This forced major retrofit programs onto already in-service systems. The first variant of Minuteman I, the "A" model (SM-80A, LGM-30A), had a range of 4,900 nautical miles—far less than the 1958 specifications for a 5,500-nautical-mile range.[280] The missiles deployed to Malmstrom AFB during the Cuban Missile Crisis required replacement at the earliest opportunity. It was later discovered that other defects existed, such as internal wiring that rendered Minuteman vulnerable to electromagnetic pulse effects at ranges in excess of 1,000 miles.[281]

The Minuteman IA missile carried a Mark 59 warhead in a Mk 5 RV; the B variant carried the Mark 56 warhead in a Mark 11 or Mark 11A RV. Early RVs, such as the Mark 5 and Mark 11, were blunt and provided antiballistic missile radars with a large cross section for targeting. The 1962 development of a large radar installation code-named DOG HOUSE 30 miles outside Moscow signaled the full-scale deployment of a Soviet antiballistic missile system.[282] In 1964, construction started on additional radar installations in Lithuania and on the Kola Peninsula, squarely along planned US ICBM and SLBM flight corridors. Moscow was gearing up the deployment of nuclear-tipped "preventive measures" against US missile systems. Mark 12 reentry vehicles were sleeker, giving a smaller radar cross section to reduce radar visibility against ABM defenses.[283]

LGM-30F Minuteman II

Improvements on the LGM-30F Minuteman II included greater range, increased throw weight, improved accuracy and reliability, multiple target selection, and greater ABM

The first LGM-30F Minuteman II is prepared by technicians. *Courtesy of the United States Air Force*

penetration capability over the Minuteman I force. Upgraded features included

- an improved first-stage motor to increase reliability,[284]
- an improved guidance system, incorporating integrated circuits and miniaturized discrete electronic parts,
- a penetration-aids system to camouflage the warhead during its reentry into an enemy environment, and
- a larger-yield warhead in the reentry vehicle to increase kill probability.

LGM-30F Emergency Rocket Communications System

Specially modified Minuteman II missiles at Whiteman AFB, Missouri, carried high-powered transmitters of the Emergency Rocket Communications System (ERCS). This system was an additional method of communication from

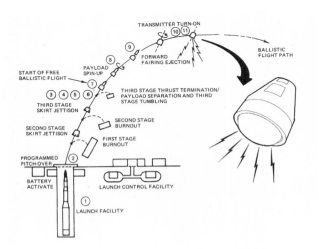

The Emergency Rocket Communications System (ERCS) was a UHF-based payload launched aboard a Minuteman II rocket. It was designed to transmit Emergency Action Messages (EAMs) to Strategic Air Command crews. It was replaced with satellite technology in the 1990s. *Courtesy of the United States Air Force*

SAC headquarters to bomber and missile crews if other methods of communication were destroyed during a nuclear attack.[285]

On select missiles, the Mark 11 warhead was replaced with two UHF transmitters. To keep maximum effectiveness as a backup system, the location of ERCS payload within the Whiteman missile complex was kept secret. Missile combat crews of the 510th Strategic Missile Squadron had uniquely modified launch control centers with ERCS command and control equipment. The missile's high trajectory would allow the payload to transmit to nuclear forces for up to thirty minutes after launch.[286]

Tests of Minuteman II with ERCS payloads at Vandenberg went under the code name GIANT MOON.[287] Ten tests of ERCS transmitters took place between 1966 and 1976. As secure means of communications over satellite links were introduced, along with the pending phaseout of the Minuteman II, ERCS was deactivated in 1991.

LGM-30G Minuteman III

Secretary of Defense McNamara initiated the STRAT-X study in late 1966, to view into a "crystal ball" to ascertain Soviet intentions and the state of nuclear forces from 1975 through 1985.[288] The twenty-volume collection was written by the Institute for Defense Analyses and provided many findings

Artist's conception of a LGM-30G Minuteman III missile launch. *Courtesy of the United States Air Force*

that would shape future nuclear planning, including the development of MIRV capability on the Minuteman III.[289]

The Minuteman III is distinguished from previous Minuteman models by the following features:[290]

- A larger third-stage rocket motor to increase flight range
- A reentry system capable of deploying penetration aids (chaff and decoys) and up to three RVs to increase payload delivery
- An added propulsion system rocket engine to increase range and maneuver the RS
- Improved electronics in the guidance system to reduce vulnerability in a nuclear environment

Minuteman and ABRES

As recounted, Atlas and Titan missiles were taken off nuclear alert and recycled either as space launch boosters or test articles for the ABRES. When the inventory of Atlas and Titan airframes dwindled, surplus Minuteman I missiles were used in the ABRES program.[291] These missiles were modified to launch inert warheads toward the Kwajalein Missile Range terminal area for acquisition of metric tracking, complex radar and optic signatures, telemetry, and reentry environmental data.[292]

Kwajalein, as the robust target area for US missile tests, provided operational realism for missile booster range and payload throw weight. Additionally, a few Minuteman III tests required land impact to test fusing techniques, as well as the requirement for Minuteman II tests to impact in shallow water so that the data-recording instrumentation package could be recovered.[293]

Force Development Evaluation

Since the stated mission of the Minuteman missile is to deter war by maintaining a survivable capability to deliver thermonuclear warheads against strategic targets from hardened underground launchers in the continental United States, constant testing is required to maintain a high level of confidence in its deterrence value. At Vandenberg, the Force Development Evaluation (FDE) program allows missile firings from a modified operational launch complex to provide experience for operations, planning, and maintenance personnel involved in Minuteman operations. Because the stated features of the Minuteman missile are high reliability, minimum maintenance with maximum operational readiness, complete remote-targeting capability, and the ability to quickly launch missiles, these characteristics must be tested frequently.

Occasionally a Minuteman test from Vandenberg will make it into the national news:

The Air Force successfully launched an unarmed Minuteman 3 missile yesterday at a target 4,200 miles away in the South Pacific, officials said.[294]

The Rocket Systems Launch Program (RSLP) converts surplus ICBMs into test launch vehicles. The Minuteman II's stages provide an ICBM class of launch vehicles for targets and experiment platforms for new concepts in weapon systems development. *Courtesy of the United States Air Force*

A Force Development Evaluation launch of a Minuteman III takes off from Launch Facility 09 (LF-09) on 5 November 2008. The Minuteman III is the backbone of US strategic deterrence and the only land-based ICBM in the inventory. *Courtesy of the United States Air Force*

Additionally, Minuteman launches will demonstrate the capability of the Airborne Launch Control System (ALCS). The ALCS provides a secure secondary command and control capability for enabling and launching of Minuteman missiles if a decapitation strike destroys a MAF or otherwise prevents the missile combat crew from launching. ALCS-launched missiles are a common part of the FDE program.

Testing for the missiles was composed of four categories: operational R&D, demonstration and shakedown operations (DASO), operational test (OT), and follow-on operational test (FOT).[295] These tests provided an operational launch environment for contractors, operators, and nuclear war planners, as well as experience for repairing and maintaining the systems. Additionally, the tests provided validation of missile combat crew training and readiness. The Minuteman I and II test programs ran concurrently until December 1971. The Minuteman I test program ceased at that time due to the LGM-30A/B force being removed from operational missile bases; however, Minuteman I testing and supporting reentry vehicle programs (ABRES) continued until the early 1990s. Testing for Minuteman II missiles ceased during 1987.

Other tests supported with Minuteman missiles, or Minuteman hardware, include Homing Overlay Experiment[296] and the Exoatmospheric Re-entry Vehicle Interception System (using an Aries booster consisting of Minuteman I second and third stages).[297]

After its creation in 1992, the mission of US Strategic Command was to integrate strategic forces under a single field commander serving a number of key characteristics involving strategic weapons; provide the primary military voice for strategic nuclear force structure, modernization, and arms control; assure the integration of strategic nuclear policies; and prepare forces for use if deterrence should fail.[298]

Today, facing multiple global threats, USSTRATCOM's (2017) mission has evolved:

> USSTRATCOM employs tailored nuclear, cyber, space, global strike, joint electronic warfare, missile defense, and intelligence capabilities to deter aggression, decisively respond if deterrence fails, assure allies, shape adversary behavior, defeat terror, and define the force of the future.[299]

To support deterrence policies, Vandenberg launches a predetermined number of Minuteman missiles per year. All missiles are selected from the operational force, shipped to Vandenberg outfitted with necessary test instrumentation, and postured to alert configuration in a Vandenberg launch facility of the same weapon system configuration as the operational base. Preparation for launching takes four to eight weeks, although the actual launch takes place during a four-hour "launch window."[300]

Abridged Chronology of Minuteman at Vandenberg[301]

- **2 February 1961:** Construction began on Minuteman ICBM test launch facilities at Vandenberg AFB.
- **28 September 1962:** First launch of a Minuteman missile from Vandenberg AFB.
- **11 April 1963:** The first successful launch of a model "A" Minuteman I ICBM from Vandenberg by a crew from the Air Force Systems Command's 6595th Aerospace Test Wing. It followed the completion of a successful flight test program from Cape Canaveral, Florida.
- **24 May 1963:** The first successful launch of a model "B" Minuteman I ICBM took place at Vandenberg AFB, California.
- **17 October 1963:** The first model "A" Minuteman I ICBM operational test (OT) launch at Vandenberg AFB, California, was a partial success. The missile, launched by a crew from the 341st Strategic Missile Wing, Malmstrom AFB, Montana, successfully flew down the Pacific Missile Range, but late third-stage thrust termination caused its reentry vehicle to impact 781 nautical miles beyond its target area.
- **17 December 1963:** Only SAC launch of an ERCS Blue Scout Jr. by the 4300th Support Squadron at Vandenberg AFB, California.

- **25 February 1964:** The first two model "B" Minuteman I ICBM OT launches at Vandenberg AFB, California, were successful. Both launches took place on the same day.
- **29 February 1964:** Two model "A" Minuteman I ICBMs were launched from Vandenberg AFB, California, in the first successful "ripple mode" launch of this weapon system. In this dual launch, primary crews from the 10th Strategic Missile Squadron at Malmstrom AFB, Montana, issued launch commands to both missiles.
- **7 July 1964:** A model "B" Minuteman I OT on this date was the 100th SAC missile launched from Vandenberg AFB, California.
- **9 November 1964:** The last model "A" Minuteman I ICBM OT launch at Vandenberg AFB, California, was successful.
- **6 July 1965:** The last model "B" Minuteman I ICBM OT launch at Vandenberg AFB, California, was successful.
- **18 August 1965:** The first attempted launch of a Minuteman II ICBM from an operationally configured underground silo at Vandenberg AFB, California, conducted by Air Force Systems Command was successful. The missile flew 5,000 miles down the Pacific Missile Range, and its reentry vehicle impacted in the target area.
- **24 February 1966:** The first attempted salvo (simultaneous) launch of two model "A" Minuteman I ICBMs at Vandenberg AFB, California, was successful. This launch demonstrated the multiple countdown and launch techniques that would be used at operational bases under actual combat conditions.
- **3 October 1966:** The last model "A" Minuteman I ICBM follow-on operational test (FOT) launch at Vandenberg AFB, California, was successful.
- **13 December 1966:** The first test and evaluation launch of the Minuteman Emergency Rocket Communications System (ERCS) was successful. A communications package was successfully launched into space aboard a Minuteman II ICBM fired from Vandenberg AFB, California, and transmitted its message successfully before reentry into the earth's atmosphere.
- **22 December 1966:** The first attempted salvo (simultaneous) launch of two model "B" Minuteman I ICBMs at Vandenberg AFB, California, was successful.
- **17 April 1967:** The last Minuteman F ERCS R&D flight test from Vandenberg AFB, California.
- **17 April 1967:** The first attempted launch of a Minuteman II ICBM by means of the Airborne Launch Control System (ALCS) conducted at Vandenberg AFB, California, was successful. The ALCS attained initial operational capability (IOC) on 31 May 1967. This system provided Headquarters SAC with the capability of launching Minuteman ICBMs from airborne command post aircraft.
- **2 June 1967:** The "Cold/Heat Soak" special test launch of a model "B" Minuteman I ICBM at Vandenberg AFB, California, was successful. The primary objective of the "Cold/Heat Soak" launches was to investigate the effects

of prolonged exposure to extreme atmospheric conditions on the operational capability of ICBMs.

- **24 October 1968:** A Minuteman II launched from Vandenberg AFB, California, was SAC's 300th missile launch.
- **10 December 1968:** The last "Cold/Heat Soak" test launch of a model "B" Minuteman I ICBM at Vandenberg AFB, California, was successful.
- **16 April 1969:** The first Minuteman II OT launch, conducted at Vandenberg AFB, California, was unsuccessful.
- **21 May 1970:** A Minuteman II ICBM was successfully launched from Vandenberg AFB, California, to the Oeno Island target area in the Southeast Pacific. This was the first time the Oeno Island target area was utilized for a Minuteman ICBM test launch.
- **4 August 1970:** First Minuteman F ERCS OT launched from Vandenberg AFB, California.
- **29 August 1970:** The first full-scale test of all major elements of the Army's Safeguard ABM system was successful. The reentry vehicle of a surplus model "B" Minuteman I ICBM launched from Vandenberg AFB, California, was successfully intercepted by a Spartan area defense interceptor missile launched from Kwajalein Atoll.
- **22 October 1970:** The first attempted salvo (simultaneous) launch of two Minuteman II ICBMs at Vandenberg AFB, California, was successful.
- **23 December 1970:** The reentry vehicle of a surplus model "B" Minuteman I ICBM launched from Vandenberg AFB, California, was successfully intercepted by a Sprint terminal-defense interceptor missile launched from Kwajalein Atoll.
- **3 February 1971:** The first Minuteman II phase II OT was launched from Vandenberg AFB, California.
- **24 March 1971:** The first Minuteman III, phase II OT launch at Vandenberg AFB, California, was successful.
- **24 May 1971:** SAC launched its 400th missile from Vandenberg AFB, California—a Minuteman II.
- **13 April 1972:** The last Minuteman II phase I OT flew from Vandenberg AFB, California.
- **13 June 1972:** At Vandenberg AFB, California, the first flight test (nicknamed GIANT PATRIOT) of the Operational Base Launch Safety System (OBLSS, launched aboard a Force Modernized Minuteman II ICBM) was successful. The OBLSS was an internally mounted destruct system that would allow the launch of a Minuteman II ICBM from an operational silo while providing ground controllers with an effective safety destruct system if the missile malfunctioned or deviated radically from its projected flight path.
- **19 September 1972:** The first Minuteman III ICBM Phase I OT launch (from a regular Minuteman II launch facility) at Vandenberg AFB, California, was successful.

Dual launches of Minuteman missiles fly westward toward Kwajalein Atoll. *Courtesy of the United States Air Force*

- **4 December 1972:** The first Minuteman III phase II OT was launched from Vandenberg AFB, California.
- **1 July 1974:** The initial training of Minuteman missile combat crews, formerly performed by Air Training Command (ATC) instructors at Vandenberg AFB, California, was incorporated into the 4315th Combat Crew Training Squadron's Operational Readiness Training (ORT) program at Vandenberg. As a result of this action, the entire Minuteman missile combat training, from beginning (initial training) to end (upgrade training), became the responsibility of SAC.
- **26 August 1976:** SAC launched its 500th missile from Vandenberg AFB, California—a Minuteman II.
- **17 September 1980:** Glory Trip 77GM—a Minuteman III OT—became the longest Minuteman flight test from Vandenberg AFB, California, when its payload impacted a broad ocean area target over 5,600 nautical miles downrange.
- **29 February 1984:** Special OTs of Minuteman II ICBMs ended with the launch of Glory Trip 146 at Vandenberg AFB, California.

- **7 February 1986:** The first class of female Minuteman combat crew officers completed initial qualification training at Vandenberg AFB, California.
- **20–21 January 1988:** Computer-aided message processing was simulated in a launch control center trainer for the first time at Vandenberg AFB, California.

Minuteman Statistics

- Most launches in one year: 55 in calendar year (CY) 1970; 60 in fiscal year (FY) 1971
- First all-SAC launch: LGM-30A on 18 June 1963 by a 394 SMS crew
- First OT launch: LGM-30A on 17 October 1963
- Most OT launches in one year: 47 in CY 1964
- Least OT launches in one year: zero in CY 1968
- Most OT launches in one month: five, 2 May to 2 June 1966
- Closest single launches: two LGM-30B missions, 12 seconds apart, 21 February 1967

- First missile launch sighted by an astronaut in space: LGM-30A on 24 August 1965 by Gemini V astronauts
- First ALCS launch: LGM-30F on 17 April 1967
- First Minuteman Emergency Rocket Communications System launch: LGM-30F on 13 December 1966
- First north–south launch: LGM-30F to Oeno Island on 21 May 1970
- First land impact mission: LGM-30G on Illeginni Island, 26 July 1979
- Longest flight test: 5,600 nautical miles by LGM-30G on 17 September 1980

Minuteman Dual Launches

#1	24 FEB 1966	LGM-30A	BROAD ARROW/SEA DEVIL
#2	22 DEC 1966	LGM-30B	STONE AXE/WILD DUCK
#3	22 OCT 1970	LGM-30F	GLORY TRIP 69F/70F
#4	10 JUL 1979	LGM-30G	GLORY TRIP 40GM/68GM

MINUTEMAN IA (LGM-30A) Launches[302]

SEQUENCE	DATE	SITE	VEHICLE	CODENAME	NOTES
170	28 SEP 62	394A-3	MINUTEMAN IA	AIR CRUSADE	FIRST MINUTEMAN 1A LAUNCH
185	10 DEC 62	394A-4	MINUTEMAN IA	AMERICAN BEAUTY	
220	11 APR 63	394A-5	MINUTEMAN IA	AFGAN RUG	
221	12 APR 63	394A-1	MINUTEMAN IA	VELVET TOUCH	
223	23 APR 63	394A-4	MINUTEMAN IA	PAT HAND	
228	30 APR 63	394A-2	MINUTEMAN IA	BOLD JOURNEY	
230	8 MAY 63	394A-5	MINUTEMAN IA	FINE SHOW	
243	18 JUN 63	394A-3	MINUTEMAN IA	WAR AXE	
246	28 JUN 63	394A-1	MINUTEMAN IA	TRIM CHIEF	
250	5 JUL 63	394A-4	MINUTEMAN IA	GRAND TOUR	
251	11 JUL 63	394A-2	MINUTEMAN IA	TRIPLE PLAY	
257	27 JUL 63	394A-5	MINUTEMAN IA	DIAL RIGHT	
261	8 AUG 63	394A-1	MINUTEMAN IA	WELL DONE	
282	17 OCT 63	394A-3	MINUTEMAN IA	CEDAR LAKE	
286	31 OCT 63	394A-5	MINUTEMAN IA	DRAG CHUTE	
287	2 NOV 63	394A-2	MINUTEMAN IA	HARD LINE	
297	29 NOV 63	394A-5	MINUTEMAN IA	ARM CHAIR	
301	13 DEC 63	394A-3	MINUTEMAN IA	BAMBOO SHOOT	
308	20 DEC 63	394A-5	MINUTEMAN IA	BENT HOOK	
316	23 JAN 64	LF-04	MINUTEMAN IA	BLACK BUSH	
320	11 FEB 64	LF-06	MINUTEMAN IA	BLUE PAINT	
328	29 FEB 64	LF-04	MINUTEMAN IA	BRASS RING	
329	29 FEB 64	LF-05	MINUTEMAN IA	BOX SEAT	
337	26 MAR 64	LF-05	MINUTEMAN IA	CIGAR SMOKE	
338	31 MAR 64	LF-04	MINUTEMAN IA	CRACKER BOX	
345	27 APR 64	LF-05	MINUTEMAN IA	DRAG OUT	
347	11 MAY 64	LF-06	MINUTEMAN IA	DIP NET	
353	9 JUN 64	LF-05	MINUTEMAN IA	GOLD CLUB	
354	11 JUN 64	LF-06	MINUTEMAN IA	HIGH OCTANE	
361	29 JUN 64	LF-04	MINUTEMAN IA	ELM BRANCH	

SEQUENCE	DATE	SITE	VEHICLE	CODENAME	NOTES
365	7 JUL 64	LF-05	MINUTEMAN IA	NORMAL TIMES	
370	27 JUL 64	LF-06	MINUTEMAN IA	GINGER FOOT	
379	17 AUG 64	LF-05	MINUTEMAN IA	LIMBER POLE	
388	1 SEP 64	LF-04	MINUTEMAN IA	DAWN PATROL	
389	8 SEP 64	LF-06	MINUTEMAN IA	LONG LINE	
411	4 NOV 64	LF-06	MINUTEMAN IA	BLACK FROST	
415	9 NOV 64	LF-05	MINUTEMAN IA	QUICK JUMP	
501	24 AUG 65	LF-06	MINUTEMAN IA	SHUTTLE TRAIN	
502	25 AUG 65	LF-04	MINUTEMAN IA	PILOT ROCK	
525	14 DEC 65	LF-04	MINUTEMAN IA	GRAND RIVER	
547	24 FEB 66	LF-04	MINUTEMAN IA	BROAD ARROW	SALVO LAUNCH
548	24 FEB 66	LF-06	MINUTEMAN IA	SEA DEVIL	SALVO LAUNCH
557	21 MAR 66	LF-06	MINUTEMAN IA	TULIP TREE	
560	25 MAR 66	LF-04	MINUTEMAN IA	WHITE BOOK	
580	16 MAY 66	LF-06	MINUTEMAN IA	SAGE GREEN	
587	31 MAY 66	LF-04	MINUTEMAN IA	NIGHT STAND	
614	16 AUG 66	LF-06	MINUTEMAN IA	WHITE ARC	
617	22 AUG 66	LF-04	MINUTEMAN IA	TOWN DOCTOR	
625	20 SEP 66	LF-04	MINUTEMAN IA	RED SPIDER	
630	3 OCT 66	LF-06	MINUTEMAN IA	GROVE HILL	FINAL LGM-30A MINUTEMAN IA LAUNCH

MINUTEMAN IB (LGM-30B) Launches[303]

SEQUENCE	DATE	SITE	VEHICLE	CODENAME	NOTES
236	24 MAY 63	394A-6	MINUTEMAN IB	HEY DAY	FIRST LGM-30B LAUNCH
267	29 AUG 63	394A-6	MINUTEMAN IB	GLASS WAND	
276	26 SEP 63	394A-7	MINUTEMAN IB	STATE PARK	
280	4 OCT 63	394A-6	MINUTEMAN IB	GOLD DUKE	
295	27 NOV 63	394A-6	MINUTEMAN IB	BIG CIRCLE	
300	13 DEC 63	394A-1	MINUTEMAN IB	ANSWER MAN	
311	10 JAN 64	LF-07	MINUTEMAN IB	CLOCK WATCH	
313	16 JAN 64	LF-02	MINUTEMAN IB	DOUBLE BARREL	
318	29 JAN 64	LF-03	MINUTEMAN IB	ECHO HILL	
324	24 FEB 64	LF-02	MINUTEMAN IB	SNAP ROLL	
325	24 FEB 64	LF-03	MINUTEMAN IB	FAST ORBIT	
331	6 MAR 64	LF-07	MINUTEMAN IB	KITE TAIL	
334	23 MAR 64	LF-02	MINUTEMAN IB	BIG TREE	
336	25 MAR 64	LF-03	MINUTEMAN IB	CHROME PLATE	
340	13 APR 64	LF-07	MINUTEMAN IB	COOPER FACE	
342	23 APR 64	LF-03	MINUTEMAN IB	DARK LADY	
346	7 MAY 64	LF-02	MINUTEMAN IB	BLACK WASP	
348	18 MAY 64	LF-03	MINUTEMAN IB	DRESS BLUES	
350	25 MAY 64	LF-07	MINUTEMAN IB	DEER HORN	
356	15 JUN 64	LF-02	MINUTEMAN IB	CRUSH PROOF	
362	29 JUN 64	LF-09	MINUTEMAN IB	BLACK PEPPER	
366	7 JUL 64	LF-02	MINUTEMAN IB	FIVE POINTS	
367	9 JUL 64	LF-07	MINUTEMAN IB	GEORGIA BOY	
369	13 JUL 64	LF-03	MINUTEMAN IB	OLD FOX	
375	7 AUG 64	LF-03	MINUTEMAN IB	GOLD REEF	
381	21 AUG 64	LF-08	MINUTEMAN IB	LIGHT HORSE	
383	25 AUG 64	LF-07	MINUTEMAN IB	IVY TOWER	
390	10 SEP 64	LF-02	MINUTEMAN IB	HOT ROOF	

SEQUENCE	DATE	SITE	VEHICLE	CODENAME	NOTES
393	15 SEP 64	LF-08	MINUTEMAN IB	QUICK LAUNCH	
394	21 SEP 64	LF-09	MINUTEMAN IB	LONG RANGE	
397	23 SEP 64	LF-03	MINUTEMAN IB	MOUNT UP	
398	29 SEP 64	LF-07	MINUTEMAN IB	PAINTED WARRIOR	
407	2 NOV 64	LF-03	MINUTEMAN IB	PARIS ROYAL	
408	2 NOV 64	LF-08	MINUTEMAN IB	NET GAIN	
412	5 NOV 64	LF-09	MINUTEMAN IB	LONG SHOT	
413	6 NOV 64	LF-07	MINUTEMAN IB	POP FLY	
414	6 NOV 64	LF-02	MINUTEMAN IB	ORANGE CHUTE	
422	9 DEC 64	LF-02	MINUTEMAN IB	NICKED BLADE	
423	9 DEC 64	LF-08	MINUTEMAN IB	TOP RAIL	
425	18 DEC 64	LF-07	MINUTEMAN IB	ROSY FUTURE	
435	20 JAN 65	LF-03	MINUTEMAN IB	PURPLE LIGHT	
438	2 FEB 65	LF-02	MINUTEMAN IB	RED BRIDGE	
439	2 FEB 65	LF-08	MINUTEMAN IB	SIDE TRIP	
440	8 FEB 65	LF-09	MINUTEMAN IB	PRONTO ROSE	
443	1 MAR 65	LF-08	MINUTEMAN IB	GOLDEN ROSE	
446	8 MAR 65	LF-07	MINUTEMAN IB	DOCK BELL	
451	16 MAR 65	LF-02	MINUTEMAN IB	TAIL FIN	
455	25 MAR 65	LF-03	MINUTEMAN IB	QUICK NOTE	
459	10 APR 65	LF-09	MINUTEMAN IB	SMOKEY RIVER	
460	13 APR 65	LF-02	MINUTEMAN IB	SEA POINT	
461	13 APR 65	LF-08	MINUTEMAN IB	YELLOW LIGHT	
466	30 APR 65	LF-03	MINUTEMAN IB	WINTER BREW	
467	10 MAY 65	LF-09	MINUTEMAN IB	VIOLET RAY	
469	18 MAY 65	LF-07	MINUTEMAN IB	SILVER CLOUD	
474	2 JUN 65	LF-08	MINUTEMAN IB	SURF SPRAY	
476	7 JUN 65	LF-03	MINUTEMAN IB	WHEEL HORSE	
480	10 JUN 65	LF-02	MINUTEMAN IB	SPEED KING	
482	23 JUN 65	LF-09	MINUTEMAN IB	WHITE GLOVE	
485	29 JUN 65	LF-08	MINUTEMAN IB	MAPLE GROVE	
488	2 JUL 65	LF-03	MINUTEMAN IB	SWEET TALK	
489	6 JUL 65	LF-07	MINUTEMAN IB	STAR DUST	
535	27 JAN 66	LF-09	MINUTEMAN IB	ANCHOR POLE	
542	11 FEB 66	LF-07	MINUTEMAN IB	CREEK BED	
550	8 MAR 66	LF-02	MINUTEMAN IB	BAIT CAN	
552	11 MAR 66	LF-03	MINUTEMAN IB	CLEAN SLATE	
564	4 APR 66	LF-09	MINUTEMAN IB	ARROW FEATHER	
565	4 APR 66	LF-02	MINUTEMAN IB	FLY BURNER	
568	15 APR 66	LF-07	MINUTEMAN IB	GAY CROWD	
572	22 APR 66	LF-03	MINUTEMAN IB	ECHO CANYON	
573	2 MAY 66	LF-02	MINUTEMAN IB	LACE STRAP	
579	16 MAY 66	LF-09	MINUTEMAN IB	DOCK WORKER	
581	17 MAY 66	LF-07	MINUTEMAN IB	TIGHT DRUM	
586	31 MAY 66	LF-03	MINUTEMAN IB	GREEN PEA	
588	2 JUN 66	LF-02	MINUTEMAN IB	FOUR ACES	
592	10 JUN 66	LF-09	MINUTEMAN IB	EBONY ANGEL	
598	11 JUL 66	LF-03	MINUTEMAN IB	SOLID GOLD	
599	12 JUL 66	LF-09	MINUTEMAN IB	SUGAR CANE	
601	13 JUL 66	LF-02	MINUTEMAN IB	YOUNG LION	
605	26 JUL 66	LF-07	MINUTEMAN IB	RED MAN	
609	5 AUG 66	LF-03	MINUTEMAN IB	PLAY BUSTER	
613	16 AUG 66	LF-02	MINUTEMAN IB	GIBSON GIRL	

SEQUENCE	DATE	SITE	VEHICLE	CODENAME	NOTES
620	29 AUG 66	LF-07	MINUTEMAN IB	MOTHER CAT	
624	16 SEP 66	LF-03	MINUTEMAN IB	SNOW HILL	
627	22 SEP 66	LF-09	MINUTEMAN IB	HOT SPRINGS	
634	13 OCT 66	LF-03	MINUTEMAN IB	SEA RAVEN	
636	21 OCT 66	LF-07	MINUTEMAN IB	MATCHED CLUBS	
642	16 NOV 66	LF-09	MINUTEMAN IB	LONG DOZEN	
643	22 NOV 66	LF-03	MINUTEMAN IB	WORKING GIRL	
649	20 DEC 66	LF-09	MINUTEMAN IB	SHELL BEACH	
651	22 DEC 66	LF-07	MINUTEMAN IB	WILD DUCK	
652	22 DEC 66	LF-03	MINUTEMAN IB	STONE AXE	
659	24 JAN 67	LF-09	MINUTEMAN IB	TRUCK TRAVEL	
661	30 JAN 67	LF-03	MINUTEMAN IB	BUCCANEER SWORD	
665	7 FEB 67	LF-07	MINUTEMAN IB	PIANO TUNER	
669	21 FEB 67	LF-09	MINUTEMAN IB	GLORY TRAIL	
670	21 FEB 67	LF-03	MINUTEMAN IB	BUDDY BOY	
674	7 MAR 67	LF-07	MINUTEMAN IB	OLD SAL	
677	22 MAR 67	LF-03	MINUTEMAN IB	GLYCOL JELL	
680	7 APR 67	LF-09	MINUTEMAN IB	BUCK PASSER	
687	21 APR 67	LF-03	MINUTEMAN IB	GIPSY CAMP	
689	27 APR 67	LF-07	MINUTEMAN IB	OLEO KNIFE	
690	28 APR 67	LF-02	MINUTEMAN IB	BUSY MUMMY	
694	17 MAY 67	LF-09	MINUTEMAN IB	GLOSSY COAT	
697	19 MAY 67	LF-02	MINUTEMAN IB	BUSY GIANT	
700	22 MAY 67	LF-03	MINUTEMAN IB	GLOSS TWINE	
706	31 MAY 67	LF-07	MINUTEMAN IB	--	
707	1 JUN 67	LF-06	MINUTEMAN IB	--	
712	21 JUN 67	LF-03	MINUTEMAN IB	--	
714	28 JUN 67	LF-02	MINUTEMAN IB	--	
716	5 JUL 67	LF-07	MINUTEMAN IB	GLOWING BRIGHT 40	
719	12 JUL 67	LF-09	MINUTEMAN IB	GLOWING BRIGHT 42	
720	13 JUL 67	LF-06	MINUTEMAN IB	OLD COIN	
721	15 JUL 67	LF-02	MINUTEMAN IB	GIN BABY I	
730	8 AUG 67	LF-09	MINUTEMAN IB	GLOWING BRIGHT 45	
733	6 SEP 67	LF-03	MINUTEMAN IB	GLOWING BRIGHT 46	
737	21 SEP 67	LF-07	MINUTEMAN IB	GLOWING BRIGHT 47	
739	26 SEP 67	LF-09	MINUTEMAN IB	GLOWING BRIGHT 48	
747	3 NOV 67	LF-02	MINUTEMAN IB	GIN BABY II	
751	14 NOV 67	LF-09	MINUTEMAN IB	GLOWING BRIGHT 52	
752	14 NOV 67	LF-07	MINUTEMAN IB	GLOWING BRIGHT 51	
755	1 DEC 67	LF-03	MINUTEMAN IB	GLOWING BRIGHT 50	
759	8 DEC 67	LF-02	MINUTEMAN IB	GIN BABY IV	
761	18 DEC 67	LF-07	MINUTEMAN IB	GLORY TRIP 01B	
763	21 DEC 67	LF-09	MINUTEMAN IB	GLORY TRIP 03B	
764	21 DEC 67	LF-03	MINUTEMAN IB	GLORY TRIP 02B	
769	16 JAN 68	LF-06	MINUTEMAN IB	GLOWING SAND	
776	2 FEB 68	LF-09	MINUTEMAN IB	OLYMPIC TRIALS B-1	
788	10 APR 68	LF-03	MINUTEMAN IB	OLYMPIC TRIALS B-2	
791	23 APR 68	LF-06	MINUTEMAN IB	GLASS POLE	
798	22 MAY 68	LF-03	MINUTEMAN IB	OLYMPIC TRIALS B-3	
801	23 MAY 68	LF-06	MINUTEMAN IB	OLD FAITHFUL	
812	12 JUL 68	LF-03	MINUTEMAN IB	OLYMPIC TRIALS B-4	
830	30 OCT 68	LF-09	MINUTEMAN IB	OLYMPIC TRIALS B-5	
840	7 DEC 68	LF-09	MINUTEMAN IB	OLYMPIC TRIALS B-6	

SEQUENCE	DATE	SITE	VEHICLE	CODENAME	NOTES
841	10 DEC 68	LF-06	MINUTEMAN IB	OLD FAITHFUL 2	
847	21 JAN 69	LF-09	MINUTEMAN IB	OLYMPIC TRIALS B-7	
853	30 JAN 69	LF-03	MINUTEMAN IB	GLORY TRIP 32B	
856	20 FEB 69	LF-09	MINUTEMAN IB	OLYMPIC TRIALS B-8	
865	24 MAR 69	LF-07	MINUTEMAN IB	GLORY TRIP 33B	
866	25 MAR 69	LF-03	MINUTEMAN IB	GLORY TRIP 34B	
873	23 APR 69	LF-07	MINUTEMAN IB	GLORY TRIP 35B	
886	18 JUN 69	LF-07	MINUTEMAN IB	GLORY TRIP 37B	
890	30 JUN 69	LF-03	MINUTEMAN IB	GLORY TRIP 38B	
891	2 JUL 69	LF-09	MINUTEMAN IB	OLYMPIC TRIALS B-9	
898	23 JUL 69	LF-07	MINUTEMAN IB	GLORY TRIP 41B	
907	28 AUG 69	LF-03	MINUTEMAN IB	--	
910	10 SEP 69	LF-07	MINUTEMAN IB	--	
913	20 SEP 69	LF-09	MINUTEMAN IB	--	
916	23 SEP 69	LF-06	MINUTEMAN IB	--	
921	2 OCT 69	LF-03	MINUTEMAN IB	--	
925	21 OCT 69	LF-07	MINUTEMAN IB	GLORY TRIP 45B	
928	6 NOV 69	LF-09	MINUTEMAN IB	--	
934	25 NOV 69	LF-03	MINUTEMAN IB	--	
937	5 DEC 69	LF-07	MINUTEMAN IB	GLORY TRIP 50B	
939	16 DEC 69	LF-06	MINUTEMAN IB	--	
946	25 FEB 70	LF-07	MINUTEMAN IB	--	
948	4 MAR 70	LF-09	MINUTEMAN IB	--	
951	10 MAR 70	LF-03	MINUTEMAN IB	--	
954	23 MAR 70	LF-07	MINUTEMAN IB	GLORY TRIP 63B	
964	4 MAY 70	LF-07	MINUTEMAN IB	--	
968	27 MAY 70	LF-03	MINUTEMAN IB	--	
970	8 JUN 70	LF-07	MINUTEMAN IB	GLORY TRIP 72B	
977	25 JUN 70	LF-03	MINUTEMAN IB	--	
981	14 JUL 70	LF-09	MINUTEMAN IB	--	
984	23 JUL 70	LF-06	MINUTEMAN IB	--	
992	20 AUG 70	LF-09	MINUTEMAN IB	--	
997	28 AUG 70	LF-06	MINUTEMAN IB	--	
998	2 SEP 70	LF-03	MINUTEMAN IB	--	
1002	25 SEP 70	LF-07	MINUTEMAN IB	--	
1007	3 OCT 70	LF-06	MINUTEMAN IB	--	
1008	5 OCT 70	LF-09	MINUTEMAN IB	--	
1013	26 OCT 70	LF-03	MINUTEMAN IB	--	
1017	8 NOV 70	LF-09	MINUTEMAN IB	--	
1024	23 DEC 70	LF-06	MINUTEMAN IB	--	
1025	11 JAN 71	LF-06	MINUTEMAN IB	--	
1028	28 JAN 71	LF-09	MINUTEMAN IB	--	
1031	8 FEB 71	LF-07	MINUTEMAN IB	--	
1035	22 FEB 71	LF-06	MINUTEMAN IB	--	
1040	2 MAR 71	LF-03	MINUTEMAN IB	--	
1041	16 MAR 71	LF-06	MINUTEMAN IB	--	
1053	26 APR 71	LF-07	MINUTEMAN IB	--	
1063	18 JUN 71	LF-07	MINUTEMAN IB	--	
1066	26 JUN 71	LF-06	MINUTEMAN IB	--	
1072	12 JUL 71	LF-09	MINUTEMAN IB	--	
1074	3 AUG 71	LF-07	MINUTEMAN IB	--	
1084	8 SEP 71	LF-07	MINUTEMAN IB	--	
1090	7 OCT 71	LF-06	MINUTEMAN IB	--	

SEQUENCE	DATE	SITE	VEHICLE	CODENAME	NOTES
1094	18 OCT 71	LF-09	MINUTEMAN IB	--	
1103	2 DEC 71	LF-09	MINUTEMAN IB	--	
1104	9 DEC 71	LF-03	MINUTEMAN IB	--	FINAL LGM-30B LAUNCH BY SAC
1117	16 MAR 72	LF-06	MINUTEMAN IB	--	
1125	5 MAY 72	LF-06	MINUTEMAN IB	--	
1138	15 JUL 72	LF-06	MINUTEMAN IB	--	
1156	27 OCT 72	LF-06	MINUTEMAN IB	--	
1163	8 DEC 72	LF-06	MINUTEMAN IB	--	
1169	19 DEC 72	LF-06	MINUTEMAN IB	--	
1175	9 MAR 73	LF-06	MINUTEMAN IB	--	
1178	25 APR 73	LF-03	MINUTEMAN IB	--	
1181	4 MAY 73	LF-06	MINUTEMAN IB	--	
1184	7 JUN 73	LF-06	MINUTEMAN IB	--	
1190	20 JUL 73	LF-06	MINUTEMAN IB	--	
1193	9 AUG 73	LF-06	MINUTEMAN IB	--	
1199	7 SEP 73	LF-06	MINUTEMAN IB	--	
1208	2 NOV 73	LF-06	MINUTEMAN IB	--	
1212	29 NOV 73	LF-06	MINUTEMAN IB	--	
1213	11 DEC 73	LF-03	MINUTEMAN IB	--	
1214	14 DEC 73	LF-06	MINUTEMAN IB	--	
1218	22 JAN 74	LF-06	MINUTEMAN IB	--	
1233	16 APR 74	LF-06	MINUTEMAN IB	--	
1234	26 APR 74	LF-03	MINUTEMAN IB	--	
1242	11 JUL 74	LF-03	MINUTEMAN IB	--	
1245	18 JUL 74	LF-06	MINUTEMAN IB	--	
1246	1 AUG 74	LF-03	MINUTEMAN IB	--	
1268	19 JAN 75	LF-03	MINUTEMAN IB	--	
1272	6 MAR 75	LF-06	MINUTEMAN IB	--	
1280	9 MAY 75	LF-06	MINUTEMAN IB	--	
1283	23 MAY 75	LF-03	MINUTEMAN IB	--	
1296	22 AUG 75	LF-06	MINUTEMAN IB	--	
1299	10 SEP 75	LF-06	MINUTEMAN IB	--	
1302	30 SEP 75	LF-03	MINUTEMAN IB	--	
1306	13 NOV 75	LF-03	MINUTEMAN IB	--	
1315	23 JAN 76	LF-06	MINUTEMAN IB	--	
1321	27 FEB 76	LF-03	MINUTEMAN IB	--	
1341	19 AUG 76	LF-06	MINUTEMAN IB	--	
1364	18 MAY 77	LF-06	MINUTEMAN IB	--	
1377	3 SEP 77	LF-06	MINUTEMAN IB	--	
1382	13 NOV 77	LF-06	MINUTEMAN IB	--	
1396	5 APR 78	LF-06	MINUTEMAN IB	--	
1403	16 JUN 78	LF-03	MINUTEMAN IB	--	
1407	4 JUL 78	LF-06	MINUTEMAN IB	--	
1415	27 NOV 78	LF-06	MINUTEMAN IB	--	
1419	19 JAN 79	LF-06	MINUTEMAN IB	--	
1420	24 JAN 79	LF-03	MINUTEMAN IB	--	
1433	6 JUL 79	LF-03	MINUTEMAN IB	--	
1438	3 AUG 79	LF-06	MINUTEMAN IB	--	
1440	22 SEP 79	LF-06	MINUTEMAN IB	--	
1445	20 DEC 79	LF-03	MINUTEMAN IB	--	
1454	15 MAR 80	LF-06	MINUTEMAN IB	--	
1456	10 APR 80	LF-03	MINUTEMAN IB	--	
1464	15 SEP 80	LF-06	MINUTEMAN IB	--	

SEQUENCE	DATE	SITE	VEHICLE	CODENAME	NOTES
1467	8 OCT 80	LF-03	MINUTEMAN IB	--	
1471	16 DEC 80	LF-06	MINUTEMAN IB	--	
1475	18 FEB 81	LF-06	MINUTEMAN IB	--	
1478	15 MAR 81	LF-03	MINUTEMAN IB	--	
1480	4 APR 81	LF-06	MINUTEMAN IB	--	
1488	12 SEP 81	LF-06	MINUTEMAN IB	--	
1489	4 OCT 81	LF-03	MINUTEMAN IB	--	
1506	8 OCT 82	LF-03	MINUTEMAN IB	--	
1511	7 JAN 83	LF-03	MINUTEMAN IB	--	
1513	7 FEB 83	LF-06	MINUTEMAN IB	--	
1520	5 MAY 83	LF-03	MINUTEMAN IB	--	
1522	28 MAY 83	LF-03	MINUTEMAN IB	--	
1537	16 DEC 83	LF-03	MINUTEMAN IB	--	
1548	10 JUN 84	LF-03	MINUTEMAN IB	--	
1559	18 OCT 84	LF-03	MINUTEMAN IB	--	
1567	22 MAY 85	LF-03	MINUTEMAN IB	--	
1584	17 MAR 86	LF-03	MINUTEMAN IB	--	
1596	20 JAN 87	LF-03	MINUTEMAN IB	--	
1611	21 SEP 87	LF-03	MINUTEMAN IB	--	
1616	18 JAN 88	LF-03	MINUTEMAN IB	--	
1643	14 FEB 90	LF-03	MINUTEMAN IB	--	
1655	28 JAN 91	LF-03	MINUTEMAN IB	--	
1659	11 MAY 91	LF-03	MINUTEMAN IB	--	
1662	20 JUN 91	LF-03	MINUTEMAN IB	--	
1672	13 MAR 92	LF-03	MINUTEMAN IB	--	
1680	24 OCT 92	LF-03	MINUTEMAN IB	--	
1686	15 JUN 93	LF-03	MINUTEMAN IB	--	

MINUTEMAN II (LGM-30F) Launches[304]

SEQUENCE	DATE	SITE	VEHICLE	CODENAME	NOTES
500	18 AUG 65	LF-21	MINUTEMAN II	REBEL RANGER	
513	6 OCT 65	LF-22	MINUTEMAN II	DICE SPOT	
518	9 NOV 65	LF-21	MINUTEMAN II	LOW TREE	
526	15 DEC 65	LF-24	MINUTEMAN II	PUSH PULL	
532	18 JAN 66	LF-26	MINUTEMAN II	RESTLES DRIFTER	
534	22 JAN 66	LF-05	MINUTEMAN II	SUPREME CHIEF	
544	16 FEB 66	LF-25	MINUTEMAN II	CALAMITY JANE	
553	17 MAR 66	LF-08	MINUTEMAN II	FAINT CLICK	
595	24 JUN 66	LF-08	MINUTEMAN II	FOX TRAP	
604	26 JUL 66	LF-08	MINUTEMAN II	TATTERED COAT	
607	1 AUG 66	LF-24	MINUTEMAN II	STAR BRIGHT	
619	26 AUG 66	LF-23	MINUTEMAN II	CAREER GIRL	
639	2 NOV 66	LF-22	MINUTEMAN II	GOLDEN AGE	
647	13 DEC 66	LF-05	MINUTEMAN II	WATER TEST	ERCS TEST
654	11 JAN 67	LF-08	MINUTEMAN II	BONUS BOY	
664	2 FEB 67	LF-05	MINUTEMAN II	SYCAMORE TREE	ERCS TEST
683	17 APR 67	LF-08	MINUTEMAN II	BUSY MISSILE	
686	21 APR 67	LF-22	MINUTEMAN II	OLYMPIC TRIALS I	
693	11 MAY 67	LF-21	MINUTEMAN II	BUSY FELLOW	
696	19 MAY 67	LF-24	MINUTEMAN II	OLYMPIC TRIALS II	
722	15 JUL 67	LF-21	MINUTEMAN II	BUSY JOKER	
723	20 JUL 67	LF-22	MINUTEMAN II	OLYMPIC TRIALS 3	

SEQUENCE	DATE	SITE	VEHICLE	CODENAME	NOTES
743	21 OCT 67	LF-24	MINUTEMAN II	OLYMPIC TRIALS 4	
753	17 NOV 67	LF-05	MINUTEMAN II	GIN BABY III	
754	21 NOV 67	LF-08	MINUTEMAN II	BUSY LOBBY	
765	23 DEC 67	LF-24	MINUTEMAN II	OLYMPIC TRIALS 5	
766	28 DEC 67	LF-05	MINUTEMAN II	GIN BABY V	
767	10 JAN 68	LF-25	MINUTEMAN II	OLYMPIC TRIALS 6	
773	25 JAN 68	LF-22	MINUTEMAN II	OLYMPIC TRIALS 7	
775	2 FEB 68	LF-24	MINUTEMAN II	OLYMPIC TRIALS 8	
777	10 FEB 68	LF-08	MINUTEMAN II	--	
784	29 MAR 68	LF-26	MINUTEMAN II	OLYMPIC TRIALS 9	
793	30 APR 68	LF-22	MINUTEMAN II	GIANT BLADE 1	
810	8 JUL 68	LF-04	MINUTEMAN II	GIANT FIST 1	
820	1 SEP 68	LF-21	MINUTEMAN II	SHORT ROUND	
829	24 OCT 68	LF-04	MINUTEMAN II	GIANT FIST 2A	
833	13 NOV 68	LF-05	MINUTEMAN II	GIANT FIST 4	
837	21 NOV 68	LF-25	MINUTEMAN II	GIANT BLADE 2	
844	20 DEC 68	LF-08	MINUTEMAN II	--	
849	29 JAN 69	LF-08	MINUTEMAN II	--	
850	29 JAN 69	LF-02	MINUTEMAN II	SPEC TEST 1	
854	2 FEB 69	LF-04	MINUTEMAN II	GIANT FIST 5	
859	7 MAR 69	LF-05	MINUTEMAN II	SPEC TEST 2	
860	12 MAR 69	LF-04	MINUTEMAN II	GIANT FIST 3	
864	22 MAR 69	LF-21	MINUTEMAN II	--	
870	16 APR 69	LF-05	MINUTEMAN II	GLORY TRIP 19M	
872	18 APR 69	LF-25	MINUTEMAN II	SPEC TEST 3	
874	25 APR 69	LF-22	MINUTEMAN II	GLORY TRIP 05F	
877	2 MAY 69	LF-21	MINUTEMAN II	--	
878	20 MAY 69	LF-26	MINUTEMAN II	GLORY TRIP 09F	
881	28 MAY 69	LF-25	MINUTEMAN II	GLORY TRIP 07F	
885	10 JUN 69	LF-24	MINUTEMAN II	GLORY TRIP 11F	
888	20 JUN 69	LF-21	MINUTEMAN II	--	
893	8 JUL 69	LF-25	MINUTEMAN II	GLORY TRIP 14F	
895	15 JUL 69	LF-22	MINUTEMAN II	GLORY TRIP 12F	
896	15 JUL 69	LF-26	MINUTEMAN II	GLORY TRIP 13F	
900	25 JUL 69	LF-08	MINUTEMAN II	--	
903	21 AUG 69	LF-24	MINUTEMAN II	GLORY TRIP 17F	
906	26 AUG 69	LF-22	MINUTEMAN II	GLORY TRIP 15F	
908	2 SEP 69	LF-26	MINUTEMAN II	GLORY TRIP 20F	
917	24 SEP 69	LF-25	MINUTEMAN II	GLORY TRIP 21F	
919	1 OCT 69	LF-21	MINUTEMAN II	--	
923	13 OCT 69	LF-24	MINUTEMAN II	GLORY TRIP 22F	
933	19 NOV 69	LF-21	MINUTEMAN II	--	
952	11 MAR 70	LF-22	MINUTEMAN II	GLORY TRIP 24F	
955	26 MAR 70	LF-05	MINUTEMAN II	GLORY TRIP 25M	
956	31 MAR 70	LF-26	MINUTEMAN II	GLORY TRIP 23F	
961	21 APR 70	LF-24	MINUTEMAN II	GLORY TRIP 48F	
963	25 APR 70	LF-22	MINUTEMAN II	GLORY TRIP 57F	
967	21 MAY 70	LF-25	MINUTEMAN II	GLORY TRIP 55F	
973	19 JUN 70	LF-05	MINUTEMAN II	GLORY TRIP 28M	
974	20 JUN 70	LF-04	MINUTEMAN II	GLORY TRIP 27M	
978	26 JUN 70	LF-22	MINUTEMAN II	GLORY TRIP 59F	
980	9 JUL 70	LF-24	MINUTEMAN II	GLORY TRIP 66F	
982	18 JUL 70	LF-04	MINUTEMAN II	GLORY TRIP 30M	

SEQUENCE	DATE	SITE	VEHICLE	CODENAME	NOTES
987	3 AUG 70	LF-25	MINUTEMAN II	GLORY TRIP 61F	
988	4 AUG 70	LF-05	MINUTEMAN II	GLORY TRIP 16L	GIANT MOON 1; ERCS TEST
989	11 AUG 70	LF-26	MINUTEMAN II	GLORY TRIP 06F	
990	14 AUG 70	LF-04	MINUTEMAN II	GLORY TRIP 31M	
993	26 AUG 70	LF-05	MINUTEMAN II	GLORY TRIP 43M	
1000	14 SEP 70	LF-25	MINUTEMAN II	GLORY TRIP 67F	
1001	17 SEP 70	LF-26	MINUTEMAN II	GLORY TRIP 68F	
1006	3 OCT 70	LF-04	MINUTEMAN II	GLORY TRIP 46M	
1009	7 OCT 70	LF-05	MINUTEMAN II	GLORY TRIP 47M	LAST LAUNCH WITH WS-133B EQUIPMENT
1010	22 OCT 70	LF-25	MINUTEMAN II	GLORY TRIP 69F	
1011	22 OCT 70	LF-26	MINUTEMAN II	GLORY TRIP 70F	
1014	2 NOV 70	LF-04	MINUTEMAN II	GLORY TRIP 51M	
1016	5 NOV 70	LF-05	MINUTEMAN II	GLORY TRIP 52M	
1020	7 DEC 70	LF-04	MINUTEMAN II	GLORY TRIP 56M	
1022	17 DEC 70	LF-05	MINUTEMAN II	GLORY TRIP 58M	
1029	3 FEB 71	LF-24	MINUTEMAN II	GLORY TRIP 101F	
1030	4 FEB 71	LF-04	MINUTEMAN II	GLORY TRIP 60M	
1036	24 FEB 71	LF-25	MINUTEMAN II	GLORY TRIP 102F	
1039	27 FEB 71	LF-04	MINUTEMAN II	GLORY TRIP 80M	
1045	31 MAR 71	LF-05	MINUTEMAN II	GLORY TRIP 82M	
1054	18 MAY 71	LF-24	MINUTEMAN II	GLORY TRIP 105F	
1055	21 MAY 71	LF-05	MINUTEMAN II	GLORY TRIP 83M	
1056	24 MAY 71	LF-22	MINUTEMAN II	GLORY TRIP 103F	
1059	4 JUN 71	LF-04	MINUTEMAN II	GLORY TRIP 81M	
1065	23 JUN 71	LF-05	MINUTEMAN II	GLORY TRIP 84M	
1075	4 AUG 71	LF-25	MINUTEMAN II	GLORY TRIP 104F-1	
1076	6 AUG 71	LF-04	MINUTEMAN II	GLORY TRIP 85M	
1079	13 AUG 71	LF-05	MINUTEMAN II	GLORY TRIP 87M	
1082	2 SEP 71	LF-04	MINUTEMAN II	GLORY TRIP 29M	
1085	10 SEP 71	LF-05	MINUTEMAN II	GLORY TRIP 89M	
1089	6 OCT 71	LF-25	MINUTEMAN II	GLORY TRIP 86F	
1097	21 OCT 71	LF-05	MINUTEMAN II	GLORY TRIP 40L	GIANT MOON 2; ERCS TEST
1119	21 MAR 72	LF-05	MINUTEMAN II	GLORY TRIP 200L	GIANT MOON 3; ERCS TEST
1121	13 APR 72	LF-05	MINUTEMAN II	GLORY TRIP 88M	
1126	12 MAY 72	LF-05	MINUTEMAN II	GLORY TRIP 106M	
1133	13 JUN 72	LF-07	MINUTEMAN II	GIANT PATRIOT I	
1135	20 JUN 72	LF-05	MINUTEMAN II	GLORY TRIP 107M	
1140	25 JUL 72	LF-07	MINUTEMAN II	GIANT PATRIOT II	
1147	25 SEP 72	LF-05	MINUTEMAN II	GLORY TRIP 108M	
1149	3 OCT 72	LF-04	MINUTEMAN II	GLORY TRIP 109M	
1155	20 OCT 72	LF-02	MINUTEMAN II	GLORY TRIP 110M	
1171	21 DEC 72	LF-07	MINUTEMAN II	GLORY TRIP 111M	
1177	17 APR 73	LF-02	MINUTEMAN II	GLORY TRIP 112M	
1186	27 JUN 73	LF-07	MINUTEMAN II	GLORY TRIP 114M	
1191	26 JUL 73	LF-05	MINUTEMAN II	GIANT MOON 4	ERCS TEST
1192	2 AUG 73	LF-04	MINUTEMAN II	GLORY TRIP 113M	
1202	25 SEP 73	LF-04	MINUTEMAN II	GLORY TRIP 115M-1	
1205	2 OCT 73	LF-07	MINUTEMAN II	GLORY TRIP 116M	
1224	12 MAR 74	LF-05	MINUTEMAN II	GIANT MOON 5	ERCS TEST
1228	27 MAR 74	LF-07	MINUTEMAN II	GLORY TRIP 117M-1	
1229	2 APR 74	LF-02	MINUTEMAN II	GLORY TRIP 119M	
1241	9 JUL 74	LF-04	MINUTEMAN II	GLORY TRIP 120M	
1255	7 OCT 74	LF-02	MINUTEMAN II	GLORY TRIP 118M	

SEQUENCE	DATE	SITE	VEHICLE	CODENAME	NOTES
1260	22 OCT 74	LF-05	MINUTEMAN II	GIANT MOON 6	ERCS TEST
1266	17 DEC 74	LF-04	MINUTEMAN II	GLORY TRIP 121M	
1294	14 AUG 75	LF-04	MINUTEMAN II	GLORY TRIP 122M-1	
1298	5 SEP 75	LF-05	MINUTEMAN II	GIANT MOON 7	ERCS TEST
1300	16 SEP 75	LF-07	MINUTEMAN II	GLORY TRIP 123M-1	
1301	23 SEP 75	LF-04	MINUTEMAN II	OSL	
1316	29 JAN 76	LF-07	MINUTEMAN II	GLORY TRIP 125M	
1319	19 FEB 76	LF-05	MINUTEMAN II	GLORY TRIP 126M	
1320	24 FEB 76	LF-04	MINUTEMAN II	GLORY TRIP 124M	
1331	8 JUN 76	LF-07	MINUTEMAN II	GLORY TRIP 127M	
1333	22 JUN 76	LF-05	MINUTEMAN II	GLORY TRIP 128M	
1342	26 AUG 76	LF-07	MINUTEMAN II	GLORY TRIP 129M	
1347	26 OCT 76	LF-05	MINUTEMAN II	GIANT MOON 8	FINAL ERCS TEST
1357	1 FEB 77	LF-07	MINUTEMAN II	GLORY TRIP 132M	
1371	28 JUN 77	LF-04	MINUTEMAN II	GLORY TRIP 134M	
1383	30 NOV 77	LF-07	MINUTEMAN II	GLORY TRIP 135M	
1400	2 JUN 78	LF-04	MINUTEMAN II	GLORY TRIP 136M	
1408	25 JUL 78	LF-09	MINUTEMAN II	GLORY TRIP 133M-1	
1414	16 NOV 78	LF-07	MINUTEMAN II	GLORY TRIP 130M-2	
1427	23 MAR 79	LF-07	MINUTEMAN II	GLORY TRIP 137M	
1436	16 JUL 79	LF-04	MINUTEMAN II	GIANT MOON 9	
1441	25 SEP 79	LF-04	MINUTEMAN II	GLORY TRIP 138M	
1444	13 DEC 79	LF-07	MINUTEMAN II	GLORY TRIP 139M	
1451	23 FEB 80	LF-04	MINUTEMAN II	GLORY TRIP 140M	
1496	18 MAR 82	LF-04	MINUTEMAN II	GLORY TRIP 141MS	
1503	19 JUL 82	LF-04	MINUTEMAN II	GLORY TRIP 142M	
1507	14 OCT 82	LF-08	MINUTEMAN II	GLORY TRIP 143MS-1	
1517	16 MAR 83	LF-08	MINUTEMAN II	GLORY TRIP 144MS	
1533	28 SEP 83	LF-04	MINUTEMAN II	GLORY TRIP 145MS	
1542	29 FEB 84	LF-04	MINUTEMAN II	GLORY TRIP 146MS	
1607	7 JUL 87	LF-04	MINUTEMAN II	GLORY TRIP 148M	
1613	28 OCT 87	LF-04	MINUTEMAN II	GLORY TRIP 150M	
1615	9 NOV 87	LF-07	MINUTEMAN II	GLORY TRIP 149M	
1732	27 SEP 96	LF-03	MINUTEMAN II	--	
1735	16 JAN 97	LF-03	MINUTEMAN II	--	
1742	23 JUN 97	LF-03	MINUTEMAN II	--	
1754	15 JAN 98	LF-03	MINUTEMAN II	--	
1784	2 OCT 99	LF-03	MINUTEMAN II	--	
1789	18 JAN 00	LF-03	MINUTEMAN II	--	
1795	28 MAY 00	LF-06	MINUTEMAN II	--	
1798	7 JUL 00	LF-03	MINUTEMAN II	--	
1806	14 JUL 01	LF-03	MINUTEMAN II	--	
1814	4 DEC 01	LF-06	MINUTEMAN II	--	
1818	15 MAR 02	LF-06	MINUTEMAN II	--	
1826	14 OCT 02	LF-06	MINUTEMAN II	--	
1829	11 DEC 02	LF-06	MINUTEMAN II	--	

MINUTEMAN III (LGM-30G) Launches[305]

SEQUENCE	DATE	SITE	VEHICLE	CODENAME	NOTES
867	11 APR 69	LF-02	MINUTEMAN III	--	FIRST LGM-30G LAUNCH
882	29 MAY 69	LF-02	MINUTEMAN III	--	
911	13 SEP 69	LF-02	MINUTEMAN III	--	

SEQUENCE	DATE	SITE	VEHICLE	CODENAME	NOTES
924	15 OCT 69	LF-02	MINUTEMAN III	--	
927	31 OCT 69	LF-02	MINUTEMAN III	--	
957	2 APR 70	LF-08	MINUTEMAN III	--	
962	22 APR 70	LF-02	MINUTEMAN III	--	
965	8 MAY 70	LF-02	MINUTEMAN III	--	
972	17 JUN 70	LF-02	MINUTEMAN III	--	
975	23 JUN 70	LF-08	MINUTEMAN III	--	
985	28 JUL 70	LF-02	MINUTEMAN III	--	
996	27 AUG 70	LF-08	MINUTEMAN III	OLD FOX 01M	
1003	25 SEP 70	LF-02	MINUTEMAN III	OLD FOX 02M	
1015	4 NOV 70	LF-21	MINUTEMAN III	STM-1W	
1018	13 NOV 70	LF-08	MINUTEMAN III	OLD FOX 03M	
1027	27 JAN 71	LF-08	MINUTEMAN III	OLD FOX 04M	
1033	16 FEB 71	LF-02	MINUTEMAN III	OLD FOX 05M	
1043	23 MAR 71	LF-08	MINUTEMAN III	GLORY TRIP 01GM	
1048	8 APR 71	LF-21	MINUTEMAN III	STM-2W	
1052	23 APR 71	LF-26	MINUTEMAN III	OLD FOX 06F	
1057	26 MAY 71	LF-08	MINUTEMAN III	GLORY TRIP 02GM	
1058	27 MAY 71	LF-02	MINUTEMAN III	GLORY TRIP 03GM	
1061	11 JUN 71	LF-21	MINUTEMAN III	STM-6W	
1071	8 JUL 71	LF-02	MINUTEMAN III	GLORY TRIP 04GM	
1083	3 SEP 71	LF-02	MINUTEMAN III	GLORY TRIP 05GM	
1092	15 OCT 71	LF-02	MINUTEMAN III	GLORY TRIP 06GM	
1095	20 OCT 71	LF-08	MINUTEMAN III	STM-3W	
1099	17 NOV 71	LF-04	MINUTEMAN III	GLORY TRIP 07GM	
1100	22 NOV 71	LF-02	MINUTEMAN III	GLORY TRIP 08GM	
1101	23 NOV 71	LF-05	MINUTEMAN III	GLORY TRIP 09GM	
1107	15 DEC 71	LF-08	MINUTEMAN III	STM-4W	
1108	17 DEC 71	LF-04	MINUTEMAN III	GLORY TRIP 10GM	
1111	26 JAN 72	LF-02	MINUTEMAN III	GLORY TRIP 11GM	
1113	4 FEB 72	LF-05	MINUTEMAN III	GLORY TRIP 12GM	
1114	9 FEB 72	LF-04	MINUTEMAN III	GLORY TRIP 13GM	
1130	31 MAY 72	LF-21	MINUTEMAN III	PVM-1	
1131	6 JUN 72	LF-04	MINUTEMAN III	GLORY TRIP 15GM	
1132	11 JUN 72	LF-02	MINUTEMAN III	GLORY TRIP 14GM	
1134	17 JUN 72	LF-08	MINUTEMAN III	STM-5W	
1143	2 AUG 72	LF-21	MINUTEMAN III	STM-7W	
1146	19 SEP 72	LF-22	MINUTEMAN III	GLORY TRIP 16GB	
1154	16 OCT 72	LF-25	MINUTEMAN III	GLORY TRIP 17GB	
1159	24 NOV 72	LF-22	MINUTEMAN III	GLORY TRIP 18GB	
1162	4 DEC 72	LF-02	MINUTEMAN III	GLORY TRIP 41GM	
1165	12 DEC 72	LF-25	MINUTEMAN III	GLORY TRIP 19GB	
1166	12 DEC 72	LF-26	MINUTEMAN III	GLORY TRIP 20GB	
1174	30 JAN 73	LF-08	MINUTEMAN III	PVM-2	
1179	26 APR 73	LF-25	MINUTEMAN III	GLORY TRIP 21GB	
1180	3 MAY 73	LF-22	MINUTEMAN III	GLORY TRIP 22GB	
1183	31 MAY 73	LF-09	MINUTEMAN III	PVM-4	
1187	6 JUL 73	LF-25	MINUTEMAN III	GLORY TRIP 23GB	
1196	23 AUG 73	LF-08	MINUTEMAN III	PVM-3	
1198	5 SEP 73	LF-02	MINUTEMAN III	GLORY TRIP 43GM	
1201	14 SEP 73	LF-26	MINUTEMAN III	GLORY TRIP 25GB	
1211	22 NOV 73	LF-04	MINUTEMAN III	GLORY TRIP 42GM-1	
1217	22 DEC 73	LF-08	MINUTEMAN III	STM-8W	

SEQUENCE	DATE	SITE	VEHICLE	CODENAME	NOTES
1219	26 JAN 74	LF-25	MINUTEMAN III	GLORY TRIP 24GB-1	
1230	4 APR 74	LF-21	MINUTEMAN III	PVM-5	
1236	2 MAY 74	LF-02	MINUTEMAN III	GLORY TRIP 44GM	
1249	17 AUG 74	LF-02	MINUTEMAN III	GLORY TRIP 45GM	
1252	28 SEP 74	LF-22	MINUTEMAN III	GLORY TRIP 46GB	
1254	4 OCT 74	LF-04	MINUTEMAN III	PVM-8	
1256	11 OCT 74	LF-21	MINUTEMAN III	PVM-6	
1257	12 OCT 74	LF-25	MINUTEMAN III	PVM-7	
1261	25 OCT 74	LF-09	MINUTEMAN III	GLORY TRIP 28GM	
1264	26 NOV 74	LF-08	MINUTEMAN III	PVM-9	
1265	3 DEC 74	LF-25	MINUTEMAN III	GLORY TRIP 47GB	
1270	29 JAN 75	LF-04	MINUTEMAN III	GLORY TRIP 48GM	
1271	5 FEB 75	LF-09	MINUTEMAN III	GLORY TRIP 29GM-1	
1279	6 MAY 75	LF-26	MINUTEMAN III	PVM-10	
1281	16 MAY 75	LF-02	MINUTEMAN III	STM-9W	PAVE PEPPER MULTIPLE RE-ENTRY VEHICLE LAUNCH
1286	11 JUN 75	LF-08	MINUTEMAN III	GLORY TRIP 30GM	
1288	20 JUN 75	LF-09	MINUTEMAN III	GLORY TRIP 31GM	
1289	1 JUL 75	LF-26	MINUTEMAN III	PVM-11	
1291	26 JUL 75	LF-02	MINUTEMAN III	STM-10W	
1297	29 AUG 75	LF-08	MINUTEMAN III	GLORY TRIP 49GM	
1307	14 NOV 75	LF-08	MINUTEMAN III	GLORY TRIP 50GM	
1313	17 DEC 75	LF-22	MINUTEMAN III	GLORY TRIP 51GB	
1314	8 JAN 76	LF-26	MINUTEMAN III	PVM-12	
1317	6 FEB 76	LF-09	MINUTEMAN III	GLORY TRIP 26GM-4	
1322	4 MAR 76	LF-25	MINUTEMAN III	GLORY TRIP 52GB	
1323	14 MAR 76	LF-26	MINUTEMAN III	PVM-13	
1332	21 JUN 76	LF-08	MINUTEMAN III	GLORY TRIP 33GM	
1335	30 JUN 76	LF-09	MINUTEMAN III	GLORY TRIP 54GM	
1338	15 JUL 76	LF-21	MINUTEMAN III	STM-11W	
1350	5 NOV 76	LF-08	MINUTEMAN III	GLORY TRIP 55GM	
1351	8 NOV 76	LF-26	MINUTEMAN III	GLORY TRIP 56GB	
1352	12 NOV 76	LF-21	MINUTEMAN III	STM-12W	
1353	30 NOV 76	LF-09	MINUTEMAN III	GLORY TRIP 32GM-1	
1355	21 JAN 77	LF-08	MINUTEMAN III	GLORY TRIP 53GM-1	
1356	30 JAN 77	LF-21	MINUTEMAN III	STM-13W	
1359	16 FEB 77	LF-09	MINUTEMAN III	GLORY TRIP 27GM-2	
1360	2 MAR 77	LF-26	MINUTEMAN III	GLORY TRIP 57GB	
1365	28 MAY 77	LF-26	MINUTEMAN III	GLORY TRIP 58GB	
1366	1 JUN 77	LF-09	MINUTEMAN III	GLORY TRIP 34GM-1	
1368	16 JUN 77	LF-21	MINUTEMAN III	STM-14W	
1374	3 AUG 77	LF-26	MINUTEMAN III	GLORY TRIP 60GB	
1375	10 AUG 77	LF-08	MINUTEMAN III	GLORY TRIP 59GM-1	
1376	19 AUG 77	LF-21	MINUTEMAN III	PVM-14	
1378	14 SEP 77	LF-09	MINUTEMAN III	GLORY TRIP 35GM	
1381	3 NOV 77	LF-21	MINUTEMAN III	PVM-15	
1384	6 DEC 77	LF-09	MINUTEMAN III	GLORY TRIP 36GM	
1387	6 JAN 78	LF-21	MINUTEMAN III	STM-15W	
1388	8 FEB 78	LF-26	MINUTEMAN III	GLORY TRIP 62GB	
1389	15 FEB 78	LF-08	MINUTEMAN III	GLORY TRIP 61GM	
1392	2 MAR 78	LF-09	MINUTEMAN III	GLORY TRIP 37GM	
1401	8 JUN 78	LF-26	MINUTEMAN III	GLORY TRIP 63GB	
1404	22 JUN 78	LF-21	MINUTEMAN III	STM-16W	
1406	27 JUN 78	LF-08	MINUTEMAN III	GLORY TRIP 64GM	

SEQUENCE	DATE	SITE	VEHICLE	CODENAME	NOTES
1410	6 SEP 78	LF-26	MINUTEMAN III	GLORY TRIP 65GB	
1416	5 DEC 78	LF-09	MINUTEMAN III	GLORY TRIP 38GM	
1417	8 DEC 78	LF-21	MINUTEMAN III	STM-17W	
1421	30 JAN 79	LF-08	MINUTEMAN III	GLORY TRIP 66GM	
1422	6 FEB 79	LF-26	MINUTEMAN III	GLORY TRIP 67GB	
1423	15 FEB 79	LF-21	MINUTEMAN III	PVM-16	
1428	28 MAR 79	LF-09	MINUTEMAN III	GLORY TRIP 39GM	
1429	19 APR 79	LF-21	MINUTEMAN III	PVM-17	
1434	10 JUL 79	LF-09	MINUTEMAN III	GLORY TRIP 40GM (DUAL)	
1435	10 JUL 79	LF-08	MINUTEMAN III	GLORY TRIP 68GM	
1437	26 JUL 79	LF-26	MINUTEMAN III	GLORY TRIP 69GB	
1439	30 AUG 79	LF-21	MINUTEMAN III	STM-18W	
1442	28 SEP 79	LF-08	MINUTEMAN III	GLORY TRIP 70GM	
1446	31 JAN 80	LF-21	MINUTEMAN III	PVM-18	
1447	5 FEB 80	LF-09	MINUTEMAN III	GLORY TRIP 71GM	
1450	21 FEB 80	LF-26	MINUTEMAN III	GLORY TRIP 72GB	
1452	27 FEB 80	LF-08	MINUTEMAN III	GLORY TRIP 73GM	
1455	27 MAR 80	LF-21	MINUTEMAN III	PVM-19	
1460	22 JUN 80	LF-08	MINUTEMAN III	GLORY TRIP 74GM	
1463	20 AUG 80	LF-26	MINUTEMAN III	GLORY TRIP 76GB	
1465	17 SEP 80	LF-09	MINUTEMAN III	GLORY TRIP 77GM	
1466	24 SEP 80	LF-08	MINUTEMAN III	GLORY TRIP 78GM	
1473	9 FEB 81	LF-08	MINUTEMAN III	GLORY TRIP 79GM	
1474	9 FEB 81	LF-09	MINUTEMAN III	GLORY TRIP 80GM	
1476	21 FEB 81	LF-26	MINUTEMAN III	GLORY TRIP 81GB	
1479	1 APR 81	LF-04	MINUTEMAN III	GLORY TRIP 75GM-2	
1483	12 JUN 81	LF-09	MINUTEMAN III	GLORY TRIP 82GM	
1485	26 JUN 81	LF-26	MINUTEMAN III	GLORY TRIP 83GB	
1491	24 NOV 81	LF-09	MINUTEMAN III	GLORY TRIP 84GM-1	
1492	9 DEC 81	LF-26	MINUTEMAN III	GLORY TRIP 85GB	
1495	29 JAN 82	LF-08	MINUTEMAN III	GLORY TRIP 86GM	
1497	31 MAR 82	LF-26	MINUTEMAN III	GLORY TRIP 87GB	
1499	22 JUN 82	LF-08	MINUTEMAN III	GLORY TRIP 88GM	
1504	4 AUG 82	LF-09	MINUTEMAN III	GLORY TRIP 89GM	
1505	24 SEP 82	LF-26	MINUTEMAN III	GLORY TRIP 90GB	
1509	2 DEC 82	LF-09	MINUTEMAN III	GLORY TRIP 91GM	
1515	24 FEB 83	LF-26	MINUTEMAN III	GLORY TRIP 92GB	
1516	11 MAR 83	LF-04	MINUTEMAN III	GLORY TRIP 93GM	
1526	25 JUN 83	LF-26	MINUTEMAN III	GLORY TRIP 95GB	
1527	25 JUN 83	LF-09	MINUTEMAN III	GLORY TRIP 94GM	
1531	21 SEP 83	LF-08	MINUTEMAN III	GLORY TRIP 96GM	
1532	21 SEP 83	LF-09	MINUTEMAN III	GLORY TRIP 97GM	
1536	22 NOV 83	LF-26	MINUTEMAN III	GLORY TRIP 98GB	
1539	25 JAN 84	LF-08	MINUTEMAN III	GLORY TRIP 99GM	
1540	25 JAN 84	LF-09	MINUTEMAN III	GLORY TRIP 100GM	
1545	8 APR 84	LF-26	MINUTEMAN III	GLORY TRIP 101GB	
1546	8 APR 84	LF-09	MINUTEMAN III	GLORY TRIP 102GM	
1554	13 SEP 84	LF-09	MINUTEMAN III	GLORY TRIP 103GM	
1555	19 SEP 84	LF-26	MINUTEMAN III	GLORY TRIP 104GB	
1557	4 OCT 84	LF-04	MINUTEMAN III	GLORY TRIP 105GM	
1563	6 FEB 85	LF-04	MINUTEMAN III	GLORY TRIP 106GM	
1565	20 FEB 85	LF-26	MINUTEMAN III	GLORY TRIP 107GB	
1569	16 JUN 85	LF-04	MINUTEMAN III	GLORY TRIP 108GM	

SEQUENCE	DATE	SITE	VEHICLE	CODENAME	NOTES
1570	16 JUN 85	LF-26	MINUTEMAN III	GLORY TRIP 109GB	
1571	15 JUL 85	LF-09	MINUTEMAN III	GLORY TRIP 110GM	
1575	26 SEP 85	LF-04	MINUTEMAN III	GLORY TRIP 111GM	
1580	14 FEB 86	LF-26	MINUTEMAN III	GLORY TRIP 112GB	
1582	15 MAR 86	LF-09	MINUTEMAN III	GLORY TRIP 113GM-1	
1583	15 MAR 86	LF-04	MINUTEMAN III	GLORY TRIP 114GM	
1587	15 JUN 86	LF-26	MINUTEMAN III	GLORY TRIP 115GB	
1588	31 JUL 86	LF-09	MINUTEMAN III	GLORY TRIP 116GM	
1590	28 AUG 86	LF-04	MINUTEMAN III	GLORY TRIP 117GM	
1593	25 SEP 86	LF-26	MINUTEMAN III	GLORY TRIP 118GB	
1597	28 JAN 87	LF-09	MINUTEMAN III	GLORY TRIP 119GM	
1598	4 FEB 87	LF-26	MINUTEMAN III	GLORY TRIP 120GB	
1601	16 MAR 87	LF-04	MINUTEMAN III	GLORY TRIP 121GM	
1603	2 APR 87	LF-06	MINUTEMAN III	IPMS	
1606	25 JUN 87	LF-26	MINUTEMAN III	GLORY TRIP 122GB-1	
1608	12 JUL 87	LF-10	MINUTEMAN III	GLORY TRIP 123GM-1	
1609	1 SEP 87	LF-06	MINUTEMAN III	IPMS	
1614	3 NOV 87	LF-09	MINUTEMAN III	GLORY TRIP 124GM	
1617	29 JAN 88	LF-26	MINUTEMAN III	GLORY TRIP 125GB-1	
1620	3 JUN 88	LF-26	MINUTEMAN III	GLORY TRIP 127GB	
1622	12 JUL 88	LF-09	MINUTEMAN III	GLORY TRIP 126GM	
1623	12 JUL 88	LF-04	MINUTEMAN III	GLORY TRIP 128GM	
1627	27 OCT 88	LF-10	MINUTEMAN III	GLORY TRIP 130GM	
1629	25 JAN 89	LF-26	MINUTEMAN III	GLORY TRIP 131GB	
1630	22 FEB 89	LF-04	MINUTEMAN III	GLORY TRIP 132GM	
1631	7 MAR 89	LF-10	MINUTEMAN III	GLORY TRIP 133GM	
1634	6 JUL 89	LF-26	MINUTEMAN III	GLORY TRIP 129GB-2	
1635	11 JUL 89	LF-09	MINUTEMAN III	GLORY TRIP 134GM	
1638	26 SEP 89	LF-26	MINUTEMAN III	GLORY TRIP 135GB	
1640	7 NOV 89	LF-10	MINUTEMAN III	GLORY TRIP 136GM	
1642	6 FEB 90	LF-26	MINUTEMAN III	GLORY TRIP 137GB	
1645	21 MAR 90	LF-09	MINUTEMAN III	GLORY TRIP 139GM	
1646	24 MAR 90	LF-04	MINUTEMAN III	GLORY TRIP 138GM	
1650	26 JUN 90	LF-26	MINUTEMAN III	GLORY TRIP 140GB	
1652	19 SEP 90	LF-09	MINUTEMAN III	GLORY TRIP 141GM	
1653	6 NOV 90	LF-04	MINUTEMAN III	GLORY TRIP 142GM	
1663	25 JUN 91	LF-26	MINUTEMAN III	GLORY TRIP 144GB	
1665	2 JUL 91	LF-10	MINUTEMAN III	GLORY TRIP 143GM	
1666	3 SEP 91	LF-04	MINUTEMAN III	GLORY TRIP 145GM	
1669	11 NOV 91	LF-09	MINUTEMAN III	GLORY TRIP 146GM	
1674	5 MAY 92	LF-10	MINUTEMAN III	GLORY TRIP 147GM-1	
1675	2 JUN 92	LF-26	MINUTEMAN III	GLORY TRIP 148GB	
1679	28 SEP 92	LF-26	MINUTEMAN III	GLORY TRIP 149GB	
1681	3 NOV 92	LF-04	MINUTEMAN III	GLORY TRIP 150GM	
1685	9 MAR 93	LF-26	MINUTEMAN III	GLORY TRIP 151GB	
1688	2 JUL 93	LF-09	MINUTEMAN III	GLORY TRIP 152GM	
1692	31 AUG 93	LF-26	MINUTEMAN III	GLORY TRIP 153GB	
1696	2 FEB 94	LF-26	MINUTEMAN III	GLORY TRIP 154GB	
1702	8 JUN 94	LF-04	MINUTEMAN III	GLORY TRIP 155GM	
1703	6 JUL 94	LF-09	MINUTEMAN III	GLORY TRIP 156GM	
1706	5 OCT 94	LF-04	MINUTEMAN III	GLORY TRIP 157GM	
1709	1 FEB 95	LF-09	MINUTEMAN III	GLORY TRIP 158GM	
1710	17 MAR 95	LF-04	MINUTEMAN III	GLORY TRIP 159GM	

SEQUENCE	DATE	SITE	VEHICLE	CODENAME	NOTES
1720	6 MAR 96	LF-09	MINUTEMAN III	GLORY TRIP 161GM	
1727	26 JUN 96	LF-10	MINUTEMAN III	GLORY TRIP 162GM	
1728	26 JUN 96	LF-04	MINUTEMAN III	GLORY TRIP 160GM	
1736	30 JAN 97	LF-26	MINUTEMAN III	GLORY TRIP 163GB	
1740	21 MAY 97	LF-04	MINUTEMAN III	GLORY TRIP 164GM	
1741	18 JUN 97	LF-10	MINUTEMAN III	GLORY TRIP 165GM	
1757	20 FEB 98	LF-04	MINUTEMAN III	GLORY TRIP 166GM	
1764	3 JUN 98	LF-26	MINUTEMAN III	GLORY TRIP 167GB	
1765	24 JUN 98	LF-09	MINUTEMAN III	IDF-1	
1766	24 JUN 98	LF-10	MINUTEMAN III	GLORY TRIP 168GM	
1768	18 SEP 98	LF-26	MINUTEMAN III	IDF-2	
1772	10 FEB 99	LF-04	MINUTEMAN III	GLORY TRIP 169GM	
1781	20 AUG 99	LF-10	MINUTEMAN III	GLORY TRIP 170GM-1	
1782	20 AUG 99	LF-09	MINUTEMAN III	GLORY TRIP 171 ????	
1785	13 NOV 99	LF-26	MINUTEMAN III	FTM-01	
1794	24 MAY 00	LF-09	MINUTEMAN III	FTM-02	
1797	9 JUN 00	LF-10	MINUTEMAN III	GLORY TRIP 172GM	
1802	28 SEP 00	LF-09	MINUTEMAN III	GLORY TRIP 174GM	
1803	28 SEP 00	LF-04	MINUTEMAN III	GLORY TRIP 173GM	
1805	7 FEB 01	LF-10	MINUTEMAN III	GLORY TRIP 175GM	
1813	7 NOV 01	LF-04	MINUTEMAN III	GLORY TRIP 176GM	
1819	8 APR 02	LF-10	MINUTEMAN III	GLORY TRIP 178GM	
1822	7 JUN 02	LF-26	MINUTEMAN III	GLORY TRIP 179GB	
1824	17 JUL 02	LF-09	MINUTEMAN III	GLORY TRIP 177GM	
1825	19 SEP 02	LF-04	MINUTEMAN III	GLORY TRIP 180GM	
1834	11 JUN 03	LF-04	MINUTEMAN III	GLORY TRIP 182GM	
1836	6 AUG 03	LF-26	MINUTEMAN III	GLORY TRIP 183GB	
1839	10 SEP 03	LF-10	MINUTEMAN III	GLORY TRIP 181GM	
1845	23 JUN 04	LF-10	MINUTEMAN III	GLORY TRIP 185GM	
1848	23 JUL 04	LF-09	MINUTEMAN III	GLORY TRIP 184GM-1	
1849	15 SEP 04	LF-26	MINUTEMAN III	GLORY TRIP 186GB	
1853	21 JUL 05	LF-10	MINUTEMAN III	SERV #1-1	
1854	25 AUG 05	LF-26	MINUTEMAN III	SERV #2	
1855	7 SEP 05	LF-04	MINUTEMAN III	GLORY TRIP 187GM-1	
1856	14 SEP 05	LF-09	MINUTEMAN III	GLORY TRIP 189GM	
1859	16 FEB 06	LF-10	MINUTEMAN III	SERV #3	
1861	7 APR 06	LF-26	MINUTEMAN III	GLORY TRIP 190GB	
1864	14 JUN 06	LF-04	MINUTEMAN III	GLORY TRIP 191GM	
1866	20 JUL 06	LF-09	MINUTEMAN III	GLORY TRIP 192GM	
1870	7 FEB 07	LF-10	MINUTEMAN III	GLORY TRIP 193GM	
1879	2 APR 08	LF-09	MINUTEMAN III	GLORY TRIP 196GM	
1880	22 MAY 08	LF-10	MINUTEMAN III	GLORY TRIP 197GM	
1882	13 AUG 08	LF-04	MINUTEMAN III	GLORY TRIP 194GM-1	
1886	5 NOV 08	LF-09	MINUTEMAN III	GLORY TRIP 198GM	
1891	29 JUN 09	LF-04	MINUTEMAN III	GLORY TRIP 199GM	
1892	23 AUG 09	LF-09	MINUTEMAN III	GLORY TRIP 195GM-2	
1899	16 JUN 10	LF-10	MINUTEMAN III	GLORY TRIP 200GM-1	
1900	30 JUN 10	LF-04	MINUTEMAN III	GLORY TRIP 201GM	
1901	17 SEP 10	LF-09	MINUTEMAN III	GLORY TRIP 202GM	
1911	22 JUN 11	LF-10	MINUTEMAN III	GLORY TRIP 204GM	
1912	27 JUL 11	LF-04	MINUTEMAN III	GLORY TRIP 205GM	
1915	25 FEB 12	LF-09	MINUTEMAN III	GLORY TRIP 203GM	
1918	14 NOV 12	LF-10	MINUTEMAN III	GLORY TRIP 206GM	

SEQUENCE	DATE	SITE	VEHICLE	CODENAME	NOTES
1921	22 MAY 13	LF-04	MINUTEMAN III	GLORY TRIP 207GM	
1925	22 SEP 13	LF-10	MINUTEMAN III	GLORY TRIP 209GM	
1926	26 SEP 13	LF-09	MINUTEMAN III	GLORY TRIP 208GM	
1929	17 DEC 13	LF-04	MINUTEMAN III	GLORY TRIP 210GM	
1934	23 SEP 14	LF-09	MINUTEMAN III	GLORY TRIP 211GM	
1937	23 MAR 15	LF-10	MINUTEMAN III	GLORY TRIP 214GM	
1938	27 MAR 15	LF-04	MINUTEMAN III	GLORY TRIP 215GM	
1939	20 MAY 15	LF-09	MINUTEMAN III	GLORY TRIP 212GM	
1940	19 AUG 15	LF-10	MINUTEMAN III	GLORY TRIP 213GM	
1942	21 OCT 15	LF-04	MINUTEMAN III	GLORY TRIP 216GM	
1946	20 FEB 16	LF-09	MINUTEMAN III	GLORY TRIP 217GM	
1947	25 FEB 16	LF-10	MINUTEMAN III	GLORY TRIP 218GM	
1948	5 SEP 16	LF-04	MINUTEMAN III	GLORY TRIP 219GM	

NIKE/AEROBEE

The Nike/Aerobee, also known as the Aerobee 170, was a high-altitude sounding rocket consisting of a solid-fuel first stage from a Nike Ajax missile and a liquid-fueled second-stage Aerobee 150. The development of the Aerobee rocket was funded by the US Navy and used US Army technology developed for the WAC Corporal rocket.[306] The manufacturer of Aerobee systems was Aerojet Engineering, the same developers of the WAC Corporal.

Integrating the Nike rocket onto the Aerobee 150 allowed payloads to reach altitudes of 125 to 168 miles.

The Nike/Aerobee combination flew from PALC-C four times. All of the Nike/Aerobee missions from Vandenberg carried experimental infrared sensors for the CHASER antiballistic missile technology missions.[307]

NIKE/AEROBEE Launches[308]

SEQUENCE	DATE	SITE	VEHICLE	CODENAME	NOTES
1068	29 JUN 71	PALC-C	NIKE/AEROBEE	--	
1102	23 NOV 71	PALC-C	NIKE/AEROBEE	--	
1136	20 JUN 72	PALC-C	NIKE/AEROBEE	--	
1152	11 OCT 72	PALC-C	NIKE/AEROBEE	--	

NIKE/ASP

The Nike/Asp was a two-stage sounding rocket consisting of a Nike booster first stage and an Asp rocket second stage. The booster pair was developed for the Naval Research Laboratory by the Cooper Development Corporation. When NASA was created in 1958, the NRL rocket group and their Nike/Asp rockets went to the civilian agency.

The Nike/Asp could lift a payload from 25 to 50 lbs.[309]

The series of Nike/Asp rockets were launched from Point Arguello Launch Complex A (PALC-A). Most of the rockets were dedicated to solar astronomy / X-ray missions, but a handful were for ionospheric research.

Note: the listings below come directly from the official Vandenberg launch listing held at the 30th Space Wing History Office, but the launch dates conflict with other resources found in print and online.

NIKE/ASP Launches[310]

SEQUENCE	DATE	SITE	VEHICLE	CODENAME	NOTES
8	14 JUL 59	PALC-A	NIKE/ASP	--	SUNFLARE II
9	24 JUL 59	PALC-A	NIKE/ASP	--	
10	24 JUL 59	PALC-A	NIKE/ASP	--	
11	17 JUL 59	PALC-A	NIKE/ASP	--	
12	1 JUL 59	PALC-A	NIKE/ASP	--	
13	1 JUL 59	PALC-A	NIKE/ASP	--	
14	1 AUG 59	PALC-A	NIKE/ASP	--	
15	1 AUG 59	PALC-A	NIKE/ASP	--	
16	1 AUG 59	PALC-A	NIKE/ASP	--	
17	1 AUG 59	PALC-A	NIKE/ASP	--	
18	1 AUG 59	PALC-A	NIKE/ASP	--	
19	1 AUG 59	PALC-A	NIKE/ASP	--	

NIKE/CAJUN

The Nike/Cajun was a two-stage sounding rocket consisting of a solid-fuel Nike first stage and a solid-fuel Cajun second stage. Following development of other Nike paired rockets, the University of Michigan and National Advisory Council on Aeronautics (NACA) developed the Nike/Cajun in the mid-1950s.

The Nike/Cajun could lift up to 100 lbs. of payload weight to an altitude of 100 miles.[311]

Three Nike/Cajun missions flew from Point Arguello Launch Complex B (PALC-B) during 1960, carrying aeronomy payloads.

NIKE/CAJUN Launches[312]

SEQUENCE	DATE	SITE	VEHICLE	CODENAME	NOTES
49	20 JUL 60	PALC-B	NIKE/CAJUN	--	
66	21 NOV 60	PALC-B	NIKE/CAJUN	--	
67	22 NOV 60	PALC-B	NIKE/CAJUN	--	

NIKE/JAVELIN

The Nike/Javelin was a two-stage, solid-propellant sounding rocket consisting of a Nike first stage and a Javelin second stage. The two Nike/Javelin launches from Point Arguello Launch Complex A (PALC-A) carried payloads for the HITAB test series. Note the inclusion of code names for both launches, unlike previous sounding-rocket launches from Point Arguello/Vandenberg.

NIKE/JAVELIN Launches[313]

SEQUENCE	DATE	SITE	VEHICLE	CODENAME	NOTES
556	19 MAR 66	PALC-A	NIKE/JAVELIN	SAGE HEN	
559	25 MAR 66	PALC-A	NIKE/JAVELIN	LEAD PENCIL	

NIKE/VIPER I

Nike Viper I was a two-stage, solid-propellant sounding rocket consisting of a Nike first-stage rocket motor and a Viper I second stage.

The Nike/Viper I booster was used as a high-altitude sampler rocket for the Atomic Energy Commission's Project TUMBLEWEED. The project's purpose was high-altitude collection of radiation data.[314]

Four launches took place at PALC-B during calendar year 1960.

NIKE/VIPER I Launches[315]

SEQUENCE	DATE	SITE	VEHICLE	CODENAME	NOTES
36	4 FEB 60	PALC-B	NIKE/VIPER I	--	AERONOMY MISSION
41	29 APR 60	PALC-B	NIKE/VIPER I	--	AERONOMY MISSION
44	27 JUN 60	PALC-B	NIKE/VIPER I	--	AERONOMY MISSION
58	30 SEP 60	PALC-B	NIKE/VIPER I	--	AERONOMY MISSION

PAIUTE TOMAHAWK

The Paiute Tomahawk was a two-stage sounding rocket consisting of a Paiute first-stage motor and a Tomahawk upper-stage motor. Developed for Sandia National Laboratory's testing program in the 1960s, the TE-416 Tomahawk was used in a one-stage configuration for a few launches but found its success as the second-stage booster.

The Paiute Tomahawk could lift either a 160 lb. payload 200 miles downrange or an 86 lb. payload to 300 miles.[316]

There was a single launch of the Paiute/Tomahawk from Vandenberg's PALC-C on 14 August 1975.

PAIUTE TOMAHAWK Launches[317]

SEQUENCE	DATE	SITE	VEHICLE	CODENAME	NOTES
1295	14 AUG 75	PLC-C	PAIUTE/TOMAHAWK	--	ONLY LAUNCH OF PAIUTE/TOMAHAWK

PEACEKEEPER

The Peacekeeper ICBM (LGM-118A) was a third-generation, solid-fueled, nuclear-tipped missile with intercontinental range and multiple independently targeted reentry vehicles (MIRVs). The Peacekeeper missile had four stages and could reach targets in excess of 7,000 miles. The first three stages were powered by solid propellants; the fourth stage was powered by hypergolic liquid bipropellants and carried the guidance and control system and reentry vehicles.

Unlike the Minuteman missile, which is considered a "hot launch" system from its silo, the Peacekeeper was housed in a launch canister and was propelled into the air by pressurized gas, ejecting the missile 110 ft. above the ground, where the first-stage engine would ignite.

The Peacekeeper flight test program combined the developmental test and evaluation (DT&E) and operational test and evaluation (OT&E) requirements through four phases of testing. Eighteen missiles flew in the test program. Flight Test Missile 18 (FTM-18), launched on 19 March 1989, was the final flight of the initial test program, and the first to be targeted and launched by the Airborne Launch Control System (ALCS).[318] The flight test program employed a variety of reentry vehicle configurations on each flight, ranging from six to ten warheads.[319]

After FTM-18, testing transitioned to SAC for follow-on test and evaluation (FOT&E). The first launch was designated Glory Trip 01PA (GT 01PA) and lifted off from LF-02 on 14 September 1989. The missile was destroyed in flight by the range safety officer.

All of the Peacekeeper missiles launched from Vandenberg carried an instrumentation and flight safety system / flight termination ordnance system (IFSS/FTOS). The IFSS consisted of two major elements: aerospace vehicle equipment (AVE) and ground support equipment (GSE). AVE was composed of various remote units and associated cabling in each of the missile stages. It transmitted data via the IFSS module on the reentry vehicle bulkhead. The IFSS avionics equipment would also receive and decode missile destruct signals and, if necessary, relay the signal to the FTOS, which would destroy the missile.

Vandenberg was also the testing location for Peacekeeper Rail Garrison. Under this concept, Peacekeeper missiles would be placed aboard railroad trains around the United States. The constant movement of trains and missiles would create a targeting problem for Soviet planners, decreasing the likelihood of a "bolt out of the blue" first-strike scenario. Located at North Vandenberg, the PK Rail Garrison loop contained a train alert shelter, missile assembly building, integration and refurbishment facility, and an aboveground launch site. After the cancellation of the Peacekeeper Rail Garrison basing mode in 1989, the facilities were reused by other Vandenberg programs.[320] As of 2016, the train alert shelter, test igloo, and missile assembly building are still standing.

The first LGM-118A Peacekeeper missile launch took place on 18 June 1983 from test pad 01 (TP-01), an aboveground site. *Courtesy of the United States Air Force*

A Peacekeeper missile takes flight from Vandenberg on 21 May 1986. *Courtesy of the United States Air Force*

Four locations at Vandenberg had Peacekeeper launches. Test pad 01 (TP-01) conducted cold launches from an aboveground launch tube during the early test phases. Launch Facilities 02, 05, and 08 (LF-02, LF-05, and LF-08) were modified from Minuteman configuration into the Peacekeeper in Minuteman Silos (PIMS) configuration as fielded in the operational missile force at F. E. Warren AFB, Wyoming.[321]

At least one Peacekeeper missile flew from Vandenberg in every year from 1983 to 2004, except for 1988, when zero launches were conducted.

Abridged Chronology of Peacekeeper Program at Vandenberg[322]

- **16 May 1975:** Special Test Missile 9W (STM-9W)—the first PAVE PEPPER flight test on a Minuteman missile—was successful. The program was designed to evaluate the use of increased numbers of Multiple Independently Targetable Reentry Vehicles (MIRV) on the MM III.

- **26 July 1975:** Special Test Missile (STM-10W) launch was successful.

- **27 January 1976:** Special Test Missile (STM-13) successfully launched.

- **15 July 1976:** STM-11W flight test successfully demonstrated the technical feasibility of the floating-ball reference sphere.

- **29 January 1982:** Air Force Secretary Verne Orr dedicated the MX Integrated Test Facility. The new facility consolidated into a single building, colocating many key activities associated with the missile's test program.

- **17 June 1983:** Air Force Systems Command successfully conducted the first flight test of a Peacekeeper ICBM. The missile—cold-launched from a canister—traveled 4,100 miles downrange and delivered six unarmed reentry vehicles to the Kwajalein Missile Range.
- **15 June 1984:** The first Peacekeeper with a Mark-21 test reentry vehicle was flight tested.
- **30 June 1985:** Air Force Systems Command conducted the final Peacekeeper launch from the aboveground launchpad.
- **23 August 1985:** The Air Force launched the first Peacekeeper from a converted Minuteman silo (LF-08). After a thirty-minute flight the missile deployed six warheads at Kwajalein Atoll.
- **21 May 1986:** The 90th Strategic Missile Wing launched its first Peacekeeper ICBM from Vandenberg in an operational test of the weapon system.
- **31 August 1986:** A Peacekeeper missile launch represented the first launch of a completely operational missile from a completely operational launch facility, and also the first Peacekeeper launch by a SAC combat crew.
- **19 March 1987:** The new $17 million Peacekeeper Missile Procedures Trainer was dedicated, featuring a state-of-the-art, computer-based simulator that would be used to train and evaluate missile crew members.
- **30 August 1995:** A crew aboard an Offutt AFB EC-135C Looking Glass airborne command post flying at 33,000 ft. conducted the first successful launch of a Peacekeeper ICBM from Launch Facility (LF) 02, using the Airborne Launch Control System.
- **21 July 2004:** The 20th Air Force conducted the final launch of a Peacekeeper ICBM at LF-04, designated GT-33PA.
- **18 October 2004:** The last class of six second lieutenants graduated from the Peacekeeper crew course conducted by the 392d Training Squadron. Gen. Lance Lord, AFSPC commander, presided at the graduation. These officers, as well as other Peacekeeper crew members, would return to Vandenberg AFB for transition training to the Minuteman III ICBM system.

A Peacekeeper missile emerges from a Vandenberg launch facility after being "popped" out by a steam generator during a "cold launch." *Courtesy of the United States Air Force*

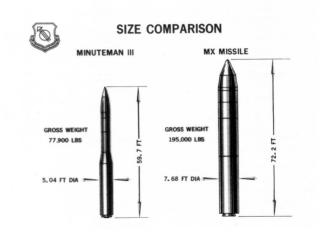

A comparison of Minuteman to Peacekeeper shows the size differences. *Courtesy of the United States Air Force*

PEACEKEEPER Launches[323]

SEQUENCE	DATE	SITE	VEHICLE	CODENAME	NOTES
1524	17 JUN 83	TP-01	PEACEKEEPER	FTM-01	
1534	14 OCT 83	TP-01	PEACEKEEPER	FTM-02	
1538	20 DEC 83	TP-01	PEACEKEEPER	FTM-03	
1544	30 MAR 84	TP-01	PEACEKEEPER	FTM-04	
1550	15 JUN 84	TP-01	PEACEKEEPER	FTM-05	
1556	1 OCT 84	TP-01	PEACEKEEPER	FTM-06	
1562	1 FEB 85	TP-01	PEACEKEEPER	FTM-07	
1568	3 JUN 85	TP-01	PEACEKEEPER	FTM-08	
1573	23 AUG 85	LF-08	PEACEKEEPER	FTM-09	
1578	13 NOV 85	LF-08	PEACEKEEPER	FTM-10	

SEQUENCE	DATE	SITE	VEHICLE	CODENAME	NOTES
1581	7 MAR 86	LF-08	PEACEKEEPER	FTM-11	
1586	21 MAY 86	LF-08	PEACEKEEPER	FTM-12	
1589	23 AUG 86	LF-02	PEACEKEEPER	FTM-15	
1592	18 SEP 86	LF-08	PEACEKEEPER	FTM-13	
1595	5 DEC 86	LF-02	PEACEKEEPER	FTM-14	
1600	13 FEB 87	LF-08	PEACEKEEPER	FTM-16	
1602	21 MAR 87	LF-08	PEACEKEEPER	FTM-17	
1632	19 MAR 89	LF-08	PEACEKEEPER	FTM-18	
1637	14 SEP 89	LF-02	PEACEKEEPER	GLORY TRIP 01PA	
1644	8 MAR 90	LF-05	PEACEKEEPER	GLORY TRIP 02PA	
1649	16 MAY 90	LF-08	PEACEKEEPER	GLORY TRIP 03PA	
1651	13 SEP 90	LF-05	PEACEKEEPER	GLORY TRIP 04PA	
1657	12 MAR 91	LF-02	PEACEKEEPER	GLORY TRIP 05PA	
1661	11 JUN 91	LF-08	PEACEKEEPER	GLORY TRIP 06PA	
1667	17 SEP 91	LF-02	PEACEKEEPER	GLORY TRIP 07PA	
1671	4 MAR 92	LF-05	PEACEKEEPER	GLORY TRIP 08PA	
1676	30 JUN 92	LF-02	PEACEKEEPER	GLORY TRIP 09PA	
1678	15 SEP 92	LF-05	PEACEKEEPER	GLORY TRIP 10PA	
1684	4 MAR 93	LF-02	PEACEKEEPER	GLORY TRIP 11PA	
1689	13 JUL 93	LF-05	PEACEKEEPER	GLORY TRIP 12PA	
1693	15 SEP 93	LF-02	PEACEKEEPER	GLORY TRIP 13PA	
1698	7 MAR 94	LF-05	PEACEKEEPER	GLORY TRIP 14PA	
1701	17 MAY 94	LF-02	PEACEKEEPER	GLORY TRIP 15PA	
1705	7 SEP 94	LF-05	PEACEKEEPER	GLORY TRIP 16PA	
1708	19 JAN 95	LF-02	PEACEKEEPER	GLORY TRIP 17PA	
1713	14 JUN 95	LF-05	PEACEKEEPER	GLORY TRIP 18PA	
1716	30 AUG 95	LF-02	PEACEKEEPER	GLORY TRIP 19PA	
1723	8 MAY 96	LF-05	PEACEKEEPER	GLORY TRIP 20PA	
1726	30 MAY 96	LF-02	PEACEKEEPER	GLORY TRIP 21PA	
1731	11 SEP 96	LF-05	PEACEKEEPER	GLORY TRIP 22PA	
1733	6 NOV 96	LF-02	PEACEKEEPER	GLORY TRIP 23PA	
1739	8 MAY 97	LF-05	PEACEKEEPER	GLORY TRIP 24PA	
1748	17 SEP 97	LF-05	PEACEKEEPER	GLORY TRIP 25PA	
1751	5 NOV 97	LF-02	PEACEKEEPER	GLORY TRIP 26PA	
1761	7 MAY 98	LF-05	PEACEKEEPER	GLORY TRIP 27PA	
1775	10 MAR 99	LF-02	PEACEKEEPER	GLORY TRIP 28PA	
1791	8 MAR 00	LF-05	PEACEKEEPER	GLORY TRIP 29PA	
1807	27 JUL 01	LF-02	PEACEKEEPER	GLORY TRIP 30PA	
1821	3 JUN 02	LF-02	PEACEKEEPER	GLORY TRIP 31PA	
1833	12 MAR 03	LF-02	PEACEKEEPER	GLORY TRIP 32PA	
1847	21 JUL 04	LF-05	PEACEKEEPER	GLORY TRIP 33PA	FINAL PEACEKEEPER LAUNCH

PEGASUS

The Pegasus rocket is a three-stage space launch booster that is launched aboard a carrier aircraft.[324] Pegasus weighs 41,000 lbs. at launch. The fuselage is 50 ft. long and approximately 50 inches in diameter. The rocket has a fixed delta wing attached to the rocket body with three control fins so it can "fly" like an airplane during the first-stage ignition. After dropping away from the aircraft at an altitude of 40,000 ft., the first-stage engine ignites. After the first stage is jettisoned, the remaining stages propel the missile into an eventual ballistic path. The Pegasus is designed to carry a payload between 450 to 600 lbs. into polar orbit.[325]

In an odd notation, the L-1011 carrier aircraft is occasionally listed as the Pegasus "first" stage (stage zero), with the subsequent three rocket motors as the additional stages.

There have been four variants of the Orbital ATK Pegasus that have flown from Vandenberg over the Western Range:
- Pegasus-H—three solid-fuel stages

- Pegasus XL—uses stretched first and second stages; 5 ft. longer than basic Pegasus
- Pegasus XL/HAPS—added a fourth stage with HAPS (Hydrazine Auxiliary Propulsion System) thrusters

The vehicle and payload are processed at Vandenberg and loaded aboard the L-1011 carrier aircraft, which takes off from the Vandenberg airfield and flies over the Pacific Ocean.

The Pegasus rocket is lifted aboard an Orbital Sciences L-1011 carrier aircraft. *Courtesy of the United States Air Force*

Technicians inspect the payload within the Pegasus's shroud prior to launch. *Courtesy of the United States Air Force*

PEGASUS Launches[326]

SEQUENCE	DATE	SITE	VEHICLE	CODENAME	NOTES
1712	3 APR 95	AIRLIFT	PEGASUS	--	ORBCOMM-1 (F1/F2); PEGASUS-H
1714	22 JUN 95	AIRLIFT	PEGASUS	--	SPACE TEST EXPERIMENT PROGRAM (STEP 3); PEGASUS XL
1721	8 MAR 96	AIRLIFT	PEGASUS	--	RADIATION EXPERIMENT (REX II); PEGASUS XL
1725	16 MAY 96	AIRLIFT	PEGASUS	--	MINIATURE SEEKER TECHNOLOGY DEMONSTRATION (MSTI); PEGASUS-H
1729	2 JUL 96	AIRLIFT	PEGASUS	--	TOTAL OZONE MAPPING SPECTROMETER - EARTH PROBE (TOMS-EP); PEGASUS XL
1730	21 AUG 96	AIRLIFT	PEGASUS	--	FAST AURORAL SNAPSHOT EXPLORER (FAST)
1744	1 AUG 97	AIRLIFT	PEGASUS	--	ORBVIEW-2; PEGASUS XL
1747	29 AUG 97	AIRLIFT	PEGASUS	--	FAST ON-ORBIT RECORDING OF TRANSIENT EVENTS (FORTE); PEGASUS XL
1758	25 FEB 98	AIRLIFT	PEGASUS	--	STUDENT NITRIC OXIDE EXPLORER (SNOE), TELEDESIC 1; PEGASUS XL
1760	1 APR 98	AIRLIFT	PEGASUS	--	TRANSITION REGION AND CORONAL EXPLORER (TRACE); PEGASUS XL
1771	5 DEC 98	AIRLIFT	PEGASUS	--	SUB-MILLIMETER ASTRONOMY SATELLITE (SWAS); PEGASUS XL
1774	4 MAR 99	AIRLIFT	PEGASUS	--	WIDE FIELD INFRARED EXPLORER (WIRE); PEGASUS XL
1778	17 MAY 99	AIRLIFT	PEGASUS	--	TERRIERS/MUBLCOM; PEGASUS XL/HAPS
1796	7 JUN 00	AIRLIFT	PEGASUS	--	TSX-5; PEGASUS XL
1835	26 JUN 03	AIRLIFT	PEGASUS	--	ORBVIEW-3; PEGASUS XL
1837	12 AUG 03	AIRLIFT	PEGASUS	--	SCISAT; PEGASUS XL
1851	15 APR 05	AIRLIFT	PEGASUS	--	DEFENSE AUTONOMOUS RENDEZVOUS TECHNOLOGY (DART); PEGASUS XL/HAPS
1860	22 MAR 06	AIRLIFT	PEGASUS	--	ST5-A/B/C; PEGASUS XL
1872	25 APR 07	AIRLIFT	PEGASUS	--	AERONOMY OF ICE IN THE MESOSPHERE (AIM); PEGASUS XL
1922	27 JUN 13	AIRLIFT	PEGASUS	--	INTERFACE REGION IMAGING SPECTROGRAPH (IRIS); PEGASUS XL

BLUE SCOUT JUNIOR

Blue Scout Junior (SLV-1B) was a four-stage, solid-rocket, spin-stabilized booster used for suborbital launches.[327] The first stage consisted of a Thiokol XM-33E7-3 (Castor) motor. The second and third stages are an ABL X-259 (Antares) and Aerojet General 30KS8000 (AJ-10), respectively. The fourth-stage motor is a 17-inch spherical NOTS 100A motor.

While the first-stage ignition is actuated by the launch blockhouse, the second stage contains a pressure switch in series with a timer. The third and fourth stages contain pressure switches connected to previous stages. The rail launcher is positioned by appropriate azimuth and elevation, containing corrections for wind weighting for proper flight path down the safety corridor. After ignition, the missile moves forward on guide rails. A spin rocket assembly is fired by lanyard pull to induce spin stabilization once the missile has departed the launcher. First-stage fins maintain the rate of spin as the rocket's speed increases.

While the Blue Scout Junior is primarily suborbital, lightweight payloads can allow the rocket to achieve escape velocity. However, the rocket cannot place a payload into orbit, since it does not have the guidance system necessary for the application of appropriate thrust along the vector needed for orbital injection.

The 4 December 1961 launch took place at PALC-A, carrying a 28.5 lb. payload to measure low-energy proton flux (solar wind) in regions beyond the outer radiation belt.[328] The rocket performed satisfactorily until the fourth-stage burn. Since there was no vehicle instrumentation aboard this flight, it was impossible to obtain accurate telemetry. Further postaccident investigation revealed that the rocket motors were allowed to fall below the recommended minimum temperature, resulting in separation of the propellant from the casing in one of the two fourth-stage motors.

All the Blue Scout Junior launches except one (detailed below) were conducted at PALC-A.

The Blue Scout Junior rocket, similar to other Scout rockets, was rail-launched as seen here inside the 4300C shelter. *Courtesy of the United States Air Force*

A rare sight of a Blue Scout Junior readied for launch from 4300C. Nothing remains of the launch site or shelter today. *Courtesy of the United States Air Force*

A Blue Scout Junior rocket sits inside its launch shelter at 4300C, just north of Space Launch Complex 10. *Courtesy of the United States Air Force*

The sole Blue Scout Junior launch from 4300C carried a Program 279L Emergency Rocket Communication System (ERCS) payload. *Courtesy of the United States Air Force*

Project Beanstalk/Program 279

One Blue Scout Junior flight was used to test the Emergency Rocket Communications System (ERCS). On 29 September 1961, SAC issued a specific operational requirement for a rocket-borne UHF communication system. The initial effort was designated Program 279 and used Blue Scout Junior rockets. The 1 kW communications payload broadcast UHF signals within line of sight of SAC bases with airborne and ICBM nuclear forces.[329] These signals carried emergency action messages (EAMs) to provide information for nuclear force direction.[330] The suborbital path of the Blue Scout Junior rockets allowed a short window of time for message broadcast to SAC forces from the earthward-descending transmitter.

While the Program 279 payload development was rapidly progressing, on 7 June 1963, SAC revised the requirement

document to request a follow-on system using Minuteman II (LGM-30F) missiles.[331] On 11 July 1963, three Blue Scout Junior ERCS sites were declared operational in Nebraska—Wisner, West Point, and Tekamah—near SAC headquarters. With the successful testing of Minuteman II ERCS at Vandenberg (see Minuteman II), the final Blue Scout Junior ERCS rockets were inactivated in Nebraska on 1 December 1967.

The sole launch of a Program 279 ERCS Blue Scout Junior took place on 17 December 1963.

Unlike the previous launches, the final two launches of Blue Scout Junior obtained code names due to the merger of NMFPA and Vandenberg AFB into the Western Test Range in 1964.

BLUE SCOUT JUNIOR Launches[332]

SEQUENCE	DATE	SITE	VEHICLE	CODENAME	NOTES
110	4 DEC 61	PALC-A	BLUE SCOUT JUNIOR	--	FIRST BLUE SCOUT JUNIOR LAUNCH
142	31 MAY 62	PALC-A	BLUE SCOUT JUNIOR	--	
157	24 JUL 62	PALC-A	BLUE SCOUT JUNIOR	--	
181	21 NOV 62	PALC-A	BLUE SCOUT JUNIOR	--	
191	18 DEC 62	PALC-A	BLUE SCOUT JUNIOR	--	
200	1 FEB 63	PALC-A	BLUE SCOUT JUNIOR	--	
209	13 MAR 63	PALC-A	BLUE SCOUT JUNIOR	--	
234	17 MAY 63	PALC-A	BLUE SCOUT JUNIOR	--	
303	17 DEC 63	4300C	BLUE SCOUT JUNIOR	--	PROGRAM 279/ERCS TEST
386	29 AUG 64	PALC-A	BLUE SCOUT JUNIOR	CANDY BAG	
428	21 DEC 64	PALC-A	BLUE SCOUT JUNIOR	QUAKER TOWN	LAST BLUE SCOUT JUNIOR LAUNCH

SCOUT

The Scout was a four-stage, solid-fuel space launch vehicle. The rocket consisted of four rocket stages that were in common use in the late 1950s to early 1960s: Algol, Castor, Antares, and Altair. From *The Origin of NASA Names*:

> The first-stage, Algol, was named for a star in the constellation Perseus; the second-stage, Castor, for the "tamer of the horses" in the constellation Gemini; the third-stage, "Antares," for the . . . brightest star in the constellation Scorpio; and the fourth stage, "Altair," for a star in the constellation Aquila.[333]

The rocket was 75 ft. in length and could lift approximately 480 lbs. into low-earth orbit.[334] Scout was designed by NASA to be reliable, inexpensive, and flexible as a launch platform. Many mission types—such as high-altitude experiments, reentry experiments, and small satellites—have flown on a Scout rocket. Scout was also the first US satellite launch vehicle to fully use solid propellants. The technology for the stages came from developments from the Polaris and Minuteman missile programs.

Scout launches at Vandenberg took place at PALC-D, which was renamed SLC-5 in the mid-1960s. The space programs launched at PALC-D/SLC-5 aboard Scout boosters supported many national-security missions. The first Scout rocket launched at Vandenberg, on 26 April 1962, carried the SOLRAD-4B mission.[335] The mission was a cover story for the Naval Research Laboratory's GRAB signals intelligence satellite. A third-stage failure prevented the satellite from achieving orbit.[336]

Prior to the launch of the first CORONA missions, it was realized that photography of the Sino-Soviet landmass would be greatly hindered by clouds. The autonomous operation of CORONA's cameras did not allow for operator input to turn the system on and off when the weather was bad. Any shots of cloudy landmass were wasted, and the photo interpreters on the ground would not know the film's photographic content until the reentry capsule was recovered. Their fears were well founded. In fact, almost half the film collected in the early days of the program (1960–1961) had images of clouds. A reliable and timely way to detect the meteorological conditions of the Soviet Union was created with the advent of a dedicated meteorological satellite alternatively named

Program II, Program 35, and Defense Meteorological Satellite Program.[337]

Early DMSP Block 1 satellites were mated to Scout rockets launched at SLC-5. Out of five launches, two satellites reached orbit. One of the two successes reached an improper orbit that hindered its primary mission. The other satellite was successful in assisting SAC forces during the Cuban Missile Crisis.[338]

The SLC-5 Scout launch complex consisted of a launcher, movable shelter, and blockhouse. The shelter rolled away from the vehicle prior to launch; the vehicle was then raised to the vertical position and rotated to the proper launch azimuth. The launcher's rotating base provided azimuth rotation up to 140°. While the first-stage ignition was actuated by the launch blockhouse, the second stage contained a pressure switch in series with a timer. The third and fourth stages contained pressure switches connected to previous stages. The rail launcher was positioned by appropriate azimuth and elevation, containing corrections for wind weighting for proper flight path down the safety corridor. After ignition, the missile moved forward on guide rails. A spin rocket assembly was fired by lanyard pull to induce spin stabilization once the missile had departed the launcher.

The final Scout launch took place in 1994, over thirty-two years from the first launch at SLC-5.

Due to vandalism and subsequent demolition, nothing remains of SLC-5's Scout launch facilities.[339]

A Scout launch vehicle takes off from Space Launch Complex 5 at South Vandenberg. *Courtesy of the United States Air Force*

SLC-5 saw sixty-nine Scout launches from 1962 to 1994. The site was pillaged and later demolished. *Courtesy of the United States Air Force*

SCOUT Launches[340]

SEQUENCE	DATE	SITE	VEHICLE	CODENAME	NOTES
134	26 APR 62	PALC-D	SCOUT	BLUE SCOUT I	
140	23 MAY 62	PALC-D	SCOUT	BLUE SCOUT II	
166	23 AUG 62	PALC-D	SCOUT	BLUE SCOUT III	
192	18 DEC 62	PALC-D	SCOUT	BLUE SCOUT IV	
204	19 FEB 63	PALC-D	SCOUT	BLUE SCOUT V	
219	5 APR 63	PALC-D	SCOUT	BLUE SCOUT VI	
225	26 APR 63	PALC-D	SCOUT	BLUE SCOUT VII	
241	15 JUN 63	PALC-D	SCOUT	BLUE SCOUT VIII	
277	27 SEP 63	PALC-D	SCOUT	BLUE SCOUT IX	
307	19 DEC 63	PALC-D	SCOUT	BLUE SCOUT X	
351	3 JUN 64	PALC-D	SCOUT	ARROW PLANT	
360	25 JUN 64	PALC-D	SCOUT	CHERRY PIE	
382	25 AUG 64	PALC-D	SCOUT	HURRY BABY	
403	9 OCT 64	PALC-D	SCOUT	GUS GOOSE	
417	21 NOV 64	PALC-D	SCOUT	IMA BIRD	
523	6 DEC 65	PALC-D	SCOUT	SQUEEKY HUB	
528	21 DEC 65	PALC-D	SCOUT	SOCIAL CIRCLE	
536	28 JAN 66	PALC-D	SCOUT	INVENTORY AID	
561	25 MAR 66	PALC-D	SCOUT	BEST GIRL	
571	22 APR 66	PALC-D	SCOUT	LABRADOR RETRIEVER	
582	18 MAY 66	PALC-D	SCOUT	DANCE LESSON	
608	4 AUG 66	SLC-5	SCOUT	RUBBER MAT	
615	17 AUG 66	SLC-5	SCOUT	MARBLE HALL	

SEQUENCE	DATE	SITE	VEHICLE	CODENAME	NOTES
637	28 OCT 66	SLC-5	SCOUT	BUSY SERVICE	
662	31 JAN 67	SLC-5	SCOUT	BUSY MASON	
682	13 APR 67	SLC-5	SCOUT	BUSY MINUTEMAN	
691	5 MAY 67	SLC-5	SCOUT	BUSY WIFE	
695	18 MAY 67	SLC-5	SCOUT	BUSY OCEAN	
704	29 MAY 67	SLC-5	SCOUT	--	
738	25 SEP 67	SLC-5	SCOUT	--	
757	4 DEC 67	SLC-5	SCOUT	--	
780	1 MAR 68	SLC-5	SCOUT	--	
796	16 MAY 68	SLC-5	SCOUT	--	
815	8 AUG 68	SLC-5	SCOUT	--	
825	3 OCT 68	SLC-5	SCOUT	--	
920	1 OCT 69	SLC-5	SCOUT	--	
929	7 NOV 69	SLC-5	SCOUT	--	
995	27 AUG 70	SLC-5	SCOUT	--	
1105	11 DEC 71	SLC-5	SCOUT	--	
1145	2 SEP 72	SLC-5	SCOUT	--	
1158	21 NOV 72	SLC-5	SCOUT	--	
1167	16 DEC 72	SLC-5	SCOUT	--	
1207	29 OCT 73	SLC-5	SCOUT	--	
1223	8 MAR 74	SLC-5	SCOUT	--	
1238	3 JUN 74	SLC-5	SCOUT	--	
1244	16 JUL 74	SLC-5	SCOUT	--	
1250	30 AUG 74	SLC-5	SCOUT	--	
1305	11 OCT 75	SLC-5	SCOUT	--	
1310	5 DEC 75	SLC-5	SCOUT	--	
1328	22 MAY 76	SLC-5	SCOUT	--	
1343	1 SEP 76	SLC-5	SCOUT	--	
1380	27 OCT 77	SLC-5	SCOUT	--	
1397	26 APR 78	SLC-5	SCOUT	--	
1443	30 OCT 79	SLC-5	SCOUT	--	
1482	14 MAY 81	SLC-5	SCOUT	--	
1528	27 JUN 83	SLC-5	SCOUT	--	
1558	11 OCT 84	SLC-5	SCOUT	--	
1572	2 AUG 85	SLC-5	SCOUT	--	
1594	13 NOV 86	SLC-5	SCOUT	--	
1610	16 SEP 87	SLC-5	SCOUT	--	
1619	25 APR 88	SLC-5	SCOUT	--	
1621	15 JUN 88	SLC-5	SCOUT	--	
1624	25 AUG 88	SLC-5	SCOUT	--	
1648	9 MAY 90	SLC-5	SCOUT	--	
1664	29 JUN 91	SLC-5	SCOUT	--	
1677	3 JUL 92	SLC-5	SCOUT	--	
1682	21 NOV 92	SLC-5	SCOUT	--	
1687	25 JUN 93	SLC-5	SCOUT	--	
1700	8 MAY 94	SLC-5	SCOUT	--	

SCUD-B

The SS-1 SCUD was a Soviet-designed, medium-range ballistic missile system with the ability to launch a 2,000 lb. conventional or 100-kiloton nuclear warhead to a range of 100 to 180 miles.[341] The missile was first used in combat in 1973, during the Yom Kippur War. It was the bane of coalition forces during Operation DESERT STORM in 1990–1991.

Under the aegis of the Ballistic Missile Defense Organization (later renamed the Missile Defense Agency, or MDA), the two tests involving SCUD-B theater ballistic missiles were performed at Vandenberg.[342] The tests were designated BLUE VELVET.[343] The objectives of the tests were to conduct two launches–one during daylight hours and one during nighttime–to collect thermal, optical, and radar signature data in support of missile-warning and defense programs.

Nothing was altered on the SCUD or its transporter-erector launcher system. This was done to realistically portray adversary use of the SCUD in combat. The missiles were flown to their maximum range and left configured as nearly as possible to the original threat missile.[344]

The logo for the BLUE VELVET test of the SCUD-B missile at Vandenberg. *Courtesy of the United States Air Force*

A Russian-made MAZ 547 transporter-erector launcher (TEL) transports a SCUD-B missile onto Vandenberg for the BLUE VELVET tests. *Courtesy of the United States Air Force*

The SCUD missile was the scourge of US forces during Operation DESERT SHIELD/STORM in the early 1990s. Here one of the SCUD-B missiles takes off from Vandenberg AFB. *Courtesy of the United States Air Force*

SCUD Launches[345]

SEQUENCE	DATE	SITE	VEHICLE	CODENAME	NOTES
1827	14 NOV 02	LF-7632	SCUD-B	--	
1828	25 NOV 02	LF-7632	SCUD-B	--	

SEAGULL

The Seagull was a single-stage, solid-fueled sounding rocket. It was used once at PALC-A on 20 December 1963 for the US Navy.[346] Little information exists on this rocket or launch.

SEAGULL Launches[347]

SEQUENCE	DATE	SITE	VEHICLE	CODENAME	NOTES
309	20 DEC 63	PALC-A	SEAGULL	--	

SMALL ICBM

The Small ICBM (MGM-134A)—nicknamed "Midgetman"—was a third-generation, solid-fueled missile with intercontinental range. The Small ICBM was a three-stage solid propellant missile with a postboost vehicle / reentry system upper-stage combination. It weighed approximately 37,000 lbs., was 53 ft. long and 46 inches in diameter, and was designed to be capable of hurling a single Mark 21 reentry vehicle with a penetration-aids (penaids) package to a planned distance of over 6,000 nautical miles. The Small ICBM was similar to the Peacekeeper missile; each was housed in a launch canister and was ejected by a gas generator system at the base of the canister. Upon clearing the canister, the missile's first-stage motor would ignite, sending the vehicle toward its intended target. Operational versions of the Small ICBM were to be deployed on hard mobile launchers (HMLs)—vehicles that resembled commercial tractor trailers.

Full-scale development of the Small ICBM was initiated by President Ronald Reagan in January 1986, with an expected initial operating capability in 1992.[348] The program focused on developing a lightweight ICBM carried on a mobile launcher and capable of surviving an attack from the Soviet Union. DoD planned to deploy SICBMs at various dispersed locations to complicate Soviet targeting during a nuclear first strike. The mobile missile's dispersal system was similar to the Peacekeeper Rail Garrison concept but did not rely on the nation's rail network. Development of SICBM floundered for a few years but was restarted by the Ballistic Missile Division with an influx of new funding.

The proposed flight test program at Vandenberg would have consisted of sixteen launches. Most of the reduction from the original twenty-two-missile flight plan was the elimination of Flight Test Mission contingency flights.

In December 1988, Congress appropriated $250 million to the Small ICBM program. The idea was to keep the program afloat long enough to allow new president George H. W. Bush adequate time to decide between keeping Small ICBM or Peacekeeper Rail Garrison. In April 1989, President Bush and a group of congressional democrats reached an agreement that appeared to keep both programs active. The president had requested $100 million for Small ICBM in FY 1990, $200 million in FY 1991, and additional increases during later years. In return, he agreed to reduce the number of Peacekeeper missiles deployed in a Rail Garrison mobile basing mode from one hundred to fifty.

The Small ICBM was given the nickname "Midgetman." It was planned as a complement to the rail-mobile LGM-118A Peacekeeper. *Courtesy of the United States Air Force*

Similar to its "big brother," the small ICBM used the "cold launch" launch method of popping the missile upward with pressure from a steam generator before igniting its first-stage rocket motor above its launcher. *Courtesy of the United States Air Force*

On 11 May 1989 the first launch of the SICBM (FTM-1) took place from test pad 01 (TP-01). The first flight test was cut short after a range safety officer destroyed the missile seventy seconds after launch.[349] The command destruct occurred approximately 1,100 miles west of Vandenberg.

The flight program was planned to resume with FTM-2 in late FY 1990. In part on the basis of the results of this operation, the remaining fourteen flights would be conducted between mid-FY 1993 and early FY 1998. FTMs 2–8 would be launched from test pad 01. Beginning with FTM-9 in 1996, all of the remaining launches were to be fired from hard mobile launchers.

In July 1989, the house voted against the $100 million requested by the administration for Small ICBM in FY 1990. The senate's version of the defense bill retained the $100 million. The issue was resolved in a joint House/Senate Conference Committee in which the president's request was passed and a house provision (Section 138) was adopted. The provision capped the number of Peacekeeper missiles

deployed at fifty. In a related action, Congress also authorized the Air Force to transfer $100 million in FY 1989 unobligated RDT&E funds to the Small ICBM program in lieu of approving a pending reprogramming request, which was to be withdrawn.

The second, and final, SICBM flight took place on 18 April 1991. FTM-2A launched from TP-01 to an apogee of 600 miles for a successful test. Changes in global politics helped hasten the end of the SICBM program. On 27 September 1991, during his nuclear de-alerting announcement, President George H. W. Bush terminated SICBM program development.

SMALL ICBM Launches[350]

SEQUENCE	DATE	SITE	VEHICLE	CODENAME	NOTES
1633	11 MAY 89	TP-01	SMALL ICBM	--	FIRST SICBM LAUNCH; FAILURE
1658	18 APR 91	TP-01	SMALL ICBM	--	LAST SICBM LAUNCH; SUCCESS

TAT/AGENA

The Thrust Augmented Thor (TAT)/Agena was a two-stage, liquid-fueled, medium-lift space launch vehicle derived from the Thor IRBM, with an Agena upper stage (Agena-B/D) for orbital insertion. The basic Thor first stage was augmented with the addition of three Thiokol Castor 1 solid-rocket strap-on motors 120° apart.[351] The TAT engine provides a thrust of 170,000 lbs., two Vernier rockets provide 2000 lbs. of thrust, and the three strap-on boosters provide thrust of 160,275 lbs. The main engine, Vernier rockets, and the boosters are ignited sequentially during liftoff. The boosters fired for forty-two seconds and were jettisoned twenty-three seconds after that, the MB-3 Block 3 main engine fired until appropriate suborbital velocity was reached, and then the Agena fired for the required time for orbital insertion.

The Agena-B/D upper-stage engine provided a thrust of 16,000 lbs. and used bipropellants of unsymmetrical dimethylhydrazine and inhibited red fuming nitric acid (IRFNA). Roll control used a cold gas attitude control system with nitrogen and tetrafluoromethane.

The TAT/Agena-B version was used only twice at Vandenberg. The first, launched on 29 June 1963, carried an undisclosed payload. The launch was also the 200th launch in the Thor program, since the serial number 101 was launched at Cape Canaveral in January 1957. The second and final TAT/Agena-B was dedicated to NASA for the Nimbus 2 weather satellite, which launched on 15 May 1966.

The TAT/Agena-D, using the "standardized Agena" upper stage, became a workhorse for the National Reconnaissance Program, lofting cameras and film in the CORONA (KH-4, KH-4A), ARGON (KH-5), and LANYARD (KH-6) series of satellites.

The CORONA series of spy satellites, flying aboard TAT/Agena-D, included the KH-4 and KH-4A models. These

heavier cameras and their film return capsules required the additional thrust provided by the TAT/Agena-D. The KH-4 had two panoramic cameras with one reentry capsule; the KH-4B upped the film amount with a second reentry capsule, in addition to the two panoramic cameras.[352] The KH-4 and KH-4A payloads were the workhorses of the CORONA program, with twenty-six and fifty-two launches, respectively.[353] The resolution of imagery obtained also improved with the change from KH-4 to the KH-4A camera, getting as low as 9 ft.[354]

The ARGON (KH-5) series objective was the covert development and operational use of a camera system with simultaneous celestial and ground collection for mapping (geodetic) purposes.[355] A total of twelve ARGON payloads were developed, with the last three being launched aboard the TAT/Agena pairing; KH-5 flights took place on 29 October 1963, 13 June 1964, and 21 August 1964. The program did not provide a huge intelligence take and was eventually supplanted by the HEXAGON mapping camera in the 1970s.

The LANYARD (KH-6) series was essentially a single-camera stereo adaptation of the first two-camera stereo reconnaissance system. The only three launches of the LANYARD series took place aboard TAT/Agena-D boosters. LANYARD Launches took place on 18 March 1963, 18 May 1963, and 30 July 1963. It was subsequently canceled after the third launch.[356]

One launch of the NRO's signals intelligence satellite series named POPPY took place on 11 January 1964. Previous (and subsequent) POPPY launches took place aboard Thor/Agena-D boosters. The satellite was developed to intercept radar signals from Soviet air defenses and relay the signals down to National Security Agency downlink stations.[357]

QUILL

QUILL was an experimental Synthetic Aperture Radar (SAR) satellite based on CORONA hardware. Because of diplomatic and security concerns, the brief mission imaged only selected targets within the United States. Those targets could be inspected on the ground to validate the intelligence value of orbital SAR without alerting the Soviets to the capability, or touching off diplomatic protest over active illumination of sovereign territory.[358] The flight used technology from the CORONA program, such as the Agena space vehicle and the

A TAT/Agena sits partially inside its launch shelter. The Agena vehicle is clearly seen, sans payload. *Courtesy of the United States Air Force*

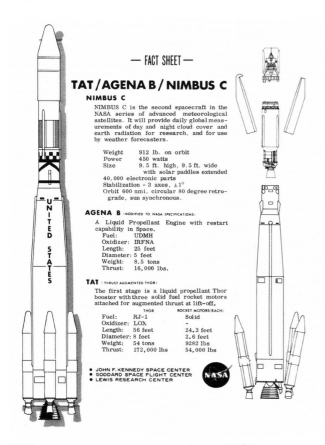

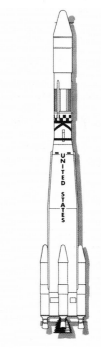

TAT/Agena rockets were also used to launch NASA meteorological satellites in the NIMBUS series. *Courtesy of the United States Air Force*

TAT/Agena serial number 360 carries CORONA 61 on 18 March 1963. Note the bright Day-Glo strap-on rockets on the aft end of the rocket. *Courtesy of the United States Air Force*

The thrust augmentation came from three strap-on rocket motors on the Thor's first stage. Later (heavier) versions of the CORONA spy satellite required more thrust to achieve orbit. *Courtesy of the United States Air Force*

A Thor booster carrying CORONA 65 on 12 June 1963 was prepared in the early morning hours. The proper hour for launch insertion was critical to photographing the Sino-Soviet landmass at the appropriate late morning / early afternoon. *Courtesy of the United States Air Force*

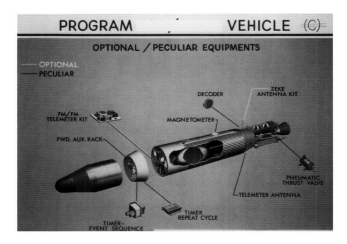

physical return of data on optical film, and merged it with a modified version of the AN/UPQ-102 pulse Doppler system produced for the RF-4C reconnaissance aircraft. The sole QUILL mission was successfully launched on 21 December 1964.[359]

During its lifetime, the TAT/Agena-D pair was launched over sixty times, with a record number of launches (20) taking place during 1964.

LEFT: The breakout diagram of the Agena-D upper stage shows a number of subsystem components required for a successful mission. The increased size of the Agena-D provided room for additional fuel and command and control features for the longer-orbital-life CORONA missions. *Courtesy of the United States Air Force*

TAT/AGENA-B/D Launches[360]

SEQUENCE	DATE	SITE	VEHICLE	CODENAME	NOTES
247	29 JUN 63	75-3-5	TAT/AGENA-B	BABY BLUE	
578	15 MAY 66	75-1-1	TAT/AGENA-B	BAD ULCER	NIMBUS 2
206	28 FEB 63	75-3-5	TAT/AGENA-D	FARM COUNTRY	CORONA MSN 9052 (KH-4)
213	18 MAR 63	75-3-4	TAT/AGENA-D	CAMP OUT	LANYARD MSN 8001 (KH-6); FIRST KH-6 LANYARD HIGH-RESOLUTION CAMERA; FAILED TO ORBIT
235	18 MAY 63	75-3-5	TAT/AGENA-D	GATE LATCH	LANYARD MSN 8002 (KH-6); SECOND LAUNCH OF KH-6 LANYARD; CAMERA NEVER ACTIVATED; RV WATER RECOVERY
239	12 JUN 63	75-3-4	TAT/AGENA-D	GREEN CASTLE	CORONA MSN 9054 (KH-4)
245	26 JUN 63	75-1-2	TAT/AGENA-D	CALICO MISS	CORONA MSN 9056 (KH-4)
259	30 JUL 63	75-1-2	TAT/AGENA-D	BIG TALK	LANYARD MSN 8003 (KH-6); LAST KH-6 LANYARD FLIGHT; CAMERAS FAILED AFTER 32 HRS., PHOTOS OUT OF FOCUS; RV MIDAIR RECOVERY
263	24 AUG 63	75-3-4	TAT/AGENA-D	GHOST DANCE	CORONA MSN 1001 (KH-4A)
274	23 SEP 63	75-1-2	TAT/AGENA-D	FELLOW KING	CORONA MSN 1002 (KH-4A)
285	29 OCT 63	75-3-4	TAT/AGENA-D	MARK DOWN	ARGON MSN 9059A (KH-5)
310	21 DEC 63	75-1-2	TAT/AGENA-D	WATER SPOUT	CORONA MSN 9062 (KH-4)
312	11 JAN 64	75-3-5	TAT/AGENA-D	EMPTY POCKET	POPPY 3
322	15 FEB 64	75-3-4	TAT/AGENA-D	GARDEN PARTY	CORONA MSN 1004 (KH-4A)
327	27 FEB 64	75-3-5	TAT/AGENA-D	FIRST QUARTER	
335	24 MAR 64	PALC-1-1	TAT/AGENA-D	HEALTH FARM	CORONA MSN 1003 (KH-4A)
344	27 APR 64	75-3-4	TAT/AGENA-D	NICE BIRD	CORONA MSN 1005 (KH-4A)
352	4 JUN 64	PALC-1-1	TAT/AGENA-D	KICK BALL	CORONA MSN 1006 (KH-4A)
355	13 JUN 64	75-1-2	TAT/AGENA-D	BEAGLE HOUND	ARGON 9065A (KH-5)
359	19 JUN 64	75-1-1	TAT/AGENA-D	GREEN DOOR	CORONA MSN 1007 (KH-4A)
363	2 JUL 64	75-3-5	TAT/AGENA-D	FIRING ORDER	
368	10 JUL 64	PALC-1-1	TAT/AGENA-D	OLD HAT	CORONA MSN 1008 (KH-4A)
373	5 AUG 64	75-3-4	TAT/AGENA-D	LONG LOOP	CORONA MSN 1009 (KH-4A)
380	21 AUG 64	75-1-2	TAT/AGENA-D	KILO KATE	ARGON MSN 9066A (KH-5); FINAL KH-5 ARGON FLIGHT
391	14 SEP 64	PALC-1-1	TAT/AGENA-D	QUIT CLAIM	CORONA MSN 1010 (KH-4A)
400	5 OCT 64	75-3-4	TAT/AGENA-D	SOLID PACK	CORONA MSN 1011 (KH-4A)
404	17 OCT 64	PALC-1-1	TAT/AGENA-D	MOOSE HORN	CORONA MSN 1012 (KH-4A)
406	2 NOV 64	75-3-4	TAT/AGENA-D	BROWN MOOSE	CORONA MSN 1013 (KH-4A)
409	3 NOV 64	75-3-5	TAT/AGENA-D	ECHO HOLE	
416	18 NOV 64	75-1-1	TAT/AGENA-D	VERBAL VENTURE	CORONA MSN 1014 (KH-4A)
426	19 DEC 64	75-3-4	TAT/AGENA-D	UTILITY TOOL	CORONA MSN 1015 (KH-4A)
427	21 DEC 64	75-1-1	TAT/AGENA-D	BARN OWL	QUILL; SYNTHETIC APERTURE RADAR PROTOTYPE
433	15 JAN 65	75-3-5	TAT/AGENA-D	BUCKET FACTORY	CORONA MSN 1016 (KH-4A)
441	25 FEB 65	PALC-1-1	TAT/AGENA-D	BOAT CAMP	CORONA MSN 1017 (KH-4A)

SEQUENCE	DATE	SITE	VEHICLE	CODENAME	NOTES
454	25 MAR 65	75-3-4	TAT/AGENA-D	PAPER ROUTE	CORONA MSN 1018 (KH-4A)
464	29 APR 65	PALC-1-1	TAT/AGENA-D	MUSK OX	CORONA MSN 1019 (KH-4A)
468	18 MAY 65	75-3-4	TAT/AGENA-D	IVY VINE	CORONA MSN 1021 (KH-4A)
478	9 JUN 65	75-3-5	TAT/AGENA-D	FEMALE LOGIC	CORONA MSN 1020 (KH-4A)
491	16 JUL 65	75-1-2	TAT/AGENA-D	LOST NOVEMBER	
492	19 JUL 65	PALC-1-1	TAT/AGENA-D	ROCKY RIVER	CORONA MSN 1022 (KH-4A)
499	17 AUG 65	PALC-1-1	TAT/AGENA-D	LIGHTS OUT	CORONA MSN 1023 (KH-4A)
508	22 SEP 65	PALC-1-1	TAT/AGENA-D	NICKLE SILVER	CORONA MSN 1024 (KH-4A)
512	5 OCT 65	75-3-5	TAT/AGENA-D	UNION LEADER	CORONA MSN 1025 (KH-4A)
514	14 OCT 65	75-1-1	TAT/AGENA-D	OLD ABBEY	OGO 2
516	28 OCT 65	PALC-1-1	TAT/AGENA-D	HIGH JOURNEY	CORONA MSN 1026 (KH-4A)
524	9 DEC 65	75-3-5	TAT/AGENA-D	LUCKY FELLOW	CORONA MSN 1027 (KH-4A)
530	24 DEC 65	75-3-4	TAT/AGENA-D	TALL STORY	CORONA MSN 1028 (KH-4A)
537	2 FEB 66	PALC-1-1	TAT/AGENA-D	SEA LEVEL	CORONA MSN 1029 (KH-4A)
539	9 FEB 66	75-1-2	TAT/AGENA-D	IRON BACK	
551	9 MAR 66	75-3-4	TAT/AGENA-D	EASY CHAIR	CORONA MSN 1030 (KH-4A)
567	7 APR 66	PALC-1-1	TAT/AGENA-D	GAPING WOUND	CORONA MSN 1031 (KH-4A)
575	3 MAY 66	75-3-5	TAT/AGENA-D	CARGO NET	CORONA MSN 1032 (KH-4A)
583	23 MAY 66	PALC-1-1	TAT/AGENA-D	SHORT TON	CORONA MSN 1033 (KH-4A)
593	21 JUN 66	75-3-5	TAT/AGENA-D	GAME LEG	CORONA MSN 1034 (KH-4A)
594	23 JUN 66	75-1-1	TAT/AGENA-D	CLOTH COAT	PAGEOS 1
626	20 SEP 66	SLC-3W	TAT/AGENA-D	BIG BADGE	CORONA MSN 1035 (KH-4A)
653	29 DEC 66	SLC-2W	TAT/AGENA-D	FRONT ROW	
656	14 JAN 67	SLC-3W	TAT/AGENA-D	LONG ROAD	CORONA MSN 1038 (KH-4A)
671	22 FEB 67	SLC-3W	TAT/AGENA-D	BUSY PAWNSHOP	CORONA MSN 1039 (KH-4A)
678	30 MAR 67	SLC-3W	TAT/AGENA-D	GIANT BANANA	CORONA MSN 1040 (KH-4A)
705	31 MAY 67	SLC-2W	TAT/AGENA-D	--	TIMATION 1
725	24-JUL-67	SLC-2W	TAT/AGENA-D	--	
727	28-JUL-67	SLC-2E	TAT/AGENA-D	--	OGO 4
770	17-JAN-68	SLC-2W	TAT/AGENA-D	--	

TAURUS

The Taurus rocket is a four-stage, solid-fuel space launch vehicle used to lift small payloads into low-earth orbit. The Taurus development was sponsored by the Defense Advanced Research Projects Agency (DARPA) for a low-cost, rapid-response launcher. As originally envisioned, Taurus launches could occur within five days of notification during crisis situations and could be launched from anywhere with a concrete slab.[361] The overall length of Taurus is 90 ft., weighing 150,000 lbs. at launch. The vehicle's lift capacity to polar orbit is around 3,000 lbs.

The Taurus upper stages use components common to the air-launched Pegasus rocket. The first stage is a Castor 120, based on the LGM-118A Peacekeeper first stage. Two launches for the Air Force used refurbished Peacekeeper first

RIGHT: The payload shroud on this Taurus contains the Orbiting Carbon Observatory (OCO). The added mass of the "stuck" fairing prevented the satellite from reaching its intended orbit. *Courtesy of the United States Air Force*

stages, since US law prohibits using government-furnished hardware for commercial satellite launches.[362]

Two payload fairing sizes and the addition of a structural adapter accommodate multiple payloads for lower launch costs.[363] As originally designed, Taurus was easily transportable and had rapid setup and launch timelines.

The launch location at Vandenberg is near Complex 576E ("E by the Sea") but does not reside inside the abandoned Atlas missile silo. Instead, a pedestal launchpad resides about 200 ft. away from the Atlas silo that remains. Command and control for the launch is conducted in a clamshell tent structure residing near the site. The pad and launch setup is designed to be ready for a subsequent launch within eight days.

Rebranding

Due to a dismal launch record of three losses out of four launches between 2001 and 2011, the Taurus booster was rebranded the "Minotaur-C" (Minotaur Commercial).[364] The new design uses Minotaur avionics and solid-fuel downstages purchased from Orbital ATK, not government-furnished missile motors as in previous models.[365] Launch listings for this variant are under "Taurus" for historical reference.

The ill-fated Taurus rocket carrying NASA's OCO satellite streaks skyward from Vandenberg on 24 February 2009. *Courtesy of the United States Air Force*

The Taurus rocket is designed to launch from a "pedestal" outside 576E at North Vandenberg. The site is austere, requiring minimal maintenance between launches. *Courtesy of the United States Air Force*

TAURUS Launches[366]

SEQUENCE	DATE	SITE	VEHICLE	CODENAME	NOTES
1699	13 MAR 94	576E	TAURUS	--	DARPASAT
1755	10 FEB 98	576E	TAURUS	--	ORBCOMM
1769	3 OCT 98	576E	TAURUS	--	STEX (NRO LAUNCH)
1788	20 DEC 99	576E	TAURUS	--	KOMPSAT/ACRIMSAT
1792	12 MAR 00	576E	TAURUS	--	MULTISPECTRAL THERMAL IMAGER
1810	21 SEP 01	576E	TAURUS	--	ORBVIEW-4
1844	20 MAY 04	576E	TAURUS XL	--	ROCSAT-2
1889	24 FEB 09	576E	TAURUS XL	--	ORBITING CARBON OBSERVATORY (OCO)
1908	4 MAR 11	576E	TAURUS XL	--	GLORY

TERRIER/ASP IV

The Terrier/Asp IV was a two-stage, solid-fuel sounding rocket used by the US Navy.[367] The Terrier first stage was a reuse of this standard Navy surface-to-air missile of the 1950s, while the Asp second stage was developed as a replacement for the Deacon rocket engine. The engine design was superior to the Deacon and was later named Atmospheric Sounding Projectile (ASP).

Two launches of the Terrier/Asp IV pairing took place, both from PALC-B during 1962.

TERRIER/ASP IV Launches[368]

SEQUENCE	DATE	SITE	VEHICLE	CODENAME	NOTES
127	14 MAR 62	PALC-B	TERRIER/ASP IV	--	
188	13 DEC 62	PALC-B	TERRIER/ASP IV	--	

THOR IRBM

The Thor IRBM (SM-75, WS-315A, PGM-17) was a first-generation, liquid-fueled, nuclear-capable missile with an intermediate range (less than 1,500 miles). Its mission was to deter an adversary by being able to deliver a thermonuclear warhead to its designated targets within minutes of receiving a launch order.

In February 1955, Dr. James Killian released his eponymous "Killian Report" to the National Security Council,[369] recommending that the USAF develop a ballistic missile for land and ship launching with an inherent range of roughly 1,500 miles. The challenges within the ICBM program were daunting; however, the problems with a shorter-range system were less complicated and could be finished sooner.

Early goals within the ballistic missile program desired a range of between 800 and 1,000 miles while carrying a payload of 3,000 lbs. of explosives (1,500 lb. payload for longer ranges). A circular error probable (CEP) of 6,000 ft. was achievable, but better accuracy was desired.

The Douglas Aircraft Company received the contract to develop the WS-315A weapon system as the program's prime contractor on 28 December 1955.[370] The WS-315A designation encompassed the entire system, whereas the XSM-75 nomenclature was for the airframe. The development period was short—only thirteen months after the ink had dried on the contract to first launch.[371]

From *The Origin of NASA Names*:
The origin of the name Thor has been traced back to Joe Rowland, Director of Public Relations at the Martin Company, who was assigned to suggest names for Martin's new intercontinental ballistic missile in preparation for a meeting at Air Research and Development Command (ARDC) Headquarters. At the meeting were to be representatives of other missile contractors, including Convair/Astronautics Division of General Dynamics Corporation and Douglas Aircraft Company. Of Rowland's list of proposed names, "Titan" was the one preferred by his colleagues, with "Thor" as second choice. At the ARDC meeting, the first-choice "Titan" was accepted as the appropriate name for the Martin Company's project. Through a misunderstanding, Douglas had prepared no name to propose for its missile. Rowland—with "Titan" now firm for his company's project—offered his alternate "Thor" to Donald Douglas, Jr. Douglas and his Vice President of Public Relations agreed it was an attractive name and proposed it to ARDC officials; it was officially adopted.[372]

The design of Thor was kept simple: an aft section with the rocket propulsion, two propellant tanks (RP-1 kerosene

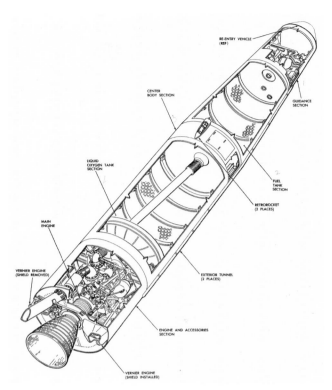

The simple design (engine, fuel, oxidizer, guidance, and warhead) of the Thor IRBM provided an infinitely flexible space launch workhorse for the early days of the US national-security space program. *Courtesy of the United States Air Force*

and liquid oxygen), and the forward section containing the guidance and warhead.[373]

The missile's final dimensions were 63 ft. long and 8 ft. in diameter through the constant portion of its cylindrical sections. The gross weight of the missile was approximately 109,800 lbs., of which 98,000 lbs. was propellants. The forward section of the missile was tapered for engagement, with a separable reentry vehicle (containing the warhead) capable of going 300 to 1,500 nautical miles.[374] The aluminum body was welded together, with internal stiffening to strengthen it throughout flight. The fuel tanks were about 6 millimeters thick, with internal baffles to prevent sloshing during flight. Additional parts of the body used skin-and-stringer construction, fastening on the aluminum skin to thin strips of material like an internal metal skeleton. Access panels along the fuselage allowed external access to the system's innards. The rear of the airframe held the Rocketdyne MB-3 engine on gimbals so the thrust chamber could be swiveled to provide pitch and yaw. Roll control used the same turbopumps as the main engine, with two 4.45 kN engines diametrically opposite each other along the outer edge of the base plate.

In January 1956, the Air Force began a search for a more suitable location to launch operational Thor missiles.[375] More than 200 government-owned sites were surveyed for favorable characteristics. Camp Cooke, a Korean War–era Army post

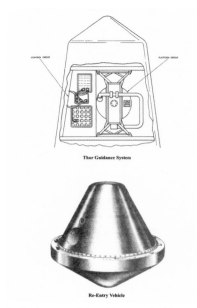

Thor Guidance System

Re-Entry Vehicle

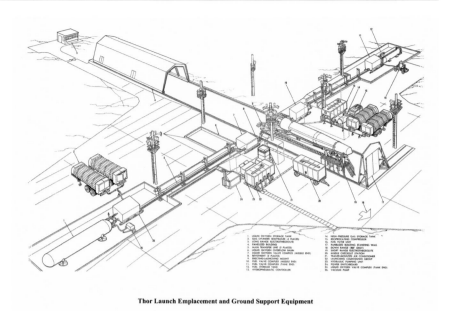

Thor Launch Emplacement and Ground Support Equipment

As is the rest of the airframe, the Thor IRBM guidance system was simplistic in design. The Mk 2 reentry vehicle used a "heat sink" design that would absorb heat from the atmosphere. *Courtesy of the United States Air Force*

An artist's conception of a Thor IRBM launch site. Sixty of these launchpads were built in the United Kingdom during the early 1960s during Project EMILY, the UK deployment of Thor IRBMs. *Courtesy of the United States Air Force*

The first missile launch from Vandenberg AFB took place on 16 December 1958. A Thor IRBM code-named TUNE UP was fired across the California skies downrange into the Pacific Ocean. This was the first of many successful rocket launches at the base. *Courtesy of the United States Air Force*

This stylized image of a Thor IRBM launch shows the clawlike "grip" provided by the transporter-erector/gantry right before launch. *Courtesy of the United States Air Force*

British Royal Air Force crew members pose in front of "their" Thor IRBM during training at Vandenberg AFB. *Courtesy of the United States Air Force*

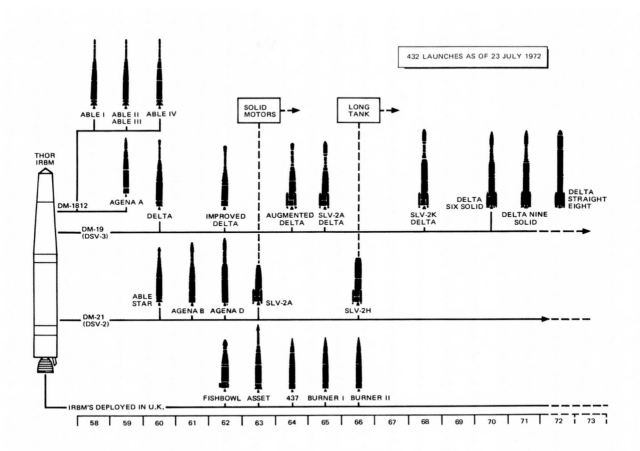

432 LAUNCHES AS OF 23 JULY 1972

Thor-Delta Family Tree 1957-1973

A simplified Thor family tree shows the development of the many variants, including the recycling of UK-based IRBMs into launch vehicles for DMSP and the nuclear-tipped Program 437 rockets. *Courtesy of the United States Air Force*

on California's central coast, was selected due to its unique characteristics:
(1) Large and remote at safe distances from nearby civilian communities (Santa Barbara, Lompoc, Santa Maria)
(2) Adequate infrastructure—such as housing, barracks, and railroad lines—was already present
(3) The post bordered the Pacific Ocean, an excellent testing ground for rockets and missiles
(4) The location was near aerospace manufacturers in San Diego and Los Angeles

The first Thor IRBM launch on the West Coast (code-named "TUNE UP") was the first missile launched from Vandenberg on 16 December 1958, at launchpad 75-1-1 (later known as SLC-2E).

While operational missiles were arriving in England for Project EMILY, RAF crews were being sent to California to begin training. The USAF activated the 392d Strategic Missile Squadron (Training) on 23 May 1957, during the buildup of facilities at what was then known as Cooke AFB. The squadron was later renamed the 392d Missile Training Squadron.[376]

The RAF launches were divided into two types: integrated weapon system training (IWST) launches and combat training launches (CTLs). The IWST launches were performed by a class that was currently in training, whereas CTLs used "graduated" RAF missile men. The IWST represented validation of the training, while CTLs validated the complete weapon system.

On 16 April 1959, Operation LIONS ROAR was successfully initiated by RAF crews at pad 75-2-8 as the first IWST launch. Subsequent launches held at SLC-10 facilities included RIFLE SHOT on 16 June 1959 (at 75-2-7), and SHORT SKIP on 14 August 1959 (at 75-2-6). SHORT SKIP was unique, since it was the only RAF launch held at 75-2-6; all SLC-10 launches afterward were at 75-2-7 or 75-2-8.[377]

The IWST training program ceased at Vandenberg on 21 January 1960 with the successful launch of the eleventh RAF Thor.[378] The twelfth CTL, code-named BLAZING CINDERS, took place on 18 June 1962 at pad 75-2-8. This would be the closeout of the RAF launch program and the last launch of a Thor IRBM at Vandenberg AFB.

In mid-1962, Secretary of Defense Robert S. McNamara informed the United Kingdom that support for Thor would end on 31 October 1964, ending a five-year agreement.

Following on the heels of Thor's acceptance into the nuclear force, the Atlas-D ICBM was declared operational by Commander in Chief, Strategic Air Command (CINCSAC), Gen. Thomas S. Power after a successful launch at Vandenberg AFB on 9 September 1959.[379] The Titan I ICBM was declared operational on 18 April 1962.[380] These two first-generation ICBMs would not last long in the operational force. Both would be withdrawn completely by 1965, in favor of the silo-launched second-generation Titan II and Minuteman missiles. Finally, increasing national-security mission requirements created a need for additional Thor boosters. Instead of programming additional airframes into the budget, the Project EMILY Thor missiles were reused as space launch boosters.

THOR IRBM Launches[381]

SEQUENCE	DATE	SITE	VEHICLE	CODENAME	NOTES
1	16 DEC 58	75-1-1	THOR	TUNE UP	FIRST THOR IRBM LAUNCH AND FIRST MISSILE LAUNCHED FROM VANDENBERG AFB
4	16 APR 59	75-2-8	THOR	LIONS ROAR	RAF IWST LAUNCH #1
6	16 JUN 59	75-2-7	THOR	RIFLE SHOT	RAF IWST LAUNCH #2
20	3 AUG 59	75-1-1	THOR	BEAN BALL	RAF IWST LAUNCH #3
22	14 AUG 59	75-2-6	THOR	SHORT SKIP	RAF IWST LAUNCH #4
25	17 SEP 59	75-1-2	THOR	GREASE GUN	RAF IWST LAUNCH #5
26	6 OCT 59	75-2-8	THOR	FOREIGN TRAVEL	RAF CTL LAUNCH #1
27	21 OCT 59	75-1-1	THOR	STAND FAST	RAF IWST LAUNCH #6
29	12 NOV 59	75-1-2	THOR	BEACH BUGGY	RAF IWST LAUNCH #7
31	1 DEC 59	75-1-1	THOR	HARD RIGHT	RAF CTL LAUNCH #2
32	14 DEC 59	75-1-2	THOR	TALL GIRL	RAF IWST LAUNCH #8
33	21 JAN 60	75-1-2	THOR	RED CABOOSE	RAF IWST LAUNCH #9
38	2 MAR 60	75-2-8	THOR	CENTER BOARD	RAF CTL LAUNCH #3
43	22 JUN 60	75-2-7	THOR	CLAN CHATTAN	RAF CTL LAUNCH #4
59	11 OCT 60	75-2-8	THOR	LEFT RUDDER	RAF CTL LAUNCH #5
70	13 DEC 60	75-2-8	THOR	ACTON TOWN	RAF CTL LAUNCH #6
80	29 MAR 61	75-2-7	THOR	SHEPHERDS BUSH	RAF CTL LAUNCH #7
88	20 JUN 61	75-2-7	THOR	WHITE BISHOP	RAF CTL LAUNCH #8
96	6 SEP 61	LE-7	THOR	SKYE BOAT	RAF CTL LAUNCH #9
111	5 DEC 61	LE-8	THOR	PIPERS DELIGHT	RAF CTL LAUNCH #10
128	19 MAR 62	LE-7	THOR	BLACK KNIFE	RAF CTL LAUNCH #11
146	18 JUN 62	LE-8	THOR	BLAZING CINDERS	RAF CTL LAUNCH #12; FINAL THOR IRBM LAUNCH

THOR/ABLE-STAR[382]

The Thor/Able-Star was a two-stage, liquid-fueled, medium-lift space launch vehicle derived from the Thor IRBM. The first stage consisted of a relatively unmodified Thor IRBM. The second stage consisted of a liquid-fueled Able-Star (also written as "Ablestar") upper stage.

A desire to increase lift capability for the Thor booster resulted in the mating of Thor with Able-Star. The simple Able-Star design complemented the simplistic Thor design. Changes within the Able engine by upgrading the thrust and utilizing a stainless-steel thrust chamber gave way to the name Able-Star. The rapid reaction capability provided by the short design and manufacturing time (eight months) allowed Able-Star to become a versatile and flexible upper stage.

The Able-Star was a modified version of the venerable Able upper stage, giving the stage an increased payload capacity (1,000 lb. payload to 300-mile orbit) and engine restart capabilities.[383] The Able-Star used UDMH and IRFNA as fuel and oxidizer, respectively.[384] It could provide 7,890 lbs. of thrust while on orbit. The restart capability gave the satellite flexibility to change orbital altitude and orbital period during a satellite's lifespan.

TRANSIT

The US Navy program called Transit was the primary user of Thor/Able-Star at Vandenberg.[385] The satellites contained a radio frequency transmitter for use as a navigational satellite system. The objectives of the Transit system were to[386]

(1) provide a means by which US Navy ships may navigate anywhere in the world,

(2) demonstrate satisfactory operation of all satellite subsystems,

(3) demonstrate satisfactory operation and potential long-life capability of the SNAP 9-A power supply,

(4) improve understanding of the effects of ionospheric refraction on radio waves,

(5) demonstrate satisfactory operation of the satellite-borne data injection memory system, and

(6) increase knowledge of the earth's shape and gravitational field.

Some satellites in the Transit series were powered by SNAP radioisotope generators. During the early stages of the program, it was decided that a portion of the Transit 5 series would use solar power, while other satellites would use nuclear generators.

The Thor/Able-Star launch on 28 September 1963 placed the Transit satellite into the correct orbit. The satellite's gravity gradient boom—needed to align orientation —was backward, giving the satellite an upside-down orientation to earth. The next launch on 5 December 1963 was successful, placing Transit 5BN-2 as the first operational navigation satellite in the world. The payload was used regularly by US Navy surface and submarine forces until the satellite's end of life in November 1964.

The final nuclear-powered Transit satellite was launched on 21 April 1964. The use of nuclear generators was halted due to the lower cost of solar panels and the bureaucratic approval process to launch a nuclear payload into orbit.

The final blocks of satellites—Transit-O—were lifted with Thor/Able-Star boosters through 1965. The remaining Transit-O series was then transitioned over to Scout boosters.[387]

Thor Able-Star was used to launch the Transit series of navigation satellites in the 1960s. These satellites provided radio frequency–based navigation signals until the advent of the global positioning system (GPS) in the 1980s. *Courtesy of the United States Air Force*

THOR ABLE-STAR Launches[388]

SEQUENCE	DATE	SITE	VEHICLE	CODENAME	
278	28 SEP 63	75-1-1	THOR/ABLE-STAR	DUCK TAIL	TRANSIT-5BN F1
298	5 DEC 63	75-1-1	THOR/ABLE-STAR	LIMIT LINE	TRANSIT-5BN F2
341	21 APR 64	75-1-1	THOR/ABLE-STAR	USEFUL TOOL	TRANSIT-5BN F3
401	6 OCT 64	75-1-2	THOR/ABLE-STAR	AIR ALARM	TRANSIT-O F1
424	12 DEC 64	75-1-2	THOR/ABLE-STAR	ASTRO ANNIE	TRANSIT-O F2
448	11 MAR 65	75-1-1	THOR/ABLE-STAR	BUSH CATTLE	TRANSIT-O F3
483	24 JUN 65	75-1-1	THOR/ABLE-STAR	PARADISE TREE	TRANSIT-O F4
497	13 AUG 65	75-1-1	THOR/ABLE-STAR	BEAUTY SHOP	TRANSIT-O F5

THOR/AGENA-A

The Thor/Agena-A was a two-stage, liquid-fueled, medium-lift space launch vehicle derived from the Thor IRBM, with an upper stage (Agena-A) for orbital insertion. The Thor booster consisted of an aft section with the rocket propulsion and two propellant tanks (RP-1 kerosene and liquid oxygen) and a forward section containing the guidance, destruct package, and upper-stage interface.

The Agena upper stage (XLR-81, RM-81) was derived from a project to develop a powered pod for the B-58 Hustler bomber. The XLR-81 engine, also known as the "Bell Hustler," was built under contract with Convair and Bell Aircraft Corporation. After contract termination in 1957, the surplus inventory of engines was given to Lockheed Aircraft Corporation and given the new name, Agena:

The Department of Defense's Advanced Research Projects Agency (ARPA) proposed to name the stage in 1958 for the star Agena in the constellation Centaurus because the rocket was an upper stage "igniting in the sky."[389]

The name "Agena" was originally published in the *Geography of the Heavens*, a collection of celestial names by astronomer Elija H. Burritt.[390] This name followed the pattern set by Lockheed to name aircraft and missiles after stellar phenomena and was approved by ARPA in June 1959.[391]

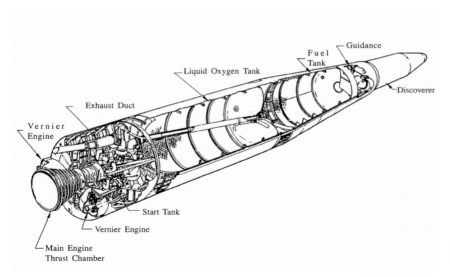

A cutaway of the Thor Agena-A shows the simplified Thor design, with the addition of an Agena-A upper stage and a payload curiously marked as "Discoverer." *Courtesy of the United States Air Force*

Thor Agena-A was the workhorse of the National Reconnaissance Program's early days. Here, the second POPPY signals-intelligence satellite awaits launch. *Courtesy of the United States Air Force*

The Agena-A primary systems include many subsystems.[392] The airframe included the main fuselage to protect the payload, a booster adapter to mate the upper stage to the booster, an explosive destruct package (if the launch goes awry), and pyrotechnics for upper-stage (or payload) separation. The propulsion system included feed and load equipment to route fuel to the main engine, pressurization equipment, the main rocket engine, a smaller ullage motor to ensure that propellant flowed to the main engine,[393] retarding rockets to slow acceleration, and backup (secondary) propulsion systems.

The propulsion power plant was a conventional turbopump-fed, gimbal-mounted engine using storable liquid propellants: unsymmetrical dimethylhydrazine (UDMH) and inhibited red fuming nitric acid (IRFNA). Some early Agena-A models used JP-1 for fuel. The electrical power subsystem included primary power sources, electrical distribution wiring, and solar power arrays (not present on all Agena-A missions).

Guidance and Control included flight control electronics, hydraulic and pneumatic attitude control equipment, sensors to maintain inertial and stellar guidance orientation, and a velocity meter. The command and control system contained tracking and command control equipment, data links, antenna and RF transmit/receive devices, and special telemetry channels.

CORONA (KH-1)

The Thor/Agena-A paring was the SLV combination for the first-generation CORONA surveillance satellite system. CORONA was the classified name for the first operational space photo reconnaissance satellite. The CORONA launches were publicly identified under the name "Discoverer"

(incorrectly identified as "Discovery" in some early documents) and a cover story:

The Discoverer [Program], beginning as a general engineering program[,] has assumed a definite set of objectives directed toward proving feasibility study assumptions, flight-testing hardware, linking ground and space elements in an integrated world-wide network, establishing a platform in space for advanced scientific and military experiments and performing ballistic re-entry.

Beyond the research payloads which are flown for various government agencies and their subcontractors, Discoverer derives a large percentage of its payload from the requirement for orbital testing of components and equipment planned for use in other USAF satellite programs.[394]

In actuality, the project was conceived to take pictures from space of the Soviet Bloc countries and eventually deorbit the photographic film for processing and exploitation.[395] The CORONA vehicle was integrated with the Agena upper stage, which provided power, attitude control, and communications with ground stations while protecting the camera, rollers, and film. The Thor booster would launch the Agena-A as an upper stage, with the CORONA camera within. After the film supply was exhausted, or when commanded from ground stations, the reentry vehicle would detach and fall through the atmosphere for aerial (or waterborne) pickup by US Air Force personnel in the Pacific Ocean.[396]

The first twelve Discoverer launches included a mixture of heartbreaking failures. As CIA Program Director Richard Bissell stated:

On 28 February 1959, a Thor Agena-A carried Discoverer 1 off the launchpad. The mission was to place the first photographic satellite into space, but the payload did not make it into orbit and was assumed to have crashed in or around Antarctica. *Courtesy of the United States Air Force*

The launch of Thor/Agena-A, serial number 231, was a watershed moment in space history. Aboard the rocket rode Discoverer 13, dubbed "Lucky 13," and the first object recovered from space—an American flag. *Courtesy of the United States Air Force*

fix, and if it fails again you know you've inferred wrong. In the case of CORONA it went on and on.[397]

On 10 August 1960, Discoverer XIII lifted off without camera and film as a diagnostic test flight.[398] After its seventeenth orbit, the reentry vehicle was deorbited and reentered over the Pacific Ocean. "Lucky Thirteen," as the flight was later dubbed, carried the first man-made object returned from space to earth—an American flag. The next flight, Discoverer XIV, would carry a camera and film and be the first photoreconnaissance satellite to return intelligence successfully.

One additional Discoverer/CORONA flight used the Thor/Agena-A combination. The launch of CORONA mission 9010 on 13 September 1960 would find successful orbital insertion and camera operation. However, the returning film capsule was lost due to the wrong reentry angle and falling outside the primary recovery zone. The capsule sank before recovery forces could reach it. Subsequent CORONA flights would use upgraded Thor boosters and Agena upper stages.

Early CORONA cameras aboard Thor/Agena-A were retroactively identified as "KH-1" (KeyHole 1) and were identified with the mission series number 9000.[399]

AFTRACK

When realizing that the Agena upper stage contained excess battery power after the end of the CORONA mission, engineers decided to include additional payloads that could "piggyback" aboard flights and provide critical intelligence. The CIA had long known that the Soviets attempted to track American space vehicles and possibly attempted to "interfere" with (jam) the Agena S-band beacon, preventing recovery.[400] A quick-reaction capability payload was created to collect against a variety of Soviet signals. The program was named AFTRACK—the location in the "aft rack" of the Agena where the SIGINT sensors were positioned. The first AFTRACK electronic intelligence (ELINT) payload —SOCTOP—flew on Discoverer 13.[401] After recovery, the ELINT equipment was removed by engineers in California before the reentry capsule (and American flag) was presented to President Eisenhower in Washington, DC.

It was a most heartbreaking business. If an airplane goes on a test fight and something malfunctions, and it gets back, the pilot can tell you about the malfunction, or you can look it over and find out. But in the case of a [reconnaissance] satellite, you fire the damn thing off and you've got some telemetry and you never get it back. There is no pilot, of course, and you've got no hardware, you never see it again. So you have to infer from telemetry what went wrong. Then you make a

THOR/AGENA-A Launches[402]

SEQUENCE	DATE	SITE	VEHICLE	CODENAME	NOTES
2	28 FEB 59	75-3-4	THOR/AGENA-A	FLYING YANKEE	R&D; FIRST USE OF THOR AS A SPACE LAUNCH VEHICLE; FIRST SUCCESSFUL USE OF AGENA-A; NO CAMERA OR FILM
3	13 APR 59	75-3-4	THOR/AGENA-A	EARLY TIME	R&D; DISCOVERER II, FIRST THREE-AXIS STABILIZED SPACECRAFT
5	3 JUN 59	75-3-4	THOR/AGENA-A	GOLD DUKE	R&D
7	25 JUN 59	75-3-5	THOR/AGENA-A	LONG ROAD	CORONA MSN 9001 (KH-1)
21	13 AUG 59	75-3-4	THOR/AGENA-A	FLY HIGH	CORONA MSN 9002 (KH-1)
23	19 AUG 59	75-3-5	THOR/AGENA-A	HURRY UP	CORONA MSN 9003 (KH-1)
28	7 NOV 59	75-3-4	THOR/AGENA-A	CARGO NET	CORONA MSN 9004 (KH-1)
30	20 NOV 59	75-3-5	THOR/AGENA-A	LIVID LADY	CORONA MSN 9005 (KH-1)

SEQUENCE	DATE	SITE	VEHICLE	CODENAME	NOTES
35	4 FEB 60	75-3-4	THOR/AGENA-A	HUNGRY EYE	CORONA MSN 9006 (KH-1)
37	19 FEB 60	75-3-5	THOR/AGENA-A	DERBY DAY	CORONA MSN 9007 (KH-1)
39	15 APR 60	75-3-5	THOR/AGENA-A	RAM HORN	CORONA MSN 9008 (KH-1)
45	29 JUN 60	75-3-4	THOR/AGENA-A	RED GARTER	CORONA FLT 12 (R&D, NO MSN NUMBER)
51	10 AUG 60	75-3-5	THOR/AGENA-A	FOGGY BOTTOM	CORONA FLT 13 (R&D, NO MSN NUMBER; SOCTOP I)
53	18 AUG 60	75-3-4	THOR/AGENA-A	LIMBER LEG	CORONA MSN 9009 (KH-1)
55	13 SEP 60	75-3-5	THOR/AGENA-A	COFFEE CALL	CORONA MSN 9010 (KH-1); SOCTOP II ELINT

THOR/AGENA-B

The Thor/Agena-B was a two-stage, liquid-fueled, medium-lift space launch vehicle derived from the Thor IRBM, with an upper stage (Agena-B) for orbital insertion. The Thor booster consisted of an aft section with the rocket propulsion and two propellant tanks (RP-1 kerosene and liquid oxygen) and a forward section containing the guidance, destruct package, and upper-stage interface.

The Agena-B, mirroring the development of the Agena-A, was designed, engineered, and manufactured on an experimental basis for military satellite systems. As originally used by NASA and the Air Force, the Agena line was produced in twenty-three different configurations in pseudo "block" releases.[403]

The "advanced Agena," as it was briefly called, provided an on-orbit engine with restart capability, double the Agena-A burn time, increased power (specific impulse), greater payload capacity, and the ability to adjust orbital altitude.[404] The earth-centered pointing requirements for the photographic CORONA program were critical to success; the Agena-B's combination of horizon sensor, inertial reference unit, and gas jet controls gave the vehicle a plus/minus of 2° of pointing accuracy.

The Agena-B contained a XLR81-BA-7 engine—improved over the previous model—to allow multiple restarts in space. The amount of propellant carried was also increased to double what the Agena-A carried. While the improvements were welcome, the Thor/Agena-B combination required a different configuration control from other Agena/booster pairings. This disparity in standardization led directly to the development of the Agena-D "Standard Agena" upper stage.

CORONA (KH-2/3/4)

The Thor/Agena-B paring was an upgrade to the combination for the first-generation CORONA surveillance satellite system. CORONA was the name for the first operational photoreconnaissance satellite system. The following KH designators were applied to the cameras lifted by the Thor/Agena-B:

An artist conception of a Thor Agena-B launch vehicle. Minor internal changes marked the creation of the Agena-B. With heavier payloads, the additional fuel and more powerful engine were welcome. *Courtesy of the United States Air Force*

An Agena-B upper stage is mated to its Thor launch vehicle for the CORONA 16 launch in October 1960. *Courtesy of the United States Air Force*

A side view of the MURAL camera used by the CORONA KH-4 system. Two cameras were paired together to produce stereoscopic imagery for photo interpreters. *Courtesy of the National Reconnaissance Office*

KEYHOLE	CAMERA	NUMBERS	TIME PERIOD	LIFETIME
KH-2	C' (C PRIME)	10 LAUNCHED	1960–1961	2–3 DAYS
KH-3	C''' (C TRIPLE PRIME)	6 LAUNCHED	1961–1962	1–4 DAYS
KH-4	M (MURAL)	26 LAUNCHED	1962–1963	6–7 DAYS

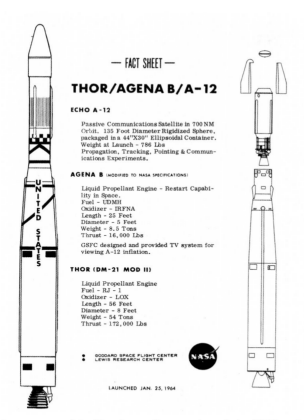

— FACT SHEET —

THOR/AGENA B/A-12

ECHO A-12

Passive Communications Satellite in 700 NM
Orbit. 135 Foot Diameter Rigidized Sphere,
packaged in a 44"X30" Ellipsoidal Container.
Weight at Launch - 786 Lbs
Propagation, Tracking, Pointing & Communications Experiments.

AGENA B (MODIFIED TO NASA SPECIFICATIONS)

Liquid Propellant Engine - Restart Capability in Space.
Fuel - UDMH
Oxidizer - IRFNA
Length - 25 Feet
Diameter - 5 Feet
Weight - 8.5 Tons
Thrust - 16,000 Lbs

GSFC designed and provided TV system for
viewing A-12 inflation.

THOR (DM-21 MOD II)

Liquid Propellant Engine
Fuel - RJ - 1
Oxidizer - LOX
Length - 56 Feet
Diameter - 8 Feet
Weight - 54 Tons
Thrust - 172,000 Lbs

● GODDARD SPACE FLIGHT CENTER
● LEWIS RESEARCH CENTER

NASA

LAUNCHED JAN. 25, 1964

An overt use of the Thor Agena-B was to launch the ECHO series of communication satellites. For the National Reconnaissance Program, the pairing launched KH-2, KH-3, and KH-4 satellites in the CORONA family. *Courtesy of the United States Air Force*

As the camera's capabilities (and weight) increased, there was a strong need for a better upper-stage booster. The changes made to the Agena-B helped increase the lifetime of subsequent camera models, such as additional on-orbit fuel and restart capability. The later cameras, such as the stereoscopic Mural, brought down the resolution to around 10 ft. from the KH-1's 40 ft. This ground resolution distance is the smallest object visible on imagery. To compare, the first image from the KH-1 series was the airfield at Mys Shmidta, showing little beyond the concrete runway near the shoreline of the Chukchi Sea. KH-4 imagery, at around 10 ft., could distinguish between missile silos, aircraft hangars, and in some cases large bomber aircraft sitting on their parking apron.

As CORONA launches increased in number, the Discoverer cover story began to run out. The last launch under this program name was Discoverer 37, launched on 13 January 1962. This mission also carried the last KH-3 C Triple Prime camera.

With the continuing development of the "Standard Agena" (Agena-D), the KH-4 missions were transitioned over to the Thor/Agena-D pairing. The final Thor/Agena-B launch for CORONA took place on 24 November 1962.

Other missions using the Thor/Agena-B include two launches for Canada's Alouette satellites, the Echo 2 communications satellite, and a Nimbus meteorological satellite.

THOR/AGENA-B Launches[405]

SEQUENCE	DATE	SITE	VEHICLE	CODENAME	NOTES
63	26 OCT 60	75-3-4	THOR/AGENA-B	SOUP SPOON	CORONA MSN 9011 (KH-2); SOCTOP IIA ELINT
65	12 NOV 60	75-3-5	THOR/AGENA-B	BOXING GLOVE	CORONA MSN 9012 (KH-2); SOCTOP III ELINT
68	7 DEC 60	75-3-4	THOR/AGENA-B	POWER TRACTOR	CORONA MSN 9013 (KH-2)
75	20 DEC 60	75-3-5	THOR/AGENA-B	TEE BIRD	DISCOVERER 19/MIDAS PAYLOAD
77	17 FEB 61	75-3-4	THOR/AGENA-B	SPIRIT LEVEL	ARGON MSN 9014A (KH-5); FIRST ARGON MISSION
78	18 FEB 61	75-3-5	THOR/AGENA-B	BENCH WARRANT	DISCOVERER 21; MIDAS PAYLOAD
81	30 MAR 61	75-3-4	THOR/AGENA-B	FEATHER CUT	CORONA MSN 9015 (KH-2); SOCTOP V ELINT
82	8 APR 61	75-3-5	THOR/AGENA-B	RUNNING BOARD	ARGON MSN 9016A (KH-5)
86	8 JUN 61	75-3-4	THOR/AGENA-B	ISLAND QUEEN	ARGON MSN 9018A (KH-5); SOCTOP IV ELINT
87	16 JUN 61	75-1-1	THOR/AGENA-B	MARKED CARDS	CORONA MSN 9017 (KH-2); TAKI I ELINT
89	7 JUL 61	75-3-5	THOR/AGENA-B	HIGH WING	CORONA MSN 9019 (KH-2); WILDBILL I ELINT
91	21 JUL 61	75-3-4	THOR/AGENA-B	STACKED DECK	ARGON MSN 9020A (KH-5)
93	3 AUG 61	75-1-1	THOR/AGENA-B	CRISP BACON	CORONA MSN 9021 (KH-2); TAKI ELINT
95	30 AUG 61	75-3-4	THOR/AGENA-B	FULL BLOWER	CORONA MSN 9023 (KH-3); TEXAS PINT I ELINT
98	12 SEP 61	75-3-5	THOR/AGENA-B	TWISTED BRAIDS	CORONA MSN 9022 (KH-3); TOPSOC I ELINT
99	17 SEP 61	75-1-1	THOR/AGENA-B	CANE POLE	CORONA MSN 9024 (KH-3); TOPSOC II ELINT
101	13 OCT 61	75-3-4	THOR/AGENA-B	CAP PISTOL	CORONA MSN 9025 (KH-3); TOPSOC III ELINT
103	23 OCT 61	75-3-5	THOR/AGENA-B	DEAD HEAT	CORONA MSN 9026 (KH-3)
104	5 NOV 61	75-1-1	THOR/AGENA-B	FOG CUTTER	CORONA MSN 9027 (KH-3); TOPSOC IV ELINT
105	15 NOV 61	75-3-4	THOR/AGENA-B	CAT FIGHT	CORONA MSN 9028 (KH-3)
114	12 DEC 61	75-3-4	THOR/AGENA-B	SILVER STRIP	CORONA MSN 9029 (KH-3); OSCAR 1; GRAPE JUICE 1 ELINT

SEQUENCE	DATE	SITE	VEHICLE	CODENAME	NOTES
116	13 JAN 62	75-3-4	THOR/AGENA-B	CANDY WRAPPER	CORONA MSN 9030 (KH-3); TAKI ELINT; LAST KH-3 CAMERA LAUNCH
122	21 FEB 62	75-3-5	THOR/AGENA-B	CABLE SPLICE	PROGJECT 698BK II/PROJECT 102 ELINT PAYLOAD
124	27 FEB 62	75-3-4	THOR/AGENA-B	CAREER GIRL	CORONA MSN 9031 (KH-4); WILDBILL ELINT
132	17 APR 62	75-3-5	THOR/AGENA-B	LONG SLICE	CORONA MSN 9032 (KH-4); GRAPE JUICE II ELINT
136	28 APR 62	75-3-4	THOR/AGENA-B	TOTAL TIME	CORONA MSN 9033 (KH-4); TAKI II ELINT
139	15 MAY 62	75-3-5	THOR/AGENA-B	HOLE PUNCH	ARGON MSN 9034A; FIRST SUCCESSFUL ARGON MISSION
141	29 MAY 62	75-1-1	THOR/AGENA-B	LEAK PROOF	CORONA MSN 9035 (KH-4)
143	1 JUN 62	75-3-4	THOR/AGENA-B	KNOTTY PINE	CORONA MSN 9036 (KH-4); OSCAR 2
145	18 JUN 62	75-3-5	THOR/AGENA-B	TASTY TREAT	PROJECT 698 BK III/PROJECT 102 ELINT PAYLOAD
147	22 JUN 62	75-3-4	THOR/AGENA-B	TIGHT SKIRT	CORONA MSN 9037 (KH-4)
156	20 JUL 62	75-3-5	THOR/AGENA-B	ADOBE HOME	CORONA MSN 9039 (KH-4)
158	27 JUL 62	75-3-4	THOR/AGENA-B	ANCHOR ROPE	CORONA MSN 9040 (KH-4); NEW JERSEY I ELINT
168	1 SEP 62	75-3-5	THOR/AGENA-B	BEADY EYE	ARGON MSN 9042A
169	17 SEP 62	75-3-4	THOR/AGENA-B	BIG FLIGHT	CORONA MSN 9043 (KH-4); GRAPE JUICE ELINT
171	28 SEP 62	75-1-1	THOR/AGENA-B	BIG GAME	ALOUETTE 1
175	9 OCT 62	75-3-4	THOR/AGENA-B	CALL BOARD	ARGON MSN 9046A
178	5 NOV 62	75-3-4	THOR/AGENA-B	BAIL OUT	CORONA MSN 9047 (KH-4)
182	24 NOV 62	75-3-4	THOR/AGENA-B	GOLDEN RUSH	CORONA MSN 9048 (KH-4); PLYMOUTH ROCK I ELINT
196	16 JAN 63	75-3-5	THOR/AGENA-B	CIRCUS BOY	PROJECT 698BK IV/PROJECT 102 ELINT PAYLOAD
317	25 JAN 64	75-1-1	THOR/AGENA-B	RAMS HORN	ECHO 2
385	28 AUG 64	75-1-1	THOR/AGENA-B	HULU MOON	NIMBUS 1
520	28 NOV 65	75-1-1	THOR/AGENA-B	REHEAT	ALOUETTE 2

THOR/AGENA-D

The Thor/Agena-D was a two-stage, liquid-fueled, medium-lift space launch vehicle derived from the Thor IRBM, with an upper stage (Agena-D) for orbital insertion. The Thor booster consisted of an aft section with the rocket propulsion and two propellant tanks (RP-1 kerosene and liquid oxygen) and a forward section containing the guidance, destruct package, and upper-stage interface.

The Agena-D upper stage consisted of an airframe with propulsion, auxiliary power, guidance and control, and space-ground communication systems.[406] After the experiences with the Agena-A and Agena-B variants, there was a great interest in "standardizing" the Agena upper stage for payloads. Propulsion system standardization was predetermined, since there was little variation in the Agena-B "blocks."[407] The power system allowed for choices—batteries, solar panels, or even nuclear generators (e.g., SNAP reactors).

The continued success of the CORONA series saw an evolutionary jump with the KH-4 series of satellite cameras. As the system capabilities increased, so did the payload weight, necessitating a change of booster to lift the heavier CORONA cameras. The few KH-4 launches enabled the troubleshooting of the Agena-D "space truck" before the transition of the standardized upper stage onto the follow-on booster, the Thorad/Agena-D.

POPPY

Another great success story with the Thor/Agena-D pairing was the SIGINT satellite program named POPPY. Three Thor/Agena-D boosters were used for the first, second, and fourth

Thor Agena-D carrying CORONA mission 9053 lifts off from SLC-1E. Photo interpreters claimed that this KH-4 mission brought back the best imagery to date. *Courtesy of the United States Air Force*

An excellent image of a Thor Agena-D lifting an ARGON mapping camera into orbit in 1963. Externally, the launch vehicle was indistinguishable from a CORONA launch. *Courtesy of the United States Air Force*

The payload atop this Thor Agena-D is distinguishably different from a CORONA Thor/Agena-D launch. This mission carried a signals intelligence satellite in the POPPY series. *Courtesy of the United States Air Force*

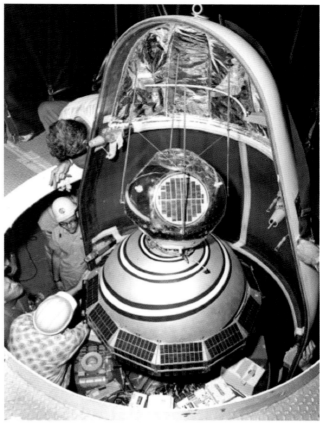

The United States' first intelligence satellite GRAB was paired with a civil system (Transit 2A) atop a Thor Agena-D. *Courtesy of the United States Air Force*

POPPY missions. Unlike the CORONA series, the Agena-D upper stage was not part of the POPPY spacecraft —the first POPPY design was initially a 20 × 24 in. quasisphere, and later a 24 × 32 in. multifaceted oblong spheroid.[408] The initial POPPY mission succeeded, as did all six additional missions. The Air Force used Thor Agena-D for POPPY 1, 2, and 4.

On occasion, errant rocket flights would be terminated early by range safety officers. One incident during a Thor/

Agena-D launch code-named WORD SCRAMBLE provided a harrowing experience:

> Debris fell on a village six miles from the base, causing minor damage and setting a number of ground fires. Three members of one serviceman's family escaped injury when the debris damaged their trailer. The Air Force identified them as the wife and children of SSgt J. P. Meachum.[409]

THOR/AGENA-D Launches[410]

SEQUENCE	DATE	SITE	VEHICLE	CODENAME	NOTES
149	27 JUN 62	75-1-1	THOR/AGENA-D	TRIAL TRACK	CORONA MSN 9038 (KH-4)
160	1 AUG 62	75-1-1	THOR/AGENA-D	APPLE GREEN	CORONA MSN 9041 (KH-4)
167	28 AUG 62	75-1-2	THOR/AGENA-D	APPLE RIND	CORONA MSN 9044 (KH-4)
172	29 SEP 62	75-1-2	THOR/AGENA-D	ARCTIC ZONE	CORONA MSN 9045 (KH-4)
176	26 OCT 62	75-1-2	THOR/AGENA-D	ANCHOR BUOY	STARAD 1
183	4 DEC 62	75-1-2	THOR/AGENA-D	CALAMITY JANE	CORONA MSN 9049 (KH-4); VINO I ELINT
187	12 DEC 62	75-1-1	THOR/AGENA-D	CORN FIELD	POPPY 1/INJUN 3/WILDBILL II ELINT/POPPY III, 2-BALL CONSTELLATION
189	14 DEC 62	75-3-5	THOR/AGENA-D	BABY DOLL	CORONA MSN 9050 (KH-4); TAKI III ELINT
195	7 JAN 63	75-1-1	THOR/AGENA-D	CANDY KISSES	CORONA MSN 9051 (KH-4); NEW JERSEY II ELINT
217	1 APR 63	75-3-5	THOR/AGENA-D	NICKEL STEEL	CORONA MSN 9053 (KH-4)

SEQUENCE	DATE	SITE	VEHICLE	CODENAME	NOTES
226	26 APR 63	75-1-1	THOR/AGENA-D	FALL HARVEST	ARGON MSN 9055A (KH-5)
242	15 JUN 63	75-1-1	THOR/AGENA-D	BUSY FLY	POPPY 2; WILDBILL IV ELINT/POPPY IV, 3-BALL CONSTELLATION
254	18 JUL 63	75-1-1	THOR/AGENA-D	CHILI WILLIE	CORONA MSN 9057 (KH-4)
266	29 AUG 63	75-3-5	THOR/AGENA-D	PELICAN PETE	ARGON MSN 9058A (KH-5)
291	9 NOV 63	75-1-2	THOR/AGENA-D	JUMP SUIT	CORONA MSN 9060 (KH-4)
296	27 NOV 63	PALC-1-1	THOR/AGENA-D	DRY DUNE	CORONA MSN 9061 (KH-4)
314	19 JAN 64	75-1-2	THOR/AGENA-D	BENCH TOP	DMSP BLOCK 1
357	17 JUN 64	75-3-4	THOR/AGENA-D	INDIO IKE	DMSP BLOCK 1
447	9 MAR 65	75-1-2	THOR/AGENA-D	DEUCE SPOT	POPPY 4B/OSCAR
505	2 SEP 65	75-3-5	THOR/AGENA-D	WORD SCRAMBLE	STARAD 2

THOR/BURNER I

The Thor/Burner I, alternately known as Thor/Altair, was a two-stage space launch booster for launching medium-sized payloads into low-earth orbit.[411] The first stage consisted of a Thor missile recycled from IRBMs returned from the United Kingdom and paired with a "cloned" Altair upper stage—not original Allegheny Ballistics Laboratory hardware.[412] The first-stage hardware was upgraded from its IRBM configuration with modified radio guidance and telemetry and flight termination equipment.

The requirement that drove the development of the Thor/Burner I was the urgent need for a meteorological satellite for the National Reconnaissance Program (NRP). As first-generation reconnaissance satellites such as CORONA and GAMBIT were launched, the fact of cloud cover over target areas became a system vulnerability. Film would be wasted photographing cloud formations over the Soviet Union instead of imaging missile sites and airfields. While NASA was in charge of the civilian Tiros weather satellite program, the NRP needed a dedicated meteorological system.

The first DMSP satellites were launched aboard Scout boosters. Due to a spotty launch record (three of five launches failed), the NRO looked to move the DMSP to the reliable Thor booster. Additionally, lack of total control of the booster program by the NRO through the Air Force helped convince program leaders to switch to another rocket. As stated in the Hexagon Mapping Camera history:

> Following a strained relationship between the Air Force and NASA, the issue of Scout responsibility was settled on 21 June 1962 by means of formal agreements which conceded control of virtually all Scout matters

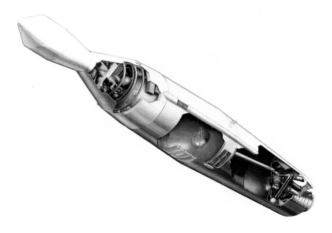

The Thor / Burner I was given alternate designations in official Air Force literature as DSV-2S or Thor/Altair, since the Burner 1 upper stage used an Altair rocket engine. *Courtesy of the United States Air Force*

to NASA, including general configuration, modification, launch stand procedures, and most related topics.[413]

After two launches aboard Thor/Agena-D boosters, the DMSP Block 1, 2 and 3 satellites were launched aboard the Thor/Burner I pair. The first Thor/Burner I, on 19 January 1965, saw a successful launch, but the payload shroud failed to separate.[414, 415] The last launch of a DMSP satellite aboard a Thor/Burner I took place on 30 March 1966.[416]

THOR/BURNER I (a.k.a. THOR/ALTAIR) Launches[417]

SEQUENCE	DATE	SITE	VEHICLE	CODENAME	NOTES
434	18 JAN 65	4300 B-6	THOR/ALTAIR	ASTRAL LAMP	DMSP BLOCK 1
452	17 MAR 65	4300 B-6	THOR/ALTAIR	ASTRAL BODY	
470	20 MAY 65	4300 B-6	THOR/ALTAIR	ROYAL EAGLE	
506	9 SEP 65	4300 B-6	THOR/ALTAIR	VICTORIA CROS	
531	6 JAN 66	4300 B-6	THOR/ALTAIR	PERSIAN LAMB	
563	30 MAR 66	4300 B-6	THOR/ALTAIR	RESORT HOTEL	

THOR/BURNER II (IIA)

The Thor/Burner II (and IIA) was a two-stage space launch booster for launching medium-sized payloads into low-earth orbit.[418] The first stage consisted of a Thor missile recycled from IRBMs returned from the United Kingdom paired with a Burner II (or IIA) upper stage.[419] The first-stage hardware was upgraded from its IRBM configuration with modified radio guidance and telemetry and flight termination equipment. The Burner II (and IIA) upper stage was a Thiokol Star 37B solid-rocket motor mounted with electronics and an attitude control system.[420]

The Thor Burner II flew a total of twelve times from SLC-10, launching ten DMSP satellites and two other payloads.

The Burner IIA upper stage used a Thiokol Star 37D—which was less powerful than the Star 37B—for a total of eight launches.[421] A variant of the Burner IIA upper stage was powered by the Star 37XE and Star 37S-IISS engines. The external fairing was virtually indistinguishable from the Burner II launches. These rockets are listed as "THOR/

A Thor / Burner II prepares for launch at Space Launch Complex 10's west pad (SLC-10W) carrying a Defense Meteorological Support Program (DMSP) satellite in 1976. *Courtesy of the United States Air Force*

BLOCK 5D-1" in the Vandenberg official launch listings, mirroring the designation of the DMSP block launched, but the five launches are listed as THOR/BURNER IIA here.

Thor serial number 197, with its Burner II upper stage, awaits launch on 24 May 1975. The Thor / Burner II combination was mainstay transportation for the DMSP satellite fleet. *Courtesy of the United States Air Force*

An earlier Thor / Burner II at SLC-10W also carries a DMSP satellite. Note the unique payload fairing atop the booster. *Courtesy of the United States Air Force*

THOR/BURNER II (IIA) Launches[422]

SEQUENCE	DATE	SITE	VEHICLE	CODENAME	NOTES
621	15 SEP 66	4300 B-6	THOR/BURNER II	IRIS DUKE	DMSP BLOCK 4A
666	8 FEB 67	4300 B-6	THOR/BURNER II	ARROW POINT	DMSP BLOCK 4A
715	29 JUN 67	LE-6	THOR/BURNER II	--	SEQUENTIAL COLLATION OF RANGE (SECOR); AURORA I
732	22 AUG 67	LE-6	THOR/BURNER II	--	DMSP BLOCK 4A
740	11 OCT 67	LE-6	THOR/BURNER II	--	DMSP BLOCK 4A
800	22 MAY 68	SLC-10W	THOR/BURNER II	--	DMSP BLOCK 4B
828	22 OCT 68	SLC-10W	THOR/BURNER II	--	DMSP BLOCK 4B
897	22 JUL 69	SLC-10W	THOR/BURNER II	--	DMSP BLOCK 4B
945	11 FEB 70	SLC-10W	THOR/BURNER II	--	DMSP BLOCK 5A
999	3 SEP 70	SLC-10W	THOR/BURNER II	--	DMSP BLOCK 5A
1032	16 FEB 71	SLC-10W	THOR/BURNER II	--	DMSP BLOCK 5A
1060	8 JUN 71	SLC-10W	THOR/BURNER II	--	SESP 1 (P70-1)

SEQUENCE	DATE	SITE	VEHICLE	CODENAME	NOTES
1091	14 OCT 71	SLC-10W	THOR/BURNER IIA	--	DMSP BLOCK 5B
1120	24 MAR 72	SLC-10W	THOR/BURNER IIA	--	DMSP BLOCK 5B
1157	8 NOV 72	SLC-10W	THOR/BURNER IIA	--	DMSP BLOCK 5B
1194	16 AUG 73	SLC-10W	THOR/BURNER IIA	--	DMSP BLOCK 5B
1225	16 MAR 74	SLC-10W	THOR/BURNER IIA	--	DMSP BLOCK 5B
1247	8 AUG 74	SLC-10W	THOR/BURNER IIA	--	DMSP BLOCK 5C
1284	23 MAY 75	SLC-10W	THOR/BURNER IIA	--	DMSP BLOCK 5C
1318	18 FEB 76	SLC-10W	THOR/BURNER IIA	--	DMSP BLOCK 5C
1344	11 SEP 76	SLC-10W	THOR/BURNER IIA	--	DMSP BLOCK 5D1
1367	4 JUN 77	SLC-10W	THOR/BURNER IIA	--	DMSP BLOCK 5D1
1398	30 APR 78	SLC-10W	THOR/BURNER IIA	--	DMSP BLOCK 5D1
1431	6 JUN 79	SLC-10W	THOR/BURNER IIA	--	DMSP BLOCK 5D1
1461	14 JUL 80	SLC-10W	THOR/BURNER IIA	--	DMSP BLOCK 5D1

THOR/DELTA

The Thor/Delta was a three-stage, liquid-fueled space launch booster for launching small to medium payloads into low-earth orbit. The rocket consisted of a Thor first stage combined with a Delta-E second stage and an Altair 2 upper stage. The vehicle was also known as the Delta E. The Thor booster consisted of an aft section with the rocket propulsion and two propellant tanks (RP-1 kerosene and liquid oxygen) and a forward section containing the guidance, destruct package, and upper-stage interface.[423] To assist in providing thrust,

The next major evolution in the Thor family was the Thor/Delta rocket. Note the "delta" triangle symbol on the upper fuselage with the serial number, indicating this is Delta number 41. *Courtesy of the United States Air Force*

A mixture of technologies are shown, with the Thor/Delta lifting off carrying ESSA 6 and the Thor shelter at SLC-2E in the foreground. *Courtesy of the United States Air Force*

three Castor 1 solid-fuel booster rockets were attached to the first stage, spaced 120° apart.

From *The Origin of NASA Names*:

When NASA was formed in 1958 it inherited from the Department of Defense's Advanced Research Projects Agency (ARPA) the booster programs using combinations of Thor or Atlas boosters with Vanguard upper stages. The first of these upper-stage configurations was designated "Able." The Delta was similar to the previous Thor-based combinations and was a fourth or "D" version. Milton W. Rosen of NASA was responsible for the name. He had been referring to the combination as "Delta," which became the firm choice in January 1959 when a name was required because NASA was signing a contract for the booster. The vehicle was variously called "Delta" and "Thor-Delta." [424]

All payloads launched aboard the Thor/Deltas from SLC-2E and SLC-2W were for NASA or launched on behalf of NASA. Many within the series launched environmental observation satellites—ESSA, Improved TIROS, or NIMBUS—into polar orbits.

THOR/DELTA Launches[425]

SEQUENCE	DATE	SITE	VEHICLE	CODENAME	NOTES
629	2 OCT 66	SLC-2E	THOR/DELTA	BUSY MALLET	ENVIRONMENTAL SURVEY SATELLITE 3 (ESSA 3)
660	26 JAN 67	SLC-2E	THOR/DELTA	BUSY PENNY	ENVIRONMENTAL SURVEY SATELLITE 4 (ESSA 4)
685	20 APR 67	SLC-2E	THOR/DELTA	BUCKLE PAINTER	ENVIRONMENTAL SURVEY SATELLITE 5 (ESSA 5)
701	24 MAY 67	SLC-2E	THOR/DELTA	--	EXPLORER 25
750	10 NOV 67	SLC-2E	THOR/DELTA	--	ENVIRONMENTAL SURVEY SATELLITE 6 (ESSA 6)
768	11 JAN 68	SLC-2E	THOR/DELTA	--	EXPLORER 36
809	4 JUL 68	SLC-2E	THOR/DELTA	--	EXPLORER 38
816	16 AUG 68	SLC-2E	THOR/DELTA	--	ENVIRONMENTAL SURVEY SATELLITE 7 (ESSA 7)
843	15 DEC 68	SLC-2E	THOR/DELTA	--	ENVIRONMENTAL SURVEY SATELLITE 8 (ESSA 8)
852	29 JAN 69	SLC-2E	THOR/DELTA	--	ISIS 1
889	21 JUN 69	SLC-2W	THOR/DELTA	--	EXPLORER 41
942	23 JAN 70	SLC-2W	THOR/DELTA	--	IMPROVED TIROS OPERATIONAL SATELLITE (ITOS 1); OSCAR 5
1021	11 DEC 70	SLC-2W	THOR/DELTA	--	NOAA 1
1046	31 MAR 71	SLC-2E	THOR/DELTA	--	ISIS 2
1096	21 OCT 71	SLC-2E	THOR/DELTA	--	ITOS B
1112	31 JAN 72	SLC-2E	THOR/DELTA	--	HIGHLY ECCENTRIC ORBITING SATELLITE (HEOS 2)
1116	11 MAR 72	SLC-2E	THOR/DELTA	--	ESRO
1139	23 JUL 72	SLC-2W	THOR/DELTA	--	LANDSAT 1
1153	15 OCT 72	SLC-2W	THOR/DELTA	--	NOAA 2/OSCAR 6
1164	10 DEC 72	SLC-2W	THOR/DELTA	--	NIMBUS 5
1189	16 JUL 73	SLC-2W	THOR/DELTA	--	ITOS E
1209	6 NOV 73	SLC-2W	THOR/DELTA	--	NOAA 3
1215	15 DEC 73	SLC-2W	THOR/DELTA	--	EXPLORER 51
1263	15 NOV 74	SLC-2W	THOR/DELTA	--	NOAA 4/INTASAT 1/OSCAR 7
1269	22 JAN 75	SLC-2W	THOR/DELTA	--	LANDSAT 2
1275	9 APR 75	SLC-2W	THOR/DELTA	--	GEODYNAMICS EXPERIMENTAL OCEAN SATELLITE 3 (GEOS 3)
1287	12 JUN 75	SLC-2W	THOR/DELTA	--	NIMBUS 6
1293	8 AUG 75	SLC-2W	THOR/DELTA	--	COS-B
1303	6 OCT 75	SLC-2W	THOR/DELTA	--	EXPLORER 54
1326	3 MAY 76	SLC-2W	THOR/DELTA	--	LASER GEODETIC SATELLITE (LAGEOS)
1339	29 JUL 76	SLC-2W	THOR/DELTA	--	NOAA 5
1393	5 MAR 78	SLC-2W	THOR/DELTA	--	LANDSAT 3/OSCAR 8
1413	24 OCT 78	SLC-2W	THOR/DELTA	--	NIMBUS 7

THORAD/AGENA-D

The Thorad/Agena-D was a two-stage, liquid-fueled, medium-lift space launch vehicle derived from the Thor IRBM (Long Tank Thrust Augmented Thor, or LTTAT), with an upper stage (Agena-D) for orbital insertion. The Thorad booster had a stretched tank (Long Tank) providing extra propellant and a burn time of 215 seconds. Thrust augmentation was provided by three Castor 2 booster rockets strapped to the side of the first stage. These boosters fired with the main engine for thirty-seven seconds, helping to lift heavier payloads such as the CORONA KH-4A and KH-4B cameras. The Agena-D upper stage consisted of an airframe with propulsion, auxiliary power, guidance and control, and space-ground communication systems.[426]

The first launch of a Thorad/Agena-D took place on 9 August 1966, lifting a CORONA KH-4A payload. The KH-4A and KH-4B carried a film payload of 160 lbs., doubled from the KH-4's 80 lb. reels. In addition, to extend the flexibility of the camera's lifespan, two film reentry vehicles were sent aloft. This provided flexibility for images to be returned early if required for intelligence analysis, yet still leave an imaging capability overhead . . . at least until the next satellite was launched.

The Thorad/Agena-D series would see the end of the CORONA program, since its photographic workload was assumed by the GAMBIT and HEXAGON series of satellites. As the program ended, Director of Central Intelligence Mr. Richard Helms stated:

> It was confidence in the ability of intelligence to monitor Soviet compliance with the commitments that enabled President Nixon to enter into the Strategic

Arms Limitation Talks and to sign the Arms Limitation Treaty. Much, but by no means all, of the intelligence necessary to verify Soviet compliance with SALT will come from photoreconnaissance satellites. CORONA, the program which pioneered the way in satellite reconnaissance, deserves the place in history which we are preserving through this small museum display.

"A Decade of Glory," as the display is entitled, must for the present remain classified. We hope, however, that as the world grows to accept satellite reconnaissance, it can be transferred to the Smithsonian Institution. Then the American public can view this work, and then the men of CORONA, like the Wright Brothers, can be recognized for the role they played in the shaping of history.[427]

This cutaway drawing of the CORONA KH-4A satellite shows two film recovery capsules at the far right illustrated by the film reel. The extended thrust of the Thorad/Agena-D was needed to get the larger camera and more film into orbit and back. *Courtesy of the United States Air Force*

As a standardized upper stage, the Agena-D gave operational planners set expectations on how it would perform during operations. Whereas previous Agena variants were assembled around a specific payload type in "blocks" with varying success rates, the Agena-D became a reliable payload that underlined the success of US space programs. *Courtesy of the United States Air Force*

The first Thorad/Agena-D took place on 9 August 1966, lifting a CORONA KH-4A satellite into low-earth orbit. *Courtesy of the United States Air Force*

THORAD/AGENA-D Launches[428]

SEQUENCE	DATE	SITE	VEHICLE	CODENAME	NOTES
611	9 AUG 66	SLC-1W	THORAD/AGENA-D	CURLY TOP	CORONA MSN 1036 (KH-4A); FIRST LONG-TANK THRUST AUGMENTED THOR/AGENA-D;
641	8 NOV 66	SLC-1W	THORAD/AGENA-D	BUSY MEETING	CORONA MSN 1037 (KH-4A)
692	9 MAY 67	SLC-1E	THORAD/AGENA-D	BUSY BANKER	CORONA MSN 1041 (KH-4A)
710	16 JUN 67	SLC-1W	THORAD/AGENA-D	--	CORONA MSN 1042 (KH-4A)
729	7 AUG 67	SLC-1E	THORAD/AGENA-D	--	CORONA MSN 1043 (KH-4A)
735	15 SEP 67	SLC-1W	THORAD/AGENA-D	--	CORONA MSN 1101 (KH-4B); FIRST KH-4B MISSION
746	2 NOV 67	SLC-1E	THORAD/AGENA-D	--	CORONA MSN 1044 (KH-4A)
760	9 DEC 67	SLC-1W	THORAD/AGENA-D	--	CORONA MSN 1102 (KH-4B)
772	24 JAN 68	SLC-1E	THORAD/AGENA-D	--	CORONA MSN 1045 (KH-4A)
783	14 MAR 68	SLC-1E	THORAD/AGENA-D	--	CORONA MSN 1046 (KH-4A)
794	1 MAY 68	SLC-3W	THORAD/AGENA-D	--	CORONA MSN 1103 (KH-4B)
797	18 MAY 68	SLC-2E	THORAD/AGENA-D	--	NIMBUS B / SECOR 10
805	20 JUN 68	SLC-1E	THORAD/AGENA-D	--	CORONA MSN 1047 (KH-4A)
814	7 AUG 68	SLC-3W	THORAD/AGENA-D	--	CORONA MSN 1104 (KH-4B)
822	18 SEP 68	SLC-1E	THORAD/AGENA-D	--	CORONA MSN 1048 (KH-4A)
826	5 OCT 68	SLC-1W	THORAD/AGENA-D	--	STRAWMAN I ELINT
831	3 NOV 68	SLC-3W	THORAD/AGENA-D	--	CORONA MSN 1105 (KH-4B)
842	12 DEC 68	SLC-3W	THORAD/AGENA-D	--	CORONA MSN 1049 (KH-4A)
855	5 FEB 69	SLC-3W	THORAD/AGENA-D	--	CORONA MSN 1106 (KH-4B)
863	19 MAR 69	SLC-3W	THORAD/AGENA-D	--	CORONA MSN 1050 (KH-4A)
868	13 APR 69	SLC-2E	THORAD/AGENA-D	--	NIMBUS 3
876	1 MAY 69	SLC-3W	THORAD/AGENA-D	--	CORONA MSN 1051 (KH-4A)
884	5 JUN 69	SLC-2E	THORAD/AGENA-D	--	OGO (ORBITING GEOPHYSICAL OBSERVATORY) 6
899	23 JUL 69	SLC-3W	THORAD/AGENA-D	--	CORONA MSN 1107 (KH-4B)
901	31 JUL 69	SLC-1W	THORAD/AGENA-D	--	STRAWMAN II ELINT
915	22 SEP 69	SLC-3W	THORAD/AGENA-D	--	CORONA MSN 1052 (KH-4A)
918	30 SEP 69	SLC-1W	THORAD/AGENA-D	--	SURCAL/TIMATION 2
936	4 DEC 69	SLC-3W	THORAD/AGENA-D	--	CORONA MSN 1108 (KH-4B)
943	3 FEB 70	SLC-2E	THORAD/AGENA-D	--	SERT 2 (SPACE ELECTRIC ROCKET TEST)
947	4 MAR 70	SLC-3W	THORAD/AGENA-D	--	CORONA MSN 1109 (KH-4B)
958	8 APR 70	SLC-2E	THORAD/AGENA-D	--	NIMBUS 4 / TOPO 1
966	20 MAY 70	SLC-3W	THORAD/AGENA-D	--	CORONA MSN 1110 (KH-4B)
983	22 JUL 70	SLC-3W	THORAD/AGENA-D	--	CORONA MSN 1111 (KH-4B)
994	26 AUG 70	SLC-1W	THORAD/AGENA-D	--	STRAWMAN III ELINT
1019	18 NOV 70	SLC-3W	THORAD/AGENA-D	--	CORONA MSN 1112 (KH-4B)
1034	17 FEB 71	SLC-3W	THORAD/AGENA-D	--	CORONA MSN 1113 (KH-4B)
1044	24 MAR 71	SLC-3W	THORAD/AGENA-D	--	CORONA MSN 1114 (KH-4B)
1073	16 JUL 71	SLC-1W	THORAD/AGENA-D	--	STRAWMAN IV ELINT
1086	10 SEP 71	SLC-3W	THORAD/AGENA-D	--	CORONA MSN 1115 (KH-4B)
1093	17 OCT 71	SLC-1W	THORAD/AGENA-D	--	ASTEX
1106	14 DEC 71	SLC-1W	THORAD/AGENA-D	--	POPPY IX ELINT; LAST POPPY SATELLITE
1123	19 APR 72	SLC-3W	THORAD/AGENA-D	--	CORONA MSN 1116 (KH-4B)
1129	25 MAY 72	SLC-3W	THORAD/AGENA-D	--	CORONA MSN 1117 (KH-4B); LAST CORONA FLIGHT; LAST KH-4 MSN.

TITAN I ICBM

The Titan I (SM-68, HGM-25A, LGM-25, WS-107A-2) was a first-generation, two-stage, liquid-fueled, nuclear-tipped missile with intercontinental range. In concert with the development of the Atlas missile, Gen. Bernard Schriever recommended a second ICBM be developed to provide a backup system in case of delays in the primary (Atlas) program. Schriever also believed that Convair—the prime contractor for Atlas—was growing complacent.[429] In October 1955, the Glenn L. Martin Company was awarded a contract to build WS-107A-2, better known as the Titan I ICBM.

The Titan I first stage was powered by two Aerojet LR87-AJ-1 engines with two thrust chambers, providing 300,000 lbs. of thrust, with the second-stage LR91-AJ-1 engine

A Titan I ICBM lifts off from its hardened launcher at Vandenberg's Complex 395A. The Titan was introduced slightly after the Atlas missile, hedging against any major technological problems that might derail the program. *Courtesy of the United States Air Force*

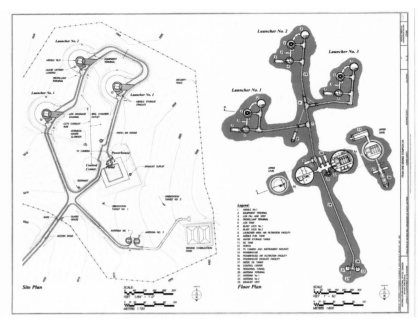

A map of Complex 395A shows the three launch silos for the Titan missiles at the top. The remaining underground structures included a launch control center, equipment building, and power facility for the site. *Courtesy of the United States Air Force*

providing 80,000 lbs. of thrust.[430] The airframe was of semimonocoque design made of lightweight aluminum, with structural members internally supporting the tank walls. Unlike the Atlas program's "stage-and-a-half" design, Titan was the first true multistage missile. After the first-stage engine fired to completion, it was jettisoned, allowing preservation of velocity and decrease of mass for the second-stage flight and enabling a greater range and heavier payload. Titan I was powered by a liquid oxygen oxidizer and RP-1 (kerosene) fuel, necessitating cryogenic storage.

The original Bell Telephone radio-inertial guidance system used a ground-based radar system to make in-flight corrections. Concerns about enemy jamming forced the adoption of an all-inertial guidance system that went into the Titan I force in 1962.

A single Mark 4 reentry vehicle—the same as on the Atlas-E and F missiles—provided the thermonuclear "punch" to the Titan I's intercontinental reach.

The basing mode for Titan I was inside super-hardened silos (withstanding blast overpressure) in a 3 × 3 configuration—three missiles at each complex, and three complexes supported by a missile support base. The missiles were raised aboveground, fueled for flight, and launched while at ground level. The Titan I was deployed with six operational squadrons:

- 395th Strategic Missile Squadron—Vandenberg AFB, CA—1 complex (3 missiles)
- 568th Strategic Missile Squadron—Larson AFB, WA—3 complexes (9 missiles)
- 569th Strategic Missile Squadron—Mt. Home AFB, ID—3 complexes (9 missiles)
- 848th/724th Strategic Missile Squadron—Lowry AFB, CO—3 complexes (9 missiles)
- 849th/725th Strategic Missile Squadron—Lowry AFB, CO—3 complexes (9 missiles)
- 850th Strategic Missile Squadron—Ellsworth AFB, SD—3 complexes (9 missiles)
- 851st Strategic Missile Squadron—Beale AFB, CA—3 complexes (9 missiles)

The two Lowry squadrons (848 SMS and 849 SMS) were renumbered to their respective designations on 1 July 1961 by Headquarters SAC.[431]

The launch sequence is detailed in *To Defend and Deter*:

The launch sequence took approximately 15 minutes. After receiving a launch order, the crew filled the missile's tanks with 200,000 pounds of liquid oxygen and RP-1. After the missile was fueled, it rode to the surface on the silo elevator and then was fired. The flight began with the ignition of the large first-stage engines that burned for 134 seconds and propelled the missile to an altitude of 35 miles. As the first-stage expired and fell away, the second-stage fired; it burned for another 156 seconds, boosting the missile to an altitude of 150 miles and a velocity of 22,554 ft. per second. After the second-stage fell silent, two small Vernier engines fired for an additional 50 seconds making final course corrections to the trajectory. After the Vernier engines burned out, the reentry vehicle carrying the warhead followed a ballistic trajectory, and at the apogee of its flight soared to an altitude of 541 miles above the earth's surface. Time elapsed for a 5,500 mile flight: 33 minutes.[432]

Titan I test flights at Vandenberg began with the launch of SILVER SADDLE from the Silo Launch Test Facility (SLTF) on 3 May 1961—incidentally the world's first in-silo launched missile. Complex 395A contained one Titan I complex, complete with three silo-lift elevators and underground power generation facilities. An additional facility, the Operational Suitability Test Facility (OSTF), was used for procedural checkout of Titan I. It experienced a destructive accident on 3 December 1960:

> The 97 ft. long Titan was being lowered into its underground concrete silo after fueling when it exploded with a roar that shook windows 25 miles away. There were no injuries —crews were in an underground building several hundred yards away. Damage from the blast . . . was estimated between $4 million and $6 million.[433]

The OSTF explosion had zero casualties but demolished the facility and obliterated the missile airframe. Remnants of the OSTF explosion can still be found at Vandenberg today. The SLTF was only used once, and the remains are still in a California hillside.

Twenty test flights of Titan I flew from Vandenberg: nineteen from Complex 395A and one from SLTF.

Even as the Titan I was joining the operational force, its replacement (Titan II) was being tested. In 1964, Secretary of Defense Robert McNamara ordered the phasing out of first-generation ICBM systems Atlas and Titan I due to numerous accidents at operational sites. The deployed Titan I inventory peaked during 1963–1964 at fifty-four missiles and plummeted to zero missiles by 1965.[434]

A network of tunnels connect the three launch tubes at Complex 395A. The Titan I program provided the United States its first experience with building underground complexes to hold its nuclear alert force. *Courtesy of the United States Air Force*

A Titan I ICBM (serial number 3698) lies on its side at Complex 395C, home of its successor missile, the Titan II. *Courtesy of the United States Air Force*

The open blast doors at Complex 395A allow a sneak peak of the Mark 4 reentry vehicle atop a Titan I ICBM. *Courtesy of the United States Air Force*

TITAN I ICBM Launches[435]

SEQUENCE	DATE	SITE	VEHICLE	CODENAME	NOTES
83	3 MAY 61	SLTF	TITAN I	SILVER SADDLE	WORLD'S FIRST IN-SILO LAUNCH
100	23 SEP 61	395A-1	TITAN I	BIG SAM	
118	20 JAN 62	395A-3	TITAN I	DOUBLE MARTINI	
123	23 FEB 62	395A-1	TITAN I	BLUE GANDER	
137	4 MAY 62	395A-1	TITAN I	SILVER TOP	
174	6 OCT 62	395A-1	TITAN I	TIGHT BRACELET	

SEQUENCE	DATE	SITE	VEHICLE	CODENAME	NOTES
184	5 DEC 62	395A-1	TITAN I	YELLOW JACKET	
198	29 JAN 63	395A-1	TITAN I	TEN MEN	
216	30 MAR 63	395A-2	TITAN I	YOUNG BLOOD	
218	4 APR 63	395A-1	TITAN I	HALF MOON	
222	13 APR 63	395A-3	TITAN I	RAMP ROOSTER	
229	1 MAY 63	395A-1	TITAN I	MARES TAIL	
253	16 JUL 63	395A-2	TITAN I	SILVER SPUR	
262	15 AUG 63	395A-1	TITAN I	HIGH RIVER	
268	30 AUG 63	395A-3	TITAN I	POLAR ROUTE	
272	17 SEP 63	395A-2	TITAN I	DAILY MAIL	
293	14 NOV 63	395A-1	TITAN I	FAST RIDE	
421	8 DEC 64	395A-1	TITAN I	WEST WING I	
432	14 JAN 65	395A-3	TITAN I	WEST WIND III	
445	5 MAR 65	395A-2	TITAN I	WEST WIND II	LAST TITAN I ICBM LAUNCH

TITAN II ICBM

The Titan II (LGM-25C) was a second-generation, liquid-fueled, nuclear-tipped, two-stage ballistic missile with intercontinental range. Its mission was to deter an adversary by maintaining a survivable capability to deliver a thermonuclear warhead more than a quarter of the way around the world (5,500-nautical-mile range) to destroy top-priority enemy targets within minutes of launch. Titan II underwent design and development while its predecessor was undergoing operational deployment. The Titan II missile was designed to overcome the limitations of Titan I. Improvements wrought by the Titan II included

- more-powerful engines,
- a larger warhead (Mark 6 warhead),
- an all-inertial guidance system,
- an onboard storable liquid oxidizer, and
- being silo launched.

The last two improvements worked in conjunction with each other. While readying the deployment of the Titan I, engineers at the Ballistic Missile Division discovered that with minor modifications the missile design could use noncryogenic propellants that could be stored aboard the missile. This would allow a decrease in launch-processing time and get the missile off the launchpad more quickly during a crisis. Additionally, this could enable the missile to reside inside, and be fired from, the hardened missile silo, negating an elevator lift to ground level for launch.

Development of all-inertial guidance allowed dispersal of individual missiles to widely separated locations, since a centralized ground-based guidance system was not needed.

Development of the Titan II was initiated in October 1959. By 1962, six Titan II squadrons were activated. Titan II was deployed in a 1 × 9 configuration, with one missile per silo complex, nine missiles per squadron, and eighteen silos (two squadrons) supported by one missile support base.

- 395th Strategic Missile Squadron—Vandenberg AFB, CA—3 complexes (3 missiles)

Images from an unidentified Titan II launch show the staging process, separating the first stage from the orbital components. *Courtesy of the United States Air Force*

- 373d Strategic Missile Squadron—Little Rock AFB, AR—9 complexes (9 missiles)
- 374d Strategic Missile Squadron—Little Rock AFB, AR—9 complexes (9 missiles)
- 532d Strategic Missile Squadron—McConnell AFB, KS—9 complexes (9 missiles)
- 533d Strategic Missile Squadron—McConnell AFB, KS—9 complexes (9 missiles)
- 570th Strategic Missile Squadron—Davis-Monthan AFB, AZ—9 complexes (9 missiles)

Titan II (serial number B-69) takes off from Complex 395C on 5 October 1973. *Courtesy of the United States Air Force*

Clearly shown is the thrust from the "W-shaped" flame deflector at the bottom of the Titan II silo. Unlike the solid-fueled Minuteman missile, the flame was directed away from the Titan II to prevent an explosion of the missile's liquid fuel and oxidizer. *Courtesy of the United States Air Force*

A rare view of a Titan II launch at Vandenberg with the site fence open (lower-left corner) and the guard post vacated (below the missile). *Courtesy of the United States Air Force*

• 571st Strategic Missile Squadron—Davis-Monthan AFB, AZ—9 complexes (9 missiles)

Three sites at Vandenberg belonged to the 395th Strategic Missile Squadron:
• 395B—Baker Site—16 launches
• 395C—Charlie Site—31 launches
• 395D—Dog Site—11 launches

Early launches of Titan II supported the development and operational testing program. Later launches provided diagnostic information for the Safeguard Anti-Ballistic Missile system. The final Titan II launch occurred on 27 June 1976 from Complex 395C.

TITAN II ICBM Launches[436]

SEQUENCE	DATE	SITE	VEHICLE	CODENAME	NOTES
203	16 FEB 63	395C	TITAN II	AWFUL TIRED	
227	27 APR 63	395C	TITAN II	DINNER PARTY	
233	13 MAY 63	395D	TITAN II	FLYING FROG	
244	20 JUN 63	395C	TITAN II	THREAD NEEDLE	
273	23 SEP 63	395D	TITAN II	TAR TOP	
290	9 NOV 63	395C	TITAN II	FIRE TRUCK	
302	16 DEC 63	395D	TITAN II	USEFUL TASK	
315	23 JAN 64	395C	TITAN II	RED SAILS	
323	17 FEB 64	395B	TITAN II	SAFE CONDUCT	
333	13 MAR 64	395C	TITAN II	APPLE PIE	
372	30 JUL 64	395D	TITAN II	COBRA SKIN	
376	11 AUG 64	395C	TITAN II	DOUBLE TALLEY	
377	13 AUG 64	395B	TITAN II	GENTLE ANNIE	
399	2 OCT 64	395C	TITAN II	BLACK WIDOW	
410	4 NOV 64	395D	TITAN II	HIGH RIDER	
453	24 MAR 65	395B	TITAN II	ARCTIC SUN	
462	16 APR 65	395C	TITAN II	BEAR HUG	
465	30 APR 65	395D	TITAN II	CARD DECK	

SEQUENCE	DATE	SITE	VEHICLE	CODENAME	NOTES
471	21 MAY 65	395B	TITAN II	FRONT SIGHT	
481	14 JUN 65	395C	TITAN II	GOLD FISH	
486	30 JUN 65	395D	TITAN II	BUSY BEE	
493	21 JUL 65	395B	TITAN II	LONG BALL	
498	16 AUG 65	395C	TITAN II	MAGIC LAMP	
503	25 AUG 65	395D	TITAN II	NEW ROLE	
507	21 SEP 65	395B	TITAN II	BOLD GUY	
515	20 OCT 65	395C	TITAN II	POWER BOX	
519	27 NOV 65	395D	TITAN II	RED WAGON	
522	30 NOV 65	395B	TITAN II	CROSS FIRE	
529	22 DEC 65	395C	TITAN II	SEA ROVER	
538	3 FEB 66	395D	TITAN II	WINTER ICE	
545	17 FEB 66	395B	TITAN II	BLACK HAWK	
558	25 MAR 66	395C	TITAN II	CLOSE TOUCH	
566	5 APR 66	395D	TITAN II	GOLD RING	
570	20 APR 66	395B	TITAN II	LONG LIGHT	
584	24 MAY 66	395C	TITAN II	SILVER BULLET	
603	22 JUL 66	395B	TITAN II	GIANT TRAIN	
622	16 SEP 66	395C	TITAN II	BLACK RIVER	
644	24 NOV 66	395B	TITAN II	BUBBLE GIRL	
676	17 MAR 67	395C	TITAN II	GIFT HORSE	
681	12 APR 67	395B	TITAN II	GLAMOUR GIRL	
713	23 JUN 67	395B	TITAN II	--	
734	11 SEP 67	395B	TITAN II	GLOWING BRIGHT 44	
779	28 FEB 68	395B	TITAN II	GLORY TRIP 04T	
785	2 APR 68	395C	TITAN II	GLORY TRIP 10T	
804	12 JUN 68	395C	TITAN II	GLORY TRIP 08T	
819	21 AUG 68	395C	TITAN II	GLORY TRIP 18T	
836	19 NOV 68	395C	TITAN II	GLORY TRIP 26T	
879	20 MAY 69	395B	TITAN II	GLORY TRIP 39T	
1064	20 JUN 71	395C	TITAN II	--	
1080	27 AUG 71	395C	TITAN II	--	
1128	24 MAY 72	395C	TITAN II	--	
1151	11 OCT 72	395C	TITAN II	--	
1206	5 OCT 73	395C	TITAN II	--	
1221	1 MAR 74	395C	TITAN II	--	
1267	9 JAN 75	395C	TITAN II	--	
1292	7 AUG 75	395C	TITAN II	--	
1309	4 DEC 75	395C	TITAN II	--	
1334	27 JUN 76	395C	TITAN II	--	LAST TITAN II ICBM LAUNCH

TITAN II SLV

The Titan II space launch vehicle was a two-stage, liquid-propellant, medium-lift booster developed from refurbished LGM-25C Titan II intercontinental ballistic missiles. The Titan II SLV used the same airframe and engines as the missile variant and was able to lift 4,200 lbs. into polar orbit.[437] The Universal Space Guidance System from the Titan III SLV replaced the missile's original inertial guidance set.[438]

The airframe was reused, as were the Stage 1 and Stage 2 engines. The Titan II SLV also incorporated modifications from the Titan III SLV, such as the payload fairing, attitude

The refurbished Titan II space launch vehicle was used to launch a variety of payloads. Note the rounded payload fairing. *Courtesy of the United States Air Force*

control system, and electrical/ordnance for destruction after launch.

In 1986, the Air Force gave Martin Marietta Company a contract to convert eight LGM-25C Titan II ICBMs into the space launch booster, and an option for five additional conversions. The contract was extended into November 1987 for one additional booster, bringing the grand total of ICBM conversion to SLVs to fourteen.[439]

While a silo launch capability for the Titan II boosters was considered, the Titan II SLVs were surface launched from SLC-4W at South Vandenberg. All launches aboard the Titan II SLV were successful.

TITAN II SLV Launches [440]

SEQUENCE	DATE	SITE	VEHICLE	CODENAME	NOTES
1625	5 SEP 88	SLC-4W	TITAN II	--	USA-32; FIRST LAUNCH OF TITAN II SLV
1636	5 SEP 89	SLC-4W	TITAN II	--	USA-45
1673	25 APR 92	SLC-4W	TITAN II	--	USA-81
1694	5 OCT 93	SLC-4W	TITAN II	--	LANDSAT 6
1695	25 JAN 94	SLC-4W	TITAN II	--	CLEMENTINE
1737	4 APR 97	SLC-4W	TITAN II	--	DMSP
1762	13 MAY 98	SLC-4W	TITAN II	--	NOAA-15
1780	19 JUN 99	SLC-4W	TITAN II	--	QUICKSCAT
1786	12 DEC 99	SLC-4W	TITAN II	--	DMSP
1801	21 SEP 00	SLC-4W	TITAN II	--	NOAA-16
1823	24 JUN 02	SLC-4W	TITAN II	--	NOAA-17
1830	6 JAN 03	SLC-4W	TITAN II	--	CORIOLIS
1840	18 OCT 03	SLC-4W	TITAN II	--	DMSP; LAST LAUNCH OF TITAN II SLV

TITAN IIIB/AGENA-D

The Titan IIIB/Agena-D was a three-stage, liquid-fueled, heavy-lift space launch booster derived from the Titan ICBM, with an upper stage (Agena-D) for orbital insertion. The primary contractor for the Titan family of boosters was Martin Marietta, building the airframe, internal fuel/oxidizer tanks, and flight control systems and ensuring compatibility with other contracted subsystems. The liquid-propellant engines were produced by Aerojet-General. The Titan IIIB consisted of the first two stages of a core Titan II. The Agena-D upper stage held the payload and provided propulsion, auxiliary power, guidance and control, and space-ground communication systems.[441]

The primary "user" for the Titan IIIB/Agena-D combination was the National Reconnaissance Office for its GAMBIT (Project 110, GAMBIT-3, KH-8) program. GAMBIT (Project 206, KH-7) was the first photographic satellite project to produce reconnaissance photographs with 2 to 3 ft. resolution.[442] The follow-on program used a Titan IIIB booster for ascent and the Agena-D as a Satellite Control Section, unlike the previous Atlas/Agena-D program.

As early as 1964, the secretary of the Air Force Special Projects branch prepared a study to replace the Atlas/Agena booster combination with a proposed Titan III(X) / Agena pairing.[443] There was a push to use the Titan III family for other Air Force space missions to provide a secure production base and ensure standardization with ground support equipment. At this time Atlas boosters were shifting over to NASA for technical control and production contracts. The final push for the Titan III(X) was the hint that a future CORONA replacement (e.g., KH-9 HEXAGON) would require a Titan III booster. In late 1964, the renamed Titan IIIB was selected as the booster of choice for the upgraded GAMBIT system.

To lessen the technological risk of failure (such as the problems with the previous GAMBIT's Orbital Control Vehicle), a "roll joint" was used between the photographic payload section and the Agena-D upper stage, allowing the pair to orbit together and use the Agena-D for orbit control, as well as orbit injection.[444] The photographic camera was a separate section that was physically connected to the Agena-D, unlike the previous GAMBIT, where the photographic payload was held *inside* the Agena-D. This allowed a revolutionary change in launch processing. The individual pieces (Titan IIIB, Agena-D upper stage, and photographic payload) were shipped separately to Vandenberg and integrated together on the launchpad.

Principal GAMBIT (Project 110) components and their manufacturers were

- Payload—Eastman Kodak Company
- Reentry Vehicle—General Electric
- Agena Stage—Lockheed Missiles and Space Company
- Command Subsystem—General Electric
- Titan III Booster—Martin Marietta

While a highly reliable system, a few GAMBIT flights had ill-fated outcomes. The Titan IIIB booster had one launch failure on 26 April 1967, when the second stage failed sixteen seconds after start of launch.[445] During two flights, the Agena-D placed the payload in an orbit with a higher velocity than planned. On the first mishap, the ground guidance station at Vandenberg allowed the Titan IIIB second stage to burn to depletion, even after achieving the proper orbit. That, coupled with the Agena-D's prescheduled burn, placed the satellite into a higher-than-expected orbit. The second mishap saw the Agena-D engine burn to depletion due to a malfunctioning injection velocity meter. The orbital altitude reached was double that specified for nominal camera operation.

The final launch of a Titan IIIB/Agena-D pair was on 11 February 1987, lifting a national-security payload.

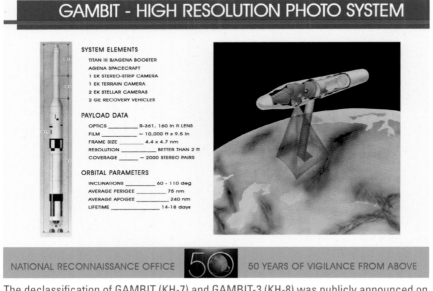

The declassification of GAMBIT (KH-7) and GAMBIT-3 (KH-8) was publicly announced on September 17, 2011 during the NRO's 50th Anniversary year. *Courtesy of the National Reconnaissance Office*

An unidentified KH-8 GAMBIT-3 satellite is lofted aboard a Titan IIIB/Agena-D combination. Previous GAMBIT (KH-7) satellites were launched on Atlas-Agena. *Courtesy of the United States Air Force*

TITAN IIIB/AGENA-D Launches[446]

SEQUENCE	DATE	SITE	VEHICLE	CODENAME	NOTES
606	29 JUL 66	SLC-4W	TITAN IIIB/AGENA-D	DAILY MAIL	GAMBIT-3 MSN 4301 (KH-8)
628	28 SEP 66	SLC-4W	TITAN IIIB/AGENA-D	BUSY SCHEME	GAMBIT-3 MSN 4302 (KH-8)
648	14 DEC 66	SLC-4W	TITAN IIIB/AGENA-D	BUSY SKYROCKET	GAMBIT-3 MSN 4303 (KH-8)
672	24 FEB 67	SLC-4W	TITAN IIIB/AGENA-D	BUSY PALEFACE	GAMBIT-3 MSN 4304 (KH-8)
688	26 APR 67	SLC-4W	TITAN IIIB/AGENA-D	BUSY TAILOR	GAMBIT-3 MSN 4305 (KH-8)
711	20 JUN 67	SLC-4W	TITAN IIIB/AGENA-D	--	GAMBIT-3 MSN 4306 (KH-8)
731	16 AUG 67	SLC-4W	TITAN IIIB/AGENA-D	--	GAMBIT-3 MSN 4307 (KH-8)
736	19 SEP 67	SLC-4W	TITAN IIIB/AGENA-D	--	GAMBIT-3 MSN 4308 (KH-8)
744	25 OCT 67	SLC-4W	TITAN IIIB/AGENA-D	--	GAMBIT-3 MSN 4309 (KH-8)
758	5 DEC 67	SLC-4W	TITAN IIIB/AGENA-D	--	GAMBIT-3 MSN 4310 (KH-8)
771	18 JAN 68	SLC-4W	TITAN IIIB/AGENA-D	--	GAMBIT-3 MSN 4311 (KH-8)
782	13 MAR 68	SLC-4W	TITAN IIIB/AGENA-D	--	GAMBIT-3 MSN 4312 (KH-8)
789	17 APR 68	SLC-4W	TITAN IIIB/AGENA-D	--	GAMBIT-3 MSN 4313 (KH-8)
803	5 JUN 68	SLC-4W	TITAN IIIB/AGENA-D	--	GAMBIT-3 MSN 4314 (KH-8)
813	6 AUG 68	SLC-4W	TITAN IIIB/AGENA-D	--	GAMBIT-3 MSN 4315 (KH-8)
821	10 SEP 68	SLC-4W	TITAN IIIB/AGENA-D	--	GAMBIT-3 MSN 4316 (KH-8)
832	6 NOV 68	SLC-4W	TITAN IIIB/AGENA-D	--	GAMBIT-3 MSN 4317 (KH-8)
839	4 DEC 68	SLC-4W	TITAN IIIB/AGENA-D	--	GAMBIT-3 MSN 4318 (KH-8)

SEQUENCE	DATE	SITE	VEHICLE	CODENAME	NOTES
848	22 JAN 69	SLC-4W	TITAN IIIB/AGENA-D	--	GAMBIT-3 MSN 4319 (KH-8)
858	4 MAR 69	SLC-4W	TITAN IIIB/AGENA-D	--	GAMBIT-3 MSN 4320 (KH-8)
869	15 APR 69	SLC-4W	TITAN IIIB/AGENA-D	--	GAMBIT-3 MSN 4321 (KH-8)
883	3 JUN 69	SLC-4W	TITAN IIIB/AGENA-D	--	GAMBIT-3 MSN 4322 (KH-8)
904	23 AUG 69	SLC-4W	TITAN IIIB/AGENA-D	--	GAMBIT-3 MSN 4323 (KH-8)
926	24 OCT 69	SLC-4W	TITAN IIIB/AGENA-D	--	GAMBIT-3 MSN 4324 (KH-8)
940	14 JAN 70	SLC-4W	TITAN IIIB/AGENA-D	--	GAMBIT-3 MSN 4325 (KH-8)
959	15 APR 70	SLC-4W	TITAN IIIB/AGENA-D	--	GAMBIT-3 MSN 4326 (KH-8)
976	25 JUN 70	SLC-4W	TITAN IIIB/AGENA-D	--	GAMBIT-3 MSN 4327 (KH-8)
991	18 AUG 70	SLC-4W	TITAN IIIB/AGENA-D	--	GAMBIT-3 MSN 4328 (KH-8)
1012	23 OCT 70	SLC-4W	TITAN IIIB/AGENA-D	--	GAMBIT-3 MSN 4329 (KH-8)
1026	21 JAN 71	SLC-4W	TITAN IIIB/AGENA-D	--	GAMBIT-3 MSN 4330 (KH-8)
1042	20 MAR 71	SLC-4W	TITAN IIIB/AGENA-D	--	
1051	22 APR 71	SLC-4W	TITAN IIIB/AGENA-D	--	GAMBIT-3 MSN 4331 (KH-8)
1078	12 AUG 71	SLC-4W	TITAN IIIB/AGENA-D	--	GAMBIT-3 MSN 4332 (KH-8)
1098	23 OCT 71	SLC-4W	TITAN IIIB/AGENA-D	--	GAMBIT-3 MSN 4333 (KH-8)
1115	16 FEB 72	SLC-4W	TITAN IIIB/AGENA-D	--	
1118	17 MAR 72	SLC-4W	TITAN IIIB/AGENA-D	--	GAMBIT-3 MSN 4334 (KH-8)
1127	20 MAY 72	SLC-4W	TITAN IIIB/AGENA-D	--	GAMBIT-3 MSN 4335 (KH-8)
1144	1 SEP 72	SLC-4W	TITAN IIIB/AGENA-D	--	GAMBIT-3 MSN 4336 (KH-8)
1170	21 DEC 72	SLC-4W	TITAN IIIB/AGENA-D	--	GAMBIT-3 MSN 4337 (KH-8)
1182	16 MAY 73	SLC-4W	TITAN IIIB/AGENA-D	--	GAMBIT-3 MSN 4338 (KH-8)
1185	26 JUN 73	SLC-4W	TITAN IIIB/AGENA-D	--	GAMBIT-3 MSN 4339 (KH-8)
1195	21 AUG 73	SLC-4W	TITAN IIIB/AGENA-D	--	
1203	27 SEP 73	SLC-4W	TITAN IIIB/AGENA-D	--	GAMBIT-3 MSN 4340 (KH-8)
1220	13 FEB 74	SLC-4W	TITAN IIIB/AGENA-D	--	GAMBIT-3 MSN 4341 (KH-8)
1239	6 JUN 74	SLC-4W	TITAN IIIB/AGENA-D	--	GAMBIT-3 MSN 4342 (KH-8)
1248	14 AUG 74	SLC-4W	TITAN IIIB/AGENA-D	--	GAMBIT-3 MSN 4343 (KH-8)
1273	9 MAR 75	SLC-4W	TITAN IIIB/AGENA-D	--	
1278	18 APR 75	SLC-4W	TITAN IIIB/AGENA-D	--	GAMBIT-3 MSN 4344 (KH-8)
1304	9 OCT 75	SLC-4W	TITAN IIIB/AGENA-D	--	GAMBIT-3 MSN 4345 (KH-8)
1324	22 MAR 76	SLC-4W	TITAN IIIB/AGENA-D	--	GAMBIT-3 MSN 4346 (KH-8)
1329	2 JUN 76	SLC-4W	TITAN IIIB/AGENA-D	--	
1340	6 AUG 76	SLC-4W	TITAN IIIB/AGENA-D	--	
1345	15 SEP 76	SLC-4W	TITAN IIIB/AGENA-D	--	GAMBIT-3 MSN 4347 (KH-8)
1361	13 MAR 77	SLC-4W	TITAN IIIB/AGENA-D	--	GAMBIT-3 MSN 4348 (KH-8)
1379	23 SEP 77	SLC-4W	TITAN IIIB/AGENA-D	--	GAMBIT-3 MSN 4349 (KH-8)
1391	24 FEB 78	SLC-4W	TITAN IIIB/AGENA-D	--	
1409	4 AUG 78	SLC-4W	TITAN IIIB/AGENA-D	--	
1430	28 MAY 79	SLC-4W	TITAN IIIB/AGENA-D	--	GAMBIT-3 MSN 4350 (KH-8)
1470	13 DEC 80	SLC-4W	TITAN IIIB/AGENA-D	--	
1477	28 FEB 81	SLC-4W	TITAN IIIB/AGENA-D	--	GAMBIT-3 MSN 4351 (KH-8)
1481	24 APR 81	SLC-4W	TITAN IIIB/AGENA-D	--	
1494	21 JAN 82	SLC-4W	TITAN IIIB/AGENA-D	--	GAMBIT-3 MSN 4352 (KH-8)
1519	15 APR 83	SLC-4W	TITAN IIIB/AGENA-D	--	GAMBIT-3 MSN 4353 (KH-8)
1530	31 JUL 83	SLC-4W	TITAN IIIB/AGENA-D	--	
1547	17 APR 84	SLC-4W	TITAN IIIB/AGENA-D	--	GAMBIT-3 MSN 4354 (KH-8)
1552	28 AUG 84	SLC-4W	TITAN IIIB/AGENA-D	--	
1564	7 FEB 85	SLC-4W	TITAN IIIB/AGENA-D	--	
1599	11 FEB 87	SLC-4W	TITAN IIIB/AGENA-D	--	

TITAN IIID

The Titan IIID was a two-stage, liquid-fueled, heavy-lift space launch booster derived from the Titan II ICBM core with thicker skin and solid-rocket motor fittings. The Titan III was one of the first rockets developed from the start as a space launch vehicle for the Department of Defense. Prior to this, space boosters were modified intermediate-range (e.g., Thor) or intercontinental-range (e.g., Atlas) missiles combined with orbital upper stages. As a heavy-lift variant of the Titan rocket family, the airframe included solid propellant strap-on boosters but lacked the transitional stage found on other Titan versions.[447] The rocket had a Titan II core, plus two two-segment solid-fuel boosters with a payload lift capacity of 11,000 lbs. Modified avionics and core engines allowed for an air start.

The Titan III system was a mixture of technology and hardware developed both for liquid- and solid-fuel ICBMs.[448] The core of the rocket was essentially a ruggedized Titan II airframe modified to accept a new third stage, guidance module, and payload. The core booster's first stage provided 430,000 lbs. of thrust, while the second stage engine gave approximately 100,000 lbs. of thrust. Two large (120-inch-diameter), strap-on, solid-rocket motors were attached to the core to produce over 1 million lbs. of total thrust.

At the start of the program, very little technology on the Titan III was new or revolutionary. This was not a slight to the rocket's design but fulfilled a requirement calling for full use of off-the-shelf (existing) technology.

HEXAGON (KH-9)

The primary "passenger" for the Titan IIID was the National Reconnaissance Office's KH-9 HEXAGON satellite. An interesting design philosophy behind Titan III stated that the rocket would not be altered to fit the payload.[449] Rather, the payload would be designed to match the booster. This fell in lockstep with previous boosters that lifted national-security payloads, such as CORONA and GAMBIT, with the cameras placed within the Agena upper-stage "space truck." As early as 1966, the decision to use a Titan IIIC or Titan IIID had not been determined.[450] It was determined that a payload weight of around 12,000 lbs. was needed, regardless of the booster selected. Excess lift capacity aboard Titan III was discovered during the GAMBIT-3 launches, even with the heavier reentry capsules and additional film load. The HEXAGON satellite was massive but fit the Titan III like a glove:

> The HEXAGON spacecraft itself was as big as a locomotive and 16.7 meters (55 feet) long, and weighed several metric tons. It contained two giant rotating optical-bar tubes, each with a 91 cm mirror and a camera. There were also four satellite recovery vehicles (SRVs) for returning film to earth and a 208,000 ft. film supply.[451]

An analogy for HEXAGON would be a Greyhound bus–sized satellite carrying over 40 miles of film aboard, taking pictures of around 2 to 3 ft. resolution from a distance of 110 miles away from its target. Comparing HEXAGON's film load to earlier satellites is mind-boggling. The first successful CORONA mission had 20 lbs. of film, later upped to 40 lbs. Early GAMBIT flights held 45 lbs. of film. HEXAGON carried 930 lbs. of film distributed between four primary reentry vehicles and one for the mapping camera.

The first Titan IIID launch took place on 15 June 1971 from SLC-4E.[452] The rocket carried a KH-9 HEXAGON satellite (Mission 1201) into low-earth orbit. The intelligence photographs obtained from the first HEXAGON mission

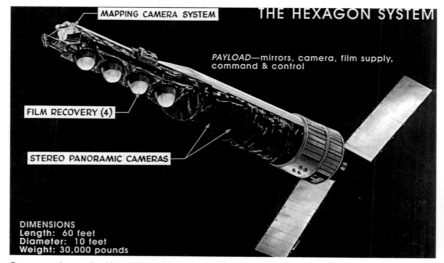

Cutaway shows the KH-9 HEXAGON surveillance satellite, colloquially known as "Big Bird." The KH-9 held four main film return capsules and one capsule for the mapping-camera system. *Courtesy of the National Reconnaissance Office*

An unidentified Titan IIID stands ready to launch its KH-9 HEXAGON payload into orbit. *Courtesy of the United States Air Force*

The last gantry at Space Launch Complex 4 was demolished in 2014 to make way for newer launch facilities. *Courtesy of the United States Air Force*

even impressed photo interpreters who had dealt with CORONA and GAMBIT photography:

My God, we never dreamed there would be this much, this good! We'll have to revamp our entire operation to handle the stuff.[453]

Titan IIIDs would carry the next sixteen HEXAGON missions through 11 May 1982. HEXAGON and GAMBIT —with differing film loads, cameras, and life spans—would be used in a "Shooter/Spotter" paring. HEXAGON would provide broad area reconnaissance, and GAMBIT would get high-resolution photography of targets of interest.

KH-11 KENNEN

On 19 December 1976 the first near-real-time electro-optical satellite was launched from SLC-4E aboard a Titan IIID.[454] The satellite, known as the KH-11 KENNEN, downlinked its images to ground stations via relay satellites, as stated inside an online brochure from the National Reconnaissance Office.[455]

The other launches from SLC-4E aboard the Titan IIID have not been characterized in print, online, or in photographs. The Titan IIID was flown twenty-two times with a 100 percent success rate, with all flights originating at Vandenberg.

TITAN IIID Launches[456]

SEQUENCE	DATE	SITE	VEHICLE	CODENAME	NOTES
1062	15 JUN 71	SLC-4E	TITAN IIID	--	HEXAGON MSN 1201
1110	20 JAN 72	SLC-4E	TITAN IIID	--	HEXAGON MSN 1202
1137	7 JUL 72	SLC-4E	TITAN IIID	--	HEXAGON MSN 1203
1150	10 OCT 72	SLC-4E	TITAN IIID	--	HEXAGON MSN 1204
1176	9 MAR 73	SLC-4E	TITAN IIID	--	HEXAGON MSN 1205
1188	13 JUL 73	SLC-4E	TITAN IIID	--	HEXAGON MSN 1206
1210	10 NOV 73	SLC-4E	TITAN IIID	--	HEXAGON MSN 1207
1231	10 APR 74	SLC-4E	TITAN IIID	--	HEXAGON MSN 1208
1262	29 OCT 74	SLC-4E	TITAN IIID	--	HEXAGON MSN 1209
1285	8 JUN 75	SLC-4E	TITAN IIID	--	HEXAGON MSN 1210
1308	4 DEC 75	SLC-4E	TITAN IIID	--	HEXAGON MSN 1211
1336	8 JUL 76	SLC-4E	TITAN IIID	--	HEXAGON MSN 1212
1354	19 DEC 76	SLC-4E	TITAN IIID	--	FIRST KH-11 KENNEN SATELLITE LAUNCH[457]
1370	27 JUN 77	SLC-4E	TITAN IIID	--	HEXAGON MSN 1213
1394	16 MAR 78	SLC-4E	TITAN IIID	--	HEXAGON MSN 1214
1402	14 JUN 78	SLC-4E	TITAN IIID	--	
1426	16 MAR 79	SLC-4E	TITAN IIID	--	HEXAGON MSN 1215
1448	6 FEB 80	SLC-4E	TITAN IIID	--	
1459	18 JUN 80	SLC-4E	TITAN IIID	--	HEXAGON MSN 1216
1487	3 SEP 81	SLC-4E	TITAN IIID	--	
1498	11 MAY 82	SLC-4E	TITAN IIID	--	HEXAGON MSN 1217
1508	17 NOV 82	SLC-4E	TITAN IIID	--	

TITAN 34D

The Titan 34D was a two-stage, liquid-fueled, heavy-lift space launch booster using a modified Titan III core. As a heavy-lift variant of the Titan rocket family, the airframe included solid propellant strap-on boosters but lacked the transitional stage found on other Titan versions.[458] The rocket had a Titan II core, plus two five-segment, solid-rocket motors providing a payload lift capacity of 32,000 lbs.

The rocket was designed as a heavy-lift follow-on to the Titan IIID series, but it did not achieve the level of success its predecessor did. Upgrades to the two solid-rocket motors provided more lift yet may have also contributed to problems involved in at least two explosions of the Titan 34D.[459]

The advent of the space shuttle in the 1980s, and the bureaucratic wrangling among NASA, the Air Force, and the NRO, forced successive presidential administrations to lay down the law.

President Ronald Reagan's administration released National Security Decision Directive 8, titled *Space Transportation System*, on 13 November 1981:

> The United States will continue to develop the STS through the National Aeronautics and Space Administration in cooperation with the Department of Defense to service all authorized space users. The STS will be the primary space launch system for both United States military and civil government missions. The transition to the Shuttle should occur as expeditiously as practical.[460]

While the space shuttle promised routine access to space with lower launch costs, some payloads were built to fit for specific launch vehicles—HEXAGON being one example. While NRO documents specifically state "no transition to the Shuttle was planned," the shuttle cargo bay was specifically designed to fit a satellite sized with HEXAGON's dimensions.[461] With shuttle schedule slips continuing, the NRO planned a launch backup capability with the Titan-34D on a "case-by-case basis."[462] Just as satellites were built to fit their launch vehicles, shuttle payloads were modified for launch from the cargo bay, and modifications for other launch vehicles were expensive and time consuming.

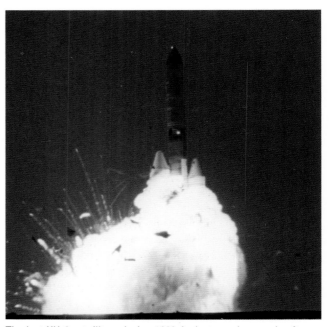

The last KH-9 satellite, mission 1220, is destroyed seconds after launch on 18 April 1986. This failure, so soon after the *Challenger* disaster, helped establish a space launch moratorium for the US government that would last almost two years. *Courtesy of the United States Air Force*

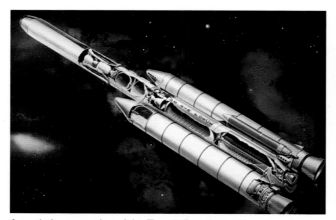

An artist's conception of the Titan 34D rocket, with cutaway showing the stage 1 and stage 2 internal structures, as well as the upper stage. While the picturesque space background is eye-catching, portions of a Titan 34D, such as the two solid-rocket motors, would have been jettisoned before it entered the realm of space. *Courtesy of the United States Air Force*

Overhead images of Space Launch Complex 4 show the debris field from the destroyed Titan 34D that carried the final KH-9 satellite. *Courtesy of the United States Air Force*

HEXAGON (KH-9)

While transition for national-security payloads to the shuttle continued, already manifested launches lifted off inside Titan 34D rockets. Seven launches of the Titan 34D took place at Vandenberg. The first Titan 34D failure occurred on 28 August 1985 while carrying an unidentified payload. The second Titan 34D failure would occur less than a year later.[463] The last three HEXAGON satellites rode aboard Titan 34Ds. Missions 1218 and 1219 successfully reached orbit, providing photographs to the intelligence community. The final flight on 18 April 1986, carrying HEXAGON Mission 1220, exploded seconds after leaving the launchpad:

> The destructive blast was the second straight failure of a Titan 34-D, considered the backbone of the military space program's ability to boost heavy payloads into orbit. [Seventy-four] people at the base, including nine civilians and two deputy sheriffs, were

treated for skin and eye irritations. Three military personnel were hospitalized, and one was held overnight for possible eye burns.[464]

The American manned space program suffered its worst disaster on 28 January 1986 with the loss of the shuttle *Challenger* and all seven crew members aboard. The loss of the Titan 34D on 18 April, in conjunction with the year's previous Titan 34D failure, caused a national stand-down on space launches, in effect "freezing" the National Reconnaissance Program to satellites already on orbit.

The final Titan 34D boosters were launched in 1987 and 1988, with unidentified payloads. After the final Titan 34D launch, the Air Force transitioned to its next heavy-lift space launch vehicle, the Titan 34D7,[465] renamed Titan IV.

TITAN 34D Launches[466]

SEQUENCE	DATE	SITE	VEHICLE	CODENAME	NOTES
1525	20 JUN 83	SLC-4E	TITAN 34D	--	HEXAGON MSN 1218
1551	25 JUN 84	SLC-4E	TITAN 34D	--	HEXAGON MSN 1219
1560	4 DEC 84	SLC-4E	TITAN 34D	--	
1574	28 AUG 85	SLC-4E	TITAN 34D	--	LAUNCH FAILURE
1585	18 APR 86	SLC-4E	TITAN 34D	--	HEXAGON MSN 1220; SPECTACULAR LAUNCH FAILURE
1612	26 OCT 87	SLC-4E	TITAN 34D	--	
1628	6 NOV 88	SLC-4E	TITAN 34D	--	

TITAN IV

The Titan IV was a two-stage, liquid-fueled, heavy-lift space launch booster derived from the Titan 34D space launch vehicle airframe. The Titan IV program originally started as the Complementary Expendable Launch Vehicle under the designation "Titan 34D7."[467] The Air Force (and NRO) believed that the space shuttle's schedule slips would prevent timely launches of critical space systems requiring a heavy-lift booster. While additional Titan 34D purchases eased the requirement, these were not long-term solutions. The program was started in the mid-1980s but was kept on minimal funding until a contract was finally awarded to Martin Marietta in February 1985 for ten Titan IVs.[468]

After the *Challenger* disaster and losses of the Titan 34Ds in 1985 and 1986, the Department of Defense moved to a force of mixed launch capabilities—medium and heavy for LEO/HEO/GEO orbits—to spread the risk over many systems. The space shuttle was directed away from lifting national-security payloads (previously configured satellites that required the shuttle were launched until 1992), and Titan IV became the primary heavy-lift expendable launch vehicle until the advent of the Evolved Expendable Launch Vehicle program in the first decade of the twenty-first century.

The Titan IV used a lengthened Titan 34D first and second stage with two seven-segment solid-rocket motors. The first stage used two Aerojet LR87-AJ-11A engines, using two independently operated sets of turbopump and thrust chambers mounted on a common frame. The second stage motor was a gimbaled Aerojet LR91-AJ-11A engine. The thrust chamber was gimbaled to provide pitch/yaw control.

Upper-stage configuration varied from no upper stage, to the Boeing Inertial Upper Stage, to the Centaur. Two variants of the Titan IV existed. The Titan IVA used steel-cased solid-rocket motors, while the Titan IVB used composite-cased solid-rocket motors, providing more thrust with less weight.

A Titan IV launch began with the ignition of the solid-rocket motors (stage zero). Around 130 seconds after ignition of the solid-rocket motors, the stage 1 engine ignited. At this point the solid-rocket motors were exhausted and jettisoned. One hundred seconds later the payload fairing was ejected and the stage 1 motors were shut down. Around one minute later, the stage 1 was jettisoned and the stage 2 motors ignited until exhaustion. After stage 2 cutoff, the stage was jettisoned and the payload flew with (or without) the upper stage to its intended orbit.

All Titan IV launches at Vandenberg took place from SLC-4E. The payloads for all flights have not been officially

A unidentified Titan IV lifts off from Vandenberg's SLC-4E. The Titan IV could place a large payload into earth orbit, comparable to the space shuttle's lift capacity.

Looking upward at a Titan IV, the two solid-fuel rocket boosters sit on pedestals, allowing the UA1207 first-stage rocket motor to hang between. *Courtesy of the United States Air Force*

The final Titan IVB launch from Vandenberg, and last launch in the Titan family, took place on 19 October 2005. The payload was identified only as NRO launch number 20 (NROL-20). *Courtesy of the United States Air Force*

identified, but the 20 December 1996 flight was the first time the US government had, in advance, acknowledged the launch of a reconnaissance satellite.[469]

The final Titan IV launch took place on 19 October 2005, ending the legacy of the Titan family of missiles and space launch vehicles.

TITAN IV Launches[470]

SEQUENCE	DATE	SITE	VEHICLE	CODENAME	NOTES
1656	8 MAR 91	SLC-4E	TITAN IV	--	TITAN IVA
1668	7 NOV 91	SLC-4E	TITAN IV	--	TITAN IVA
1683	28 NOV 92	SLC-4E	TITAN IV	--	TITAN IVA
1690	2 AUG 93	SLC-4E	TITAN IV	--	TITAN IVA; LAUNCH FAILURE
1718	5 DEC 95	SLC-4E	TITAN IV	--	TITAN IVA
1724	12 MAY 96	SLC-4E	TITAN IV	--	TITAN IVA
1734	20 DEC 96	SLC-4E	TITAN IV	--	NROL-2; TITAN IVA
1750	23 OCT 97	SLC-4E	TITAN IV	--	NROL-3; TITAN IVA
1779	22 MAY 99	SLC-4E	TITAN IV	--	NROL-9; FIRST TITAN IVB LAUNCH
1800	17 AUG 00	SLC-4E	TITAN IV	--	NROL-11; TITAN IVB
1811	4 OCT 01	SLC-4E	TITAN IV	--	NROL-14; TITAN IVB
1858	19 OCT 05	SLC-4E	TITAN IV	--	NROL-20; LAST TITAN IVB LAUNCH

UTE TOMAHAWK

The Ute Tomahawk was a two-stage, solid-fuel sounding rocket developed by Thiokol Chemical Corporation for Sandia National Laboratory in the 1960s. While the TE-416 Tomahawk was used in a single-stage configuration, adding the TU-715 Ute booster as a first stage provided a robust small-payload launch capability for NASA and the Air Force.[471]

As stated in a Thiokol Chemical Corporation study, the Ute-Tomahawk rocket family

provide[s] proven transportation to carry scientific payloads for investigation of the upper atmosphere.

In addition to the competitive cost of these systems, they offer advantages including: a wide range of payload-weight/apogee altitude performance, capability for operations over a wide range of temperatures and in a variety of environments, complete interchangeability of flight hardware, and relative ease in field handling, assembly, and launch.[472]

One launch of the Ute Tomahawk booster combination took place at Vandenberg. On 10 December 1975, a Ute Tomahawk was launched from PLC-C carrying a payload called ESCAPE-II for Air Force Systems Command.[473] The payload reached an altitude of 101 miles.

UTE TOMAHAWK Launches[474]

SEQUENCE	DATE	SITE	VEHICLE	CODENAME	NOTES
1311	10 DEC 75	PLC-C	UTE TOMAHAWK	--	ONLY FLIGHT OF UTE TOMAHAWK

CHAPTER 3:
Select Chronology of Vandenberg Air Force Base

Note: This chronology of activities at Vandenberg is neither complete nor exhaustive. The base housed many military units over the span of sixty years as an Air Force base and conducted over 1,900 launches. That number does not include the Army units at Camp Cooke during the World War II and Korean War years. The events were taken directly from the official chronologies of Vandenberg's annual history from 1958 through 2014.[1]

- **5 October 1941:** United States Army activated Camp Cooke, California. Used during World War II as an armored and infantry training site.
- **1 February 1946:** Camp Cooke placed on inactive status.
- **7 August 1950:** Camp Cooke reactivated and used during the Korean War as an armored and infantry training site.
- **1 February 1953:** Camp Cooke again inactivated.
- **16 November 1956:** The secretary of defense directed the United States Army to transfer 64,000 acres of Camp

Cooke's 86,000 acres to the Air Force to establish an ICBM/IRBM operational training site at Camp Cooke, California.

- **1 January 1957:** The Air Force obtained a use permit for its new facility at Camp Cooke (formally transferred by the Army effective 21 June 1957).
- **15 February 1957:** The 6591st Support Squadron (Air Force) organized at Camp Cooke and assigned to Air Research and Development Command (ARDC).
- **15 April 1957:** ARDC, later renamed Air Force Systems Command (AFSC), activated Headquarters, 1st Missile Division, at Los Angeles, California, and Headquarters, 392d Air Base Group, at Camp Cooke while inactivating the 6591st Support Squadron.
- **23 April 1957:** The Air Force garrison at Camp Cooke was established by ARDC on the northern 64,047 acres, equaling approximately 100 square miles.
- **9 May 1957:** New facility construction and major building renovation starts at Camp Cooke.
- **7 June 1957:** The Air Force portion of Camp Cooke is renamed Cooke Air Force Base.
- **1 July 1957:** Air Research and Development Command activated the 704th Strategic Missile Wing (Atlas) at Cooke AFB.
- **16 July 1957:** Headquarters 1st Missile Division relocated from Los Angeles to Cooke AFB.
- **1 August 1957:** 1st Missile Division assumed operational control of the 704th Strategic Missile Wing.
- **7 December 1957:** The secretary of defense directed the transfer of South Camp Cooke (almost 20,000 acres) from the Army to the Navy for use in a projected national missile range on the West Coast.
- **1 January 1958:** Cooke AFB (with major operational and training units) transferred from Air Research and Development Command to Strategic Air Command. Launch facility construction, as well as research and development activities at Cooke AFB, was the responsibility of the Air Force Ballistic Missile Division (with headquarters at Inglewood, California).
- **14 February 1958:** 19,861 acres of South Camp Cooke transferred from the Army to the Navy on an interim permit basis (actual transfer on 27 May).
- **5 March 1958:** The Joint Navy–Air Force (Burke-White) Agreement was completed. This agreement defined the areas of responsibility between the projected Pacific Missile Range and Cooke Air Force Base.
- **4 April 1958:** Establishment of the US Naval Missile Facility at Point Arguello, the southern portion of former Camp Cooke (facility formally commissioned on 10 May).
- **16 June 1958:** Formal establishment of the Navy's Pacific Missile Range (with its headquarters at Point Mugu and its major launch head at Point Arguello).
- **31 July 1958:** A memorandum of agreement establishing a field office at Cooke AFB by the Air Force Ballistic

Missile Division (ARDC) was signed with the 1st Missile Division to oversee the design and buildup of missile installations, and to flight test launch vehicles to be turned over to the Strategic Air Command for operational deployment.

- **4 October 1958:** Cooke AFB redesignated Vandenberg AFB, honoring the late Gen. Hoyt S. Vandenberg, the Air Force's second chief of staff.
- **16 December 1958:** First missile launch from Vandenberg AFB—a Thor IRBM. The mission was a success.
- **28 February 1959:** World's first polar-orbiting satellite (Discoverer 1) launched on first Thor/Agena booster/upper-stage combination.
- **9 September 1959:** First West Coast launch of an Atlas (12D). Afterward, Gen. Thomas S. Power, commander in chief of Strategic Air Command, declared the Atlas system to be operational.
- **1 July 1960:** Major expansion of Pacific Missile Range with incorporation of Eniwetok and Kwajalein Atolls in the Marshall Islands by the United States Navy for instrumentation complexes (in support of Air Force launches from Vandenberg AFB).
- **10 August 1960:** A Thor/Agena-A launched from Vandenberg AFB placed Discoverer XIII into orbit. On 11 August, the data capsule was ejected and recovered by Pacific Missile Range ship *Longview*. This marked the first successful recovery of a man-made object ejected from an orbiting satellite.
- **11 October 1960:** Initial West Coast launch of an Atlas/Agena space booster.
- **20 October 1960:** Air Force Ballistic Missile Division Field Office at Vandenberg AFB replaced by the 6565th Test Wing (Ballistic Missiles and Space Systems).
- **1 December 1960:** 6565th Test Wing (Ballistic Missiles and Space Systems) renamed the 6565th Test Wing (Development).
- **3 December 1960:** A Titan missile exploded while being lowered into the OSTF.
- **20 December 1960:** 704th Instrumentation Squadron was deactivated.
- **21 January 1961:** The division formally accepted a T-600 Trainer for the Atlas-E program.
- **30 January 1961:** The first Atlas-E series academic and missile procedure training got underway.
- **2 February 1961:** Groundbreaking ceremonies were held to mark the beginning of Minuteman construction.
- **10 March 1961:** The first Atlas-E launch crew personnel from the 576th Strategic Missile Squadron graduated after completing their Phase I Operational Readiness Training.
- **1 April 1961:** 6565th Test Wing (Development) assigned to Space Systems Division (renamed Space and Missile Systems Organization on 1 July 1967) in Los Angeles, California.

- **3 May 1961:** The first Titan in-silo launch was successfully completed at the silo launch test facility (SLTF).
- **19 May 1961:** The Atlas-D ORT program was completed with graduation of Class #10 from the 566th Strategic Missile Squadron.
- **7 June 1961:** An Atlas-E missile exploded during the first attempt to launch an "E" missile.
- **14 June 1961:** The 3901st Strategic Standardization Squadron, later renamed the Strategic Missile Evaluation Squadron, was activated to standardize operational procedures at all ICBM bases.
- **21 June 1961:** The first Atlas-F missile arrived at Vandenberg.
- **21 July 1961:** 1st Missile Division (SAC) at Vandenberg renamed the 1st Strategic Aerospace Division.
- **25 August 1961:** Government officials dedicated the 50,000th Capehart house in the US at Vandenberg. The house stood at 1119 Timberlane.
- **23 September 1961:** The first launch from Titan silo-lift facilities. One hundredth launch from Vandenberg/Point Arguello.
- **4 October 1961:** Vice President Lyndon B. Johnson visited Vandenberg AFB for an orientation and tour of the base and its mission.
- **18 October 1961:** The 392d Strategic Missile Wing is activated at Vandenberg.
- **1 November 1961:** 6565th Test Wing (Development) renamed the 6595th Aerospace Test Wing.
- **1 November 1961:** The first Minuteman ICBM to be delivered to Vandenberg—an inert training missile—arrived.
- **20 December 1961:** The 392d Strategic Missile Wing was discontinued; the 4392d Aerospace Support Wing was renamed the 4392d Aerospace Support Group.
- **9 January 1962:** Initial instruction of Atlas-F launch crews begins.
- **12 February 1962:** Titan I hardware operational readiness training began, initially training launch crews and maintenance personnel from Lowry AFB, Colorado.
- **19 February 1962:** Atlas-F hardware ORT began, initially training maintenance teams from Schilling AFB, Kansas.
- **9 March 1962:** ORT of the original force of Atlas-E crews completed.
- **23 March 1962:** President John F. Kennedy toured Atlas-D, Titan I, and Minuteman facilities and witnessed the launch of Atlas 134D ("CURRY COMB I").
- **26 April 1962:** First West Coast launch of a Scout space booster.
- **15 June 1962:** The 392d MTS received the USAF Missile Safety Award for 1961.
- **18 June 1962:** The last Thor IRBM combat training launch took place ("BLAZING CINDERS").
- **26 June 1962:** First launch of an Army Nike-Zeus from Kwajalein against an Atlas from Vandenberg AFB.
- **26 June 1962:** The base's first Titan II (an inert testing device) arrived.
- **19 July 1962:** Atlas 13D boosted a target vehicle that was intercepted by an Army Nike-Zeus rocket off Kwajalein Atoll.
- **1 August 1962:** First launch of an Atlas-F ICBM.
- **28 September 1962:** Initial launch of a Minuteman I.
- **28 September 1962:** First international satellite (Canada's Alouette) launched aboard a Thor/Agena booster.
- **1 February 1963:** The 392d MTS was inactivated.
- **16 February 1963:** First West Coast launch of a Titan II ICBM from an underground silo.
- **28 February 1963:** First use of a Thrust-Augmented-Thor/Agena space booster.
- **28 September 1963:** Initial launch of Thor/Able-Star.
- **4 November 1963:** First launch in the Advanced Ballistic Reentry System (ABRES) program. Vehicle used for this mission was an Atlas-D.
- **16 November 1963:** To improve management and operation of DoD Ranges and Flight Test Facilities, the secretary of defense directed several changes, including establishment within the Air Force of a central authority to coordinate planning of ICBM and space vehicle launching and tracking, and transfer to the Air Force major portions of the Navy's Pacific Missile Range, including its launching base at Point Arguello, California.
- **3 December 1963:** Air Staff decision to keep the Strategic Air Command as host organization over the combined Point Arguello / Vandenberg AFB (effective 1 July 1964), with Air Force Systems Command responsible for all matters pertaining to management and operation of range support facilities and services.
- **25 January 1964:** The National Aeronautics and Space Administration's ECHO II passive communications satellite, placed in a near-polar orbit by a Thor/Agena-B launched from Vandenberg AFB, included among its tests one-way transmissions from England to Russia. First cooperative space program between Russia and the United States.
- **15 May 1964:** Activation of the Air Force Western Test Range at Vandenberg AFB.
- **1 July 1964:** The US Navy's Point Arguello facility was transferred from the Navy to the Air Force, adding approximately 20,000 acres to Vandenberg AFB.
- **18 January 1965:** Initial West Coast launch of a Thor/Altair.
- **1 February 1965:** Five months ahead of the original schedule, Air Force Western Test Range (AFWTR) assumed responsibilities for intercontinental ballistic missile and space vehicle support functions from the Navy's Pacific Missile Range. Fixed and mobile facilities transferred included the former PMR instrumentation at the expanded Vandenberg complex (Point Arguello), Pillar Point (near San Francisco), South Point and Kokee

Park (Hawaii), Midway and Wake Islands, Canton Island, Eniwetok Atoll (including Bikini Atoll) in the Marshall Islands, and six range instrumentation ships (*Range Tracker, Longview, Richfield, Sunnyvale, Watertown,* and *Huntsville*).

- **1 March 1965:** Atlas programs at Vandenberg transferred from SAC to Air Force Systems Command.
- **5 March 1965:** Last launch of a Titan I (first launch on 3 May 1961).
- **3 April 1965:** The Atomic Energy Commission's Snapshot spacecraft carrying the Snap-10A nuclear reactor successfully launched by an Atlas/Agena. The onboard reactor provided electrical power for a 2.2 lb. ion engine, marking the first attempt to test a reactor-ion system in orbit.
- **1 June 1965:** Transfer of Kokee Park (Hawaii) Tracking Station management from AFWTR to NASA.
- **13 August 1965:** Last launch of Thor/Able-Star (first launch on 28 September 1963).
- **18 August 1965:** First launch of a Minuteman II. Five hundredth missile launched from Vandenberg / Point Arguello.
- **24 August 1965:** One hundredth launch of a Minuteman ICBM since 1962.
- **25 August 1965:** DoD revealed that the newly authorized Manned Orbiting Laboratory (MOL) program (announced by the president the same day) would be launched both from the Air Force Eastern and Western Test Ranges.
- **28 November 1965:** Last Thor/Agena launch (first mission on 28 February 1959).
- **1 March 1966:** Vandenberg AFB acquired the Sudden Ranch area south of the base and added almost 15,000 acres to the installation, increasing the installation's size to its current 99,090 acres.
- **12 March 1966:** Start of construction (site preparation) for Space Launch Complex 6 facilities at the former Sudden Ranch property.
- **30 March 1966:** Final mission of the Thor/Altair (first launch on 18 January 1965).
- **29 July 1966:** First launch of a Titan IIIB / Agena space booster carrying the first Gambit-3 (Mission 4301).
- **9 August 1966:** Initial launch of a Long Tank Thor / Agena-D (Thorad/Agena-D) space booster.
- **25 August 1966:** AFWTR supported the Navy's first launch of a BOMARC-A target missile.
- **15 September 1966:** First launch of a Thor/Burner II.
- **2 October 1966:** First Thor/Delta launch at Vandenberg AFB.
- **1 December 1966:** Initial launch of Atlas/Prime.
- **13 December 1966:** First Minuteman launch (WATER TEST) with Emergency Rocket Communication System payload.
- **29 December 1966:** Liftoff of a Thrust-Augmented-Thor/Agena-D space booster combination marked the 123rd

major launch operation from Vandenberg AFB since January. This record still stands today.

- **11 January 1967:** First and only launch of a Castor/Scramjet.
- **21 February 1967:** Vice President Hubert Humphrey, accompanied by his wife and a small entourage, viewed a Minuteman I ripple launch.
- **3 March 1967:** First Minuteman launch (BUSY LOBBY) with the Airborne Launch Control System, a modified EC-135 aircraft with two missile combat crew members aboard.
- **17 March 1967:** AFWTR assumed operational control of the range instrumentation ship *Vanguard.*
- **19 April 1967:** Last of three successful Atlas/Prime missions (first launch on 21 December 1966).
- **7 November 1967:** Final launch of an Atlas-D missile (first operational at Vandenberg on 9 September 1959).
- **17 January 1968:** Final launch of a Thrust-Augmented-Thor/Agena space booster from Vandenberg (first launch on 28 February 1963).
- **16 August 1968:** First of two Atlas/Burner II space launches.
- **11 April 1969:** First Minuteman III flight test missile launched.
- **10 June 1969:** Department of Defense announced cancellation of the planned Manned Orbiting Laboratory (MOL) program from Space Launch Complex 6 at Vandenberg AFB.
- **1 October 1969:** Eniwetok Atoll (Marshall Islands) placed on caretaker status.
- **21 November 1969:** Bikini Atoll (Marshall Islands) turned over to UN Trust Territory of the Pacific Islands.
- **1 April 1970:** Headquarters Space and Missile Test Center (SAMTEC) activated at Vandenberg AFB with assignment to Air Force Systems Command.
- **14 September 1970:** Minuteman II (GLORY TRIP 67F) was the one hundredth missile launched from Vandenberg.
- **8 June 1971:** Final launch of the Thor / Burner II (first launch on 15 September 1966).
- **15 June 1971:** Initial launch of a Titan IIID space booster.
- **14 October 1971:** The first of eight Thor / Burner IIA launches.
- **25 May 1972:** Last launch of a Thorad/Agena (first launch on 9 August 1966).
- **2 October 1972:** Last of two Atlas / Burner II space launches (first launch on 16 August 1968).
- **12 October 1974:** Final use of an Atlas booster in the Advanced Ballistic Reentry System (ABRES) program.
- **1 January 1975:** The USNS *Sunnyvale,* the last Air Force Western Test Range instrumentation ship, is transferred to the Maritime Administration.
- **23 May 1975:** First use of the Minuteman I booster—replacing the Atlas—for the ABRES program.

- **8 February 1976:** Final launch of a Thor / Burner IIA (first launch on 14 October 1971).
- **27 June 1976:** Last launch of a Titan II ICBM (first West Coast launch on 16 February 1963).
- **11 September 1976:** Initial launch of a Thor / Block 5D-1 from the West Coast.
- **26 October 1976:** Five hundredth launch of a Minuteman ICBM since 1962.
- **19 December 1976:** First launch of a near-real-time electro-optical reconnaissance satellite from SLC-4E aboard a Titan IIID.
- **29 December 1977:** South Vandenberg AFB brush fire consumed 9,040 acres and claimed the lives of the base commander, both fire chiefs, and, a few days later, a civilian bulldozer operator.
- **26 June 1978:** Final launch of an Atlas/Agena booster/upper-stage combination (first launch on 11 October 1960).
- **1 January 1979:** Demolition and construction work began at Space Launch Complex 6 in preparation for the space shuttle program.
- **1 October 1979:** Space and Missile Test Center (SAMTEC) renamed the Space and Missile Test Organization (SAMTO). At the same time, the Western Space and Missile Center (WSMC) was created and assigned to SAMTO.
- **14 July 1980:** Fifth and final launch of a Thor / Block 5D-1.
- **23 June 1981:** Final launch of an Atlas-F booster.
- **14 July 1982:** Last two launches of the Navy's BOMARC target missile program.
- **17 November 1982:** Final launch of a Titan IIID.
- **7 February 1983:** Six hundredth launch of a Minuteman ICBM since 1962.
- **9 February 1983:** Initial launch of an Atlas-H space booster.
- **1 May 1983:** All 1STRAD space units transferred to the newly established Air Force Space Command (AFSPC).
- **17 June 1983:** The first launch of a LGM-118A Peacekeeper missile.
- **20 June 1983:** First of seven Titan 34D launches from the West Coast.
- **6 November 1983:** Space shuttle orbiter *Discovery* arrived at Vandenberg for a series of fit checks at the orbiter-lifting frame.
- **16 November 1984:** Space shuttle test article *Enterprise* arrived at Vandenberg for a series of facility verification tests.
- **23 August 1985:** First Peacekeeper ICBM "cold launch" from an underground silo (LF-08). First eight launches conducted from an aboveground launch stand at test pad 01.
- **15 October 1985:** SLC-6, the site of future space shuttle operations, is declared operational.

- **22 October 1985:** First (and last) Vandenberg launch of a ground-launched cruise missile.
- **31 July 1986:** Secretary of the Air Force Edward C. Aldridge Jr. announced that the Vandenberg space shuttle program would be placed in operational caretaker status seven months after the space shuttle *Challenger* accident.
- **1 January 1987:** The 6595th Shuttle Test Group was inactivated.
- **1 February 1987:** A Peacekeeper ICBM became the 1,600th vehicle launched from VAFB since the first launch in 1958.
- **11 February 1987:** Last launch of a Titan IIIB / Agena.
- **20 February 1987:** SLC-6 moved into minimum caretaker status.
- **1 March 1987:** 4315 CCTS activated the first Peacekeeper Missile Procedures Trainer for instruction.
- **1 April 1987:** First Minuteman III launched from recently converted LF-06.
- **15 May 1987:** Last launch of an Atlas-H space launch vehicle.
- **1 September 1987:** First Peacekeeper class graduated from the 4315 CCTS.
- **9 November 1987:** Last launch of a Minuteman II.
- **1 December 1987:** Dedication of SLC-10 as the Missile Heritage Center.
- **13 May 1988:** Air Force Secretary Edward C. Aldridge Jr. directed the Air Force to mothball or transfer space shuttle assets at Vandenberg to other organizations by 30 September 1989.
- **1 August 1988:** The 20,000th student, Capt. Bruce W. Young, graduated from the 4315 CCTS.
- **6 November 1988:** Final Titan 34D launch (first launch on 20 June 1983).
- **11 May 1989:** Initial launch of the Small ICBM.
- **20 September 1989:** Space Launch Complex 6 placed on mothball status.
- **1 October 1989:** Inactivation of HQ SAMTO at Vandenberg AFB.
- **5 October 1989:** First attempt by a commercial firm—American Rocket Company (AMROC)—to launch its SET-1/SMLV (Single Engine Test, 1/Single Module Launch Vehicle) failed on the pad at Vandenberg AFB.
- **26 December 1989:** Air Force Secretary Aldridge directed the Air Force to officially terminate the space shuttle program at Vandenberg. Estimated cost of the shuttle program at Vandenberg is $4 billion.
- **6 June 1990:** Completion of Peacekeeper Rail Garrison system facilities at Vandenberg AFB.
- **6 July 1990:** Lockheed Space Operations Company awarded an Air Force ground support system contract to modify Space Launch Complex 6 to a Titan IV / Centaur launch complex. Site work was scheduled to begin in late fiscal year (FY) 1992 and lead to an initial launch capability in FY 1996.

- **5 August 1990:** First flight of the air-launched Pegasus space booster employing a B-52 carrier aircraft over the Western Range. Aircraft was staged from Edwards AFB, California.
- **1 October 1990:** WSMC realigned from Air Force Systems Command to Air Force Space Command.
- **15 January 1991:** Host base responsibilities for Vandenberg AFB transferred from Strategic Air Command to Air Force Space Command. Additionally, the 4392d Aerospace Support Wing, the 392d Communications Group, and the base hospital were reassigned to WSMC as the new host organization.
- **8 March 1991:** First West Coast launch of a Titan IV space booster.
- **22 March 1991:** HQ USAF announced the termination of the planned Titan IV / Centaur program at SLC-6. The project was canceled because of "insufficient Titan IV launch requirements from the West Coast to support the construction of a new launchpad." The contract with Lockheed was closed out several months later.
- **18 April 1991:** Final launch of the MGM-134A Small ICBM missile (first launch on 11 May 1989).
- **23 July 1991:** Vice President Danforth Quayle visited Vandenberg AFB.
- **19 November 1991:** WSMC renamed the 30th Space Wing. Simultaneously, the word "Test" was removed from the geographic designation "Western Test Range."
- **20 July 1992:** In keeping with the objective wing structure of "one base, one boss," the ambiguous titles "installation commander" and "base commander" were reexamined. The latter term was abandoned in favor of installation commander, who was dual-hatted as the operational wing commander.
- **1 July 1993:** HQ AFSPC activated HQ 14th Air Force and assigned the unit to Vandenberg AFB. At the same time, Air Combat Command's 310th Training and Test Wing at Vandenberg was reassigned to the 30th Space Wing.
- **4 February 1994:** First (and only) flight of the ASTRID (Advanced Single-Stage Technology Rapid Insertion Demonstration) interceptor vehicle.
- **13 March 1994:** First launch of the Taurus space booster.
- **14 April 1994:** The previously designated Titan Division of the 6595th Aerospace Test Group and Detachment 9, Space and Missile Systems Center, Titan Division, was combined and transferred to the 30th Space Wing as the 4th Space Launch Squadron.
- **8 May 1994:** Final launch of the Scout booster (first launch on 26 April 1962).
- **16 March 1995:** The Western Commercial Space Center signed a twenty-five-year lease with the Air Force, retroactive to 6 March 1995, enabling the company to begin development of its spaceport facilities at South Vandenberg AFB.
- **24 March 1995:** Final launch of an Atlas-E booster (first launch on 7 June 1961).
- **3 April 1995:** The eighth air-launched Pegasus rocket carrying two commercial communications satellites and a scientific satellite was the first Pegasus mission to be fully integrated and flown from Vandenberg AFB. All previous Pegasus missions originated from Edwards AFB, California. This was also the first successful launch of a commercial satellite from Vandenberg.
- **15 August 1995:** First launch from SLC-6 was Lockheed's Launch Vehicle 1 (LLV-1), carrying the commercial communications satellite GEMstar.
- **26 October 1995:** A ribbon-cutting ceremony opening the new military family housing project was held at 114 Hillside Circle.
- **17 January 1996:** NASA awarded Spaceport Systems International (SSI) a contract to process two satellites at Vandenberg AFB, with an option for up to ten additional payloads. Total contract value for all twelve spacecraft was $9 million.
- **19 September 1996:** Vandenberg AFB became the site of the world's first commercial spaceport, following the award of the first such license to SSI by the Federal Aviation Administration. SSI would operate the site and planned to begin launching small- and medium-sized satellites in early 1998.
- **22 October 1996:** The 30th Space Wing hosted an activation ceremony for the newly constructed Space Launch Complex 3 East pad to be used for Atlas II space boosters. The $300 million facility replaced the original structure built in 1959.
- **21 May 1997:** Seven hundredth launch of Minuteman ICBM since 1962.
- **18 January 2000:** National Missile Defense Program test fails to intercept Vandenberg-launched Minuteman II ICBM target.
- **14 September 2000:** Retired general Bernard Schriever, chief architect of the Air Force missile program, celebrated his ninetieth birthday at Vandenberg.
- **28 September 2000:** Two Minuteman III ICBMs were launched under a short-time interval launch (STIL) two hours apart toward Kwajalein Atoll.
- **29 June 2001:** A 576 FLTS transporter-erector vehicle overturns on North Vandenberg, causing $2.3 million in damages.
- **14 July 2001:** Greenpeace activists "invade" Vandenberg, attempting to delay a Minuteman launch. Seventeen protesters were arrested.
- **11 September 2001:** Attacks on the World Trade Center and the Pentagon force base officials to declare Force Protection Condition DELTA, canceling two scheduled Minuteman III flights.

- **18 March 2003:** AFSPC cancels the space and missile competition GUARDIAN CHALLENGE due to the pending invasion of Iraq.
- **1 December 2003:** The California Spaceport at South Base is officially renamed Space Launch Complex 8 (SLC-8).
- **2 December 2003:** Last Atlas IIAS launch.
- **19 October 2005:** Last Titan IVB launch.
- **10 April 2006:** Missile Defense Agency facilities are dedicated as "Ronald Reagan Missile Defense Site."
- **27 June 2006:** First Delta IV launch.
- **12 September 2006:** US Strategic Command's Joint Functional Component Command for Space (JFCC SPACE) is activated at Vandenberg.
- **1 December 2006:** Boeing and Lockheed Martin launch companies merge to create the United Launch Alliance.
- **14 December 2006:** First NRO launch aboard a Delta II.
- **13 March 2008:** First Atlas V launch.
- **22 April 2010:** First Minotaur IV "Lite" booster launch.
- **15 June 2010:** Secretary of the Air Force Michael Donley visits, touring the Joint Space Operations Center (JSpOC).
- **3 December 2010:** X-37B space plane lands at Vandenberg. The spacecraft was launched from Cape Canaveral on 22 April 2010.
- **20 January 2011:** First launch of Delta IV Heavy.
- **1 January 2012:** Highly accurate measurements using GIS measurements officially state that Vandenberg encompasses 99,099 acres of land with 41 miles of coastline.
- **3 April 2012:** First Delta IV Medium launch.
- **16 June 2012:** X-37B space plane lands at Vandenberg.
- **21 September 2012:** Space shuttle *Endeavour* overflies Vandenberg atop its 747 carrier transport aircraft as a tribute to the space shuttle program at the base.
- **3 April 2014:** DMSP-19 successfully launched aboard an Atlas V Evolved Expendable Launch vehicle from Space Launch Complex 3.
- **13 August 2014:** WorldView-3 successfully launched aboard an Atlas V Evolved Expendable Launch Vehicle from Space Launch Complex 3.
- **7 October 2014:** Secretary of the Air Force Deborah Lee James visited Vandenberg Air Force Base, met with airmen, and observed the successful launch of an unarmed Minuteman III intercontinental ballistic missile.
- **17 October 2014:** Boeing X-37 Orbital Test Vehicle landed on the flight line and was successfully recovered by the 30th Space Wing and Boeing personnel.
- **12 December 2014:** NROL-35 successfully launched aboard an Atlas V EELV from SLC-3.

Complete List of Vandenberg Air Force Base Launches

NO.	DATE	COMPLEX	PAD	LAUNCH VEHICLE	UPPER STAGE	TYPE	CODENAME
1	16-DEC-58	75-1-1		THOR	--	IRBM	TUNE UP
2	28-FEB-59	75-3-4		THOR	AGENA-A	SLV	FLYING YANKEE
3	13-APR-59	75-3-4		THOR	AGENA-A	SLV	EARLY TIME
4	16-APR-59	75-2-8		THOR	--	IRBM	LIONS ROAR
5	3-JUN-59	75-3-4		THOR	AGENA-A	SLV	GOLD DUKE
6	16-JUN-59	75-2-7		THOR	--	IRBM	RIFLE SHOT
7	25-JUN-59	75-3-5		THOR	AGENA-A	SLV	LONG ROAD
8	1-JUL-59	PALC	A	NIKE	ASP	SOUNDING ROCKET	--
9	1-JUL-59	PALC	A	NIKE	ASP	SOUNDING ROCKET	--
10	14-JUL-59	PALC	A	NIKE	ASP	SOUNDING ROCKET	--
11	17-JUL-59	PALC	A	NIKE	ASP	SOUNDING ROCKET	--
12	24-JUL-59	PALC	A	NIKE	ASP	SOUNDING ROCKET	--
13	24-JUL-59	PALC	A	NIKE	ASP	SOUNDING ROCKET	--
14	1-AUG-59	PALC	A	NIKE	ASP	SOUNDING ROCKET	--
15	1-AUG-59	PALC	A	NIKE	ASP	SOUNDING ROCKET	--
16	1-AUG-59	PALC	A	NIKE	ASP	SOUNDING ROCKET	--
17	1-AUG-59	PALC	A	NIKE	ASP	SOUNDING ROCKET	--
18	1-AUG-59	PALC	A	NIKE	ASP	SOUNDING ROCKET	--
19	1-AUG-59	PALC	A	NIKE	ASP	SOUNDING ROCKET	--
20	3-AUG-59	75-1-1		THOR	--	IRBM	BEAN BALL
21	13-AUG-59	75-3-4		THOR	AGENA-A	SLV	FLY HIGH
22	14-AUG-59	75-2-6		THOR	--	IRBM	SHORT SKIP
23	19-AUG-59	75-3-5		THOR	AGENA-A	SLV	HURRY UP
24	9-SEP-59	576	A-2	ATLAS-D	(NONE)	ICBM	DESERT HEAT
25	17-SEP-59	75-1-2		THOR	--	IRBM	GREASE GUN
26	6-OCT-59	75-2-8		THOR	--	IRBM	FOREIGN TRAVEL
27	21-OCT-59	75-1-1		THOR	--	IRBM	STAND FAST
28	7-NOV-59	75-3-4		THOR	AGENA-A	SLV	CARGO NET
29	12-NOV-59	75-1-2		THOR	--	IRBM	BEACH BUGGY
30	20-NOV-59	75-3-5		THOR	AGENA-A	SLV	LIVID LADY
31	1-DEC-59	75-1-1		THOR	--	IRBM	HARD RIGHT
32	14-DEC-59	75-1-2		THOR	--	IRBM	TALL GIRL
33	21-JAN-60	75-1-2		THOR	--	IRBM	RED CABOOSE
34	26-JAN-60	576	A-3	ATLAS-D	(NONE)	ICBM	DUAL EXHAUST
35	4-FEB-60	75-3-4		THOR	AGENA-A	SLV	HUNGRY EYE
36	4-FEB-60	PALC	B	NIKE	VIPER I	SOUNDING ROCKET	--
37	19-FEB-60	75-3-5		THOR	AGENA-A	SLV	DERBY DAY
38	2-MAR-60	75-2-8		THOR	--	IRBM	CENTER BOARD
39	15-APR-60	75-3-5		THOR	AGENA-A	SLV	RAM HORN
40	22-APR-60	576	B-2	ATLAS-D	(NONE)	ICBM	QUICK START
41	29-APR-60	PALC	B	NIKE	VIPER I	SOUNDING ROCKET	--
42	6-MAY-60	576	B-1	ATLAS-D	(NONE)	ICBM	LUCKY DRAGON
43	22-JUN-60	75-2-7		THOR	--	IRBM	CLAN CHATTAN
44	27-JUN-60	PALC	B	NIKE	VIPER I	SOUNDING ROCKET	--
45	29-JUN-60	75-3-4		THOR	AGENA-A	SLV	RED GARTER
46	1-JUL-60	PALC	B	DEACON	ARROW II	SOUNDING ROCKET	--
47	8-JUL-60	PALC	B	DEACON	ARROW II	SOUNDING ROCKET	--
48	14-JUL-60	PALC	B	DEACON	ARROW II	SOUNDING ROCKET	--
49	20-JUL-60	PALC	B	NIKE	CAJUN	SOUNDING ROCKET	--
50	22-JUL-60	576	B-1	ATLAS-D	(NONE)	ICBM	TIGER SKIN

NO.	DATE	COMPLEX	PAD	LAUNCH VEHICLE	UPPER STAGE	TYPE	CODENAME
51	10-AUG-60	75-3-5		THOR	AGENA-A	SLV	FOGGY BOTTOM
52	12-AUG-60	PALC	B	KIVA/HOPI		SOUNDING ROCKET	--
53	18-AUG-60	75-3-4		THOR	AGENA-A	SLV	LIMBER LEG
54	12-SEP-60	576	B-3	ATLAS-D	(NONE)	ICBM	GOLDEN JOURNEY
55	13-SEP-60	75-3-5		THOR	AGENA-A	SLV	COFFEE CALL
56	19-SEP-60	PALC-A		ARGO D-8		SOUNDING ROCKET	--
57	29-SEP-60	576	B-2	ATLAS-D	(NONE)	ICBM	HIGH ARROW
58	30-SEP-60	PALC	B	NIKE	VIPER I	SOUNDING ROCKET	--
59	11-OCT-60	75-2-8		THOR	--	IRBM	LEFT RUDDER
60	11-OCT-60	PALC-1-1		ATLAS	AGENA-A	SLV	GIBSON GIRL
61	12-OCT-60	576	B-1	ATLAS-D	(NONE)	ICBM	DIAMOND JUBILEE
62	12-OCT-60	PALC	B	KIVA/HOPI		SOUNDING ROCKET	--
63	26-OCT-60	75-3-4		THOR	AGENA-B	SLV	SOUP SPOON
64	27-OCT-60	PALC	B	KIVA/HOPI		SOUNDING ROCKET	--
65	12-NOV-60	75-3-5		THOR	AGENA-B	SLV	BOXING GLOVE
66	21-NOV-60	PALC	B	NIKE	CAJUN	SOUNDING ROCKET	--
67	22-NOV-60	PALC	B	NIKE	CAJUN	SOUNDING ROCKET	--
68	7-DEC-60	75-3-4		THOR	AGENA-B	SLV	POWER TRACTOR
69	7-DEC-60	PALC	B	KIVA/HOPI		SOUNDING ROCKET	--
70	13-DEC-60	75-2-8		THOR	--	IRBM	ACTON TOWN
71	14-DEC-60	PALC	B	KIVA/HOPI		SOUNDING ROCKET	--
72	14-DEC-60	PALC	B	KIVA/HOPI		SOUNDING ROCKET	--
73	16-DEC-60	576	B-3	ATLAS-D	(NONE)	ICBM	HOT SHOT
74	16-DEC-60	PALC	B	KIVA/HOPI		SOUNDING ROCKET	--
75	20-DEC-60	75-3-5		THOR	AGENA-B	SLV	TEE BIRD
76	31-JAN-61	PALC-1-1		ATLAS	AGENA-A	SLV	JAYHAWK JAMBOREE
77	17-FEB-61	75-3-4		THOR	AGENA-B	SLV	SPIRIT LEVEL
78	18-FEB-61	75-3-5		THOR	AGENA-B	SLV	BENCH WARRANT
79	27-MAR-61	PALC	B	DEACON	ARROW II	SOUNDING ROCKET	--
80	29-MAR-61	75-2-7		THOR	--	IRBM	SHEPHERDS BUSH
81	30-MAR-61	75-3-4		THOR	AGENA-B	SLV	FEATHER CUT
82	8-APR-61	75-3-5		THOR	AGENA-B	SLV	RUNNING BOARD
83	3-MAY-61	395	SLTF	TITAN I	--	ICBM	SILVER SADDLE
84	24-MAY-61	576	B-2	ATLAS-D	(NONE)	ICBM	LITTLE SATIN
85	7-JUN-61	576	F	ATLAS-E	(NONE)	ICBM	SURE SHOT
86	8-JUN-61	75-3-4		THOR	AGENA-B	SLV	ISLAND QUEEN
87	16-JUN-61	75-1-1		THOR	AGENA-B	SLV	MARKED CARDS
88	20-JUN-61	75-2-7		THOR	--	IRBM	WHITE BISHOP
89	7-JUL-61	75-3-5		THOR	AGENA-B	SLV	HIGH WING
90	12-JUL-61	PALC-1-2		ATLAS	AGENA-B	SLV	POLAR ORBIT
91	21-JUL-61	75-3-4		THOR	AGENA-B	SLV	STACKED DECK
92	1-AUG-61	PALC-A		ASTROBEE 1500		SOUNDING ROCKET	--
93	3-AUG-61	75-1-1		THOR	AGENA-B	SLV	CRISP BACON
94	22-AUG-61	576	B-3	ATLAS-D	(NONE)	ICBM	NEW NICKLE
95	30-AUG-61	75-3-4		THOR	AGENA-B	SLV	FULL BLOWER
96	6-SEP-61	LE-7		THOR	--	IRBM	SKYE BOAT
97	9-SEP-61	PALC-1-1		ATLAS	AGENA-B	SLV	FIRST MOTION
98	12-SEP-61	75-3-5		THOR	AGENA-B	SLV	TWISTED BRAIDS
99	17-SEP-61	75-1-1		THOR	AGENA-B	SLV	CANE POLE
100	23-SEP-61	395	A-1	TITAN I	--	ICBM	BIG SAM
101	13-OCT-61	75-3-4		THOR	AGENA-B	SLV	CAP PISTOL
102	21-OCT-61	PALC-1-2		ATLAS	AGENA-B	SLV	BIG TOWN
103	23-OCT-61	75-3-5		THOR	AGENA-B	SLV	DEAD HEAT
104	5-NOV-61	75-1-1		THOR	AGENA-B	SLV	FOG CUTTER
105	15-NOV-61	75-3-4		THOR	AGENA-B	SLV	CAT FIGHT

NO.	DATE	COMPLEX	PAD	LAUNCH VEHICLE	UPPER STAGE	TYPE	CODENAME
106	15-NOV-61	PALC-A		ARGO D-8		SOUNDING ROCKET	--
107	18-NOV-61	PALC-A		ARGO D-8		SOUNDING ROCKET	--
108	22-NOV-61	PALC-1-1		ATLAS	AGENA-B	SLV	ROUND TRIP
109	29-NOV-61	576	B-2	ATLAS-D	(NONE)	ICBM	BIG PUSH
110	4-DEC-61	PALC-A		SCOUT JUNIOR		SLV	--
111	5-DEC-61	LE-8		THOR	--	IRBM	PIPERS DELIGHT
112	7-DEC-61	576	B-3	ATLAS-D	(NONE)	ICBM	BIG CHIEF
113	8-DEC-61	PALC-A		ASTROBEE 1500		SOUNDING ROCKET	--
114	12-DEC-61	75-3-4		THOR	AGENA-B	SLV	SILVER STRIP
115	22-DEC-61	PALC-1-2		ATLAS	AGENA-B	SLV	OCEAN WAY
116	13-JAN-62	75-3-4		THOR	AGENA-B	SLV	CANDY WRAPPER
117	17-JAN-62	576	B-2	ATLAS-D	(NONE)	ICBM	BLUE FIN
118	20-JAN-62	395	A-3	TITAN I	--	ICBM	DOUBLE MARTINI
119	23-JAN-62	576	B-3	ATLAS-D	(NONE)	ICBM	BLUE MOSS
120	16-FEB-62	576	B-2	ATLAS-D	(NONE)	ICBM	BIG JOHN
121	21-FEB-62	576	B-3	ATLAS-D	(NONE)	ICBM	CHAIN SMOKE
122	21-FEB-62	75-3-5		THOR	AGENA-B	SLV	CABLE SPLICE
123	23-FEB-62	395	A-1	TITAN I	--	ICBM	BLUE GANDER
124	27-FEB-62	75-3-4		THOR	AGENA-B	SLV	CAREER GIRL
125	28-FEB-62	OSTF-1		ATLAS-E	(NONE)	ICBM	SILVER SPUR
126	7-MAR-62	PALC-1-2		ATLAS	AGENA-B	SLV	LOOSE TOOTH
127	14-MAR-62	PALC	B	TERRIER	ASP IV	SOUNDING ROCKET	--
128	19-MAR-62	LE-7		THOR	--	IRBM	BLACK KNIFE
129	23-MAR-62	576	B-2	ATLAS-D	(NONE)	ICBM	CURRY COMB I
130	9-APR-62	PALC-1-2		ATLAS	AGENA-B	SLV	NIGHT HUNT
131	11-APR-62	576	B-2	ATLAS-D	(NONE)	ICBM	CURRY COMB II
132	17-APR-62	75-3-5		THOR	AGENA-B	SLV	LONG SLICE
133	26-APR-62	PALC-1-1		ATLAS	AGENA-B	SLV	DAINTY DOLL
134	26-APR-62	PALC-D		SCOUT		SLV	BLUE SCOUT I
135	27-APR-62	576	B-2	ATLAS-D	(NONE)	ICBM	BLUE BALL
136	28-APR-62	75-3-4		THOR	AGENA-B	SLV	TOTAL TIME
137	4-MAY-62	395	A-1	TITAN I	--	ICBM	SILVER TOP
138	11-MAY-62	576	B-3	ATLAS-D	(NONE)	ICBM	CANNONBALL FLYER
139	15-MAY-62	75-3-5		THOR	AGENA-B	SLV	HOLE PUNCH
140	23-MAY-62	PALC-D		SCOUT		SLV	BLUE SCOUT II
141	29-MAY-62	75-1-1		THOR	AGENA-B	SLV	LEAK PROOF
142	31-MAY-62	PALC-A		SCOUT JUNIOR		SLV	--
143	1-JUN-62	75-3-4		THOR	AGENA-B	SLV	KNOTTY PINE
144	17-JUN-62	PALC-1-1		ATLAS	AGENA-B	SLV	RUBBER GUN
145	18-JUN-62	75-3-5		THOR	AGENA-B	SLV	TASTY TREAT
146	18-JUN-62	LE-8		THOR	--	IRBM	BLAZING CIDERS
147	22-JUN-62	75-3-4		THOR	AGENA-B	SLV	TIGHT SKIRT
148	26-JUN-62	576	B-3	ATLAS-D	(NONE)	ICBM	ALL JAZZ
149	27-JUN-62	75-1-1		THOR	AGENA-D	SLV	TRIAL TRACK
150	9-JUL-62	PALC-A		ARGO D-8		SOUNDING ROCKET	--
151	9-JUL-62	PALC-B		ASTROBEE 1500		SOUNDING ROCKET	--
152	12-JUL-62	576	B-2	ATLAS-D	(NONE)	ICBM	LONG LADY
153	13-JUL-62	OSTF-1		ATLAS-E	(NONE)	ICBM	EXTRA BONUS
154	18-JUL-62	PALC-1-1		ATLAS	AGENA-B	SLV	ARMORED CAR
155	19-JUL-62	576	B-1	ATLAS-D	(NONE)	ICBM	FIRST TRY
156	20-JUL-62	75-3-5		THOR	AGENA-B	SLV	ADOBE HOME
157	24-JUL-62	PALC-A		SCOUT JUNIOR		SLV	--
158	27-JUL-62	75-3-4		THOR	AGENA-B	SLV	ANCHOR ROPE
159	1-AUG-62	576	E	ATLAS-F		ICBM	HIS NIBS
160	1-AUG-62	75-1-1		THOR	AGENA-D	SLV	APPLE GREEN

NO.	DATE	COMPLEX	PAD	LAUNCH VEHICLE	UPPER STAGE	TYPE	CODENAME
162	5-AUG-62	PALC	B	KIVA/HOPI		SOUNDING ROCKET	--
161	5-AUG-62	PALC-1-1		ATLAS	AGENA-B	SLV	AIR SCOUT
164	9-AUG-62	576	B-2	ATLAS-D	(NONE)	ICBM	PEG BOARD II
163	9-AUG-62	576	B-3	ATLAS-D	(NONE)	ICBM	PEG BOARD
165	10-AUG-62	OSTF-2		ATLAS-F		ICBM	CRASH TRUCK
166	23-AUG-62	PALC-D		SCOUT		SLV	BLUE SCOUT III
167	28-AUG-62	75-1-2		THOR	AGENA-D	SLV	APPLE RIND
168	1-SEP-62	75-3-5		THOR	AGENA-B	SLV	BEADY EYE
169	17-SEP-62	75-3-4		THOR	AGENA-B	SLV	BIG FLIGHT
170	28-SEP-62	394	A-3	MINUTEMAN IA	--	ICBM	AIR CRUSADE
171	28-SEP-62	75-1-1		THOR	AGENA-B	SLV	BIG GAME
172	29-SEP-62	75-1-2		THOR	AGENA-D	SLV	ARCTIC ZONE
173	2-OCT-62	576	B-2	ATLAS-D	(NONE)	ICBM	BRIAR STREET
174	6-OCT-62	395	A-1	TITAN I	--	ICBM	TIGHT BRACELET
175	9-OCT-62	75-3-4		THOR	AGENA-B	SLV	CALL BOARD
177	26-OCT-62	576	A-1	ATLAS-D	(NONE)	ICBM	CLOSED CIRCUITS
176	26-OCT-62	75-1-2		THOR	AGENA-D	SLV	ANCHOR BUOY
178	5-NOV-62	75-3-4		THOR	AGENA-B	SLV	BAIL OUT
179	11-NOV-62	PALC-1-1		ATLAS	AGENA-B	SLV	AFTER DECK
180	14-NOV-62	OSTF-2		ATLAS-F		ICBM	ACTION TIME
181	21-NOV-62	PALC-A		SCOUT JUNIOR		SLV	--
182	24-NOV-62	75-3-4		THOR	AGENA-B	SLV	GOLDEN RUSH
183	4-DEC-62	75-1-2		THOR	AGENA-D	SLV	CALAMITY JANE
184	5-DEC-62	395	A-1	TITAN I	--	ICBM	YELLOW JACKET
185	10-DEC-62	394	A-4	MINUTEMAN IA	--	ICBM	AMERICAN BEAUTY
186	12-DEC-62	576	A-3	ATLAS-D	(NONE)	ICBM	DEER PARK
187	12-DEC-62	75-1-1		THOR	AGENA-D	SLV	CORN FIELD
188	13-DEC-62	PALC	B	TERRIER	ASP IV	SOUNDING ROCKET	--
189	14-DEC-62	75-3-5		THOR	AGENA-D	SLV	BABY DOLL
190	17-DEC-62	PALC-1-2		ATLAS	AGENA-B	SLV	BARGIN COUNTER
193	18-DEC-62	OSTF-1		ATLAS-E	(NONE)	ICBM	OAK TREE
191	18-DEC-62	PALC-A		SCOUT JUNIOR		SLV	--
192	18-DEC-62	PALC-D		SCOUT		SLV	BLUE SCOUT IV
194	22-DEC-62	576	A-1	ATLAS-D	(NONE)	ICBM	FLY HIGH
195	7-JAN-63	75-1-1		THOR	AGENA-D	SLV	CANDY KISSES
196	16-JAN-63	75-3-5		THOR	AGENA-B	SLV	CIRCUS BOY
197	25-JAN-63	576	B-2	ATLAS-D	(NONE)	ICBM	BIG SUE
198	29-JAN-63	395	A-1	TITAN I	--	ICBM	TEN MEN
199	31-JAN-63	576	A-3	ATLAS-D	(NONE)	ICBM	FAINT CLICK
200	1-FEB-63	PALC-A		SCOUT JUNIOR		SLV	--
201	11-FEB-63	PALC-A		ARGO D-8		SOUNDING ROCKET	--
202	13-FEB-63	576	A-1	ATLAS-D	(NONE)	ICBM	FLAG RACE
203	16-FEB-63	395	C	TITAN II	--	ICBM	AWFUL TIRED
204	19-FEB-63	PALC-D		SCOUT		SLV	BLUE SCOUT V
205	28-FEB-63	576	A-3	ATLAS-D	(NONE)	ICBM	PITCH PINE
206	28-FEB-63	75-3-5		THRUST AUGMENTED THOR	AGENA-D	SLV	FARM COUNTRY
207	9-MAR-63	576	B-3	ATLAS-D	(NONE)	ICBM	TALL TREE 3
208	11-MAR-63	576	B-2	ATLAS-D	(NONE)	ICBM	TALL TREE 2
209	13-MAR-63	PALC-A		SCOUT JUNIOR		SLV	--
210	15-MAR-63	576	B-1	ATLAS-D	(NONE)	ICBM	TALL TREE 1
211	15-MAR-63	576	D	ATLAS-F		ICBM	TALL TREE 5
212	16-MAR-63	576	A-1	ATLAS-D	(NONE)	ICBM	LEADING EDGE
213	18-MAR-63	75-3-4		THRUST AUGMENTED THOR	AGENA-D	SLV	CAMP OUT
214	21-MAR-63	OSTF-2		ATLAS-F		ICBM	KENDALL GREEN
215	23-MAR-63	576	E	ATLAS-F		ICBM	TALL TREE 4

NO.	DATE	COMPLEX	PAD	LAUNCH VEHICLE	UPPER STAGE	TYPE	CODENAME
216	30-MAR-63	395	A-2	TITAN I	--	ICBM	YOUNG BLOOD
217	1-APR-63	75-3-5		THOR	AGENA-D	SLV	NICKEL STEEL
218	4-APR-63	395	A-1	TITAN I	--	ICBM	HALF MOON
219	5-APR-63	PALC-D		SCOUT		SLV	BLUE SCOUT VI
220	11-APR-63	394	A-5	MINUTEMAN IA	--	ICBM	AFGAN RUG
221	12-APR-63	394	A-1	MINUTEMAN IA	--	ICBM	VELVET TOUCH
222	13-APR-63	395	A-3	TITAN I	--	ICBM	RAMP ROOSTER
223	23-APR-63	394	A-4	MINUTEMAN IA	--	ICBM	PAT HAND
224	24-APR-63	OSTF-1		ATLAS-E	(NONE)	ICBM	BLACK BUCK
226	26-APR-63	75-1-1		THOR	AGENA-D	SLV	FALL HARVEST
225	26-APR-63	PALC-D		SCOUT		SLV	BLUE SCOUT VII
227	27-APR-63	395	C	TITAN II	--	ICBM	DINNER PARTY
228	30-APR-63	394	A-2	MINUTEMAN IA	--	ICBM	BOLD JOURNEY
229	1-MAY-63	395	A-1	TITAN I	--	ICBM	MARES TAIL
230	8-MAY-63	394	A-5	MINUTEMAN IA	--	ICBM	FINE SHOW
231	9-MAY-63	PALC-1-2		ATLAS	AGENA-B	SLV	DAMP CLAY
232	11-MAY-63	PALC	B	KIVA/HOPI		SOUNDING ROCKET	--
233	13-MAY-63	395	D	TITAN II	--	ICBM	FLYING FROG
234	17-MAY-63	PALC-A		SCOUT JUNIOR		SLV	--
235	18-MAY-63	75-3-5		THRUST AUGMENTED THOR	AGENA-D	SLV	GATE LATCH
236	24-MAY-63	394	A-6	MINUTEMAN IB	--	ICBM	HEY DAY
237	4-JUN-63	OSTF-1		ATLAS-E	(NONE)	ICBM	DOCK HAND
238	12-JUN-63	576	A-3	ATLAS-D	(NONE)	ICBM	HARPOON GUN
239	12-JUN-63	75-3-4		THRUST AUGMENTED THOR	AGENA-D	SLV	GREEN CASTLE
240	12-JUN-63	PALC-1-2		ATLAS	AGENA-B	SLV	BIG FOUR
242	15-JUN-63	75-1-1		THOR	AGENA-D	SLV	BUSY FLY
241	15-JUN-63	PALC-D		SCOUT		SLV	BLUE SCOUT VIII
243	18-JUN-63	394	A-3	MINUTEMAN IA	--	ICBM	WAR AXE
244	20-JUN-63	395	C	TITAN II	--	ICBM	THREAD NEEDLE
245	26-JUN-63	75-1-2		THRUST AUGMENTED THOR	AGENA-D	SLV	CALICO MISS
246	28-JUN-63	394	A-1	MINUTEMAN IA	--	ICBM	TRIM CHIEF
247	29-JUN-63	75-3-5		THRUST AUGMENTED THOR	AGENA-B	SLV	BABY BLUE
248	1-JUL-63	PALC	A	BLACK BRANT III		SOUNDING ROCKET	--
249	3-JUL-63	576	C	ATLAS-E	(NONE)	ICBM	GO BOY
250	5-JUL-63	394	A-4	MINUTEMAN IA	--	ICBM	GRAND TOUR
251	11-JUL-63	394	A-2	MINUTEMAN IA	--	ICBM	TRIPLE PLAY
252	12-JUL-63	PALC-2-3		ATLAS	AGENA-D	SLV	FISH POOL
253	16-JUL-63	395	A-2	TITAN I	--	ICBM	SILVER SPUR
254	18-JUL-63	75-1-1		THOR	AGENA-D	SLV	CHILI WILLIE
255	18-JUL-63	PALC-1-2		ATLAS	AGENA-B	SLV	DAMP DUCK
256	26-JUL-63	576	F	ATLAS-E	(NONE)	ICBM	SILVER DOLL
257	27-JUL-63	394	A-5	MINUTEMAN IA	--	ICBM	DIAL RIGHT
258	30-JUL-63	576	C	ATLAS-E	(NONE)	ICBM	BIG FLIGHT
259	30-JUL-63	75-1-2		THRUST AUGMENTED THOR	AGENA-D	SLV	BIG TALK
260	31-JUL-63	576	B-1	ATLAS-D	(NONE)	ICBM	COOL WATER I
261	8-AUG-63	394	A-1	MINUTEMAN IA	--	ICBM	WELL DONE
262	15-AUG-63	395	A-1	TITAN I	--	ICBM	HIGH RIVER
264	24-AUG-63	576	F	ATLAS-E	(NONE)	ICBM	PIPE DREAM
263	24-AUG-63	75-3-4		THRUST AUGMENTED THOR	AGENA-D	SLV	GHOST DANCE
265	28-AUG-63	576	B-3	ATLAS-D	(NONE)	ICBM	COOL WATER II
267	29-AUG-63	394	A-6	MINUTEMAN IB	--	ICBM	GLASS WAND
266	29-AUG-63	75-3-5		THOR	AGENA-D	SLV	PELICAN PETE
268	30-AUG-63	395	A-3	TITAN I	--	ICBM	POLAR ROUTE
269	6-SEP-63	576	B-2	ATLAS-D	(NONE)	ICBM	COOL WATER III
270	6-SEP-63	PALC-2-3		ATLAS	AGENA-D	SLV	FIXED FEE

NO.	DATE	COMPLEX	PAD	LAUNCH VEHICLE	UPPER STAGE	TYPE	CODENAME
271	11-SEP-63	576	B-1	ATLAS-D	(NONE)	ICBM	COOL WATER IV
272	17-SEP-63	395	A-2	TITAN I	--	ICBM	DAILY MAIL
273	23-SEP-63	395	D	TITAN II	--	ICBM	TAR TOP
274	23-SEP-63	75-1-2		THRUST AUGMENTED THOR	AGENA-D	SLV	FELLOW KING
275	25-SEP-63	576	C	ATLAS-E	(NONE)	ICBM	FILTER TIP
276	26-SEP-63	394	A-7	MINUTEMAN IB	--	ICBM	STATE PARK
277	27-SEP-63	PALC-D		SCOUT		SLV	BLUE SCOUT IX
278	28-SEP-63	75-1-1		THOR	ABLE-STAR	SLV	DUCK TAIL
279	3-OCT-63	576	G	ATLAS-F		ICBM	HOT RUM
280	4-OCT-63	394	A-6	MINUTEMAN IB	--	ICBM	GOLD DUKE
281	7-OCT-63	576	B-3	ATLAS-D	(NONE)	ICBM	COOL WATER V
282	17-OCT-63	394	A-3	MINUTEMAN IA	--	ICBM	CEDAR LAKE
283	24-OCT-63	PALC	A	DAC ROC		SOUNDING ROCKET	--
284	25-OCT-63	PALC-2-3		ATLAS	AGENA-D	SLV	HAY BAILER
285	29-OCT-63	75-3-4		THRUST AUGMENTED THOR	AGENA-D	SLV	MARK DOWN
286	31-OCT-63	394	A-5	MINUTEMAN IA	--	ICBM	DRAG CHUTE
287	2-NOV-63	394	A-2	MINUTEMAN IA	--	ICBM	HARD LINE
288	4-NOV-63	4300	A-1	ATLAS-D	(NONE)	ICBM	HICKORY HOLLOW
289	7-NOV-63	PALC	A	BLACK BRANT III		SOUNDING ROCKET	--
290	9-NOV-63	395	C	TITAN II	--	ICBM	FIRE TRUCK
291	9-NOV-63	75-1-2		THOR	AGENA-D	SLV	JUMP SUIT
292	13-NOV-63	576	B-2	ATLAS-D	(NONE)	ICBM	COOL WATER VI
293	14-NOV-63	395	A-1	TITAN I	--	ICBM	FAST RIDE
294	18-NOV-63	PALC	A	HONEST JOHN	NIKE/NIKE	MRBM	--
295	27-NOV-63	394	A-6	MINUTEMAN IB	--	ICBM	BIG CIRCLE
296	27-NOV-63	PALC-1-1		THOR	AGENA-D	SLV	DRY DUNE
297	29-NOV-63	394	A-5	MINUTEMAN IA	--	ICBM	ARM CHAIR
298	5-DEC-63	75-1-1		THOR	ABLE-STAR	SLV	LIMIT LINE
299	10-DEC-63	PALC	A	DAC ROC		SOUNDING ROCKET	--
300	13-DEC-63	394	A-1	MINUTEMAN IB	--	ICBM	ANSWER MAN
301	13-DEC-63	394	A-3	MINUTEMAN IA	--	ICBM	BAMBOO SHOOT
302	16-DEC-63	395	D	TITAN II	--	ICBM	USEFUL TASK
303	17-DEC-63	4300C		SCOUT JUNIOR		SLV	--
306	18-DEC-63	576	G	ATLAS-F		ICBM	DAY BOOK
304	18-DEC-63	4300	A-1	ATLAS-D	(NONE)	ICBM	LENS COVER
305	18-DEC-63	PALC-2-3		ATLAS	AGENA-D	SLV	REST EASY
307	19-DEC-63	PALC-D		SCOUT		SLV	BLUE SCOUT X
308	20-DEC-63	394	A-5	MINUTEMAN IA	--	ICBM	BENT HOOK
309	20-DEC-63	PALC	A	SEAGULL		SOUNDING ROCKET	--
310	21-DEC-63	75-1-2		THRUST AUGMENTED THOR	AGENA-D	SLV	WATER SPOUT
311	10-JAN-64	LF-07		MINUTEMAN IB	--	ICBM	CLOCK WATCH
312	11-JAN-64	75-3-5		THRUST AUGMENTED THOR	AGENA-D	SLV	EMPTY POCKET
313	16-JAN-64	LF-02		MINUTEMAN IB	--	ICBM	DOUBLE BARREL
314	19-JAN-64	75-1-2		THOR	AGENA-D	SLV	BENCH TOP
315	23-JAN-64	395	C	TITAN II	--	ICBM	RED SAILS
316	23-JAN-64	LF-04		MINUTEMAN IA	--	ICBM	BLACK BUSH
317	25-JAN-64	75-1-1		THOR	AGENA-B	SLV	RAMS HORN
318	29-JAN-64	LF-03		MINUTEMAN IB	--	ICBM	ECHO HILL
319	6-FEB-64	PALC	A	HONEST JOHN	NIKE/NIKE	MRBM	--
320	11-FEB-64	LF-06		MINUTEMAN IA	--	ICBM	BLUE PAINT
321	12-FEB-64	576	F	ATLAS-E	(NONE)	ICBM	BLUE BAY
322	15-FEB-64	75-3-4		THRUST AUGMENTED THOR	AGENA-D	SLV	GARDEN PARTY
323	17-FEB-64	395	B	TITAN II	--	ICBM	SAFE CONDUCT
324	24-FEB-64	LF-02		MINUTEMAN IB	--	ICBM	SNAP ROLL
325	24-FEB-64	LF-03		MINUTEMAN IB	--	ICBM	FAST ORBIT

NO.	DATE	COMPLEX	PAD	LAUNCH VEHICLE	UPPER STAGE	TYPE	CODENAME
326	25-FEB-64	PALC-2-3		ATLAS	AGENA-D	SLV	UPPER OCTANE
327	27-FEB-64	75-3-5		THRUST AUGMENTED THOR	AGENA-D	SLV	FIRST QUARTER
328	29-FEB-64	LF-04		MINUTEMAN IA	--	ICBM	BRASS RING
329	29-FEB-64	LF-05		MINUTEMAN IA	--	ICBM	BOX SEAT
330	3-MAR-64	PALC	A	HONEST JOHN	NIKE/NIKE	MRBM	--
331	6-MAR-64	LF-07		MINUTEMAN IB	--	ICBM	KITE TAIL
332	11-MAR-64	PALC-2-3		ATLAS	AGENA-D	SLV	INK BLOTTER
333	13-MAR-64	395	C	TITAN II	--	ICBM	APPLE PIE
334	23-MAR-64	LF-02		MINUTEMAN IB	--	ICBM	BIG TREE
335	24-MAR-64	PALC-1-1		THRUST AUGMENTED THOR	AGENA-D	SLV	HEALTH FARM
336	25-MAR-64	LF-03		MINUTEMAN IB	--	ICBM	CHROME PLATE
337	26-MAR-64	LF-05		MINUTEMAN IA	--	ICBM	CIGAR SMOKE
338	31-MAR-64	LF-04		MINUTEMAN IA	--	ICBM	CRACKER BOX
339	3-APR-64	576	G	ATLAS-F		ICBM	HIGH BALL
340	13-APR-64	LF-07		MINUTEMAN IB	--	ICBM	COOPER FACE
341	21-APR-64	75-1-1		THOR	ABLE-STAR	SLV	USEFUL TOOL
342	23-APR-64	LF-03		MINUTEMAN IB	--	ICBM	DARK LADY
343	23-APR-64	PALC-2-3		ATLAS	AGENA-D	SLV	ANCHOR DAN
344	27-APR-64	75-3-4		THRUST AUGMENTED THOR	AGENA-D	SLV	NICE BIRD
345	27-APR-64	LF-05		MINUTEMAN IA	--	ICBM	DRAG OUT
346	7-MAY-64	LF-02		MINUTEMAN IB	--	ICBM	BLACK WASP
347	11-MAY-64	LF-06		MINUTEMAN IA	--	ICBM	DIP NET
348	18-MAY-64	LF-03		MINUTEMAN IB	--	ICBM	DRESS BLUES
349	19-MAY-64	PALC-2-3		ATLAS	AGENA-D	SLV	BIG FRED
350	25-MAY-64	LF-07		MINUTEMAN IB	--	ICBM	DEER HORN
351	3-JUN-64	PALC-D		SCOUT		SLV	ARROW PLANT
352	4-JUN-64	PALC-1-1		THRUST AUGMENTED THOR	AGENA-D	SLV	KICK BALL
353	9-JUN-64	LF-05		MINUTEMAN IA	--	ICBM	GOLD CLUB
354	11-JUN-64	LF-06		MINUTEMAN IA	--	ICBM	HIGH OCTANE
355	13-JUN-64	75-1-2		THRUST AUGMENTED THOR	AGENA-D	SLV	BEAGLE HOUND
356	15-JUN-64	LF-02		MINUTEMAN IB	--	ICBM	CRUSH PROOF
357	17-JUN-64	75-3-4		THOR	AGENA-D	SLV	INDIO IKE
358	18-JUN-64	4300	A-1	ATLAS-D	(NONE)	ICBM	IRON LUNG
359	19-JUN-64	75-1-1		THRUST AUGMENTED THOR	AGENA-D	SLV	GREEN DOOR
360	25-JUN-64	PALC-D		SCOUT		SLV	CHERRY PIE
361	29-JUN-64	LF-04		MINUTEMAN IA	--	ICBM	ELM BRANCH
362	29-JUN-64	LF-09		MINUTEMAN IB	--	ICBM	BLACK PEPPER
363	2-JUL-64	75-3-5		THRUST AUGMENTED THOR	AGENA-D	SLV	FIRING ORDER
364	6-JUL-64	PALC-2-3		ATLAS	AGENA-D	SLV	QUARTER ROUND
366	7-JUL-64	LF-02		MINUTEMAN IB	--	ICBM	FIVE POINTS
365	7-JUL-64	LF-05		MINUTEMAN IA	--	ICBM	NORMAL TIMES
367	9-JUL-64	LF-07		MINUTEMAN IB	--	ICBM	GEORGIA BOY
368	10-JUL-64	PALC-1-1		THRUST AUGMENTED THOR	AGENA-D	SLV	OLD HAT
369	13-JUL-64	LF-03		MINUTEMAN IB	--	ICBM	OLD FOX
370	27-JUL-64	LF-06		MINUTEMAN IA	--	ICBM	GINGER FOOT
371	29-JUL-64	4300	A-3	ATLAS-D	(NONE)	ICBM	KNOCK WOOD
372	30-JUL-64	395	D	TITAN II	--	ICBM	COBRA SKIN
373	5-AUG-64	75-3-4		THRUST AUGMENTED THOR	AGENA-D	SLV	LONG LOOP
374	7-AUG-64	576	E	ATLAS-F		ICBM	LARGE CHARGE
375	7-AUG-64	LF-03		MINUTEMAN IB	--	ICBM	GOLD REEF
376	11-AUG-64	395	C	TITAN II	--	ICBM	DOUBLE TALLEY
377	13-AUG-64	395	B	TITAN II	--	ICBM	GENTLE ANNIE
378	14-AUG-64	PALC-2-4		ATLAS	AGENA-D	SLV	BIG SICKLE
379	17-AUG-64	LF-05		MINUTEMAN IA	--	ICBM	LIMBER POLE
380	21-AUG-64	75-1-2		THRUST AUGMENTED THOR	AGENA-D	SLV	KILO KATE

NO.	DATE	COMPLEX	PAD	LAUNCH VEHICLE	UPPER STAGE	TYPE	CODENAME
381	21-AUG-64	LF-08		MINUTEMAN IB	--	ICBM	LIGHT HORSE
383	25-AUG-64	LF-07		MINUTEMAN IB	--	ICBM	IVY TOWER
382	25-AUG-64	PALC-D		SCOUT		SLV	HURRY BABY
384	27-AUG-64	576	F	ATLAS-E	(NONE)	ICBM	GALLANT GAL
385	28-AUG-64	75-1-1		THOR	AGENA-B	SLV	HULU MOON
386	29-AUG-64	PALC-A		SCOUT JUNIOR		SLV	CANDY BAG
387	31-AUG-64	576	D	ATLAS-F		ICBM	BIG DEAL
388	1-SEP-64	LF-04		MINUTEMAN IA	--	ICBM	DAWN PATROL
389	8-SEP-64	LF-06		MINUTEMAN IA	--	ICBM	LONG LINE
390	10-SEP-64	LF-02		MINUTEMAN IB	--	ICBM	HOT ROOF
391	14-SEP-64	PALC-1-1		THRUST AUGMENTED THOR	AGENA-D	SLV	QUIT CLAIM
392	15-SEP-64	4300	A-1	ATLAS-D	(NONE)	ICBM	BUTTERFLY NET
393	15-SEP-64	LF-08		MINUTEMAN IB	--	ICBM	QUICK LAUNCH
394	21-SEP-64	LF-09		MINUTEMAN IB	--	ICBM	LONG RANGE
395	22-SEP-64	4300	A-3	ATLAS-D	(NONE)	ICBM	BUZZING BEE
397	23-SEP-64	LF-03		MINUTEMAN IB	--	ICBM	MOUNT UP
396	23-SEP-64	PALC-2-4		ATLAS	AGENA-D	SLV	SLOW PACE
398	29-SEP-64	LF-07		MINUTEMAN IB	--	ICBM	PAINTED WARRIOR
399	2-OCT-64	395	C	TITAN II	--	ICBM	BLACK WIDOW
400	5-OCT-64	75-3-4		THRUST AUGMENTED THOR	AGENA-D	SLV	SOLID PACK
401	6-OCT-64	75-1-2		THOR	ABLE-STAR	SLV	AIR ALARM
402	8-OCT-64	PALC-2-4		ATLAS	AGENA-D	SLV	BUSY LINE
403	9-OCT-64	PALC-D		SCOUT		SLV	GUS GOOSE
404	17-OCT-64	PALC-1-1		THRUST AUGMENTED THOR	AGENA-D	SLV	MOOSE HORN
405	23-OCT-64	PALC-2-3		ATLAS	AGENA-D	SLV	BOON DECKER
406	2-NOV-64	75-3-4		THRUST AUGMENTED THOR	AGENA-D	SLV	BROWN MOOSE
407	2-NOV-64	LF-03		MINUTEMAN IB	--	ICBM	PARIS ROYAL
408	2-NOV-64	LF-08		MINUTEMAN IB	--	ICBM	NET GAIN
409	3-NOV-64	75-3-5		THRUST AUGMENTED THOR	AGENA-D	SLV	ECHO HOLE
410	4-NOV-64	395	D	TITAN II	--	ICBM	HIGH RIDER
411	4-NOV-64	LF-06		MINUTEMAN IA	--	ICBM	BLACK FROST
412	5-NOV-64	LF-09		MINUTEMAN IB	--	ICBM	LONG SHOT
414	6-NOV-64	LF-02		MINUTEMAN IB	--	ICBM	ORANGE CHUTE
413	6-NOV-64	LF-07		MINUTEMAN IB	--	ICBM	POP FLY
415	9-NOV-64	LF-05		MINUTEMAN IA	--	ICBM	QUICK JUMP
416	18-NOV-64	75-1-1		THRUST AUGMENTED THOR	AGENA-D	SLV	VERBAL VENTURE
417	21-NOV-64	PALC-D		SCOUT		SLV	IMA BIRD
418	1-DEC-64	576	A-1	ATLAS-D	(NONE)	ICBM	BROOK TROUT
419	4-DEC-64	576	A-3	ATLAS-D	(NONE)	ICBM	OPERA GLASS
420	4-DEC-64	PALC-2-4		ATLAS	AGENA-D	SLV	BATTLE ROYAL
421	8-DEC-64	395	A-1	TITAN I	--	ICBM	WEST WING I
422	9-DEC-64	LF-02		MINUTEMAN IB	--	ICBM	NICKED BLADE
423	9-DEC-64	LF-08		MINUTEMAN IB	--	ICBM	TOP RAIL
424	12-DEC-64	75-1-2		THOR	ABLE-STAR	SLV	ASTRO ANNIE
425	18-DEC-64	LF-07		MINUTEMAN IB	--	ICBM	ROSY FUTURE
426	19-DEC-64	75-3-4		THRUST AUGMENTED THOR	AGENA-D	SLV	UTILITY TOOL
427	21-DEC-64	75-1-1		THRUST AUGMENTED THOR	AGENA-D	SLV	BARN OWL
428	21-DEC-64	PALC-A		SCOUT JUNIOR		SLV	QUAKER TOWN
429	22-DEC-64	576	E	ATLAS-F		ICBM	STEP OVER
430	8-JAN-65	576	G	ATLAS-F		ICBM	PILOT LIGHT
431	12-JAN-65	576	B1	ATLAS-D	(NONE)	ICBM	PENSIL SET
432	14-JAN-65	395	A-3	TITAN I	--	ICBM	WEST WIND III
433	15-JAN-65	75-3-5		THRUST AUGMENTED THOR	AGENA-D	SLV	BUCKET FACTORY
434	18-JAN-65	4300	B-6	THOR	ALTAIR	SLV	ASTRAL LAMP
435	20-JAN-65	LF-03		MINUTEMAN IB	--	ICBM	PURPLE LIGHT

NO.	DATE	COMPLEX	PAD	LAUNCH VEHICLE	UPPER STAGE	TYPE	CODENAME
436	21-JAN-65	576	B-3	ATLAS-D	(NONE)	ICBM	BEAVERS DAM
437	23-JAN-65	PALC-2-3		ATLAS	AGENA-D	SLV	SAND LARK
438	2-FEB-65	LF-02		MINUTEMAN IB	--	ICBM	RED BRIDGE
439	2-FEB-65	LF-08		MINUTEMAN IB	--	ICBM	SIDE TRIP
440	8-FEB-65	LF-09		MINUTEMAN IB	--	ICBM	PRONTO ROSE
441	25-FEB-65	PALC-1-1		THRUST AUGMENTED THOR	AGENA-D	SLV	BOAT CAMP
442	27-FEB-65	576	A-1	ATLAS-D	(NONE)	ICBM	DRAG BAR
443	1-MAR-65	LF-08		MINUTEMAN IB	--	ICBM	GOLDEN ROSE
444	2-MAR-65	576	A-3	ATLAS-D	(NONE)	ICBM	PORK BARREL
445	5-MAR-65	395	A-2	TITAN I	--	ICBM	WEST WIND II
446	8-MAR-65	LF-07		MINUTEMAN IB	--	ICBM	DOCK BELL
447	9-MAR-65	75-1-2		THOR	AGENA-D	SLV	DEUCE SPOT
448	11-MAR-65	75-1-1		THOR	ABLE-STAR	SLV	BUSH CATTLE
450	12-MAR-65	576	B-3	ATLAS-D	(NONE)	ICBM	ANGEL CAMP
449	12-MAR-65	PALC-2-3		ATLAS	AGENA-D	SLV	SHIP RAIL
451	16-MAR-65	LF-02		MINUTEMAN IB	--	ICBM	TAIL FIN
452	17-MAR-65	4300	B-6	THOR	ALTAIR	SLV	ASTRAL BODY
453	24-MAR-65	395	B	TITAN II	--	ICBM	ARCTIC SUN
454	25-MAR-65	75-3-4		THRUST AUGMENTED THOR	AGENA-D	SLV	PAPER ROUTE
455	25-MAR-65	LF-03		MINUTEMAN IB	--	ICBM	QUICK NOTE
456	26-MAR-65	576	A-1	ATLAS-D	(NONE)	ICBM	FRESH FROG
457	3-APR-65	PALC-2-4		ATLAS	AGENA-D	SLV	AIR PUMP
458	6-APR-65	576	B-1	ATLAS-D	(NONE)	ICBM	FLIP SIDE
459	10-APR-65	LF-09		MINUTEMAN IB	--	ICBM	SMOKEY RIVER
460	13-APR-65	LF-02		MINUTEMAN IB	--	ICBM	SEA POINT
461	13-APR-65	LF-08		MINUTEMAN IB	--	ICBM	YELLOW LIGHT
462	16-APR-65	395	C	TITAN II	--	ICBM	BEAR HUG
463	28-APR-65	PALC-2-4		ATLAS	AGENA-D	SLV	DWARF TREE
464	29-APR-65	PALC-1-1		THRUST AUGMENTED THOR	AGENA-D	SLV	MUSK OX
465	30-APR-65	395	D	TITAN II	--	ICBM	CARD DECK
466	30-APR-65	LF-03		MINUTEMAN IB	--	ICBM	WINTER BREW
467	10-MAY-65	LF-09		MINUTEMAN IB	--	ICBM	VIOLET RAY
468	18-MAY-65	75-3-4		THRUST AUGMENTED THOR	AGENA-D	SLV	IVY VINE
469	18-MAY-65	LF-07		MINUTEMAN IB	--	ICBM	SILVER CLOUD
470	20-MAY-65	4300	B-6	THOR	ALTAIR	SLV	ROYAL EAGLE
471	21-MAY-65	395	B	TITAN II	--	ICBM	FRONT SIGHT
473	27-MAY-65	576	B-3	ATLAS-D	(NONE)	ICBM	TENNIS MATCH
472	27-MAY-65	PALC-2-4		ATLAS	AGENA-D	SLV	BOTTOM LAND
474	2-JUN-65	LF-08		MINUTEMAN IB	--	ICBM	SURF SPRAY
475	3-JUN-65	576	B-2	ATLAS-D	(NONE)	ICBM	OLD FOGEY
476	7-JUN-65	LF-03		MINUTEMAN IB	--	ICBM	WHEEL HORSE
477	8-JUN-65	576	A-1	ATLAS-D	(NONE)	ICBM	LEA RING
478	9-JUN-65	75-3-5		THRUST AUGMENTED THOR	AGENA-D	SLV	FEMALE LOGIC
479	10-JUN-65	576	A-3	ATLAS-D	(NONE)	ICBM	STOCK BOY
480	10-JUN-65	LF-02		MINUTEMAN IB	--	ICBM	SPEED KING
481	14-JUN-65	395	C	TITAN II	--	ICBM	GOLD FISH
482	23-JUN-65	LF-09		MINUTEMAN IB	--	ICBM	WHITE GLOVE
483	24-JUN-65	75-1-1		THOR	ABLE-STAR	SLV	PARADISE TREE
484	25-JUN-65	PALC-2-4		ATLAS	AGENA-D	SLV	WORN FACE
485	29-JUN-65	LF-08		MINUTEMAN IB	--	ICBM	MAPLE GROVE
486	30-JUN-65	395	D	TITAN II	--	ICBM	BUSY BEE
487	1-JUL-65	576	B-1	ATLAS-D	(NONE)	ICBM	BLIND SPOT
488	2-JUL-65	LF-03		MINUTEMAN IB	--	ICBM	SWEET TALK
489	6-JUL-65	LF-07		MINUTEMAN IB	--	ICBM	STAR DUST
490	12-JUL-65	PALC-2-4		ATLAS	AGENA-D	SLV	WHITE PINE

NO.	DATE	COMPLEX	PAD	LAUNCH VEHICLE	UPPER STAGE	TYPE	CODENAME
491	16-JUL-65	75-1-2		THRUST AUGMENTED THOR	AGENA-D	SLV	LOST NOVEMBER
492	19-JUL-65	PALC-1-1		THRUST AUGMENTED THOR	AGENA-D	SLV	ROCKY RIVER
493	21-JUL-65	395	B	TITAN II	--	ICBM	LONG BALL
494	3-AUG-65	PALC-2-4		ATLAS	AGENA-D	SLV	WATER TOWER
495	4-AUG-65	576	B-1	ATLAS-D	(NONE)	ICBM	PIANO WIRE
496	5-AUG-65	576	A-2	ATLAS-F		ICBM	SEA TRAMP
497	13-AUG-65	75-1-1		THOR	ABLE-STAR	SLV	BEAUTY SHOP
498	16-AUG-65	395	C	TITAN II	--	ICBM	MAGIC LAMP
499	17-AUG-65	PALC-1-1		THRUST AUGMENTED THOR	AGENA-D	SLV	LIGHTS OUT
500	18-AUG-65	LF-21		MINUTEMAN II	--	ICBM	REBEL RANGER
501	24-AUG-65	LF-06		MINUTEMAN IA	--	ICBM	SHUTTLE TRAIN
503	25-AUG-65	395	D	TITAN II	--	ICBM	NEW ROLE
502	25-AUG-65	LF-04		MINUTEMAN IA	--	ICBM	PILOT ROCK
504	26-AUG-65	576	B-2	ATLAS-D	(NONE)	ICBM	TONTO RIM
505	2-SEP-65	75-3-5		THOR	AGENA-D	SLV	WORD SCRAMBLE
506	9-SEP-65	4300	B-6	THOR	ALTAIR	SLV	VICTORIA CROSS
507	21-SEP-65	395	B	TITAN II	--	ICBM	BOLD GUY
508	22-SEP-65	PALC-1-1		THRUST AUGMENTED THOR	AGENA-D	SLV	NICKLE SILVER
509	29-SEP-65	576	B-1	ATLAS-D	(NONE)	ICBM	WATER SNAKE
510	30-SEP-65	PALC-2-4		ATLAS	AGENA-D	SLV	LOG FOG
511	5-OCT-65	576	B-3	ATLAS-D	(NONE)	ICBM	SEETHING CITY
512	5-OCT-65	75-3-5		THRUST AUGMENTED THOR	AGENA-D	SLV	UNION LEADER
513	6-OCT-65	LF-22		MINUTEMAN II	--	ICBM	DICE SPOT
514	14-OCT-65	75-1-1		THRUST AUGMENTED THOR	AGENA-D	SLV	OLD ABBEY
515	20-OCT-65	395	C	TITAN II	--	ICBM	POWER BOX
516	28-OCT-65	PALC-1-1		THRUST AUGMENTED THOR	AGENA-D	SLV	HIGH JOURNEY
517	8-NOV-65	PALC-2-4		ATLAS	AGENA-D	SLV	SHOP DEGREE
518	9-NOV-65	LF-21		MINUTEMAN II	--	ICBM	LOW TREE
519	27-NOV-65	395	D	TITAN II	--	ICBM	RED WAGON
520	28-NOV-65	75-1-1		THOR	AGENA-B	SLV	REHEAT
521	29-NOV-65	576	A-1	ATLAS-D	(NONE)	ICBM	WILD GOAT
522	30-NOV-65	395	B	TITAN II	--	ICBM	CROSS FIRE
523	6-DEC-65	PALC-D		SCOUT		SLV	SQUEEKY HUB
524	9-DEC-65	75-3-5		THRUST AUGMENTED THOR	AGENA-D	SLV	LUCKY FELLOW
525	14-DEC-65	LF-04		MINUTEMAN IA	--	ICBM	GRAND RIVER
526	15-DEC-65	LF-24		MINUTEMAN II	--	ICBM	PUSH PULL
527	20-DEC-65	576	B-2	ATLAS-D	(NONE)	ICBM	TAG DAY
528	21-DEC-65	PALC-D		SCOUT		SLV	SOCIAL CIRCLE
529	22-DEC-65	395	C	TITAN II	--	ICBM	SEA ROVER
530	24-DEC-65	75-3-4		THRUST AUGMENTED THOR	AGENA-D	SLV	TALL STORY
531	6-JAN-66	4300	B-6	THOR	ALTAIR	SLV	PERSIAN LAMB
532	18-JAN-66	LF-26		MINUTEMAN II	--	ICBM	RESTLES DRIFTER
533	19-JAN-66	PALC-2-4		ATLAS	AGENA-D	SLV	BLANKET PARTY
534	22-JAN-66	LF-05		MINUTEMAN II	--	ICBM	SUPREME CHIEF
535	27-JAN-66	LF-09		MINUTEMAN IB	--	ICBM	ANCHOR POLE
536	28-JAN-66	PALC-D		SCOUT		SLV	INVENTORY AID
537	2-FEB-66	PALC-1-1		THRUST AUGMENTED THOR	AGENA-D	SLV	SEA LEVEL
538	3-FEB-66	395	D	TITAN II	--	ICBM	WINTER ICE
539	9-FEB-66	75-1-2		THRUST AUGMENTED THOR	AGENA-D	SLV	IRON BACK
540	10-FEB-66	576	A-1	ATLAS-D	(NONE)	ICBM	YEAST CAKE
541	11-FEB-66	576	B-2	ATLAS-D	(NONE)	ICBM	LONELY MOUNTAIN
542	11-FEB-66	LF-07		MINUTEMAN IB	--	ICBM	CREEK BED
543	15-FEB-66	PALC-2-4		ATLAS	AGENA-D	SLV	MUCHO GRANDE
544	16-FEB-66	LF-25		MINUTEMAN II	--	ICBM	CALAMITY JANE
545	17-FEB-66	395	B	TITAN II	--	ICBM	BLACK HAWK

NO.	DATE	COMPLEX	PAD	LAUNCH VEHICLE	UPPER STAGE	TYPE	CODENAME
546	19-FEB-66	576	B-1	ATLAS-D	(NONE)	ICBM	SYCAMORE RIDGE
547	24-FEB-66	LF-04		MINUTEMAN IA	--	ICBM	BROAD ARROW
548	24-FEB-66	LF-06		MINUTEMAN IA	--	ICBM	SEA DEVIL
549	4-MAR-66	576	A-1	ATLAS-D	(NONE)	ICBM	ETERNAL CAMP
550	8-MAR-66	LF-02		MINUTEMAN IB	--	ICBM	BAIT CAN
551	9-MAR-66	75-3-4		THRUST AUGMENTED THOR	AGENA-D	SLV	EASY CHAIR
552	11-MAR-66	LF-03		MINUTEMAN IB	--	ICBM	CLEAN SLATE
553	17-MAR-66	LF-08		MINUTEMAN II	--	ICBM	FAINT CLICK
554	18-MAR-66	PALC-2-4		ATLAS	AGENA-D	SLV	DUMB DORA
555	19-MAR-66	576	A-1	ATLAS-D	(NONE)	ICBM	WHITE BEAR
556	19-MAR-66	PALC	A	NIKE	JAVELIN	SOUNDING ROCKET	SAGE HEN
557	21-MAR-66	LF-06		MINUTEMAN IA	--	ICBM	TULIP TREE
558	25-MAR-66	395	C	TITAN II	--	ICBM	CLOSE TOUCH
560	25-MAR-66	LF-04		MINUTEMAN IA	--	ICBM	WHITE BOOK
559	25-MAR-66	PALC	A	NIKE	JAVELIN	SOUNDING ROCKET	LEAD PENCIL
561	25-MAR-66	PALC-D		SCOUT		SLV	BEST GIRL
562	30-MAR-66	576	B-3	ATLAS-D	(NONE)	ICBM	BRONZE BELL
563	30-MAR-66	4300	B-6	THOR	ALTAIR	SLV	RESORT HOTEL
565	4-APR-66	LF-02		MINUTEMAN IB	--	ICBM	FLY BURNER
564	4-APR-66	LF-09		MINUTEMAN IB	--	ICBM	ARROW FEATHER
566	5-APR-66	395	D	TITAN II	--	ICBM	GOLD RING
567	7-APR-66	PALC-1-1		THRUST AUGMENTED THOR	AGENA-D	SLV	GAPING WOUND
568	15-APR-66	LF-07		MINUTEMAN IB	--	ICBM	GAY CROWD
569	19-APR-66	PALC-2-4		ATLAS	AGENA-D	SLV	SHALLOW STREAM
570	20-APR-66	395	B	TITAN II	--	ICBM	LONG LIGHT
572	22-APR-66	LF-03		MINUTEMAN IB	--	ICBM	ECHO CANYON
571	22-APR-66	PALC-D		SCOUT		SLV	LABRADOR RETRIEVER
573	2-MAY-66	LF-02		MINUTEMAN IB	--	ICBM	LACE STRAP
574	3-MAY-66	576	A-1	ATLAS-D	(NONE)	ICBM	CRAB CLAW
575	3-MAY-66	75-3-5		THRUST AUGMENTED THOR	AGENA-D	SLV	CARGO NET
576	13-MAY-66	576	B-1	ATLAS-D	(NONE)	ICBM	SUPPLY ROOM
577	14-MAY-66	PALC-2-4		ATLAS	AGENA-D	SLV	PUMP HANDLE
578	15-MAY-66	75-1-1		THRUST AUGMENTED THOR	AGENA-B	SLV	BAD ULCER
580	16-MAY-66	LF-06		MINUTEMAN IA	--	ICBM	SAGE GREEN
579	16-MAY-66	LF-09		MINUTEMAN IB	--	ICBM	DOCK WORKER
581	17-MAY-66	LF-07		MINUTEMAN IB	--	ICBM	TIGHT DRUM
582	18-MAY-66	PALC-D		SCOUT		SLV	DANCE LESSON
583	23-MAY-66	PALC-1-1		THRUST AUGMENTED THOR	AGENA-D	SLV	SHORT TON
584	24-MAY-66	395	C	TITAN II	--	ICBM	SILVER BULLET
585	26-MAY-66	576	B-2	ATLAS-D	(NONE)	ICBM	SAND SHARK
586	31-MAY-66	LF-03		MINUTEMAN IB	--	ICBM	GREEN PEA
587	31-MAY-66	LF-04		MINUTEMAN IA	--	ICBM	NIGHT STAND
588	2-JUN-66	LF-02		MINUTEMAN IB	--	ICBM	FOUR ACES
589	3-JUN-66	PALC-2-4		ATLAS	AGENA-D	SLV	POWER DRILL
590	9-JUN-66	PALC-1-2		ATLAS	AGENA-D	SLV	MAMAS BOY
591	10-JUN-66	576	B-1	ATLAS-D	(NONE)	ICBM	VENEER PANEL
592	10-JUN-66	LF-09		MINUTEMAN IB	--	ICBM	EBONY ANGEL
593	21-JUN-66	75-3-5		THRUST AUGMENTED THOR	AGENA-D	SLV	GAME LEG
594	23-JUN-66	75-1-1		THRUST AUGMENTED THOR	AGENA-D	SLV	CLOTH COAT
595	24-JUN-66	LF-08		MINUTEMAN II	--	ICBM	FOX TRAP
596	26-JUN-66	576	B-2	ATLAS-D	(NONE)	ICBM	GOLDEN MOUNTAIN
597	30-JUN-66	576	A-1	ATLAS-D	(NONE)	ICBM	HEAVY ARTILLERY
598	11-JUL-66	LF-03		MINUTEMAN IB	--	ICBM	SOLID GOLD
599	12-JUL-66	LF-09		MINUTEMAN IB	--	ICBM	SUGAR CANE
600	12-JUL-66	SLC-4	EAST	ATLAS	AGENA-D	SLV	SNAKE CREEK

NO.	DATE	COMPLEX	PAD	LAUNCH VEHICLE	UPPER STAGE	TYPE	CODENAME
602	13-JUL-66	576	B-3	ATLAS-D	(NONE)	ICBM	STONY ISLAND
601	13-JUL-66	LF-02		MINUTEMAN IB	--	ICBM	YOUNG LION
603	22-JUL-66	395	B	TITAN II	--	ICBM	GIANT TRAIN
605	26-JUL-66	LF-07		MINUTEMAN IB	--	ICBM	RED MAN
604	26-JUL-66	LF-08		MINUTEMAN II	--	ICBM	TATTERED COAT
606	29-JUL-66	SLC-4	WEST	TITAN IIIB	AGENA-D	SLV	DAILY MAIL
607	1-AUG-66	LF-24		MINUTEMAN II	--	ICBM	STAR BRIGHT
608	4-AUG-66	SLC-5		SCOUT		SLV	RUBBER MAT
609	5-AUG-66	LF-03		MINUTEMAN IB	--	ICBM	PLAY BUSTER
610	8-AUG-66	576	A-2	ATLAS-F		ICBM	BUSY RAMROD
611	9-AUG-66	SLC-1	WEST	THORAD	AGENA-D	SLV	CURLY TOP
613	16-AUG-66	LF-02		MINUTEMAN IB	--	ICBM	GIBSON GIRL
614	16-AUG-66	LF-06		MINUTEMAN IA	--	ICBM	WHITE ARC
612	16-AUG-66	SLC-4	EAST	ATLAS	AGENA-D	SLV	SILVER DOLL
615	17-AUG-66	SLC-5		SCOUT		SLV	MARBLE HALL
616	19-AUG-66	SLC-3	EAST	ATLAS	AGENA-D	SLV	HAPPY MOUNTAIN
617	22-AUG-66	LF-04		MINUTEMAN IA	--	ICBM	TOWN DOCTOR
618	25-AUG-66	BOM	2	BOMARC-A		TARGET DRONE	AUGUST CORN
619	26-AUG-66	LF-23		MINUTEMAN II	--	ICBM	CAREER GIRL
620	29-AUG-66	LF-07		MINUTEMAN IB	--	ICBM	MOTHER CAT
621	15-SEP-66	4300	B-6	THOR	BURNER II	SLV	IRIS DUKE
622	16-SEP-66	395	C	TITAN II	--	ICBM	BLACK RIVER
624	16-SEP-66	LF-03		MINUTEMAN IB	--	ICBM	SNOW HILL
623	16-SEP-66	SLC-4	EAST	ATLAS	AGENA-D	SLV	TAXI DRIVER
625	20-SEP-66	LF-04		MINUTEMAN IA	--	ICBM	RED SPIDER
626	20-SEP-66	SLC-3	WEST	THRUST AUGMENTED THOR	AGENA-D	SLV	BIG BADGE
627	22-SEP-66	LF-09		MINUTEMAN IB	--	ICBM	HOT SPRINGS
628	28-SEP-66	SLC-4	WEST	TITAN IIIB	AGENA-D	SLV	BUSY SCHEME
629	2-OCT-66	SLC-2	EAST	THOR/DELTA		SLV	BUSY MALLET
630	3-OCT-66	LF-06		MINUTEMAN IA	--	ICBM	GROVE HILL
631	5-OCT-66	SLC-3	EAST	ATLAS	AGENA-D	SLV	DWARF KILLER
632	11-OCT-66	576	A-2	ATLAS-F		ICBM	LOW HILL
633	12-OCT-66	SLC-4	EAST	ATLAS	AGENA-D	SLV	GLEAMING STAR
634	13-OCT-66	LF-03		MINUTEMAN IB	--	ICBM	SEA RAVEN
635	14-OCT-66	BOM	1	BOMARC-A		TARGET DRONE	FALL HARVEST
636	21-OCT-66	LF-07		MINUTEMAN IB	--	ICBM	MATCHED CLUBS
637	28-OCT-66	SLC-5		SCOUT		SLV	BUSY SERVICE
638	1-NOV-66	BOM	2	BOMARC-A		TARGET DRONE	BLUE HAWK
639	2-NOV-66	LF-22		MINUTEMAN II	--	ICBM	GOLDEN AGE
640	2-NOV-66	SLC-4	EAST	ATLAS	AGENA-D	SLV	RED CABOOSE
641	8-NOV-66	SLC-1	WEST	THORAD	AGENA-D	SLV	BUSY MEETING
642	16-NOV-66	LF-09		MINUTEMAN IB	--	ICBM	LONG DOZEN
643	22-NOV-66	LF-03		MINUTEMAN IB	--	ICBM	WORKING GIRL
644	24-NOV-66	395	B	TITAN II	--	ICBM	BUBBLE GIRL
645	5-DEC-66	SLC-4	EAST	ATLAS	AGENA-D	SLV	BUSY MERMAID
646	11-DEC-66	576	B-3	ATLAS-D	(NONE)	ICBM	BUSY PANAMA
647	13-DEC-66	LF-05		MINUTEMAN II	--	ICBM	WATER TEST
648	14-DEC-66	SLC-4	WEST	TITAN IIIB	AGENA-D	SLV	BUSY SKYROCKET
649	20-DEC-66	LF-09		MINUTEMAN IB	--	ICBM	SHELL BEACH
650	21-DEC-66	SLC-3	EAST	ATLAS	PRIME	SLV	BUSY PEACOCK
652	22-DEC-66	LF-03		MINUTEMAN IB	--	ICBM	STONE AXE
651	22-DEC-66	LF-07		MINUTEMAN IB	--	ICBM	WILD DUCK
653	29-DEC-66	SLC-2	WEST	THRUST AUGMENTED THOR	AGENA-D	SLV	FRONT ROW
655	11-JAN-67	4300		CASTOR/SCRAMJET		SOUNDING ROCKET	TREE MOSS
654	11-JAN-67	LF-08		MINUTEMAN II	--	ICBM	BONUS BOY

NO.	DATE	COMPLEX	PAD	LAUNCH VEHICLE	UPPER STAGE	TYPE	CODENAME
656	14-JAN-67	SLC-3	WEST	THRUST AUGMENTED THOR	AGENA-D	SLV	LONG ROAD
657	17-JAN-67	576	A-2	ATLAS-F		ICBM	BUSY STEPSON
658	22-JAN-67	576	B-2	ATLAS-D	(NONE)	ICBM	BUSY NIECE
659	24-JAN-67	LF-09		MINUTEMAN IB	--	ICBM	TRUCK TRAVEL
660	26-JAN-67	SLC-2	EAST	THOR/DELTA		SLV	BUSY PENNY
661	30-JAN-67	LF-03		MINUTEMAN IB	--	ICBM	BUCCANEER SWORD
662	31-JAN-67	SLC-5		SCOUT		SLV	BUSY MASON
664	2-FEB-67	LF-05		MINUTEMAN II	--	ICBM	SYCAMORE TREE
663	2-FEB-67	SLC-4	EAST	ATLAS	AGENA-D	SLV	BUSY PARTY
665	7-FEB-67	LF-07		MINUTEMAN IB	--	ICBM	PIANO TUNER
666	8-FEB-67	4300	B-6	THOR	BURNER II	SLV	ARROW POINT
667	8-FEB-67	BOM	1	BOMARC-A		TARGET DRONE	BUSY NEEDLE
668	13-FEB-67	576	A-3	ATLAS-F		ICBM	BUSY BOXER
670	21-FEB-67	LF-03		MINUTEMAN IB	--	ICBM	BUDDY BOY
669	21-FEB-67	LF-09		MINUTEMAN IB	--	ICBM	GLORY TRAIL
671	22-FEB-67	SLC-3	WEST	THRUST AUGMENTED THOR	AGENA-D	SLV	BUSY PAWNSHOP
672	24-FEB-67	SLC-4	WEST	TITAN IIIB	AGENA-D	SLV	BUSY PALEFACE
673	5-MAR-67	SLC-3	EAST	ATLAS	PRIME	SLV	GIANT CHIEF
674	7-MAR-67	LF-07		MINUTEMAN IB	--	ICBM	OLD SAL
675	16-MAR-67	576	A-2	ATLAS-F		ICBM	LITTLE CHURCH
676	17-MAR-67	395	C	TITAN II	--	ICBM	GIFT HORSE
677	22-MAR-67	LF-03		MINUTEMAN IB	--	ICBM	GLYCOL JELL
678	30-MAR-67	SLC-3	WEST	THRUST AUGMENTED THOR	AGENA-D	SLV	GIANT BANANA
679	7-APR-67	576	B-2	ATLAS-D	(NONE)	ICBM	BUSY SUNRISE
680	7-APR-67	LF-09		MINUTEMAN IB	--	ICBM	BUCK PASSER
681	12-APR-67	395	B	TITAN II	--	ICBM	GLAMOUR GIRL
682	13-APR-67	SLC-5		SCOUT		SLV	BUSY MINUTEMAN
683	17-APR-67	LF-08		MINUTEMAN II	--	ICBM	BUSY MISSILE
684	19-APR-67	SLC-3	EAST	ATLAS	PRIME	SLV	BUSY TOURNAMENT
685	20-APR-67	SLC-2	EAST	THOR/DELTA		SLV	BUCKLE PAINTER
687	21-APR-67	LF-03		MINUTEMAN IB	--	ICBM	GIPSY CAMP
686	21-APR-67	LF-22		MINUTEMAN II	--	ICBM	OLYMPIC TRIALS I
688	26-APR-67	SLC-4	WEST	TITAN IIIB	AGENA-D	SLV	BUSY TAILOR
689	27-APR-67	LF-07		MINUTEMAN IB	--	ICBM	OLEO KNIFE
690	28-APR-67	LF-02		MINUTEMAN IB	--	ICBM	BUSY MUMMY
691	5-MAY-67	SLC-5		SCOUT		SLV	BUSY WIFE
692	9-MAY-67	SLC-1	EAST	THORAD	AGENA-D	SLV	BUSY BANKER
693	11-MAY-67	LF-21		MINUTEMAN II	--	ICBM	BUSY FELLOW
694	17-MAY-67	LF-09		MINUTEMAN IB	--	ICBM	GLOSSY COAT
695	18-MAY-67	SLC-5		SCOUT		SLV	BUSY OCEAN
698	19-MAY-67	576	A-1	ATLAS-F		ICBM	BUSY PIGSKIN
697	19-MAY-67	LF-02		MINUTEMAN IB	--	ICBM	BUSY GIANT
696	19-MAY-67	LF-24		MINUTEMAN II	--	ICBM	OLYMPIC TRIALS II
700	22-MAY-67	LF-03		MINUTEMAN IB	--	ICBM	GLOSS TWINE
699	22-MAY-67	SLC-4	EAST	ATLAS	AGENA-D	SLV	BUSY CAMPER
701	24-MAY-67	SLC-2	EAST	THOR/DELTA		SLV	--
703	25-MAY-67	BOM	1	BOMARC-A		TARGET DRONE	--
702	25-MAY-67	BOM	2	BOMARC-A		TARGET DRONE	BUSY SPOTTER
704	29-MAY-67	SLC-5		SCOUT		SLV	
706	31-MAY-67	LF-07		MINUTEMAN IB	--	ICBM	
705	31-MAY-67	SLC-2	WEST	THRUST AUGMENTED THOR	AGENA-D	SLV	
707	1-JUN-67	LF-06		MINUTEMAN IB	--	ICBM	
708	4-JUN-67	SLC-4	EAST	ATLAS	AGENA-D	SLV	--
709	9-JUN-67	576	A-3	ATLAS-F		ICBM	
710	16-JUN-67	SLC-1	WEST	THORAD	AGENA-D	SLV	

NO.	DATE	COMPLEX	PAD	LAUNCH VEHICLE	UPPER STAGE	TYPE	CODENAME
711	20-JUN-67	SLC-4	WEST	TITAN IIIB	AGENA-D	SLV	
712	21-JUN-67	LF-03		MINUTEMAN IB	--	ICBM	
713	23-JUN-67	395	B	TITAN II	--	ICBM	
714	28-JUN-67	LF-02		MINUTEMAN IB	--	ICBM	
715	29-JUN-67	LE-6	--	THOR	BURNER II	SLV	--
716	5-JUL-67	LF-07		MINUTEMAN IB	--	ICBM	GLOWING BRIGHT 40
717	6-JUL-67	576	B-2	ATLAS-D	(NONE)	ICBM	--
718	6-JUL-67	BOM	1	BOMARC-A		TARGET DRONE	BUCKBOARD SEAT
719	12-JUL-67	LF-09		MINUTEMAN IB	--	ICBM	GLOWING BRIGHT 42
720	13-JUL-67	LF-06		MINUTEMAN IB	--	ICBM	OLD COIN
721	15-JUL-67	LF-02		MINUTEMAN IB	--	ICBM	GIN BABY I
722	15-JUL-67	LF-21		MINUTEMAN II	--	ICBM	BUSY JOKER
723	20-JUL-67	LF-22		MINUTEMAN II	--	ICBM	OLYMPIC TRIALS 3
724	22-JUL-67	576	A-3	ATLAS-F		ICBM	--
725	24-JUL-67	SLC-2	WEST	THRUST AUGMENTED THOR	AGENA-D	SLV	--
726	27-JUL-67	576	B-3	ATLAS-D	(NONE)	ICBM	--
727	28-JUL-67	SLC-2	EAST	THRUST AUGMENTED THOR	AGENA-D	SLV	--
728	29-JUL-67	576	A-2	ATLAS-F		ICBM	BREAD HOOK
729	7-AUG-67	SLC-1	EAST	THORAD	AGENA-D	SLV	--
730	8-AUG-67	LF-09		MINUTEMAN IB	--	ICBM	GLOWING BRIGHT 45
731	16-AUG-67	SLC-4	WEST	TITAN IIIB	AGENA-D	SLV	--
732	22-AUG-67	LE-6	--	THOR	BURNER II	SLV	--
733	6-SEP-67	LF-03		MINUTEMAN IB	--	ICBM	GLOWING BRIGHT 46
734	11-SEP-67	395	B	TITAN II	--	ICBM	GLOWING BRIGHT 44
735	15-SEP-67	SLC-1	WEST	THORAD	AGENA-D	SLV	--
736	19-SEP-67	SLC-4	WEST	TITAN IIIB	AGENA-D	SLV	--
737	21-SEP-67	LF-07		MINUTEMAN IB	--	ICBM	GLOWING BRIGHT 47
738	25-SEP-67	SLC-5		SCOUT		SLV	--
739	26-SEP-67	LF-09		MINUTEMAN IB	--	ICBM	GLOWING BRIGHT 48
741	11-OCT-67	576	B-3	ATLAS-D	(NONE)	ICBM	--
740	11-OCT-67	LE-6	--	THOR	BURNER II	SLV	--
742	14-OCT-67	576	A-2	ATLAS-F		ICBM	--
743	21-OCT-67	LF-24		MINUTEMAN II	--	ICBM	OLYMPIC TRIALS 4
744	25-OCT-67	SLC-4	WEST	TITAN IIIB	AGENA-D	SLV	--
745	27-OCT-67	576	A-3	ATLAS-F		ICBM	--
746	2-NOV-67	SLC-1	EAST	THORAD	AGENA-D	SLV	--
747	3-NOV-67	LF-02		MINUTEMAN IB	--	ICBM	GIN BABY II
748	7-NOV-67	576	B-2	ATLAS-D	(NONE)	ICBM	--
749	10-NOV-67	576	A-1	ATLAS-F		ICBM	--
750	10-NOV-67	SLC-2	EAST	THOR/DELTA		SLV	--
752	14-NOV-67	LF-07		MINUTEMAN IB	--	ICBM	GLOWING BRIGHT 51
751	14-NOV-67	LF-09		MINUTEMAN IB	--	ICBM	GLOWING BRIGHT 52
753	17-NOV-67	LF-05		MINUTEMAN II	--	ICBM	GIN BABY III
754	21-NOV-67	LF-08		MINUTEMAN II	--	ICBM	BUSY LOBBY
756	1-DEC-67	BOM	1	BOMARC-A		TARGET DRONE	--
755	1-DEC-67	LF-03		MINUTEMAN IB	--	ICBM	GLOWING BRIGHT 50
757	4-DEC-67	SLC-5		SCOUT		SLV	--
758	5-DEC-67	SLC-4	WEST	TITAN IIIB	AGENA-D	SLV	--
759	8-DEC-67	LF-02		MINUTEMAN IB	--	ICBM	GIN BABY IV
760	9-DEC-67	SLC-1	WEST	THORAD	AGENA-D	SLV	--
761	18-DEC-67	LF-07		MINUTEMAN IB	--	ICBM	GLORY TRIP 01B
762	21-DEC-67	576	A-3	ATLAS-F		ICBM	--
764	21-DEC-67	LF-03		MINUTEMAN IB	--	ICBM	GLORY TRIP 02B
763	21-DEC-67	LF-09		MINUTEMAN IB	--	ICBM	GLORY TRIP 03B
765	23-DEC-67	LF-24		MINUTEMAN II	--	ICBM	OLYMPIC TRIALS 5

NO.	DATE	COMPLEX	PAD	LAUNCH VEHICLE	UPPER STAGE	TYPE	CODENAME
766	28-DEC-67	LF-05		MINUTEMAN II	--	ICBM	GIN BABY V
767	10-JAN-68	LF-25		MINUTEMAN II	--	ICBM	OLYMPIC TRIALS 6
768	11-JAN-68	SLC-2	EAST	THOR/DELTA		SLV	
769	16-JAN-68	LF-06		MINUTEMAN IB	--	ICBM	GLOWING SAND
770	17-JAN-68	SLC-2	WEST	THRUST AUGMENTED THOR	AGENA-D	SLV	--
771	18-JAN-68	SLC-4	WEST	TITAN IIIB	AGENA-D	SLV	
772	24-JAN-68	SLC-1	EAST	THORAD	AGENA-D	SLV	
773	25-JAN-68	LF-22		MINUTEMAN II	--	ICBM	OLYMPIC TRIALS 7
774	31-JAN-68	576	A-3	ATLAS-F		ICBM	
776	2-FEB-68	LF-09		MINUTEMAN IB	--	ICBM	OLYMPIC TRIALS B-1
775	2-FEB-68	LF-24		MINUTEMAN II	--	ICBM	OLYMPIC TRIALS 8
777	10-FEB-68	LF-08		MINUTEMAN II	--	ICBM	--
778	26-FEB-68	576	A-1	ATLAS-F		ICBM	
779	28-FEB-68	395	B	TITAN II	--	ICBM	GLORY TRIP 04T
780	1-MAR-68	SLC-5		SCOUT		SLV	
781	6-MAR-68	576	A-3	ATLAS-E	(NONE)	ICBM	
782	13-MAR-68	SLC-4	WEST	TITAN IIIB	AGENA-D	SLV	
783	14-MAR-68	SLC-1	EAST	THORAD	AGENA-D	SLV	
784	29-MAR-68	LF-26		MINUTEMAN II	--	ICBM	OLYMPIC TRIALS 9
785	2-APR-68	395	C	TITAN II	--	ICBM	GLORY TRIP 10T
786	4-APR-68	BOM	1	BOMARC-A		TARGET DRONE	--
787	6-APR-68	576	A-2	ATLAS-F		ICBM	
788	10-APR-68	LF-03		MINUTEMAN IB	--	ICBM	OLYMPIC TRIALS B-2
789	17-APR-68	SLC-4	WEST	TITAN IIIB	AGENA-D	SLV	
790	18-APR-68	576	A-1	ATLAS-E	(NONE)	ICBM	
791	23-APR-68	LF-06		MINUTEMAN IB	--	ICBM	GLASS POLE
792	27-APR-68	576	A-3	ATLAS-E	(NONE)	ICBM	
793	30-APR-68	LF-22		MINUTEMAN II	--	ICBM	GIANT BLADE 1
794	1-MAY-68	SLC-3	WEST	THORAD	AGENA-D	SLV	
795	3-MAY-68	576	A-2	ATLAS-F		ICBM	
796	16-MAY-68	SLC-5		SCOUT		SLV	
797	18-MAY-68	SLC-2	EAST	THORAD	AGENA-D	SLV	
799	22-MAY-68	BOM	1	BOMARC-A		TARGET DRONE	--
798	22-MAY-68	LF-03		MINUTEMAN IB	--	ICBM	OLYMPIC TRIALS B-3
800	22-MAY-68	SLC-10	WEST	THOR	BURNER II	SLV	--
801	23-MAY-68	LF-06		MINUTEMAN IB	--	ICBM	OLD FAITHFUL
802	1-JUN-68	576	A-2	ATLAS-F		ICBM	--
803	5-JUN-68	SLC-4	WEST	TITAN IIIB	AGENA-D	SLV	
804	12-JUN-68	395	C	TITAN II	--	ICBM	GLORY TRIP 08T
805	20-JUN-68	SLC-1	EAST	THORAD	AGENA-D	SLV	
806	22-JUN-68	576	A-3	ATLAS-F		ICBM	--
807	27-JUN-68	BOM	1	BOMARC-A		TARGET DRONE	--
808	29-JUN-68	576	A-1	ATLAS-F		ICBM	--
809	4-JUL-68	SLC-2	EAST	THOR/DELTA		SLV	--
810	8-JUL-68	LF-04		MINUTEMAN II	--	ICBM	GIANT FIST 1
811	11-JUL-68	576	A-2	ATLAS-F		ICBM	
812	12-JUL-68	LF-03		MINUTEMAN IB	--	ICBM	OLYMPIC TRIALS B-4
813	6-AUG-68	SLC-4	WEST	TITAN IIIB	AGENA-D	SLV	
814	7-AUG-68	SLC-3	WEST	THORAD	AGENA-D	SLV	
815	8-AUG-68	SLC-5		SCOUT		SLV	
816	16-AUG-68	SLC-2	EAST	THOR/DELTA		SLV	--
817	16-AUG-68	SLC-3	EAST	ATLAS	BURNER II	SLV	--
818	19-AUG-68	BOM	2	BOMARC-A		TARGET DRONE	--
819	21-AUG-68	395	C	TITAN II	--	ICBM	GLORY TRIP 18T
820	1-SEP-68	LF-21		MINUTEMAN II	--	ICBM	SHORT ROUND

NO.	DATE	COMPLEX	PAD	LAUNCH VEHICLE	UPPER STAGE	TYPE	CODENAME
821	10-SEP-68	SLC-4	WEST	TITAN IIIB	AGENA-D	SLV	--
822	18-SEP-68	SLC-1	EAST	THORAD	AGENA-D	SLV	--
823	25-SEP-68	576	A-3	ATLAS-F		ICBM	--
824	27-SEP-68	576	A-1	ATLAS-F		ICBM	--
825	3-OCT-68	SLC-5		SCOUT		SLV	--
826	5-OCT-68	SLC-1	WEST	THORAD	AGENA-D	SLV	--
827	7-OCT-68	BOM	1	BOMARC-A		TARGET DRONE	--
828	22-OCT-68	SLC-10	WEST	THOR	BURNER II	SLV	--
829	24-OCT-68	LF-04		MINUTEMAN II	--	ICBM	GIANT FIST 2A
830	30-OCT-68	LF-09		MINUTEMAN IB	--	ICBM	OLYMPIC TRIALS B-5
831	3-NOV-68	SLC-3	WEST	THORAD	AGENA-D	SLV	--
832	6-NOV-68	SLC-4	WEST	TITAN IIIB	AGENA-D	SLV	--
834	13-NOV-68	BOM	2	BOMARC-A		TARGET DRONE	--
833	13-NOV-68	LF-05		MINUTEMAN II	--	ICBM	GIANT FIST 4
835	16-NOV-68	576	A-3	ATLAS-F		ICBM	--
836	19-NOV-68	395	C	TITAN II	--	ICBM	GLORY TRIP 26T
837	21-NOV-68	LF-25		MINUTEMAN II	--	ICBM	GIANT BLADE 2
838	24-NOV-68	576	A-1	ATLAS-F		ICBM	--
839	4-DEC-68	SLC-4	WEST	TITAN IIIB	AGENA-D	SLV	--
840	7-DEC-68	LF-09		MINUTEMAN IB	--	ICBM	OLYMPIC TRIALS B-6
841	10-DEC-68	LF-06		MINUTEMAN IB	--	ICBM	OLD FAITHFUL 2
842	12-DEC-68	SLC-3	WEST	THORAD	AGENA-D	SLV	--
843	15-DEC-68	SLC-2	EAST	THOR/DELTA		SLV	--
844	20-DEC-68	LF-08		MINUTEMAN II	--	ICBM	--
845	8-JAN-69	BOM	2	BOMARC-A		TARGET DRONE	--
846	16-JAN-69	576	A-3	ATLAS-F		ICBM	--
847	21-JAN-69	LF-09		MINUTEMAN IB	--	ICBM	OLYMPIC TRIALS B-7
848	22-JAN-69	SLC-4	WEST	TITAN IIIB	AGENA-D	SLV	--
851	29-JAN-69	BOM	1	BOMARC-A		TARGET DRONE	--
850	29-JAN-69	LF-02		MINUTEMAN II	--	ICBM	SPEC TEST 1
849	29-JAN-69	LF-08		MINUTEMAN II	--	ICBM	--
852	29-JAN-69	SLC-2	EAST	THOR/DELTA		SLV	--
853	30-JAN-69	LF-03		MINUTEMAN IB	--	ICBM	GLORY TRIP 32B
854	2-FEB-69	LF-04		MINUTEMAN II	--	ICBM	GIANT FIST 5
855	5-FEB-69	SLC-3	WEST	THORAD	AGENA-D	SLV	--
856	20-FEB-69	LF-09		MINUTEMAN IB	--	ICBM	OLYMPIC TRIALS B-8
857	21-FEB-69	BOM	2	BOMARC-A		TARGET DRONE	--
858	4-MAR-69	SLC-4	WEST	TITAN IIIB	AGENA-D	SLV	--
859	7-MAR-69	LF-05		MINUTEMAN II	--	ICBM	SPEC TEST 2
860	12-MAR-69	LF-04		MINUTEMAN II	--	ICBM	GIANT FIST 3
861	15-MAR-69	BOM	1	BOMARC-A		TARGET DRONE	--
862	17-MAR-69	576	A-2	ATLAS-F		ICBM	--
863	19-MAR-69	SLC-3	WEST	THORAD	AGENA-D	SLV	--
864	22-MAR-69	LF-21		MINUTEMAN II	--	ICBM	--
865	24-MAR-69	LF-07		MINUTEMAN IB	--	ICBM	GLORY TRIP 33B
866	25-MAR-69	LF-03		MINUTEMAN IB	--	ICBM	GLORY TRIP 34B
867	11-APR-69	LF-02		MINUTEMAN III	--	ICBM	--
868	13-APR-69	SLC-2	EAST	THORAD	AGENA-D	SLV	--
869	15-APR-69	SLC-4	WEST	TITAN IIIB	AGENA-D	SLV	--
870	16-APR-69	LF-05		MINUTEMAN II	--	ICBM	GLORY TRIP 19M
871	17-APR-69	BOM	2	BOMARC-A		TARGET DRONE	--
872	18-APR-69	LF-25		MINUTEMAN II	--	ICBM	SPEC TEST 3
873	23-APR-69	LF-07		MINUTEMAN IB	--	ICBM	GLORY TRIP 35B
874	25-APR-69	LF-22		MINUTEMAN II	--	ICBM	GLORY TRIP 05F
875	30-APR-69	BOM	1	BOMARC-A		TARGET DRONE	--

NO.	DATE	COMPLEX	PAD	LAUNCH VEHICLE	UPPER STAGE	TYPE	CODENAME
876	1-MAY-69	SLC-3	WEST	THORAD	AGENA-D	SLV	--
877	2-MAY-69	LF-21		MINUTEMAN II	--	ICBM	--
879	20-MAY-69	395	B	TITAN II	--	ICBM	GLORY TRIP 39T
878	20-MAY-69	LF-26		MINUTEMAN II	--	ICBM	GLORY TRIP 09F
880	21-MAY-69	BOM	2	BOMARC-A		TARGET DRONE	--
881	28-MAY-69	LF-25		MINUTEMAN II	--	ICBM	GLORY TRIP 07F
882	29-MAY-69	LF-02		MINUTEMAN III	--	ICBM	--
883	3-JUN-69	SLC-4	WEST	TITAN IIIB	AGENA-D	SLV	--
884	5-JUN-69	SLC-2	EAST	THORAD	AGENA-D	SLV	--
885	10-JUN-69	LF-24		MINUTEMAN II	--	ICBM	GLORY TRIP 11F
886	18-JUN-69	LF-07		MINUTEMAN IB	--	ICBM	GLORY TRIP 37B
887	19-JUN-69	BOM	1	BOMARC-A		TARGET DRONE	--
888	20-JUN-69	LF-21		MINUTEMAN II	--	ICBM	--
889	21-JUN-69	SLC-2	WEST	THOR/DELTA		SLV	--
890	30-JUN-69	LF-03		MINUTEMAN IB	--	ICBM	GLORY TRIP 38B
891	2-JUL-69	LF-09		MINUTEMAN IB	--	ICBM	OLYMPIC TRIALS B-9
892	3-JUL-69	BOM	1	BOMARC-A		TARGET DRONE	
893	8-JUL-69	LF-25		MINUTEMAN II		ICBM	GLORY TRIP 14F
894	12-JUL-69	BOM	2	BOMARC-A		TARGET DRONE	--
895	15-JUL-69	LF-22		MINUTEMAN II	--	ICBM	GLORY TRIP 12F
896	15-JUL-69	LF-26		MINUTEMAN II	--	ICBM	GLORY TRIP 13F
897	22-JUL-69	SLC-10	WEST	THOR	BURNER II	SLV	--
898	23-JUL-69	LF-07		MINUTEMAN IB	--	ICBM	GLORY TRIP 41B
899	23-JUL-69	SLC-3	WEST	THORAD	AGENA-D	SLV	--
900	25-JUL-69	LF-08		MINUTEMAN II	--	ICBM	--
901	31-JUL-69	SLC-1	WEST	THORAD	AGENA-D	SLV	--
902	20-AUG-69	BMRS	A-1	ATLAS-F		ICBM	--
903	21-AUG-69	LF-24		MINUTEMAN II	--	ICBM	GLORY TRIP 17F
904	23-AUG-69	SLC-4	WEST	TITAN IIIB	AGENA-D	SLV	
905	24-AUG-69	BOM	1	BOMARC-A		TARGET DRONE	--
906	26-AUG-69	LF-22		MINUTEMAN II	--	ICBM	GLORY TRIP 15F
907	28-AUG-69	LF-03		MINUTEMAN IB	--	ICBM	
908	2-SEP-69	LF-26		MINUTEMAN II	--	ICBM	GLORY TRIP 20F
909	3-SEP-69	BOM	2	BOMARC-A		TARGET DRONE	--
910	10-SEP-69	LF-07		MINUTEMAN IB	--	ICBM	
911	13-SEP-69	LF-02		MINUTEMAN III	--	ICBM	
912	16-SEP-69	BMRS	A-3	ATLAS-F		ICBM	--
914	20-SEP-69	BOM	1	BOMARC-A		TARGET DRONE	--
913	20-SEP-69	LF-09		MINUTEMAN IB	--	ICBM	
915	22-SEP-69	SLC-3	WEST	THORAD	AGENA-D	SLV	--
916	23-SEP-69	LF-06		MINUTEMAN IB	--	ICBM	
917	24-SEP-69	LF-25		MINUTEMAN II	--	ICBM	GLORY TRIP 21F
918	30-SEP-69	SLC-1	WEST	THORAD	AGENA-D	SLV	--
919	1-OCT-69	LF-21		MINUTEMAN II	--	ICBM	
920	1-OCT-69	SLC-5		SCOUT		SLV	
921	2-OCT-69	LF-03		MINUTEMAN IB	--	ICBM	
922	10-OCT-69	BMRS	A-3	ATLAS-F		ICBM	
923	13-OCT-69	LF-24		MINUTEMAN II	--	ICBM	GLORY TRIP 22F
924	15-OCT-69	LF-02		MINUTEMAN III	--	ICBM	
925	21-OCT-69	LF-07		MINUTEMAN IB	--	ICBM	GLORY TRIP 45B
926	24-OCT-69	SLC-4	WEST	TITAN IIIB	AGENA-D	SLV	
927	31-OCT-69	LF-02		MINUTEMAN III	--	ICBM	
928	6-NOV-69	LF-09		MINUTEMAN IB	--	ICBM	
929	7-NOV-69	SLC-5		SCOUT		SLV	--
931	13-NOV-69	BOM	1	BOMARC-A		TARGET DRONE	--

NO.	DATE	COMPLEX	PAD	LAUNCH VEHICLE	UPPER STAGE	TYPE	CODENAME
930	13-NOV-69	BOM	2	BOMARC-A		TARGET DRONE	--
932	18-NOV-69	BOM	1	BOMARC-A		TARGET DRONE	--
933	19-NOV-69	LF-21		MINUTEMAN II	--	ICBM	--
934	25-NOV-69	LF-03		MINUTEMAN IB	--	ICBM	
935	3-DEC-69	BMRS	A-1	ATLAS-F		ICBM	--
936	4-DEC-69	SLC-3	WEST	THORAD	AGENA-D	SLV	--
937	5-DEC-69	LF-07		MINUTEMAN IB	--	ICBM	GLORY TRIP 50B
938	12-DEC-69	BMRS	A-3	ATLAS-F		ICBM	--
939	16-DEC-69	LF-06		MINUTEMAN IB	--	ICBM	
940	14-JAN-70	SLC-4	WEST	TITAN IIIB	AGENA-D	SLV	
941	15-JAN-70	BOM	1	BOMARC-A		TARGET DRONE	--
942	23-JAN-70	SLC-2	WEST	THOR/DELTA		SLV	--
943	3-FEB-70	SLC-2	EAST	THORAD	AGENA-D	SLV	--
944	8-FEB-70	BMRS	A-3	ATLAS-F		ICBM	--
945	11-FEB-70	SLC-10	WEST	THOR	BURNER II	SLV	--
946	25-FEB-70	LF-07		MINUTEMAN IB	--	ICBM	
948	4-MAR-70	LF-09		MINUTEMAN IB	--	ICBM	
947	4-MAR-70	SLC-3	WEST	THORAD	AGENA-D	SLV	
949	7-MAR-70	BOM	1	BOMARC-A		TARGET DRONE	--
950	7-MAR-70	BOM	2	BOMARC-A		TARGET DRONE	--
951	10-MAR-70	LF-03		MINUTEMAN IB	--	ICBM	
952	11-MAR-70	LF-22		MINUTEMAN II	--	ICBM	GLORY TRIP 24F
953	13-MAR-70	BMRS	A-3	ATLAS-F		ICBM	--
954	23-MAR-70	LF-07		MINUTEMAN IB	--	ICBM	GLORY TRIP 63B
955	26-MAR-70	LF-05		MINUTEMAN II	--	ICBM	GLORY TRIP 25M
956	31-MAR-70	LF-26		MINUTEMAN II	--	ICBM	GLORY TRIP 23F
957	2-APR-70	LF-08		MINUTEMAN III	--	ICBM	
958	8-APR-70	SLC-2	EAST	THORAD	AGENA-D	SLV	--
959	15-APR-70	SLC-4	WEST	TITAN IIIB	AGENA-D	SLV	
960	18-APR-70	BOM	1	BOMARC-A		TARGET DRONE	--
961	21-APR-70	LF-24		MINUTEMAN II	--	ICBM	GLORY TRIP 48F
962	22-APR-70	LF-02		MINUTEMAN III	--	ICBM	
963	25-APR-70	LF-22		MINUTEMAN II	--	ICBM	GLORY TRIP 57F
964	4-MAY-70	LF-07		MINUTEMAN IB	--	ICBM	
965	8-MAY-70	LF-02		MINUTEMAN III	--	ICBM	
966	20-MAY-70	SLC-3	WEST	THORAD	AGENA-D	SLV	--
967	21-MAY-70	LF-25		MINUTEMAN II	--	ICBM	GLORY TRIP 55F
968	27-MAY-70	LF-03		MINUTEMAN IB	--	ICBM	
969	30-MAY-70	BMRS	A-3	ATLAS-F		ICBM	--
970	8-JUN-70	LF-07		MINUTEMAN IB	--	ICBM	GLORY TRIP 72B
971	9-JUN-70	BMRS	A-1	ATLAS-F		ICBM	--
972	17-JUN-70	LF-02		MINUTEMAN III	--	ICBM	
973	19-JUN-70	LF-05		MINUTEMAN II	--	ICBM	GLORY TRIP 28M
974	20-JUN-70	LF-04		MINUTEMAN II	--	ICBM	GLORY TRIP 27M
975	23-JUN-70	LF-08		MINUTEMAN III	--	ICBM	
977	25-JUN-70	LF-03		MINUTEMAN IB	--	ICBM	
976	25-JUN-70	SLC-4	WEST	TITAN IIIB	AGENA-D	SLV	
978	26-JUN-70	LF-22		MINUTEMAN II	--	ICBM	GLORY TRIP 59F
979	2-JUL-70	BOM	1	BOMARC-A		TARGET DRONE	--
980	9-JUL-70	LF-24		MINUTEMAN II	--	ICBM	GLORY TRIP 66F
981	14-JUL-70	LF-09		MINUTEMAN IB	--	ICBM	
982	18-JUL-70	LF-04		MINUTEMAN II	--	ICBM	GLORY TRIP 30M
983	22-JUL-70	SLC-3	WEST	THORAD	AGENA-D	SLV	--
984	23-JUL-70	LF-06		MINUTEMAN IB	--	ICBM	
985	28-JUL-70	LF-02		MINUTEMAN III	--	ICBM	

NO.	DATE	COMPLEX	PAD	LAUNCH VEHICLE	UPPER STAGE	TYPE	CODENAME
986	29-JUL-70	BOM	2	BOMARC-A		TARGET DRONE	--
987	3-AUG-70	LF-25		MINUTEMAN II	--	ICBM	GLORY TRIP 61F
988	4-AUG-70	LF-05		MINUTEMAN II	--	ICBM	GLORY TRIP 16L
989	11-AUG-70	LF-26		MINUTEMAN II	--	ICBM	GLORY TRIP 06F
990	14-AUG-70	LF-04		MINUTEMAN II	--	ICBM	GLORY TRIP 31M
991	18-AUG-70	SLC-4	WEST	TITAN IIIB	AGENA-D	SLV	
992	20-AUG-70	LF-09		MINUTEMAN IB	--	ICBM	
993	26-AUG-70	LF-05		MINUTEMAN II	--	ICBM	GLORY TRIP 43M
994	26-AUG-70	SLC-1	WEST	THORAD	AGENA-D	SLV	--
996	27-AUG-70	LF-08		MINUTEMAN III	--	ICBM	OLD FOX 01M
995	27-AUG-70	SLC-5		SCOUT		SLV	--
997	28-AUG-70	LF-06		MINUTEMAN IB	--	ICBM	
998	2-SEP-70	LF-03		MINUTEMAN IB	--	ICBM	
999	3-SEP-70	SLC-10	WEST	THOR	BURNER II	SLV	--
1000	14-SEP-70	LF-25		MINUTEMAN II	--	ICBM	GLORY TRIP 67F
1001	17-SEP-70	LF-26		MINUTEMAN II	--	ICBM	GLORY TRIP 68F
1003	25-SEP-70	LF-02		MINUTEMAN III	--	ICBM	OLD FOX 02M
1002	25-SEP-70	LF-07		MINUTEMAN IB	--	ICBM	
1004	26-SEP-70	BOM	1	BOMARC-A		TARGET DRONE	--
1005	26-SEP-70	BOM	2	BOMARC-A		TARGET DRONE	--
1006	3-OCT-70	LF-04		MINUTEMAN II	--	ICBM	GLORY TRIP 46M
1007	3-OCT-70	LF-06		MINUTEMAN IB	--	ICBM	
1008	5-OCT-70	LF-09		MINUTEMAN IB	--	ICBM	
1009	7-OCT-70	LF-05		MINUTEMAN II	--	ICBM	GLORY TRIP 47M
1010	22-OCT-70	LF-25		MINUTEMAN II	--	ICBM	GLORY TRIP 69F
1011	22-OCT-70	LF-26		MINUTEMAN II	--	ICBM	GLORY TRIP 70F
1012	23-OCT-70	SLC-4	WEST	TITAN IIIB	AGENA-D	SLV	
1013	26-OCT-70	LF-03		MINUTEMAN IB	--	ICBM	
1014	2-NOV-70	LF-04		MINUTEMAN II	--	ICBM	GLORY TRIP 51M
1015	4-NOV-70	LF-21		MINUTEMAN III	--	ICBM	STM-1W
1016	5-NOV-70	LF-05		MINUTEMAN II	--	ICBM	GLORY TRIP 52M
1017	8-NOV-70	LF-09		MINUTEMAN IB	--	ICBM	
1018	13-NOV-70	LF-08		MINUTEMAN III	--	ICBM	OLD FOX 03M
1019	18-NOV-70	SLC-3	WEST	THORAD	AGENA-D	SLV	--
1020	7-DEC-70	LF-04		MINUTEMAN II	--	ICBM	GLORY TRIP 56M
1021	11-DEC-70	SLC-2	WEST	THOR/DELTA		SLV	--
1022	17-DEC-70	LF-05		MINUTEMAN II	--	ICBM	GLORY TRIP 58M
1023	22-DEC-70	BMRS	A-3	ATLAS-F		ICBM	--
1024	23-DEC-70	LF-06		MINUTEMAN IB	--	ICBM	
1025	11-JAN-71	LF-06		MINUTEMAN IB	--	ICBM	
1026	21-JAN-71	SLC-4	WEST	TITAN IIIB	AGENA-D	SLV	
1027	27-JAN-71	LF-08		MINUTEMAN III	--	ICBM	OLD FOX 04M
1028	28-JAN-71	LF-09		MINUTEMAN IB	--	ICBM	
1029	3-FEB-71	LF-24		MINUTEMAN II	--	ICBM	GLORY TRIP 101F
1030	4-FEB-71	LF-04		MINUTEMAN II	--	ICBM	GLORY TRIP 60M
1031	8-FEB-71	LF-07		MINUTEMAN IB	--	ICBM	
1033	16-FEB-71	LF-02		MINUTEMAN III	--	ICBM	OLD FOX 05M
1032	16-FEB-71	SLC-10	WEST	THOR	BURNER II	SLV	--
1034	17-FEB-71	SLC-3	WEST	THORAD	AGENA-D	SLV	--
1035	22-FEB-71	LF-06		MINUTEMAN IB	--	ICBM	
1036	24-FEB-71	LF-25		MINUTEMAN II	--	ICBM	GLORY TRIP 102F
1037	27-FEB-71	BOM	1	BOMARC-A		TARGET DRONE	--
1038	27-FEB-71	BOM	2	BOMARC-A		TARGET DRONE	--
1039	27-FEB-71	LF-04		MINUTEMAN II	--	ICBM	GLORY TRIP 80M
1040	2-MAR-71	LF-03		MINUTEMAN IB	--	ICBM	

NO.	DATE	COMPLEX	PAD	LAUNCH VEHICLE	UPPER STAGE	TYPE	CODENAME
1041	16-MAR-71	LF-06		MINUTEMAN IB	--	ICBM	
1042	20-MAR-71	SLC-4	WEST	TITAN IIIB	AGENA-D	SLV	
1043	23-MAR-71	LF-08		MINUTEMAN III	--	ICBM	GLORY TRIP 01GM
1044	24-MAR-71	SLC-3	WEST	THORAD	AGENA-D	SLV	--
1045	31-MAR-71	LF-05		MINUTEMAN II	--	ICBM	GLORY TRIP 82M
1046	31-MAR-71	SLC-2	EAST	THOR/DELTA		SLV	--
1047	5-APR-71	BMRS	A-1	ATLAS-F		ICBM	--
1048	8-APR-71	LF-21		MINUTEMAN III	--	ICBM	STM-2W
1049	14-APR-71	BOM	1	BOMARC-A		TARGET DRONE	--
1050	14-APR-71	BOM	2	BOMARC-A		TARGET DRONE	--
1051	22-APR-71	SLC-4	WEST	TITAN IIIB	AGENA-D	SLV	
1052	23-APR-71	LF-26		MINUTEMAN III	--	ICBM	OLD FOX 06F
1053	26-APR-71	LF-07		MINUTEMAN IB	--	ICBM	
1054	18-MAY-71	LF-24		MINUTEMAN II	--	ICBM	GLORY TRIP 105F
1055	21-MAY-71	LF-05		MINUTEMAN II	--	ICBM	GLORY TRIP 83M
1056	24-MAY-71	LF-22		MINUTEMAN II	--	ICBM	GLORY TRIP 103F
1057	26-MAY-71	LF-08		MINUTEMAN III	--	ICBM	GLORY TRIP 02GM
1058	27-MAY-71	LF-02		MINUTEMAN III	--	ICBM	GLORY TRIP 03GM
1059	4-JUN-71	LF-04		MINUTEMAN II	--	ICBM	GLORY TRIP 81M
1060	8-JUN-71	SLC-10	WEST	THOR	BURNER II	SLV	--
1061	11-JUN-71	LF-21		MINUTEMAN III	--	ICBM	STM-6W
1062	15-JUN-71	SLC-4	EAST	TITAN IIID	--	SLV	
1063	18-JUN-71	LF-07		MINUTEMAN IB	--	ICBM	
1064	20-JUN-71	395	C	TITAN II	--	ICBM	
1065	23-JUN-71	LF-05		MINUTEMAN II	--	ICBM	GLORY TRIP 84M
1066	26-JUN-71	LF-06		MINUTEMAN IB	--	ICBM	
1067	29-JUN-71	BMRS	A-3	ATLAS-F		ICBM	--
1069	29-JUN-71	BOM	1	BOMARC-A		TARGET DRONE	--
1070	29-JUN-71	BOM	2	BOMARC-A		TARGET DRONE	--
1068	29-JUN-71	PALC	C	NIKE	AEROBEE	SOUNDING ROCKET	--
1071	8-JUL-71	LF-02		MINUTEMAN III	--	ICBM	GLORY TRIP 04GM
1072	12-JUL-71	LF-09		MINUTEMAN IB	--	ICBM	
1073	16-JUL-71	SLC-1	WEST	THORAD	AGENA-D	SLV	--
1074	3-AUG-71	LF-07		MINUTEMAN IB	--	ICBM	
1075	4-AUG-71	LF-25		MINUTEMAN II	--	ICBM	GLORY TRIP 104F-1
1077	6-AUG-71	BMRS	A-2	ATLAS-F		ICBM	--
1076	6-AUG-71	LF-04		MINUTEMAN II	--	ICBM	GLORY TRIP 85M
1078	12-AUG-71	SLC-4	WEST	TITAN IIIB	AGENA-D	SLV	
1079	13-AUG-71	LF-05		MINUTEMAN II	--	ICBM	GLORY TRIP 87M
1080	27-AUG-71	395	C	TITAN II	--	ICBM	
1081	1-SEP-71	BMRS	A-1	ATLAS-F		ICBM	--
1082	2-SEP-71	LF-04		MINUTEMAN II	--	ICBM	GLORY TRIP 29M
1083	3-SEP-71	LF-02		MINUTEMAN III	--	ICBM	GLORY TRIP 05GM
1084	8-SEP-71	LF-07		MINUTEMAN IB	--	ICBM	
1085	10-SEP-71	LF-05		MINUTEMAN II	--	ICBM	GLORY TRIP 89M
1086	10-SEP-71	SLC-3	WEST	THORAD	AGENA-D	SLV	--
1088	16-SEP-71	BOM	1	BOMARC-A		TARGET DRONE	--
1087	16-SEP-71	BOM	2	BOMARC-		TARGET DRONE	--
1089	6-OCT-71	LF-25		MINUTEMAN II	--	ICBM	GLORY TRIP 86F
1090	7-OCT-71	LF-06		MINUTEMAN IB	--	ICBM	
1091	14-OCT-71	SLC-10	WEST	THOR	BURNER IIA	SLV	--
1092	15-OCT-71	LF-02		MINUTEMAN III	--	ICBM	GLORY TRIP 06GM
1093	17-OCT-71	SLC-1	WEST	THORAD	AGENA-D	SLV	--
1094	18-OCT-71	LF-09		MINUTEMAN IB	--	ICBM	
1095	20-OCT-71	LF-08		MINUTEMAN III	--	ICBM	STM-3W

NO.	DATE	COMPLEX	PAD	LAUNCH VEHICLE	UPPER STAGE	TYPE	CODENAME
1097	21-OCT-71	LF-05		MINUTEMAN II	--	ICBM	GLORY TRIP 40L
1096	21-OCT-71	SLC-2	EAST	THOR/DELTA		SLV	--
1098	23-OCT-71	SLC-4	WEST	TITAN IIIB	AGENA-D	SLV	
1099	17-NOV-71	LF-04		MINUTEMAN III	--	ICBM	GLORY TRIP 07GM
1100	22-NOV-71	LF-02		MINUTEMAN III	--	ICBM	GLORY TRIP 08GM
1101	23-NOV-71	LF-05		MINUTEMAN III	--	ICBM	GLORY TRIP 09GM
1102	23-NOV-71	PALC	C	NIKE	AEROBEE	SOUNDING ROCKET	--
1103	2-DEC-71	LF-09		MINUTEMAN IB	--	ICBM	
1104	9-DEC-71	LF-03		MINUTEMAN IB	--	ICBM	
1105	11-DEC-71	SLC-5		SCOUT		SLV	--
1106	14-DEC-71	SLC-1	WEST	THORAD	AGENA-D	SLV	--
1107	15-DEC-71	LF-08		MINUTEMAN III	--	ICBM	STM-4W
1108	17-DEC-71	LF-04		MINUTEMAN III	--	ICBM	GLORY TRIP 10GM
1109	19-JAN-72	BOM	1	BOMARC-A		TARGET DRONE	--
1110	20-JAN-72	SLC-4	EAST	TITAN IIID	--	SLV	
1111	26-JAN-72	LF-02		MINUTEMAN III	--	ICBM	GLORY TRIP 11GM
1112	31-JAN-72	SLC-2	EAST	THOR/DELTA		SLV	--
1113	4-FEB-72	LF-05		MINUTEMAN III	--	ICBM	GLORY TRIP 12GM
1114	9-FEB-72	LF-04		MINUTEMAN III	--	ICBM	GLORY TRIP 13GM
1115	16-FEB-72	SLC-4	WEST	TITAN IIIB	AGENA-D	SLV	
1116	11-MAR-72	SLC-2	EAST	THOR/DELTA		SLV	--
1117	16-MAR-72	LF-06		MINUTEMAN IB	--	ICBM	
1118	17-MAR-72	SLC-4	WEST	TITAN IIIB	AGENA-D	SLV	
1119	21-MAR-72	LF-05		MINUTEMAN II	--	ICBM	GLORY TRIP 200L
1120	24-MAR-72	SLC-10	WEST	THOR	BURNER IIA	SLV	--
1121	13-APR-72	LF-05		MINUTEMAN II	--	ICBM	GLORY TRIP 88M
1122	14-APR-72	BOM	1	BOMARC-A		TARGET DRONE	--
1123	19-APR-72	SLC-3	WEST	THORAD	AGENA-D	SLV	--
1124	21-APR-72	BOM	2	BOMARC-A		TARGET DRONE	--
1125	5-MAY-72	LF-06		MINUTEMAN IB	--	ICBM	
1126	12-MAY-72	LF-05		MINUTEMAN II	--	ICBM	GLORY TRIP 106M
1127	20-MAY-72	SLC-4	WEST	TITAN IIIB	AGENA-D	SLV	
1128	24-MAY-72	395	C	TITAN II	--	ICBM	
1129	25-MAY-72	SLC-3	WEST	THORAD	AGENA-D	SLV	--
1130	31-MAY-72	LF-21		MINUTEMAN III	--	ICBM	PVM-1
1131	6-JUN-72	LF-04		MINUTEMAN III	--	ICBM	GLORY TRIP 15GM
1132	11-JUN-72	LF-02		MINUTEMAN III	--	ICBM	GLORY TRIP 14GM
1133	13-JUN-72	LF-07		MINUTEMAN II	--	ICBM	GIANT PATRIOT I
1134	17-JUN-72	LF-08		MINUTEMAN III	--	ICBM	STM-5W
1135	20-JUN-72	LF-05		MINUTEMAN II	--	ICBM	GLORY TRIP 107M
1136	20-JUN-72	PALC	C	NIKE	AEROBEE	SOUNDING ROCKET	--
1137	7-JUL-72	SLC-4	EAST	TITAN IIID	--	SLV	
1138	15-JUL-72	LF-06		MINUTEMAN IB	--	ICBM	
1139	23-JUL-72	SLC-2	WEST	THOR/DELTA		SLV	--
1140	25-JUL-72	LF-07		MINUTEMAN II	--	ICBM	GIANT PATRIOT II
1141	27-JUL-72	BOM	1	BOMARC-A		TARGET DRONE	--
1142	27-JUL-72	BOM	2	BOMARC-A		TARGET DRONE	--
1143	2-AUG-72	LF-21		MINUTEMAN III	--	ICBM	STM-7W
1144	1-SEP-72	SLC-4	WEST	TITAN IIIB	AGENA-D	SLV	
1145	2-SEP-72	SLC-5		SCOUT		SLV	--
1146	19-SEP-72	LF-22		MINUTEMAN III	--	ICBM	GLORY TRIP 16GB
1147	25-SEP-72	LF-05		MINUTEMAN II	--	ICBM	GLORY TRIP 108M
1148	2-OCT-72	BMRS	A-1	ATLAS	BURNER IIA	SLV	--
1149	3-OCT-72	LF-04		MINUTEMAN II	--	ICBM	GLORY TRIP 109M
1150	10-OCT-72	SLC-4	EAST	TITAN IIID	--	SLV	

NO.	DATE	COMPLEX	PAD	LAUNCH VEHICLE	UPPER STAGE	TYPE	CODENAME
1151	11-OCT-72	395	C	TITAN II	--	ICBM	
1152	11-OCT-72	PALC	C	NIKE	AEROBEE	SOUNDING ROCKET	--
1153	15-OCT-72	SLC-2	WEST	THOR/DELTA		SLV	--
1154	16-OCT-72	LF-25		MINUTEMAN III	--	ICBM	GLORY TRIP 17GB
1155	20-OCT-72	LF-02		MINUTEMAN II	--	ICBM	GLORY TRIP 110M
1156	27-OCT-72	LF-06		MINUTEMAN IB	--	ICBM	
1157	8-NOV-72	SLC-10	WEST	THOR	BURNER IIA	SLV	--
1158	21-NOV-72	SLC-5		SCOUT		SLV	--
1159	24-NOV-72	LF-22		MINUTEMAN III	--	ICBM	GLORY TRIP 18GB
1160	29-NOV-72	BOM	1	BOMARC-A		TARGET DRONE	--
1161	1-DEC-72	BOM	2	BOMARC-A		TARGET DRONE	--
1162	4-DEC-72	LF-02		MINUTEMAN III	--	ICBM	GLORY TRIP 41GM
1163	8-DEC-72	LF-06		MINUTEMAN IB	--	ICBM	
1164	10-DEC-72	SLC-2	WEST	THOR/DELTA		SLV	
1165	12-DEC-72	LF-25		MINUTEMAN III	--	ICBM	GLORY TRIP 19GB
1166	12-DEC-72	LF-26		MINUTEMAN III	--	ICBM	GLORY TRIP 20GB
1167	16-DEC-72	SLC-5		SCOUT		SLV	
1168	18-DEC-72	BOM	1	BOMARC-A		TARGET DRONE	--
1169	19-DEC-72	LF-06		MINUTEMAN IB	--	ICBM	
1171	21-DEC-72	LF-07		MINUTEMAN II	--	ICBM	GLORY TRIP 111M
1170	21-DEC-72	SLC-4	WEST	TITAN IIIB	AGENA-D	SLV	
1172	27-DEC-72	BOM	1	BOMARC-A		TARGET DRONE	--
1173	29-DEC-72	BOM	2	BOMARC-A		TARGET DRONE	--
1174	30-JAN-73	LF-08		MINUTEMAN III	--	ICBM	PVM-2
1175	9-MAR-73	LF-06		MINUTEMAN IB	--	ICBM	
1176	9-MAR-73	SLC-4	EAST	TITAN IIID	--	SLV	
1177	17-APR-73	LF-02		MINUTEMAN II	--	ICBM	GLORY TRIP 112M
1178	25-APR-73	LF-03		MINUTEMAN IB	--	ICBM	
1179	26-APR-73	LF-25		MINUTEMAN III	--	ICBM	GLORY TRIP 21GB
1180	3-MAY-73	LF-22		MINUTEMAN III	--	ICBM	GLORY TRIP 22GB
1181	4-MAY-73	LF-06		MINUTEMAN IB	--	ICBM	
1182	16-MAY-73	SLC-4	WEST	TITAN IIIB	AGENA-D	SLV	
1183	31-MAY-73	LF-09		MINUTEMAN III	--	ICBM	PVM-4
1184	7-JUN-73	LF-06		MINUTEMAN IB	--	ICBM	
1185	26-JUN-73	SLC-4	WEST	TITAN IIIB	AGENA-D	SLV	
1186	27-JUN-73	LF-07		MINUTEMAN II	--	ICBM	GLORY TRIP 114M
1187	6-JUL-73	LF-25		MINUTEMAN III	--	ICBM	GLORY TRIP 23GB
1188	13-JUL-73	SLC-4	EAST	TITAN IIID	--	SLV	
1189	16-JUL-73	SLC-2	WEST	THOR/DELTA		SLV	--
1190	20-JUL-73	LF-06		MINUTEMAN IB		ICBM	
1191	26-JUL-73	LF-05		MINUTEMAN II	--	ICBM	GIANT MOON 4
1192	2-AUG-73	LF-04		MINUTEMAN II	--	ICBM	GLORY TRIP 113M
1193	9-AUG-73	LF-06		MINUTEMAN IB	--	ICBM	
1194	16-AUG-73	SLC-10	WEST	THOR	BURNER IIA	SLV	--
1195	21-AUG-73	SLC-4	WEST	TITAN IIIB	AGENA-D	SLV	
1196	23-AUG-73	LF-08		MINUTEMAN III	--	ICBM	PVM-3
1197	29-AUG-73	BMRS	A-3	ATLAS-F		ICBM	--
1198	5-SEP-73	LF-02		MINUTEMAN III	--	ICBM	GLORY TRIP 43GM
1199	7-SEP-73	LF-06		MINUTEMAN IB	--	ICBM	
1200	11-SEP-73	BOM	1	BOMARC-B		TARGET DRONE	--
1201	14-SEP-73	LF-26		MINUTEMAN III	--	ICBM	GLORY TRIP 25GB
1202	25-SEP-73	LF-04		MINUTEMAN II	--	ICBM	GLORY TRIP 115M-1
1203	27-SEP-73	SLC-4	WEST	TITAN IIIB	AGENA-D	SLV	
1204	30-SEP-73	BMRS	A-1	ATLAS-F		ICBM	--
1205	2-OCT-73	LF-07		MINUTEMAN II	--	ICBM	GLORY TRIP 116M

NO.	DATE	COMPLEX	PAD	LAUNCH VEHICLE	UPPER STAGE	TYPE	CODENAME
1206	5-OCT-73	395	C	TITAN II	--	ICBM	
1207	29-OCT-73	SLC-5		SCOUT		SLV	--
1208	2-NOV-73	LF-06		MINUTEMAN IB	--	ICBM	
1209	6-NOV-73	SLC-2	WEST	THOR/DELTA		SLV	--
1210	10-NOV-73	SLC-4	EAST	TITAN IIID	--	SLV	
1211	22-NOV-73	LF-04		MINUTEMAN III	--	ICBM	GLORY TRIP 42GM-1
1212	29-NOV-73	LF-06		MINUTEMAN IB	--	ICBM	
1213	11-DEC-73	LF-03		MINUTEMAN IB	--	ICBM	
1214	14-DEC-73	LF-06		MINUTEMAN IB	--	ICBM	
1215	15-DEC-73	SLC-2	WEST	THOR/DELTA		SLV	--
1216	17-DEC-73	BOM	1	BOMARC-B		TARGET DRONE	--
1217	22-DEC-73	LF-08		MINUTEMAN III	--	ICBM	STM-8W
1218	22-JAN-74	LF-06		MINUTEMAN IB	--	ICBM	
1219	26-JAN-74	LF-25		MINUTEMAN III	--	ICBM	GLORY TRIP 24GB-1
1220	13-FEB-74	SLC-4	WEST	TITAN IIIB	AGENA-D	SLV	
1221	1-MAR-74	395	C	TITAN II	--	ICBM	
1222	6-MAR-74	BMRS	A-1	ATLAS-F		ICBM	--
1223	8-MAR-74	SLC-5		SCOUT		SLV	--
1224	12-MAR-74	LF-05		MINUTEMAN II	--	ICBM	GIANT MOON 5
1225	16-MAR-74	SLC-10	WEST	THOR	BURNER IIA	SLV	
1226	20-MAR-74	BOM	1	BOMARC-B		TARGET DRONE	--
1227	23-MAR-74	BMRS	A-3	ATLAS-F		ICBM	--
1228	27-MAR-74	LF-07		MINUTEMAN II	--	ICBM	GLORY TRIP 117M-1
1229	2-APR-74	LF-02		MINUTEMAN II	--	ICBM	GLORY TRIP 119M
1230	4-APR-74	LF-21		MINUTEMAN III	--	ICBM	PVM-5
1232	10-APR-74	BOM	2	BOMARC-B		TARGET DRONE	--
1231	10-APR-74	SLC-4	EAST	TITAN IIID	--	SLV	
1233	16-APR-74	LF-06		MINUTEMAN IB	--	ICBM	
1234	26-APR-74	LF-03		MINUTEMAN IB	--	ICBM	
1235	1-MAY-74	BMRS	A-1	ATLAS-F		ICBM	--
1236	2-MAY-74	LF-02		MINUTEMAN III	--	ICBM	GLORY TRIP 44GM
1237	30-MAY-74	BOM	1	BOMARC-B		TARGET DRONE	--
1238	3-JUN-74	SLC-5		SCOUT		SLV	--
1239	6-JUN-74	SLC-4	WEST	TITAN IIIB	AGENA-D	SLV	
1240	28-JUN-74	BMRS	A-1	ATLAS-F		ICBM	--
1241	9-JUL-74	LF-04		MINUTEMAN II	--	ICBM	GLORY TRIP 120M
1242	11-JUL-74	LF-03		MINUTEMAN IB	--	ICBM	
1243	13-JUL-74	SLC-3	WEST	ATLAS-F		SLV	--
1244	16-JUL-74	SLC-5		SCOUT		SLV	--
1245	18-JUL-74	LF-06		MINUTEMAN IB	--	ICBM	
1246	1-AUG-74	LF-03		MINUTEMAN IB	--	ICBM	
1247	8-AUG-74	SLC-10	WEST	THOR	BURNER IIA	SLV	--
1248	14-AUG-74	SLC-4	WEST	TITAN IIIB	AGENA-D	SLV	
1249	17-AUG-74	LF-02		MINUTEMAN III	--	ICBM	GLORY TRIP 45GM
1250	30-AUG-74	SLC-5		SCOUT		SLV	--
1251	8-SEP-74	BMRS	A-1	ATLAS-F		ICBM	--
1252	28-SEP-74	LF-22		MINUTEMAN III	--	ICBM	GLORY TRIP 46GB
1253	1-OCT-74	BOM	1	BOMARC-B		TARGET DRONE	--
1254	4-OCT-74	LF-04		MINUTEMAN III	--	ICBM	PVM-8
1255	7-OCT-74	LF-02		MINUTEMAN II	--	ICBM	GLORY TRIP 118M
1256	11-OCT-74	LF-21		MINUTEMAN III	--	ICBM	PVM-6
1258	12-OCT-74	BMRS	A-3	ATLAS-F		ICBM	--
1257	12-OCT-74	LF-25		MINUTEMAN III	--	ICBM	PVM-7
1259	16-OCT-74	BOM	2	BOMARC-B		TARGET DRONE	--
1260	22-OCT-74	LF-05		MINUTEMAN II	--	ICBM	GIANT MOON 6

NO.	DATE	COMPLEX	PAD	LAUNCH VEHICLE	UPPER STAGE	TYPE	CODENAME
1261	25-OCT-74	LF-09		MINUTEMAN III	--	ICBM	GLORY TRIP 28GM
1262	29-OCT-74	SLC-4	EAST	TITAN IIID	--	SLV	
1263	15-NOV-74	SLC-2	WEST	THOR/DELTA		SLV	--
1264	26-NOV-74	LF-08		MINUTEMAN III	--	ICBM	PVM-9
1265	3-DEC-74	LF-25		MINUTEMAN III	--	ICBM	GLORY TRIP 47GB
1266	17-DEC-74	LF-04		MINUTEMAN II	--	ICBM	GLORY TRIP 121M
1267	9-JAN-75	395	C	TITAN II	--	ICBM	
1268	19-JAN-75	LF-03		MINUTEMAN IB	--	ICBM	
1269	22-JAN-75	SLC-2	WEST	THOR/DELTA		SLV	--
1270	29-JAN-75	LF-04		MINUTEMAN III	--	ICBM	GLORY TRIP 48GM
1271	5-FEB-75	LF-09		MINUTEMAN III	--	ICBM	GLORY TRIP 29GM-1
1272	6-MAR-75	LF-06		MINUTEMAN IB	--	ICBM	
1273	9-MAR-75	SLC-4	WEST	TITAN IIIB	AGENA-D	SLV	
1274	20-MAR-75	BOM	1	BOMARC-B		TARGET DRONE	--
1275	9-APR-75	SLC-2	WEST	THOR/DELTA		SLV	
1276	10-APR-75	BOM	2	BOMARC-B		TARGET DRONE	--
1277	12-APR-75	SLC-3	WEST	ATLAS-F		SLV	
1278	18-APR-75	SLC-4	WEST	TITAN IIIB	AGENA-D	SLV	
1279	6-MAY-75	LF-26		MINUTEMAN III	--	ICBM	PVM-10
1280	9-MAY-75	LF-06		MINUTEMAN IB	--	ICBM	
1281	16-MAY-75	LF-02		MINUTEMAN III	--	ICBM	STM-9W
1282	22-MAY-75	BOM	1	BOMARC-B		TARGET DRONE	--
1283	23-MAY-75	LF-03		MINUTEMAN IB	--	ICBM	
1284	23-MAY-75	SLC-10	WEST	THOR	BURNER IIA	SLV	--
1285	8-JUN-75	SLC-4	EAST	TITAN IIID	--	SLV	
1286	11-JUN-75	LF-08		MINUTEMAN III	--	ICBM	GLORY TRIP 30GM
1287	12-JUN-75	SLC-2	WEST	THOR/DELTA		SLV	--
1288	20-JUN-75	LF-09		MINUTEMAN III	--	ICBM	GLORY TRIP 31GM
1289	1-JUL-75	LF-26		MINUTEMAN III	--	ICBM	PVM-11
1290	23-JUL-75	BOM	2	BOMARC-B		TARGET DRONE	--
1291	26-JUL-75	LF-02		MINUTEMAN III	--	ICBM	STM-10W
1292	7-AUG-75	395	C	TITAN II	--	ICBM	
1293	8-AUG-75	SLC-2	WEST	THOR/DELTA		SLV	--
1294	14-AUG-75	LF-04		MINUTEMAN II	--	ICBM	GLORY TRIP 122M-1
1295	14-AUG-75	PLC-C		PAIUTE	TOMAHAWK	SOUNDING ROCKET	--
1296	22-AUG-75	LF-06		MINUTEMAN IB	--	ICBM	
1297	29-AUG-75	LF-08		MINUTEMAN III	--	ICBM	GLORY TRIP 49GM
1298	5-SEP-75	LF-05		MINUTEMAN II	--	ICBM	GIANT MOON 7
1299	10-SEP-75	LF-06		MINUTEMAN IB	--	ICBM	
1300	16-SEP-75	LF-07		MINUTEMAN II	--	ICBM	GLORY TRIP 123M-1
1301	23-SEP-75	LF-04		MINUTEMAN II	--	ICBM	OSL
1302	30-SEP-75	LF-03		MINUTEMAN IB	--	ICBM	
1303	6-OCT-75	SLC-2	WEST	THOR/DELTA		SLV	
1304	9-OCT-75	SLC-4	WEST	TITAN IIIB	AGENA-D	SLV	
1305	11-OCT-75	SLC-5		SCOUT		SLV	--
1306	13-NOV-75	LF-03		MINUTEMAN IB	--	ICBM	
1307	14-NOV-75	LF-08		MINUTEMAN III	--	ICBM	GLORY TRIP 50GM
1309	4-DEC-75	395	C	TITAN II	--	ICBM	
1308	4-DEC-75	SLC-4	EAST	TITAN IIID	--	SLV	
1310	5-DEC-75	SLC-5		SCOUT		SLV	--
1311	10-DEC-75	PLC-C		UTE TOMAHAWK	--	SOUNDING ROCKET	
1312	16-DEC-75	BOM	1	BOMARC-B		TARGET DRONE	--
1313	17-DEC-75	LF-22		MINUTEMAN III	--	ICBM	GLORY TRIP 51GB
1314	8-JAN-76	LF-26		MINUTEMAN III	--	ICBM	PVM-12
1315	23-JAN-76	LF-06		MINUTEMAN IB	--	ICBM	

NO.	DATE	COMPLEX	PAD	LAUNCH VEHICLE	UPPER STAGE	TYPE	CODENAME
1316	29-JAN-76	LF-07		MINUTEMAN II	--	ICBM	GLORY TRIP 125M
1317	6-FEB-76	LF-09		MINUTEMAN III	--	ICBM	GLORY TRIP 26GM-4
1318	18-FEB-76	SLC-10	WEST	THOR	BURNER IIA	SLV	--
1319	19-FEB-76	LF-05		MINUTEMAN II	--	ICBM	GLORY TRIP 126M
1320	24-FEB-76	LF-04		MINUTEMAN II	--	ICBM	GLORY TRIP 124M
1321	27-FEB-76	LF-03		MINUTEMAN IB	--	ICBM	
1322	4-MAR-76	LF-25		MINUTEMAN III	--	ICBM	GLORY TRIP 52GB
1323	14-MAR-76	LF-26		MINUTEMAN III	--	ICBM	PVM-13
1324	22-MAR-76	SLC-4	WEST	TITAN IIIB	AGENA-D	SLV	
1325	30-APR-76	SLC-3	WEST	ATLAS-F		SLV	--
1326	3-MAY-76	SLC-2	WEST	THOR/DELTA		SLV	
1327	5-MAY-76	BOM	2	BOMARC-B		TARGET DRONE	--
1328	22-MAY-76	SLC-5		SCOUT		SLV	--
1329	2-JUN-76	SLC-4	WEST	TITAN IIIB	AGENA-D	SLV	
1330	3-JUN-76	BOM	1	BOMARC-B		TARGET DRONE	--
1331	8-JUN-76	LF-07		MINUTEMAN II	--	ICBM	GLORY TRIP 127M
1332	21-JUN-76	LF-08		MINUTEMAN III	--	ICBM	GLORY TRIP 33GM
1333	22-JUN-76	LF-05		MINUTEMAN II	--	ICBM	GLORY TRIP 128M
1334	27-JUN-76	395	C	TITAN II	--	ICBM	
1335	30-JUN-76	LF-09		MINUTEMAN III	--	ICBM	GLORY TRIP 54GM
1336	8-JUL-76	SLC-4	EAST	TITAN IIID	--	SLV	
1337	13-JUL-76	BOM	2	BOMARC-B		TARGET DRONE	--
1338	15-JUL-76	LF-21		MINUTEMAN III	--	ICBM	STM-11W
1339	29-JUL-76	SLC-2	WEST	THOR/DELTA		SLV	--
1340	6-AUG-76	SLC-4	WEST	TITAN IIIB	AGENA-D	SLV	
1341	19-AUG-76	LF-06		MINUTEMAN IB		ICBM	
1342	26-AUG-76	LF-07		MINUTEMAN II	--	ICBM	GLORY TRIP 129M
1343	1-SEP-76	SLC-5		SCOUT		SLV	--
1344	11-SEP-76	SLC-10	WEST	THOR	BURNER IIA	SLV	--
1345	15-SEP-76	SLC-4	WEST	TITAN IIIB	AGENA-D	SLV	
1346	23-SEP-76	BOM	2	BOMARC-B		TARGET DRONE	--
1347	26-OCT-76	LF-05		MINUTEMAN II	--	ICBM	GIANT MOON 8
1348	28-OCT-76	BOM	1	BOMARC-B		TARGET DRONE	--
1349	28-OCT-76	BOM	2	BOMARC-B		TARGET DRONE	--
1350	5-NOV-76	LF-08		MINUTEMAN III	--	ICBM	GLORY TRIP 55GM
1351	8-NOV-76	LF-26		MINUTEMAN III	--	ICBM	GLORY TRIP 56GB
1352	12-NOV-76	LF-21		MINUTEMAN III	--	ICBM	STM-12W
1353	30-NOV-76	LF-09		MINUTEMAN III	--	ICBM	GLORY TRIP 32GM-1
1354	19-DEC-76	SLC-4	EAST	TITAN IIID	--	SLV	
1355	21-JAN-77	LF-08		MINUTEMAN III	--	ICBM	GLORY TRIP 53GM-1
1356	30-JAN-77	LF-21		MINUTEMAN III	--	ICBM	STM-13W
1357	1-FEB-77	LF-07		MINUTEMAN II	--	ICBM	GLORY TRIP 132M
1358	4-FEB-77	BOM	2	BOMARC-B		TARGET DRONE	--
1359	16-FEB-77	LF-09		MINUTEMAN III	--	ICBM	GLORY TRIP 27GM-2
1360	2-MAR-77	LF-26		MINUTEMAN III	--	ICBM	GLORY TRIP 57GB
1361	13-MAR-77	SLC-4	WEST	TITAN IIIB	AGENA-D	SLV	
1362	31-MAR-77	BOM	2	BOMARC-B		TARGET DRONE	--
1363	11-MAY-77	BOM	1	BOMARC-B		TARGET DRONE	--
1364	18-MAY-77	LF-06		MINUTEMAN IB		ICBM	
1365	28-MAY-77	LF-26		MINUTEMAN III	--	ICBM	GLORY TRIP 58GB
1366	1-JUN-77	LF-09		MINUTEMAN III	--	ICBM	GLORY TRIP 34GM-1
1367	4-JUN-77	SLC-10	WEST	THOR	BURNER IIA	SLV	--
1368	16-JUN-77	LF-21		MINUTEMAN III	--	ICBM	STM-14W
1369	23-JUN-77	SLC-3	WEST	ATLAS-F		SLV	--
1370	27-JUN-77	SLC-4	EAST	TITAN IIID	--	SLV	

NO.	DATE	COMPLEX	PAD	LAUNCH VEHICLE	UPPER STAGE	TYPE	CODENAME
1371	28-JUN-77	LF-04		MINUTEMAN II	--	ICBM	GLORY TRIP 134M
1372	13-JUL-77	BOM	2	BOMARC-B		TARGET DRONE	--
1373	14-JUL-77	BOM	1	BOMARC-B		TARGET DRONE	--
1374	3-AUG-77	LF-26		MINUTEMAN III	--	ICBM	GLORY TRIP 60GB
1375	10-AUG-77	LF-08		MINUTEMAN III	--	ICBM	GLORY TRIP 59GM-1
1376	19-AUG-77	LF-21		MINUTEMAN III	--	ICBM	PVM-14
1377	3-SEP-77	LF-06		MINUTEMAN IB	--	ICBM	
1378	14-SEP-77	LF-09		MINUTEMAN III	--	ICBM	GLORY TRIP 35GM
1379	23-SEP-77	SLC-4	WEST	TITAN IIIB	AGENA-D	SLV	
1380	27-OCT-77	SLC-5		SCOUT		SLV	--
1381	3-NOV-77	LF-21		MINUTEMAN III	--	ICBM	PVM-15
1382	13-NOV-77	LF-06		MINUTEMAN IB		ICBM	
1383	30-NOV-77	LF-07		MINUTEMAN II	--	ICBM	GLORY TRIP 135M
1384	6-DEC-77	LF-09		MINUTEMAN III	--	ICBM	GLORY TRIP 36GM
1385	8-DEC-77	SLC-3	WEST	ATLAS-F		SLV	--
1386	9-DEC-77	BOM	1	BOMARC-B		TARGET DRONE	--
1387	6-JAN-78	LF-21		MINUTEMAN III	--	ICBM	STM-15W
1388	8-FEB-78	LF-26		MINUTEMAN III	--	ICBM	GLORY TRIP 62GB
1389	15-FEB-78	LF-08		MINUTEMAN III	--	ICBM	GLORY TRIP 61GM
1390	22-FEB-78	SLC-3	EAST	ATLAS-F		SLV	
1391	24-FEB-78	SLC-4	WEST	TITAN IIIB	AGENA-D	SLV	
1392	2-MAR-78	LF-09		MINUTEMAN III	--	ICBM	GLORY TRIP 37GM
1393	5-MAR-78	SLC-2	WEST	THOR/DELTA		SLV	--
1394	16-MAR-78	SLC-4	EAST	TITAN IIID		SLV	
1395	24-MAR-78	BOM	2	BOMARC-B		TARGET DRONE	--
1396	5-APR-78	LF-06		MINUTEMAN IB	--	ICBM	
1397	26-APR-78	SLC-5		SCOUT		SLV	--
1398	30-APR-78	SLC-10	WEST	THOR	BURNER IIA	SLV	--
1399	13-MAY-78	SLC-3	EAST	ATLAS-F		SLV	--
1400	2-JUN-78	LF-04		MINUTEMAN II	--	ICBM	GLORY TRIP 136M
1401	8-JUN-78	LF-26		MINUTEMAN III	--	ICBM	GLORY TRIP 63GB
1402	14-JUN-78	SLC-4	EAST	TITAN IIID		SLV	
1403	16-JUN-78	LF-03		MINUTEMAN IB	--	ICBM	
1404	22-JUN-78	LF-21		MINUTEMAN III	--	ICBM	STM-16W
1405	26-JUN-78	SLC-3	WEST	ATLAS	AGENA-D	SLV	--
1406	27-JUN-78	LF-08		MINUTEMAN III	--	ICBM	GLORY TRIP 64GM
1407	4-JUL-78	LF-06		MINUTEMAN IB	--	ICBM	
1408	25-JUL-78	LF-09		MINUTEMAN II	--	ICBM	GLORY TRIP 133M-1
1409	4-AUG-78	SLC-4	WEST	TITAN IIIB	AGENA-D	SLV	
1410	6-SEP-78	LF-26		MINUTEMAN III	--	ICBM	GLORY TRIP 65GB
1411	6-OCT-78	SLC-3	EAST	ATLAS-F		SLV	--
1412	13-OCT-78	SLC-3	WEST	ATLAS-F		SLV	--
1413	24-OCT-78	SLC-2	WEST	THOR/DELTA		SLV	--
1414	16-NOV-78	LF-07		MINUTEMAN II	--	ICBM	GLORY TRIP 130M-2
1415	27-NOV-78	LF-06		MINUTEMAN IB		ICBM	
1416	5-DEC-78	LF-09		MINUTEMAN III	--	ICBM	GLORY TRIP 38GM
1417	8-DEC-78	LF-21		MINUTEMAN III	--	ICBM	STM-17W
1418	10-DEC-78	SLC-3	EAST	ATLAS-F		SLV	--
1419	19-JAN-79	LF-06		MINUTEMAN IB		ICBM	
1420	24-JAN-79	LF-03		MINUTEMAN IB	--	ICBM	
1421	30-JAN-79	LF-08		MINUTEMAN III	--	ICBM	GLORY TRIP 66GM
1422	6-FEB-79	LF-26		MINUTEMAN III	--	ICBM	GLORY TRIP 67GB
1423	15-FEB-79	LF-21		MINUTEMAN III	--	ICBM	PVM-16
1424	24-FEB-79	SLC-3	WEST	ATLAS-F		SLV	
1425	27-FEB-79	BOM	1	BOMARC-B		TARGET DRONE	--

NO.	DATE	COMPLEX	PAD	LAUNCH VEHICLE	UPPER STAGE	TYPE	CODENAME
1426	16-MAR-79	SLC-4	EAST	TITAN IIID		SLV	
1427	23-MAR-79	LF-07		MINUTEMAN II	--	ICBM	GLORY TRIP 137M
1428	28-MAR-79	LF-09		MINUTEMAN III	--	ICBM	GLORY TRIP 39GM
1429	19-APR-79	LF-21		MINUTEMAN III	--	ICBM	PVM-17
1430	28-MAY-79	SLC-4	WEST	TITAN IIIB	AGENA-D	SLV	
1431	6-JUN-79	SLC-10	WEST	THOR	BURNER IIA	SLV	--
1432	27-JUN-79	SLC-3	WEST	ATLAS-F		SLV	--
1433	6-JUL-79	LF-03		MINUTEMAN IB	--	ICBM	
1435	10-JUL-79	LF-08		MINUTEMAN III	--	ICBM	GLORY TRIP 68GM
1434	10-JUL-79	LF-09		MINUTEMAN III	--	ICBM	GLORY TRIP 40GM (DUAL)
1436	16-JUL-79	LF-04		MINUTEMAN II	--	ICBM	GIANT MOON 9
1437	26-JUL-79	LF-26		MINUTEMAN III	--	ICBM	GLORY TRIP 69GB
1438	3-AUG-79	LF-06		MINUTEMAN IB	--	ICBM	
1439	30-AUG-79	LF-21		MINUTEMAN III	--	ICBM	STM-18W
1440	22-SEP-79	LF-06		MINUTEMAN IB	--	ICBM	
1441	25-SEP-79	LF-04		MINUTEMAN II	--	ICBM	GLORY TRIP 138M
1442	28-SEP-79	LF-08		MINUTEMAN III	--	ICBM	GLORY TRIP 70GM
1443	30-OCT-79	SLC-5		SCOUT		SLV	--
1444	13-DEC-79	LF-07		MINUTEMAN II	--	ICBM	GLORY TRIP 139M
1445	20-DEC-79	LF-03		MINUTEMAN IB	--	ICBM	
1446	31-JAN-80	LF-21		MINUTEMAN III	--	ICBM	PVM-18
1447	5-FEB-80	LF-09		MINUTEMAN III	--	ICBM	GLORY TRIP 71GM
1448	6-FEB-80	SLC-4	EAST	TITAN IIID		SLV	
1449	9-FEB-80	SLC-3	EAST	ATLAS-F		SLV	--
1450	21-FEB-80	LF-26		MINUTEMAN III	--	ICBM	GLORY TRIP 72GB
1451	23-FEB-80	LF-04		MINUTEMAN II	--	ICBM	GLORY TRIP 140M
1452	27-FEB-80	LF-08		MINUTEMAN III	--	ICBM	GLORY TRIP 73GM
1453	3-MAR-80	SLC-3	WEST	ATLAS-F		SLV	--
1454	15-MAR-80	LF-06		MINUTEMAN IB	--	ICBM	
1455	27-MAR-80	LF-21		MINUTEMAN III	--	ICBM	PVM-19
1456	10-APR-80	LF-03		MINUTEMAN IB	--	ICBM	
1457	26-APR-80	SLC-3	EAST	ATLAS-F		SLV	--
1458	29-MAY-80	SLC-3	WEST	ATLAS-F		SLV	--
1459	18-JUN-80	SLC-4	EAST	TITAN IIID		SLV	
1460	22-JUN-80	LF-08		MINUTEMAN III	--	ICBM	GLORY TRIP 74GM
1461	14-JUL-80	SLC-10	WEST	THOR	BURNER IIA	SLV	--
1462	1-AUG-80	BOM	2	BOMARC-B		TARGET DRONE	--
1463	20-AUG-80	LF-26		MINUTEMAN III	--	ICBM	GLORY TRIP 76GB
1464	15-SEP-80	LF-06		MINUTEMAN IB	--	ICBM	
1465	17-SEP-80	LF-09		MINUTEMAN III	--	ICBM	GLORY TRIP 77GM
1466	24-SEP-80	LF-08		MINUTEMAN III	--	ICBM	GLORY TRIP 78GM
1467	8-OCT-80	LF-03		MINUTEMAN IB	--	ICBM	
1468	17-NOV-80	BOM	1	BOMARC-B		TARGET DRONE	--
1469	8-DEC-80	SLC-3	WEST	ATLAS-E		SLV	--
1470	13-DEC-80	SLC-4	WEST	TITAN IIIB	AGENA-D	SLV	
1471	16-DEC-80	LF-06		MINUTEMAN IB	--	ICBM	
1472	19-DEC-80	BOM	2	BOMARC-B		TARGET DRONE	
1473	9-FEB-81	LF-08		MINUTEMAN III	--	ICBM	GLORY TRIP 79GM
1474	9-FEB-81	LF-09		MINUTEMAN III	--	ICBM	GLORY TRIP 80GM
1475	18-FEB-81	LF-06		MINUTEMAN IB	--	ICBM	
1476	21-FEB-81	LF-26		MINUTEMAN III	--	ICBM	GLORY TRIP 81GB
1477	28-FEB-81	SLC-4	WEST	TITAN IIIB	AGENA-D	SLV	
1478	15-MAR-81	LF-03		MINUTEMAN IB	--	ICBM	
1479	1-APR-81	LF-04		MINUTEMAN III	--	ICBM	GLORY TRIP 75GM-2
1480	4-APR-81	LF-06		MINUTEMAN IB	--	ICBM	

NO.	DATE	COMPLEX	PAD	LAUNCH VEHICLE	UPPER STAGE	TYPE	CODENAME
1481	24-APR-81	SLC-4	WEST	TITAN IIIB	AGENA-D	SLV	
1482	14-MAY-81	SLC-5		SCOUT		SLV	--
1483	12-JUN-81	LF-09		MINUTEMAN III	--	ICBM	GLORY TRIP 82GM
1484	23-JUN-81	SLC-3	WEST	ATLAS-F		SLV	--
1485	26-JUN-81	LF-26		MINUTEMAN III	--	ICBM	GLORY TRIP 83GB
1486	3-AUG-81	SLC-2	WEST	DELTA		SLV	--
1487	3-SEP-81	SLC-4	EAST	TITAN IIID		SLV	
1488	12-SEP-81	LF-06		MINUTEMAN IB	--	ICBM	
1489	4-OCT-81	LF-03		MINUTEMAN IB	--	ICBM	
1490	6-OCT-81	SLC-2	WEST	DELTA		SLV	--
1491	24-NOV-81	LF-09		MINUTEMAN III	--	ICBM	GLORY TRIP 84GM-1
1492	9-DEC-81	LF-26		MINUTEMAN III	--	ICBM	GLORY TRIP 85GB
1493	18-DEC-81	SLC-3	EAST	ATLAS-E		SLV	--
1494	21-JAN-82	SLC-4	WEST	TITAN IIIB	AGENA-D	SLV	
1495	29-JAN-82	LF-08		MINUTEMAN III	--	ICBM	GLORY TRIP 86GM
1496	18-MAR-82	LF-04		MINUTEMAN II	--	ICBM	GLORY TRIP 141MS
1497	31-MAR-82	LF-26		MINUTEMAN III	--	ICBM	GLORY TRIP 87GB
1498	11-MAY-82	SLC-4	EAST	TITAN IIID		SLV	
1499	22-JUN-82	LF-08		MINUTEMAN III	--	ICBM	GLORY TRIP 88GM
1501	14-JUL-82	BOM	1	BOMARC-B		TARGET DRONE	--
1500	14-JUL-82	BOM	2	BOMARC-B		TARGET DRONE	--
1502	16-JUL-82	SLC-2	WEST	DELTA		SLV	--
1503	19-JUL-82	LF-04		MINUTEMAN II	--	ICBM	GLORY TRIP 142M
1504	4-AUG-82	LF-09		MINUTEMAN III	--	ICBM	GLORY TRIP 89GM
1505	24-SEP-82	LF-26		MINUTEMAN III	--	ICBM	GLORY TRIP 90GB
1506	8-OCT-82	LF-03		MINUTEMAN IB	--	ICBM	
1507	14-OCT-82	LF-08		MINUTEMAN II	--	ICBM	GLORY TRIP 143MS-1
1508	17-NOV-82	SLC-4	EAST	TITAN IIID		SLV	
1509	2-DEC-82	LF-09		MINUTEMAN III	--	ICBM	GLORY TRIP 91GM
1510	20-DEC-82	SLC-3	WEST	ATLAS-E		SLV	--
1511	7-JAN-83	LF-03		MINUTEMAN IB	--	ICBM	
1512	25-JAN-83	SLC-2	WEST	DELTA		SLV	--
1513	7-FEB-83	LF-06		MINUTEMAN IB	--	ICBM	
1514	9-FEB-83	SLC-3	EAST	ATLAS-H		SLV	--
1515	24-FEB-83	LF-26		MINUTEMAN III	--	ICBM	GLORY TRIP 92GB
1516	11-MAR-83	LF-04		MINUTEMAN III	--	ICBM	GLORY TRIP 93GM
1517	16-MAR-83	LF-08		MINUTEMAN II	--	ICBM	GLORY TRIP 144MS
1518	28-MAR-83	SLC-3	WEST	ATLAS-E		SLV	--
1519	15-APR-83	SLC-4	WEST	TITAN IIIB	AGENA-D	SLV	
1520	5-MAY-83	LF-03		MINUTEMAN IB	--	ICBM	
1521	26-MAY-83	SLC-2	WEST	DELTA		SLV	--
1522	28-MAY-83	LF-03		MINUTEMAN IB	--	ICBM	
1523	9-JUN-83	SLC-3	EAST	ATLAS-H		SLV	--
1524	17-JUN-83	TP-01		PEACEKEEPER	--	ICBM	FTM-01
1525	20-JUN-83	SLC-4	EAST	TITAN 34D	--	SLV	
1527	25-JUN-83	LF-09		MINUTEMAN III	--	ICBM	GLORY TRIP 94GM
1526	25-JUN-83	LF-26		MINUTEMAN III	--	ICBM	GLORY TRIP 95GB
1528	27-JUN-83	SLC-5		SCOUT		SLV	--
1529	14-JUL-83	SLC-3	WEST	ATLAS-E		SLV	--
1530	31-JUL-83	SLC-4	WEST	TITAN IIIB	AGENA-D	SLV	
1531	21-SEP-83	LF-08		MINUTEMAN III	--	ICBM	GLORY TRIP 96GM
1532	21-SEP-83	LF-09		MINUTEMAN III	--	ICBM	GLORY TRIP 97GM
1533	28-SEP-83	LF-04		MINUTEMAN II	--	ICBM	GLORY TRIP 145MS
1534	14-OCT-83	TP-01		PEACEKEEPER	--	ICBM	FTM-02
1535	17-NOV-83	SLC-3	WEST	ATLAS-E		SLV	--

NO.	DATE	COMPLEX	PAD	LAUNCH VEHICLE	UPPER STAGE	TYPE	CODENAME
1536	22-NOV-83	LF-26		MINUTEMAN III	--	ICBM	GLORY TRIP 98GB
1537	16-DEC-83	LF-03		MINUTEMAN IB	--	ICBM	
1538	20-DEC-83	TP-01		PEACEKEEPER	--	ICBM	FTM-03
1539	25-JAN-84	LF-08		MINUTEMAN III	--	ICBM	GLORY TRIP 99GM
1540	25-JAN-84	LF-09		MINUTEMAN III	--	ICBM	GLORY TRIP 100GM
1541	5-FEB-84	SLC-3	EAST	ATLAS-H		SLV	--
1542	29-FEB-84	LF-04		MINUTEMAN II	--	ICBM	GLORY TRIP 146MS
1543	1-MAR-84	SLC-2	WEST	DELTA		SLV	--
1544	30-MAR-84	TP-01		PEACEKEEPER	--	ICBM	FTM-04
1546	8-APR-84	LF-09		MINUTEMAN III	--	ICBM	GLORY TRIP 102GM
1545	8-APR-84	LF-26		MINUTEMAN III	--	ICBM	GLORY TRIP 101GB
1547	17-APR-84	SLC-4	WEST	TITAN IIIB	AGENA-D	SLV	
1548	10-JUN-84	LF-03		MINUTEMAN IB		ICBM	
1549	13-JUN-84	SLC-3	WEST	ATLAS-E		SLV	--
1550	15-JUN-84	TP-01		PEACEKEEPER	--	ICBM	FTM-05
1551	25-JUN-84	SLC-4	EAST	TITAN 34D	--	SLV	
1552	28-AUG-84	SLC-4	WEST	TITAN IIIB	AGENA-D	SLV	
1553	8-SEP-84	SLC-3	WEST	ATLAS-E		SLV	--
1554	13-SEP-84	LF-09		MINUTEMAN III	--	ICBM	GLORY TRIP 103GM
1555	19-SEP-84	LF-26		MINUTEMAN III	--	ICBM	GLORY TRIP 104GB
1556	1-OCT-84	TP-01		PEACEKEEPER	--	ICBM	FTM-06
1557	4-OCT-84	LF-04		MINUTEMAN III	--	ICBM	GLORY TRIP 105GM
1558	11-OCT-84	SLC-5		SCOUT		SLV	--
1559	18-OCT-84	LF-03		MINUTEMAN IB	--	ICBM	
1560	4-DEC-84	SLC-4	EAST	TITAN 34D	--	SLV	
1561	12-DEC-84	SLC-3	WEST	ATLAS-E		SLV	--
1562	1-FEB-85	TP-01		PEACEKEEPER	--	ICBM	FTM-07
1563	6-FEB-85	LF-04		MINUTEMAN III	--	ICBM	GLORY TRIP 106GM
1564	7-FEB-85	SLC-4	WEST	TITAN IIIB	AGENA-D	SLV	
1565	20-FEB-85	LF-26		MINUTEMAN III	--	ICBM	GLORY TRIP 107GB
1566	12-MAR-85	SLC-3	WEST	ATLAS-E		SLV	--
1567	22-MAY-85	LF-03		MINUTEMAN IB		ICBM	
1568	3-JUN-85	TP-01		PEACEKEEPER		ICBM	FTM-08
1569	16-JUN-85	LF-04		MINUTEMAN III	--	ICBM	GLORY TRIP 108GM
1570	16-JUN-85	LF-26		MINUTEMAN III	--	ICBM	GLORY TRIP 109GB
1571	15-JUL-85	LF-09		MINUTEMAN III	--	ICBM	GLORY TRIP 110GM
1572	2-AUG-85	SLC-5		SCOUT		SLV	--
1573	23-AUG-85	LF-08		PEACEKEEPER	--	ICBM	FTM-09
1574	28-AUG-85	SLC-4	EAST	TITAN 34D	--	SLV	
1575	26-SEP-85	LF-04		MINUTEMAN III	--	ICBM	GLORY TRIP 111GM
1576	8-OCT-85	SLC-3	WEST	ATLAS-E		SLV	--
1577	22-OCT-85	HP-06		GLCM		CRUISE MISSILE	--
1578	13-NOV-85	LF-08		PEACEKEEPER	--	ICBM	FTM-10
1579	9-FEB-86	SLC-3	EAST	ATLAS-H		SLV	--
1580	14-FEB-86	LF-26		MINUTEMAN III	--	ICBM	GLORY TRIP 112GB
1581	7-MAR-86	LF-08		PEACEKEEPER	--	ICBM	FTM-11
1583	15-MAR-86	LF-04		MINUTEMAN III	--	ICBM	GLORY TRIP 114GM
1582	15-MAR-86	LF-09		MINUTEMAN III	--	ICBM	GLORY TRIP 113GM-1
1584	17-MAR-86	LF-03		MINUTEMAN IB	--	ICBM	
1585	18-APR-86	SLC-4	EAST	TITAN 34D	--	SLV	
1586	21-MAY-86	LF-08		PEACEKEEPER	--	ICBM	FTM-12
1587	15-JUN-86	LF-26		MINUTEMAN III	--	ICBM	GLORY TRIP 115GB
1588	31-JUL-86	LF-09		MINUTEMAN III	--	ICBM	GLORY TRIP 116GM
1589	23-AUG-86	LF-02		PEACEKEEPER	--	ICBM	FTM-15
1590	28-AUG-86	LF-04		MINUTEMAN III	--	ICBM	GLORY TRIP 117GM

NO.	DATE	COMPLEX	PAD -	LAUNCH VEHICLE	UPPER STAGE	TYPE	CODENAME
1591	17-SEP-86	SLC-3	WEST	ATLAS-E		SLV	--
1592	18-SEP-86	LF-08		PEACEKEEPER	--	ICBM	FTM-13
1593	25-SEP-86	LF-26		MINUTEMAN III	--	ICBM	GLORY TRIP 118GB
1594	13-NOV-86	SLC-5		SCOUT		SLV	
1595	5-DEC-86	LF-02		PEACEKEEPER	--	ICBM	FTM-14
1596	20-JAN-87	LF-03		MINUTEMAN IB	--	ICBM	
1597	28-JAN-87	LF-09		MINUTEMAN III	--	ICBM	GLORY TRIP 119GM
1598	4-FEB-87	LF-26		MINUTEMAN III	--	ICBM	GLORY TRIP 120GB
1599	11-FEB-87	SLC-4	WEST	TITAN IIIB	AGENA-D	SLV	
1600	13-FEB-87	LF-08		PEACEKEEPER	--	ICBM	FTM-16
1601	16-MAR-87	LF-04		MINUTEMAN III	--	ICBM	GLORY TRIP 121GM
1602	21-MAR-87	LF-08		PEACEKEEPER	--	ICBM	FTM-17
1603	2-APR-87	LF-06		MINUTEMAN III	--	ICBM	IPMS
1604	15-MAY-87	SLC-3	EAST	ATLAS-H		SLV	--
1605	19-JUN-87	SLC-3	WEST	ATLAS-E		SLV	--
1606	25-JUN-87	LF-26		MINUTEMAN III	--	ICBM	GLORY TRIP 122GB-1
1607	7-JUL-87	LF-04		MINUTEMAN II	--	ICBM	GLORY TRIP 148M
1608	12-JUL-87	LF-10		MINUTEMAN III	--	ICBM	GLORY TRIP 123GM-1
1609	1-SEP-87	LF-06		MINUTEMAN III	--	ICBM	IPMS
1610	16-SEP-87	SLC-5		SCOUT		SLV	--
1611	21-SEP-87	LF-03		MINUTEMAN IB	--	ICBM	
1612	26-OCT-87	SLC-4	EAST	TITAN 34D	--	SLV	
1613	28-OCT-87	LF-04		MINUTEMAN II	--	ICBM	GLORY TRIP 150M
1614	3-NOV-87	LF-09		MINUTEMAN III	--	ICBM	GLORY TRIP 124GM
1615	9-NOV-87	LF-07		MINUTEMAN II	--	ICBM	GLORY TRIP 149M
1616	18-JAN-88	LF-03		MINUTEMAN IB	--	ICBM	
1617	29-JAN-88	LF-26		MINUTEMAN III	--	ICBM	GLORY TRIP 125GB-1
1618	2-FEB-88	SLC-3	WEST	ATLAS-E		SLV	--
1619	25-APR-88	SLC-5		SCOUT		SLV	--
1620	3-JUN-88	LF-26		MINUTEMAN III	--	ICBM	GLORY TRIP 127GB
1621	15-JUN-88	SLC-5		SCOUT		SLV	--
1623	12-JUL-88	LF-04		MINUTEMAN III	--	ICBM	GLORY TRIP 128GM
1622	12-JUL-88	LF-09		MINUTEMAN III	--	ICBM	GLORY TRIP 126GM
1624	25-AUG-88	SLC-5		SCOUT		SLV	--
1625	5-SEP-88	SLC-4	WEST	TITAN II	--	SLV	
1626	24-SEP-88	SLC-3	WEST	ATLAS-E		SLV	--
1627	27-OCT-88	LF-10		MINUTEMAN III	--	ICBM	GLORY TRIP 130GM
1628	6-NOV-88	SLC-4	EAST	TITAN 34D	--	SLV	
1629	25-JAN-89	LF-26		MINUTEMAN III	--	ICBM	GLORY TRIP 131GB
1630	22-FEB-89	LF-04		MINUTEMAN III	--	ICBM	GLORY TRIP 132GM
1631	7-MAR-89	LF-10		MINUTEMAN III	--	ICBM	GLORY TRIP 133GM
1632	19-MAR-89	LF-08		PEACEKEEPER	--	ICBM	FTM-18
1633	11-MAY-89	TP-01		SMALL ICBM		ICBM	--
1634	6-JUL-89	LF-26		MINUTEMAN III	--	ICBM	GLORY TRIP 129GB-2
1635	11-JUL-89	LF-09		MINUTEMAN III	--	ICBM	GLORY TRIP 134GM
1636	5-SEP-89	SLC-4	WEST	TITAN II	--	SLV	
1637	14-SEP-89	LF-02		PEACEKEEPER	--	ICBM	GLORY TRIP 01PA
1638	26-SEP-89	LF-26		MINUTEMAN III	--	ICBM	GLORY TRIP 135GB
1639	5-OCT-89	BMRS	A-3	AMROC/IRR		SLV	
1640	7-NOV-89	LF-10		MINUTEMAN III	--	ICBM	GLORY TRIP 136GM
1641	18-NOV-89	SLC-2	WEST	DELTA		SLV	--
1642	6-FEB-90	LF-26		MINUTEMAN III	--	ICBM	GLORY TRIP 137GB
1643	14-FEB-90	LF-03		MINUTEMAN IB	--	ICBM	
1644	8-MAR-90	LF-05		PEACEKEEPER	--	ICBM	GLORY TRIP 02PA
1645	21-MAR-90	LF-09		MINUTEMAN III	--	ICBM	GLORY TRIP 139GM

NO.	DATE	COMPLEX	PAD	LAUNCH VEHICLE	UPPER STAGE	TYPE	CODENAME
1646	24-MAR-90	LF-04		MINUTEMAN III	--	ICBM	GLORY TRIP 138GM
1647	11-APR-90	SLC-3	WEST	ATLAS-E		SLV	--
1648	9-MAY-90	SLC-5		SCOUT		SLV	--
1649	16-MAY-90	LF-08		PEACEKEEPER	--	ICBM	GLORY TRIP 03PA
1650	26-JUN-90	LF-26		MINUTEMAN III	--	ICBM	GLORY TRIP 140GB
1651	13-SEP-90	LF-05		PEACEKEEPER	--	ICBM	GLORY TRIP 04PA
1652	19-SEP-90	LF-09		MINUTEMAN III	--	ICBM	GLORY TRIP 141GM
1653	6-NOV-90	LF-04		MINUTEMAN III	--	ICBM	GLORY TRIP 142GM
1654	1-DEC-90	SLC-3	WEST	ATLAS-E		SLV	--
1655	28-JAN-91	LF-03		MINUTEMAN IB	--	ICBM	
1656	8-MAR-91	SLC-4	EAST	TITAN IV		SLV	
1657	12-MAR-91	LF-02		PEACEKEEPER	--	ICBM	GLORY TRIP 05PA
1658	18-APR-91	TP-01		SMALL ICBM		ICBM	--
1659	11-MAY-91	LF-03		MINUTEMAN IB	--	ICBM	
1660	14-MAY-91	SLC-3	WEST	ATLAS-E		SLV	--
1661	11-JUN-91	LF-08		PEACEKEEPER	--	ICBM	GLORY TRIP 06PA
1662	20-JUN-91	LF-03		MINUTEMAN IB	--	ICBM	
1663	25-JUN-91	LF-26		MINUTEMAN III	--	ICBM	GLORY TRIP 144GB
1664	29-JUN-91	SLC-5		SCOUT		SLV	--
1665	2-JUL-91	LF-10		MINUTEMAN III	--	ICBM	GLORY TRIP 143GM
1666	3-SEP-91	LF-04		MINUTEMAN III	--	ICBM	GLORY TRIP 145GM
1667	17-SEP-91	LF-02		PEACEKEEPER	--	ICBM	GLORY TRIP 07PA
1668	7-NOV-91	SLC-4	EAST	TITAN IV		SLV	
1669	11-NOV-91	LF-09		MINUTEMAN III	--	ICBM	GLORY TRIP 146GM
1670	28-NOV-91	SLC-3	WEST	ATLAS-E		SLV	--
1671	4-MAR-92	LF-05		PEACEKEEPER	--	ICBM	GLORY TRIP 08PA
1672	13-MAR-92	LF-03		MINUTEMAN IB	--	ICBM	
1673	25-APR-92	SLC-4	WEST	TITAN II	--	SLV	
1674	5-MAY-92	LF-10		MINUTEMAN III	--	ICBM	GLORY TRIP 147GM-1
1675	2-JUN-92	LF-26		MINUTEMAN III	--	ICBM	GLORY TRIP 148GB
1676	30-JUN-92	LF-02		PEACEKEEPER	--	ICBM	GLORY TRIP 09PA
1677	3-JUL-92	SLC-5		SCOUT		SLV	--
1678	15-SEP-92	LF-05		PEACEKEEPER	--	ICBM	GLORY TRIP 10PA
1679	28-SEP-92	LF-26		MINUTEMAN III	--	ICBM	GLORY TRIP 149GB
1680	24-OCT-92	LF-03		MINUTEMAN IB	--	ICBM	
1681	3-NOV-92	LF-04		MINUTEMAN III	--	ICBM	GLORY TRIP 150GM
1682	21-NOV-92	SLC-5		SCOUT		SLV	--
1683	28-NOV-92	SLC-4	EAST	TITAN IV		SLV	
1684	4-MAR-93	LF-02		PEACEKEEPER	--	ICBM	GLORY TRIP 11PA
1685	9-MAR-93	LF-26		MINUTEMAN III	--	ICBM	GLORY TRIP 151GB
1686	15-JUN-93	LF-03		MINUTEMAN IB	--	ICBM	
1687	25-JUN-93	SLC-5		SCOUT		SLV	--
1688	2-JUL-93	LF-09		MINUTEMAN III	--	ICBM	GLORY TRIP 152GM
1689	13-JUL-93	LF-05		PEACEKEEPER	--	ICBM	GLORY TRIP 12 PA
1690	2-AUG-93	SLC-4	EAST	TITAN IV		SLV	
1691	9-AUG-93	SLC-3	WEST	ATLAS-E		SLV	--
1692	31-AUG-93	LF-26		MINUTEMAN III	--	ICBM	GLORY TRIP 153GB
1693	15-SEP-93	LF-02		PEACEKEEPER	--	ICBM	GLORY TRIP 13PA
1694	5-OCT-93	SLC-4	WEST	TITAN II	--	SLV	
1695	25-JAN-94	SLC-4	WEST	TITAN II	--	SLV	
1696	2-FEB-94	LF-26		MINUTEMAN III	--	ICBM	GLORY TRIP 154GB
1697	4-FEB-94	LF-08		ASTRID		SOUNDING ROCKET	--
1698	7-MAR-94	LF-05		PEACEKEEPER	--	ICBM	GLORY TRIP 14PA
1699	13-MAR-94	576	(NEAR E)	TAURUS		SLV	--
1700	8-MAY-94	SLC-5		SCOUT		SLV	--

NO.	DATE	COMPLEX	PAD	LAUNCH VEHICLE	UPPER STAGE	TYPE	CODENAME
1701	17-MAY-94	LF-02		PEACEKEEPER	--	ICBM	GLORY TRIP 15PA
1702	8-JUN-94	LF-04		MINUTEMAN III	--	ICBM	GLORY TRIP 155GM
1703	6-JUL-94	LF-09		MINUTEMAN III	--	ICBM	GLORY TRIP 156GM
1704	29-AUG-94	SLC-3	WEST	ATLAS-E		SLV	--
1705	7-SEP-94	LF-05		PEACEKEEPER	--	ICBM	GLORY TRIP 16PA
1706	5-OCT-94	LF-04		MINUTEMAN III	--	ICBM	GLORY TRIP 157GM
1707	30-DEC-94	SLC-3	WEST	ATLAS-E		SLV	--
1708	19-JAN-95	LF-02		PEACEKEEPER	--	ICBM	GLORY TRIP 17PA
1709	1-FEB-95	LF-09		MINUTEMAN III	--	ICBM	GLORY TRIP 158GM
1710	17-MAR-95	LF-04		MINUTEMAN III	--	ICBM	GLORY TRIP 159GM ?
1711	24-MAR-95	SLC-3	WEST	ATLAS-E		SLV	--
1712	3-APR-95	AIRLIFT		PEGASUS		SLV	--
1713	14-JUN-95	LF-05		PEACEKEEPER	--	ICBM	GLORY TRIP 18PA
1714	22-JUN-95	AIRLIFT		PEGASUS		SLV	--
1715	15-AUG-95	SLC-6		LLV-1		SLV	--
1716	30-AUG-95	LF-02		PEACEKEEPER	--	ICBM	GLORY TRIP 19PA
1717	4-NOV-95	SLC-2	WEST	DELTA II		SLV	--
1718	5-DEC-95	SLC-4	EAST	TITAN IV		SLV	
1719	24-FEB-96	SLC-2	WEST	DELTA II		SLV	
1720	6-MAR-96	LF-09		MINUTEMAN III	--	ICBM	GLORY TRIP 161GM
1721	8-MAR-96	AIRLIFT		PEGASUS		SLV	
1722	24-APR-96	SLC-2	WEST	DELTA II		SLV	--
1723	8-MAY-96	LF-05		PEACEKEEPER	--	ICBM	GLORY TRIP 20PA
1724	12-MAY-96	SLC-4	EAST	TITAN IV		SLV	
1725	16-MAY-96	AIRLIFT		PEGASUS		SLV	--
1726	30-MAY-96	LF-02		PEACEKEEPER	--	ICBM	GLORY TRIP 21PA
1728	26-JUN-96	LF-04		MINUTEMAN III	--	ICBM	GLORY TRIP 160GM
1727	26-JUN-96	LF-10		MINUTEMAN III	--	ICBM	GLORY TRIP 162GM
1729	2-JUL-96	AIRLIFT		PEGASUS		SLV	--
1730	21-AUG-96	AIRLIFT		PEGASUS		SLV	--
1731	11-SEP-96	LF-05		PEACEKEEPER	--	ICBM	GLORY TRIP 22PA
1732	27-SEP-96	LF-03		MINUTEMAN II		ICBM	
1733	6-NOV-96	LF-02		PEACEKEEPER	--	ICBM	GLORY TRIP 23PA
1734	20-DEC-96	SLC-4	EAST	TITAN IV		SLV	
1735	16-JAN-97	LF-03		MINUTEMAN II		ICBM	
1736	30-JAN-97	LF-26		MINUTEMAN III	--	ICBM	GLORY TRIP 163GB
1737	4-APR-97	SLC-4	WEST	TITAN II		SLV	
1738	5-MAY-97	SLC-2	WEST	DELTA II		SLV	--
1739	8-MAY-97	LF-05		PEACEKEEPER	--	ICBM	GLORY TRIP 24PA
1740	21-MAY-97	LF-04		MINUTEMAN III	--	ICBM	GLORY TRIP 164GM
1741	18-JUN-97	LF-10		MINUTEMAN III	--	ICBM	GLORY TRIP 165GM
1742	23-JUN-97	LF-03		MINUTEMAN II	--	ICBM	
1743	9-JUL-97	SLC-2	WEST	DELTA II		SLV	--
1744	1-AUG-97	AIRLIFT		PEGASUS		SLV	--
1745	20-AUG-97	SLC-2	WEST	DELTA II		SLV	--
1746	22-AUG-97	SLC-6		LMLV-1		SLV	
1747	29-AUG-97	AIRLIFT		PEGASUS		SLV	
1748	17-SEP-97	LF-05		PEACEKEEPER	--	ICBM	GLORY TRIP 25PA
1749	26-SEP-97	SLC-2	WEST	DELTA II		SLV	--
1750	23-OCT-97	SLC-4	EAST	TITAN IV		SLV	
1751	5-NOV-97	LF-02		PEACEKEEPER	--	ICBM	GLORY TRIP 26PA
1752	8-NOV-97	SLC-2	WEST	DELTA II		SLV	--
1753	20-DEC-97	SLC-2	WEST	DELTA II		SLV	--
1754	15-JAN-98	LF-03		MINUTEMAN II	--	ICBM	
1755	10-FEB-98	576	E	TAURUS		SLV	--

NO.	DATE	COMPLEX	PAD	LAUNCH VEHICLE	UPPER STAGE	TYPE	CODENAME
1756	18-FEB-98	SLC-2	WEST	DELTA II		SLV	--
1757	20-FEB-98	LF-04		MINUTEMAN III	--	ICBM	GLORY TRIP 166GM
1758	25-FEB-98	AIRLIFT		PEGASUS		SLV	
1759	29-MAR-98	SLC-2	WEST	DELTA II		SLV	--
1760	1-APR-98	AIRLIFT		PEGASUS		SLV	
1761	7-MAY-98	LF-05		PEACEKEEPER	--	ICBM	GLORY TRIP 27PA
1762	13-MAY-98	SLC-4	WEST	TITAN II	--	SLV	
1763	17-MAY-98	SLC-2	WEST	DELTA II		SLV	
1764	3-JUN-98	LF-26		MINUTEMAN III	--	ICBM	GLORY TRIP 167GB
1765	24-JUN-98	LF-09		MINUTEMAN III	--	ICBM	IDF-1
1766	24-JUN-98	LF-10		MINUTEMAN III	--	ICBM	GLORY TRIP 168GM
1767	8-SEP-98	SLC-2	WEST	DELTA II		SLV	--
1768	18-SEP-98	LF-26		MINUTEMAN III	--	ICBM	IDF-2
1769	3-OCT-98	576	E	TAURUS		SLV	--
1770	6-NOV-98	SLC-2	WEST	DELTA II		SLV	--
1771	5-DEC-98	AIRLIFT		PEGASUS		SLV	
1772	10-FEB-99	LF-04		MINUTEMAN III	--	ICBM	GLORY TRIP 169GM
1773	23-FEB-99	SLC-2	WEST	DELTA II		SLV	
1774	4-MAR-99	AIRLIFT		PEGASUS		SLV	--
1775	10-MAR-99	LF-02		PEACEKEEPER	--	ICBM	GLORY TRIP 28PA
1776	15-APR-99	SLC-2	WEST	DELTA II		SLV	--
1777	27-APR-99	SLC-6		ATHENA II		SLV	--
1778	17-MAY-99	AIRLIFT		PEGASUS		SLV	--
1779	22-MAY-99	SLC-4	EAST	TITAN IV		SLV	
1780	19-JUN-99	SLC-4	WEST	TITAN II	--	SLV	
1782	20-AUG-99	LF-09		MINUTEMAN III	--	ICBM	GLORY TRIP 171 ????
1781	20-AUG-99	LF-10		MINUTEMAN III	--	ICBM	GLORY TRIP 170GM-1
1783	24-SEP-99	SLC-6		ATHENA II		SLV	--
1784	2-OCT-99	LF-03		MINUTEMAN II	--	ICBM	
1785	13-NOV-99	LF-26		MINUTEMAN III	--	ICBM	FTM-01
1786	12-DEC-99	SLC-4	WEST	TITAN II	--	SLV	
1787	18-DEC-99	SLC-3	EAST	ATLAS IIAS		SLV	--
1788	20-DEC-99	576	E	TAURUS		SLV	--
1789	18-JAN-00	LF-03		MINUTEMAN II	--	ICBM	
1790	26-JAN-00	SLF		MINOTAUR/OSPSLV		SLV	
1791	8-MAR-00	LF-05		PEACEKEEPER	--	ICBM	GLORY TRIP 29PA
1792	12-MAR-00	576	E	TAURUS		SLV	--
1793	25-MAR-00	SLC-2	WEST	DELTA II		SLV	--
1794	24-MAY-00	LF-09		MINUTEMAN III	--	ICBM	FTM-02
1795	28-MAY-00	LF-06		MINUTEMAN II	--	ICBM	
1796	7-JUN-00	AIRLIFT		PEGASUS		SLV	--
1797	9-JUN-00	LF-10		MINUTEMAN III	--	ICBM	GLORY TRIP 172GM
1798	7-JUL-00	LF-03		MINUTEMAN II	--	ICBM	
1799	19-JUL-00	SLF		MINOTAUR/OSPSLV		SLV	
1800	17-AUG-00	SLC-4	EAST	TITAN IV		SLV	
1801	21-SEP-00	SLC-4	WEST	TITAN II	--	SLV	
1803	28-SEP-00	LF-04		MINUTEMAN III	--	ICBM	GLORY TRIP 173GM
1802	28-SEP-00	LF-09		MINUTEMAN III	--	ICBM	GLORY TRIP 174GM
1804	21-NOV-00	SLC-2	WEST	DELTA II		SLV	--
1805	7-FEB-01	LF-10		MINUTEMAN III	--	ICBM	GLORY TRIP 175GM
1806	14-JUL-01	LF-03		MINUTEMAN II	--	ICBM	
1807	27-JUL-01	LF-02		PEACEKEEPER	--	ICBM	GLORY TRIP 30PA
1808	31-AUG-01	LF-21		GMD		ICBM	--
1809	8-SEP-01	SLC-3	EAST	ATLAS IIAS		SLV	--
1810	21-SEP-01	576	E	TAURUS		SLV	--

NO.	DATE	COMPLEX	PAD	LAUNCH VEHICLE	UPPER STAGE	TYPE	CODENAME
1811	4-OCT-01	SLC-4	EAST	TITAN IV		SLV	
1812	18-OCT-01	SLC-2	WEST	DELTA II		SLV	--
1813	7-NOV-01	LF-04		MINUTEMAN III	--	ICBM	GLORY TRIP 176GM
1814	4-DEC-01	LF-06		MINUTEMAN II		ICBM	
1815	7-DEC-01	SLC-2	WEST	DELTA II		SLV	
1816	13-DEC-01	LF-21		GMD		ICBM	--
1817	11-FEB-02	SLC-2	WEST	DELTA II		SLV	--
1818	15-MAR-02	LF-06		MINUTEMAN II	--	ICBM	
1819	8-APR-02	LF-10		MINUTEMAN III	--	ICBM	GLORY TRIP 178GM
1820	4-MAY-02	SLC-2	WEST	DELTA II		SLV	--
1821	3-JUN-02	LF-02		PEACEKEEPER	--	ICBM	GLORY TRIP 31PA
1822	7-JUN-02	LF-26		MINUTEMAN III	--	ICBM	GLORY TRIP 179GB
1823	24-JUN-02	SLC-4	WEST	TITAN II	--	SLV	
1824	17-JUL-02	LF-09		MINUTEMAN III	--	ICBM	GLORY TRIP 177GM
1825	19-SEP-02	LF-04		MINUTEMAN III	--	ICBM	GLORY TRIP 180GM
1826	14-OCT-02	LF-06		MINUTEMAN II	--	ICBM	
1827	14-NOV-02	LF-7632		SCUD-B		MRBM	--
1828	25-NOV-02	LF-7632		SCUD-B		MRBM	--
1829	11-DEC-02	LF-06		MINUTEMAN II		ICBM	
1830	6-JAN-03	SLC-4	WEST	TITAN II	--	SLV	
1831	12-JAN-03	SLC-2	WEST	DELTA II		SLV	
1832	6-FEB-03	576	E	TAURUS LITE		SLV	
1833	12-MAR-03	LF-02		PEACEKEEPER	--	ICBM	GLORY TRIP 32PA
1834	11-JUN-03	LF-04		MINUTEMAN III	--	ICBM	GLORY TRIP 182GM
1835	26-JUN-03	AIRLIFT		PEGASUS		SLV	--
1836	6-AUG-03	LF-26		MINUTEMAN III	--	ICBM	GLORY TRIP 183GB
1837	12-AUG-03	AIRLIFT		PEGASUS		SLV	--
1838	16-AUG-03	LF-23		GMD		ICBM	--
1839	10-SEP-03	LF-10		MINUTEMAN III	--	ICBM	GLORY TRIP 181GM
1840	18-OCT-03	SLC-4	WEST	TITAN II	--	SLV	
1841	2-DEC-03	SLC-3	EAST	ATLAS IIAS		SLV	--
1842	9-JAN-04	LF-21		GMD		ICBM	--
1843	20-APR-04	SLC-2	WEST	DELTA II		SLV	--
1844	20-MAY-04	576	E	TAURUS XL		SLV	--
1845	23-JUN-04	LF-10		MINUTEMAN III	--	ICBM	GLORY TRIP 185GM
1846	15-JUL-04	SLC-2	WEST	DELTA II		SLV	--
1847	21-JUL-04	LF-05		PEACEKEEPER	--	ICBM	GLORY TRIP 33PA
1848	23-JUL-04	LF-09		MINUTEMAN III	--	ICBM	GLORY TRIP 184GM-1
1849	15-SEP-04	LF-26		MINUTEMAN III	--	ICBM	GLORY TRIP 186GB
1850	11-APR-05	SLC-8		MINOTAUR		SLV	
1851	15-APR-05	AIRLIFT		PEGASUS		SLV	--
1852	20-MAY-05	SLC-2	WEST	DELTA II		SLV	--
1853	21-JUL-05	LF-10		MINUTEMAN III	--	ICBM	SERV #1-1
1854	25-AUG-05	LF-26		MINUTEMAN III	--	ICBM	SERV #2
1855	7-SEP-05	LF-04		MINUTEMAN III	--	ICBM	GLORY TRIP 187GM-1
1856	14-SEP-05	LF-09		MINUTEMAN III	--	ICBM	GLORY TRIP 189GM
1857	22-SEP-05	SLC-8		MINOTAUR		SLV	
1858	19-OCT-05	SLC-4	EAST	TITAN IV		SLV	
1859	16-FEB-06	LF-10		MINUTEMAN III	--	ICBM	SERV #3
1860	22-MAR-06	AIRLIFT		PEGASUS		SLV	--
1861	7-APR-06	LF-26		MINUTEMAN III	--	ICBM	GLORY TRIP 190GB
1862	14-APR-06	SLC-8		MINOTAUR		SLV	
1863	28-APR-06	SLC-2	WEST	DELTA II		SLV	--
1864	14-JUN-06	LF-04		MINUTEMAN III	--	ICBM	GLORY TRIP 191GM
1865	27-JUN-06	SLC-6		DELTA IV		SLV	--

NO.	DATE	COMPLEX	PAD	LAUNCH VEHICLE	UPPER STAGE	TYPE	CODENAME
1866	20-JUL-06	LF-09		MINUTEMAN III	--	ICBM	GLORY TRIP 192GM
1867	1-SEP-06	LF-23		GMD		ICBM	--
1868	4-NOV-06	SLC-6		DELTA IV		SLV	--
1869	14-DEC-06	SLC-2	WEST	DELTA II		SLV	--
1870	7-FEB-07	LF-10		MINUTEMAN III	--	ICBM	GLORY TRIP 193GM
1871	20-MAR-07	LF-06		TLV-5 (MINUTEMAN F)		ICBM	
1872	25-APR-07	AIRLIFT		PEGASUS		SLV	--
1873	7-JUN-07	SLC-2	WEST	DELTA II		SLV	--
1874	23-AUG-07	LF-06		TLV-7 (MINUTEMAN F)		ICBM	
1875	18-SEP-07	SLC-2	WEST	DELTA II		SLV	--
1876	28-SEP-07	LF-23		GMD		ICBM	--
1877	8-DEC-07	SLC-2	WEST	DELTA II		SLV	--
1878	13-MAR-08	SLC-3	EAST	ATLAS V		SLV	--
1879	2-APR-08	LF-09		MINUTEMAN III	--	ICBM	GLORY TRIP 196GM
1880	22-MAY-08	LF-10		MINUTEMAN III	--	ICBM	GLORY TRIP 197GM
1881	20-JUN-08	SLC-2	WEST	DELTA II		SLV	--
1882	13-AUG-08	LF-04		MINUTEMAN III	--	ICBM	GLORY TRIP 194GM-1
1883	6-SEP-08	SLC-2	WEST	DELTA II		SLV	--
1884	23-SEP-08	LF-06		TLV-8 (MINUTEMAN F)		ICBM	
1885	24-OCT-08	SLC-2	WEST	DELTA II		SLV	--
1886	5-NOV-08	LF-09		MINUTEMAN III	--	ICBM	GLORY TRIP 198GM
1887	5-DEC-08	LF-23		GMD		ICBM	--
1888	6-FEB-09	SLC-2	WEST	DELTA II		SLV	--
1889	24-FEB-09	576	E	TAURUS XL		SLV	--
1890	5-MAY-09	SLC-2	WEST	DELTA II		SLV	--
1891	29-JUN-09	LF-04		MINUTEMAN III	--	ICBM	GLORY TRIP 199GM
1892	23-AUG-09	LF-09		MINUTEMAN III	--	ICBM	GLORY TRIP 195GM-2
1893	8-OCT-09	SLC-2	WEST	DELTA II		SLV	--
1894	18-OCT-09	SLC-3	EAST	ATLAS V		SLV	--
1895	14-DEC-09	SLC-2	WEST	DELTA II		SLV	--
1896	31-JAN-10	LF-23		GMD		ICBM	--
1897	22-APR-10	SLC-8		MINOTAUR IV (LITE)		SLV	
1898	6-JUN-10	LF-24		GMD		ICBM	--
1899	16-JUN-10	LF-10		MINUTEMAN III	--	ICBM	GLORY TRIP 200GM-1
1900	30-JUN-10	LF-04		MINUTEMAN III	--	ICBM	GLORY TRIP 201GM
1901	17-SEP-10	LF-09		MINUTEMAN III	--	ICBM	GLORY TRIP 202GM
1902	20-SEP-10	SLC-3	EAST	ATLAS V		SLV	--
1903	25-SEP-10	SLC-8		MINOTAUR IV		SLV	
1904	5-NOV-10	SLC-2	WEST	DELTA II		SLV	--
1905	15-DEC-10	LF-23		GMD	--	ICBM	--
1906	20-JAN-11	SLC-6		DELTA IV		SLV	--
1907	6-FEB-11	SLC-8		MINOTAUR I		SLV	
1908	4-MAR-11	576E		TAURUS XL		SLV	--
1909	14-APR-11	SLC-3	EAST	ATLAS V		SLV	--
1910	10-JUN-11	SLC-2	WEST	DELTA II		SLV	--
1911	22-JUN-11	LF-10		MINUTEMAN III	--	ICBM	GLORY TRIP 204GM
1912	27-JUL-11	LF-04		MINUTEMAN III	--	ICBM	GLORY TRIP 205GM
1913	11-AUG-11	SLC-8		MINOTAUR IV		SLV	
1914	28-OCT-11	SLC-2	WEST	DELTA II		SLV	--
1915	25-FEB-12	LF-09		MINUTEMAN III	--	ICBM	GLORY TRIP 203GM
1916	3-APR-12	SLC-6		DELTA IV		SLV	--
N/A	16-JUN-12	N/A		X-37B	--	--	
1917	13-SEP-12	SLC-3	EAST	ATLAS V		SLV	--
1918	14-NOV-12	LF-10		MINUTEMAN III	--	ICBM	GLORY TRIP 206GM
N/A	3-DEC-12	N/A		X-37B	--	--	

NO.	DATE	COMPLEX	PAD	LAUNCH VEHICLE	UPPER STAGE	TYPE	CODENAME
1919	26-JAN-13	LF-23		GMD	--	ICBM	--
1920	11-FEB-13	SLC-3	EAST	ATLAS V		SLV	--
1921	22-MAY-13	LF-04		MINUTEMAN III	--	ICBM	GLORY TRIP 207GM
1922	27-JUN-13	AIR LIFT		PEGASUS		SLV	
1923	5-JUL-13	LF-24		GMD		ICBM	--
1924	28-AUG-13	SLC-6		DELTA IV		SLV	--
1925	22-SEP-13	LF-10		MINUTEMAN III	--	ICBM	GLORY TRIP 209GM
1926	26-SEP-13	LF-09		MINUTEMAN III	--	ICBM	GLORY TRIP 208GM
1927	29-SEP-13	SLC-4	EAST	FALCON 9		SLV	--
1928	6-DEC-13	SLC-3	EAST	ATLAS V		SLV	--
1929	17-DEC-13	LF-04		MINUTEMAN III	--	ICBM	GLORY TRIP 210GM
1930	3-APR-14	SLC-3	EAST	ATLAS V		SLV	--
1931	22-JUN-14	LF-23		GMD		ICBM	
1932	2-JUL-14	SLC-2	WEST	DELTA II		SLV	--
1933	13-AUG-14	SLC-3	EAST	ATLAS V		SLV	--
1934	23-SEP-14	LF-09		MINUTEMAN III	--	ICBM	GLORY TRIP 211GM
N/A	17-OCT-14	N/A		X-37B		--	
1935	12-DEC-14	SLC-3	EAST	ATLAS V		SLV	--
1936	31-JAN-15	SLC-2	WEST	DELTA II		SLV	--
1937	23-MAR-15	LF-10		MINUTEMAN III	--	ICBM	GLORY TRIP 214GM
1938	27-MAR-15	LF-04		MINUTEMAN III	--	ICBM	GLORY TRIP 215GM
1939	20-MAY-15	LF-09		MINUTEMAN III	--	ICBM	GLORY TRIP 212GM
1940	19-AUG-15	LF-10		MINUTEMAN III	--	ICBM	GLORY TRIP 213GM
1941	8-OCT-15	SLC-3	EAST	ATLAS V		SLV	--
1942	21-OCT-15	LF-04		MINUTEMAN III	--	ICBM	GLORY TRIP 216GM
1943	18-JAN-16	SLC-4	EAST	FALCON-9		SLV	--
1944	28-JAN-16	LF-23		GMD		ICBM	--
1945	10-FEB-16	SLC-6		DELTA IV		SLV	--
1946	20-FEB-16	LF-09		MINUTEMAN III	--	ICBM	GLORY TRIP 217GM
1947	25-FEB-16	LF-10		MINUTEMAN III	--	ICBM	GLORY TRIP 218GM
1948	5-SEP-16	LF-04		MINUTEMAN III	--	ICBM	GLORY TRIP 219GM

List of Rocket & Missile Launch Facilities

Missile Launch Facilities

CURRENT NAME	PREVIOUS NAME
395A	N/A
395B	N/A
395C	N/A
395D	N/A
576C	N/A
576D	N/A
576E	N/A
576F	OSTF-1
576G	OSTF-2
ABRES B-1	576 B-1
ABRES B-2	576 B-2
ABRES B-3	576 B-3
BMRS A-1	576 A-1
BMRS A-2	576 A-2
BMRS A-3	576 A-3
BOMARC-1	N/A
BOMARC-2	N/A
LF-02	394 A-1
LF-03	394 A-2
LF-04	394 A-3
LF-05	394 A-4
LF-06	394 A-5
LF-07	394 A-6
LF-08	394 A-7
LF-09	N/A
LF-10	LF-22
LF-21	N/A
LF-23	N/A
LF-24	N/A
LF-25	N/A
LF-26	N/A
OSTF	N/A
SLTF	N/A
TP-01	N/A

Space Launch Facilities

CURRENT NAME	PREVIOUS NAME
SLC-1E	75-3-5
SLC-1W	75-3-4
SLC-2E	75-1-1
SLC-2W	75-1-2
SLC-3E	PALC-1-2
SLC-3W	PALC-1-1
SLC-4E	PALC-2-4
SLC-4W	PALC-2-3
SLC-5	PALC-D
SLC-6	N/A
SLC-7	PROPOSED NAME; NOT USED
SLC-8	SLF
SLC-10E	75-2-7
SLC-10W	75-2-6
LE-8	75-2-8
4300C	N/A
PAD B	PALC-B
PLC-C	PALC-C
PLC-A	PALC-A

Glossary

ABRES: Advanced Ballistic Reentry Systems

ABRV: Advanced Ballistic Reentry Vehicle [formerly LBRV]

ACC: Air Combat Command

ADC: Aerospace Defense Command

AEC: Atomic Energy Commission

AFGSC: Air Force Global Strike Command

AFMC: Air Force Materiel Command

AFRCO: Air Force Rapid Capabilities Office

AFSC: Air Force Systems Command

AFSPC: Air Force Space Command

ALCS: Airborne Launch Control System

AMROC: American Rocket Company

ARDC: Air Research and Development Command

ARPA: Advanced Research Projects Agency

ASTRID: Advanced Single-Stage Technology, Rapid Insertion Demonstration

BIOS: Biological Investigations of Space

BMDO: Ballistic Missile Defense Organization

BMRS : Ballistic Missile Reentry Systems

BOMARC: Boeing and Michigan Aeronautical Research Center

BVT: Boost Vehicle Test

CBC: Common Booster Core

CCTS: Combat Crew Training Squadron

CRL: USAF Cambridge Research Laboratories

CTL: Combat Training Launch

CTV: Controlled Test Vehicle

DAC ROC: Douglas Aircraft Rocket

DARPA: Defense Advanced Research Projects Agency

DASO: Demonstration and Shakedown Operations

DMSP: Defense Meteorological Satellite Program

DMSS: Defense Meteorological Satellite System

DT: Dedicated Target

DT&E: Development Test & Evaluation

DT&E PHASE I: Development Test & Evaluation (Missile Functional Performance)

DT&E PHASE II: Development Test & Evaluation (Missile Reentry Vehicle Capabilities)

DUAL LAUNCH: The launch of two missiles one after another within the same launch window

EELV: Evolved Expendable Launch Vehicle

EKV: Exoatmospheric Kill Vehicle

EO: electro-optical

EOS: Earth Observation System [or Satellite]

ERCS: Emergency Rocket Communications System (494L)

FDE: Force Development Evaluation

FOT: Follow-On Operational Test

FTG: Flight Test Ground

FTM: Flight Test Missile

GBI: Ground-Based Interceptor

GEOS: Geodetic Earth Orbiting Satellite

GEOSAT: Geodetic Satellite [Navy]

GERTS: General Electric Radio Tracking System

GFO: Geosat Follow-On

GLCM: Ground Launch Cruise Missile

GMD: Ground-Based Midcourse Defense

GOTS: Government Off-the-Shelf

GPALS: Global Protection against Limited Strikes

GRP: Guidance Replacement Program

HAP: High-Altitude Probe

HAS: High-Altitude Sampler [Program]

HTV: Hypersonic Technology Vehicle

ICBM: Intercontinental Ballistic Missile

IDF: Integrated Demonstration Flight

IFT: Integrated Flight Test [initially called ITF]

IGY: International Geophysical Year

IOC: Initial Operational Capability

IPA: ICBM Penetration Aids

IPMS: Inertial [navigation system] Performance Measurement System

IRAS: Infrared Astronomical Satellite

IRBM: Intermediate-Range Ballistic Missile

IRIS: International Radiation Investigation Satellite

IRR: Industrial Research Rocket

IRS: Interim Recovery System

ITF: Integrated Test Flight

ITOS: Improved Tiros Operational Satellite

IWST: Integrated Weapons System Training (RAF/SAC)

LANDSAT: Earth Resources Satellite

LBRV: Large Ballistic Reentry Vehicle (See ABRV)

LDCM: Landsat Data Continuity Mission

LE: Launch Emplacement

LEO: Low-Earth Orbiting

LF: Launch Facility

LLL: Lawrence Livermore Laboratory

LLV-1: Lockheed Launch Vehicle 1

LM: Lockheed Martin (Corporation)

LMLV-1: Lockheed Martin Launch Vehicle

LORV: Low Observable Reentry Vehicle

MACSAT: Multiple Access Communications Satellite

MAGSAT: Magnetic Field Measurement Satellite

MAPCE: Mobile Automatic Programmed Checkout Equipment

MaST: Maneuvering Systems Technology

MD: McDonnell Douglas

MDA: Missile Defense Agency

MINT: Miniaturized Instrumented Nose Tip

MLV: Medium-Lift [Launch] Vehicle

MOD: Modernized Minuteman (R&D, DASO)

MSLS: Multi-service Launch System

MSTI: Miniature Sensor Technology Integration

MSX: Midcourse Space Experiment

MTI: Multispectral Thermal Imager

MUBLCOM: Multiple Path Beyond Line of Sight Communications

N/A: Not Applicable

NASA: National Aeronautics and Space Administration

NAVSTAR: Navigation Satellite Timing and Ranging

NDS: Navigation Development Satellite

NERV: Nuclear Emulsion Recovery Vehicle

NFIRE: Near Field Infrared Experiment

NOAA: National Oceanic and Atmospheric Administration

NPOESS: National Polar-Orbiting Operational Environmental Satellite System

NPP: NPOESS Preparatory Project

NRO: National Reconnaissance Office

NROL: National Reconnaissance Office Launch

NRP: National Reconnaissance Program

NTS: Navigation Technology Satellite

NTV: Nosetip Vehicle

OBLSS: Operational Base Launch Safety System

OCO: Orbiting Carbon Observatory

OGO: Orbiting Geophysical Laboratory

OPADEC: Optical Particle Decoy

ORBCOMM (FM): Orbital Communications (Flight Module)

ORBVIEW: Orbital View

ORT: Operational Readiness Test

OSC: Orbital Sciences Corporation

OSL: Ogden Special Launch

OSPSLV: Orbital Suborbital Program Space Launch Vehicle

OSP/TLV: Orbital Suborbital Program/Target Launch Vehicle

OSTF: Operational System Test Facility

OSTM: Ocean Surface Topography Mission

OT: Operational Test

OTV: Orbital Test Vehicle

OV: Orbiting Vehicle

PALC: Point Arguello Launch Complex

PAS: Penetration Aids Study

PENAID: Penetration Aids

PLC: Probe Launch Complex (later renamed PALC)

PMR: Pacific Missile Range

PRIME: Precision Recovery Including Maneuvering Entry

PRP: Propulsion Replacement System

PVM: Production Verification Missile

QUICKSCAT: Quick Scatterometer

QUICK TOMS: Quick Total Ozone Mapping Spectrometer

R&D: Research and Development

RADARSAT: Radar Satellite

RADCAL: Radar Calibration

RAE: Radio Astronomy Explorer

RAF: Royal Air Force

REX: Radiation Experiment

RM: Radio Meter

ROCSAT: Republic of China Satellite

RSLP: Reentry Systems Launch Program

SAC: Strategic Air Command

SAC-C: Satelite de Aplicaciones Científicas-C [Argentine satellite]

SAFEGUARD: An Antiballistic Missile (ABM) test program

SALVO: Simultaneous launching of two or more missiles

SAMAST: Sandia ABRES Material Systems Test

SAMPEX: Solar, Anomalous, and Magnetospheric Particle Explorer

SBSS: Space-Based Space Surveillance

SCISAT: Science Satellite

SEASAT: Sea [Observation] Satellite

SENT: Severe Nose-Tip Environment Test

SERV: Safety Enhanced Reentry Vehicle

SET: Single Engine Test

SFT: Supplemental Flight Test

SLC: Space Launch Complex

SLF: Space Launch Facility

SLTF: Silo Launch Test Facility

SLV: Space Launch Vehicle

SM: Solar Mesosphere

SMC: Space and Missile Systems Center

SMLV: Single-Module Launch Vehicle

SNOE: Student Nitric Oxide Explorer

SOOS: Stacked Oscar On Scout

SOT: Special Operational Test

SPACE PROBE: A nonorbital space operation

ST: Special Test

STEP: Space Test Experiment Platform

STEX: Space Technology Experiment

STM: Special Test Missile

STP: Special [Space] Test Program

STREP: System Technology Reentry Experiments Program

STRR-ATRR: Space Tracking and Surveillance System, Advanced Technology Risk Reduction

SWAS: Submillimeter Wave Astronomy Satellite

TAC: Tactical Air Command

TARGET: Missile target for surface-to-air/air-to-air missile-firing practice

TAT: Thrust-Augmented Thor

TD: Technology Demonstration

TDT: Target Development Test

TDV: Technology Development Vehicle

TERRIERS: Tomographic Experiment Using Radioactive Recombinative Ionospheric Extreme Ultraviolet and Radio Sources

TIMED: Thermosphere, Ionosphere, Mesosphere, Energetics, and Dynamics

TIP: Transition Improvement Program

TLV: Target Launch Vehicle

TOMS-EP: Total Ozone Mapping Spectrometer–Earth Probe

TRACE: Transition Region and Coronal Explorer

TREP: Thrusted Replica

TP: Test Pad

TSX: Tri-Service Experiments

ULA: United Launch Alliance

UTE: Unified Test Equipment

WIRE: Wide-Field Infrared Explorer

WISE: Wide-Field Infrared Survey Explorer

XSS: Experimental Satellite System

Bibliography

ARTICLES

Alamogordo Daily News. "AFMDC Role Not Changed by 'Shifts.'" *Alamogordo Daily News* (Alamogordo, NM), 8 Dec. 1957.

Anselmo, Joseph. "Bigger Satellites Drive Plans for New Atlas, Athena Launchers." AWST Archive, 13 Apr. 1998.

———. "OrbImage and Spot Link Up: Ikonos Readied for Launch." AWST Archive, 20 Sep. 1999.

Associated Press. "Management Had Agreed to Let Board Act." *AP Archive*s, 21 Oct. 1941.

———. "Guardsmen Get Ready For Speed-Up Duties." *AP Archives*, 3 Aug. 1950.

———. "'Scared Down to My Toes' Says GI from A-Bomb Area." *AP Archives*, Nov. 2, 1951.

———. "Oil Forces Army to Put Camp on Inactive Status." *AP Archives*, 8 Nov. 1952.

———. "AF Building Ballistic Missile Base." *AP Archives*, 10 May 1957.

———. "Air Force Starts Construction on First Strategic Rocket Base." *AP Archives*, 10 May 1957.

———. "Work Underway on First Ballistic Missile Center." *AP Archives*, 13 May 1957.

———. "Air Force Announces New Ballistic Division." *AP Archives*, 13 Sep. 1957.

———. "Air Force Confirms Anti-missile Missile Now on Drawing Boards." *AP Archives*, 30 Nov. 1957.

———. "Pacific Missile Range Established." *AP Archives*, 30 Jan. 1958.

———. "Camp Cooke Gets Name Change." *Alamogordo Daily News* (Alamogordo, NM), 6 Oct. 1958.

———. "Rocket Range is Maximum Security Area." *Santa Fe New Mexican* (Santa Fe, NM), 14 Nov. 1958.

———. "IRBMs May Be Used Awhile Yet." *Alamogordo Daily News* (Alamogordo, NM), 16 Nov. 1958.

———. "AF Satellite Launch Dec. 15 Is Predicted." *Alamogordo Daily News* (Alamogordo, NM), 24 Nov. 1958.

———. "Combat Ready Unit Fires Giant Rocket." *AP Archives*, 17 Dec. 1958.

———. "Rockets to Test Space Radiation." *AP Archive*, 19 May 1960.

———. "Pacific Test to Study High Radiation Belt." *AP Archive*, 16 Sep. 1960.

———. "Experts Study Ruins of Titan." *Eugene Register-Guard* (Eugene, OR), 5 Dec. 1960.

———. "Rocket Shot for Flares in Space." *AP Archives*, 8 Dec. 1961.

———. "Secret Satellite Launched by AF." *Toledo Blade* (Toledo, OH), 18 Sep. 1962.

———. "Rocket Probes Radiation Belt." *AP Archives*, 12 Feb. 1963.

———. "Across the Nation." *Reading Eagle* (Reading, PA), 19 Oct. 1963.

———. "Satellite Attempt Fails." *Lawrence Journal-World* (Lawrence, KS), 22 Jan. 1965.

———. "Across the Nation." *Reading Eagle* (Reading, PA) Sep. 3, 1965.

———. "2 Missiles Test-Fired." *Spokesman-Review* (Spokane, WA), 22 Feb. 1967.

———. "Space Shuttle to Cape, Vandenberg." *AP Archive*, 14 Apr. 1972.

———. "Studying the Earth's Pulse." *AP Archive*, 20 Apr. 1986.

———. "Missile Test Succeeds." *Pittsburgh Post-Gazette* (Pittsburgh, PA), 29 Jan. 1987.

———. "U.S. Rocket Makers Frustrated by Red Tape." *AP Archives*, 16 Sep. 1987.

———. "Getting into Orbit on the Cheap." *Los Angeles Times* (Los Angeles, CA), 8 May 1989.

———. "Midgetman Test Flight Cut Short." *Milwaukee Journal* (Milwaukee, WI), 12 May 1989.

———. "Obituaries: George A. Koopman." *Santa Fe New Mexican* (Santa Fe, NM), 21 Jul. 1989.

———. "Major Space Role for State Envisioned." *AP Archive*, 5 Oct. 1990.

———. "Missile Launch Provides a Spectacular Light Show." *AP Archives*, 20 Sep. 2002.

Aviation Week and Space Technology. "Ballistic Missile Chronology." AWST Archive, 6 Aug. 1956.

———. "Convair Will Use Four Atlas Bases." AWST Archive, 19 Nov. 1956.

———. "New Rocket Research Vehicles Detailed." AWST Archive, 3 Dec. 1956.

———. "Guidance Changes Made on Atlas, Titan." AWST Archive, 28 Jul. 1958.

———. "Convair-Astronautics Fabricates Atlas Pressurized Fuel Tankage." AWST Archive, 25 May 1959.

———. "Rocket Probe Nuclear Blasts." AWST Archive, 10 Aug. 1959.

———. "All-SAC Crew Fires Initial Atlas ICBM." AWST Archive, 14 Sep. 1959.

———. "SAC Fires Atlas ICBM from Horizontal Pad." AWST Archive, 9 May 1960.

———. "SAC Cuts ICBM Crews, Maintenance." AWST Archive, 20 Jun. 1960.

———. "SAC Shapes Missile Force for Survival." AWST Archive, 20 Jun. 1960.

———. "Project GOLDEN RAM." AWST Archive, 19 Dec. 1960.

———. "GOLDEN RAM Produces Successful Atlas Shot." AWST Archive, 26 Dec. 1960.

———. "Service Use Modifies Missile Concepts." AWST Archive, 13 Mar. 1961.

———. "Atlas Coffin Firing Fails." AWST Archive, 12 Jun. 1961.

———. "Atlas E Fails." AWST Archive, 3 Jul. 1961.

———. "Atlas E Flight Test Program Reviewed." AWST Archive, 10 Jul. 1961.

———. "Atlas ICBM Geared to Total Deployment." AWST Archive, 25 Sep. 1961.

———. "Vandenberg Coordinates Ballistic Effort." AWST Archive, 25 Sep. 1961.

———. "Second BIOS Launching Fails." AWST Archive, 27 Nov. 1961.

———. "Project Cambridge Flash Flares Photographed over Pacific Ocean." AWST Archive, 18 Dec. 1961.

———. "Department of Defense Restricts Nike Zeus Testing Information." AWST Archive, 5 Feb. 1962.

———. "Golden Ram Payoff." AWST Archive, 12 Mar. 1962.

———. "Advanced Missile Re-entry Flight Tests Planned." AWST Archive, 10 Dec. 1962.

———. "Nike Zeus Intercepts Atlas Re-entry Body." AWST Archive, 17 Dec. 1962.

———. "U.S. Research Rockets." AWST Archive, 16 Mar. 1964.

———. "USAF Had 13 Straight Atlas Failures." AWST Archive, 20 Apr. 1964.

———. "Atlas-D Phase-Out." AWST Archive, 21 Sep. 1964.

———. "Industry Observer." AWST Archive, 1 Mar. 1965.

———. "Titan 3D Award." AWST Archive, 4 Dec. 1967.

———. "First Atlas/Burner 2 Launch Fails." AWST Archive, 26 Aug. 1968.

———. "Minuteman 3 Launch." AWST Archive, 30 Jun. 1969.

———. "Minuteman 3 Deployment Slated." AWST Archive, 16 Mar. 1970.

———. "Leading U.S., International Research Rockets." AWST Archive, 13 Mar. 1972.

———. "U.S. Rocket Motors." AWST Archive, 13 Mar. 1972.

———. "AMROC Rocket in Launch Position." AWST Archive, 4 Sep. 1989.

———. "Launch Vehicles." AWST Archive, 13 Jan. 1997.

———. "LMLV Readies for Return." AWST Archive, 7 Apr. 1997.

———. "World News Roundup." AWST Archive, 31 Jan. 2000.

———. "World News Roundup." AWST Archive, 20 Aug. 2001.

———. "Atlas V Debuts at Vandenberg." AWST Archive, 17 Mar. 2008.

———. "Minotaur IV Launches SBSS." AWST Archive, 4 Oct. 2010.

———. "The World." AWST Archive, 21 Feb. 2011.

———. "The World: Space." AWST Archive, 3 Mar. 2014.

Bako, Stacee. "Team Vandenberg Launches Scud Missile on Data-Seeking Mission." *Space & Missile Times,* 22 Nov. 2002, www.techexpo.com/WWW/opto-knowledge/Mssile-Defense.pdf.

Bender, Averam. "From Tanks to Missiles: Camp Cooke / Cooke Air Force Base, 1941–1958." *Arizona and the West* 9 (Autumn 1967): 219–42.

Berkowitz, Bruce D. "The Nine Lives of Slick Six: Vandenberg's Space Launch Complex 6." *Air & Space,* 1 Mar. 1997, http://infoweb.newsbank.com/resources/doc/nb/news/13E65206FB8C5AB0?p=NewsBank.

"Bomber Crew Reunites." *Lewiston Daily Sun* (Lewiston, ME), 14 Jul. 1987.

Broad, William. "What's Next for 'Star Wars' 'Brilliant Pebbles.'" *New York Times,* 25 Apr. 1989, www.nytimes.com/1989/04/25/science/what-s-next-for-star-wars-brilliant-pebbles.html.

Brooks, David. "Launch Failure Haunts AMROC." *The Telegraph* (Nashua, NH), 5 Nov. 1989.

"Business Friday: Failed Launch." *Milwaukee Journal* (Milwaukee, WI), 6 Oct. 1989.

Chicago Tribune Press Service. "Pacific Missile Range Goes from Navy to Air Force." *Chicago Tribune,* 21 Nov. 1963.

Clark, Stephen. "Taurus Rocket on the Market with New Name, Upgrades." *Spaceflight Now,* 24 Feb. 2014, http://spaceflightnow.com/news/n1402/24minotaurc/.

"Company Introduces New Rocket Engine." *Times-News* (Hendersonville, NC), 21 Feb. 1993.

Covault, Craig. "Launch Surge Begins for Secret NRO Missions." AWST Archive, 10 Sep. 2001.

Day, Dwayne A. "Death of a Monster." *Space Review,* 15 Dec. 2008, www.thespacereview.com/article/1268/1.

Diltz, Douglas. "Missiles-Men Are Married at Vandenberg." *St. Petersburg Times* (St. Petersburg, FL), 1 Mar. 1963.

Dornheim, Michael. "AMROC Retains Key Personnel despite Cutbacks after Pad Fire." *Aviation Week and Space Technology,* 30 Oct. 1989.

———. "Lockheed Completes LLV Mockup Stacking." AWST Archive, 1 Aug. 1994.

———. "ITT to Invest $31 Million in California Spaceport." AWST Archive, 5 Dec. 1994.

———. "Lockheed Must Prove LLV Reliability by June." AWST Archive, 21 Aug. 1995.

———. "Vectoring, IMU Destroyed LLV-1." AWST Archive, 18 Dec. 1995.

———. "LMLV-1 Gives Good Delivery to Orbit." AWST Archive, Sep. 1, 1997.

———. "Rendezvous Trials." AWST Archive, 18 Apr. 2005.

———. "The World: Space." AWST Archive, 3 Mar. 2014.

Ferrell, J. E. "Little Rocket Company Set to Compete." *The Telegraph* (Nashua, NH), 27 Jan. 1987.

"Force Improvement Program Gives Airmen Direct Line to Air Force Leaders." *Targeted News Service,* 7 Feb. 2014 / *Infotrac Newsstand* (web), 9 Aug. 2016.

Furniss, Tim. "The Thirteenth Delta." *Flight International,* 7 Jan. 1989.

Garwood, Darrell. "2 More Year-End Roundups on What to Expect in 1959." *UPI Archives,* 18 Dec. 1958.

Greer, Kenneth E. "CORONA." *Studies in Intelligence*, Central Intelligence Agency, 1973.

Grier, Peter. "STRAT-X." *Air Force Magazine*, Jan. 2010: 52–55, www.airforcemag.com/MagazineArchive/Documents/2010/January%202010/0110stratx.pdf.

Henry, Bonnie, "Famous Airman's Son Had Own Remarkable Air Force Career." *Arizona Daily Star* (Tucson, AZ), 1 Oct. 2007.

"Improved Bomarc Offers Greater U.S. Protection." *Albuquerque Tribune*, 21 Nov. 1958.

Kolcum, Edward. "Defense Dept. to Retain Expendable Launchers as Backup to Shuttle." AWST Archive, 18 Mar. 1985.

Lenorovitz, Jeffrey M. "Lockheed Develops Low-End Launch Vehicle." AWST Archive, 10 May 1993.

Mecham, Michael. "Faulty Athena Shroud Ruins Ikonos 1 Launch." AWST Archive, 3 May 1999.

———. "Ikonos Launch to Open New Earth-Imaging Era." AWST Archive, 4 Oct. 1999.

———. "Terra Launch Puts EOS Program on Track." AWST Archive, 1 Jan. 2000.

———. "New Pad Signals Shift for NRO." AWST Archive, 10 Jan. 2000.

Miller, Barry. "Studies of Penetration Aids Broadening." AWST Archive, 20 Jan. 1964.

Morring, Frank, Jr. "In Orbit: Indefinite Delay." AWST Archive, 12 Oct. 2009.

Petit, Charles. "Rockets for the Rest of Us." *Air & Space*, 1 Mar. 1998.

Picariello, Erica. "Historic Training Squadrons Merge, Missions Continue at Vandenberg." *30th Space Wing Public Affairs*, 13 Jul. 2013, www.vandenberg.af.mil/news/story.asp?id=123309905.

Powell, J. W., and G. R. Richards. "The Atlas E/F Launch Vehicle—an Unsung Workhorse." *Journal of the British Interplanetary Society* 44 (May 1991): 229–40, www.atlasmissilesilo.com/Documents/Operational/AZ-D-O-999-99-ZZ-00005_Atlas_E_F_LaunchVehicle_UnsungWorkhorse.pdf.

Quicksilver. "Entering Vandenberg Air Force Base." *Earth First! Journal* 23, no. 5 (Jul.–Aug. 2003).

Ray, Justin. "What to Do with the Final Delta 2 Rocket?" *Spaceflight Now*, 8 Apr. 2015, https://spaceflightnow.com/2015/04/08/what-to-do-with-the-final-delta-2-rocket/.

Richards, G. R., and J. W. Powell. "Waste Not—the Use of Ex-RAF Thor Vehicles." *Journal of the British Interplanetary Society* 50 (1977): 189–200.

Scully, Janene. "Firms Team to Revive Athena Rocket." *Lompoc Record*, 26 Mar. 2010, http://lompocrecord.com/news/local/military/article_aa462caa-3897-11df-b796-001cc4c002e0.html.

Souza, Ed. "Israelis Monitor VAFB Launch." *Santa Barbara News-Press*, 26 Nov. 2002, www.techexpo.com/WWW/opto-knowledge/Mssile-Defense.pdf.

Stone, Brad. "Pushing That Frontier." *Newsweek*, 21 Nov. 2003.

Stone, Irving. "U.S. Schedules Additional SAMOS Launches." AWST Archive, 17 Oct. 1960.

Sweeney, Richard. "Atlas Generate Fabrication Advances." AWST Archive, 4 Jan. 1960.

"Tech Update: Blastoff from the Middle of Nowhere." *Popular Mechanics* 170, no. 7 (Jul. 1993): 17.

Totemeier, Carl. "Gardening; Marigolds: America's Beautiful Native." *New York Times*, 31 May 1987, www.nytimes.com/1987/05/31/nyregion/gardening-marigolds-america-s-beautiful-native-by-carl-totemeier.html.

United Press International. "Camp Cooke May Become Missile Site." UPI Archives, 2 Jan. 1958.

———. "Missile Testing Center Commissioned by Navy." UPI Archives, 10 May 1958.

———. "Moon Shot Set on West Coast." *Albuquerque Journal* (Albuquerque, NM), 28 Oct. 1958.

———. "Titan Roars Aloft in 'Routine' Launch." *Eugene Register-Guard* (Eugene, OR), 12 Apr. 1963.

———. "Air Force Plans Manned Space Lab by '70." UPI Archives, 12 Jun. 1966.

———. "Rocket's Explosion Deals U.S. a Blow." *Mohave Daily Miner* (Kingman, AZ), 20 Apr. 1986.

———. "Private Rocket Readied for Launch." UPI Archives, 25 Aug. 1989.

———. "Shuttle May Put Vandenberg Back in the Space Business." UPI Archives: Domestic News, 30 Nov. 1980 / *Infotrac Newsstand* (web), 9 Aug. 2016.

Wattles, Jackie, and Robert McLean. "SpaceX Rocket Explodes after Landing." CNN, 18 Jan. 2016, http://money.cnn.com/2016/01/17/technology/spacex-launch/.

Whitehead, John. "ASTRID Rocket Flight Test." *Energy and Technology Review* (University of California, Lawrence Livermore National Laboratory), Jul. 1994, https://str.llnl.gov/etr/pdfs/07_94.2.pdf.

BOOKS

Arnold, David C. *Spying from Space: Constructing America's Satellite Command and Control Systems*. College Station: Texas A&M University Press, 2005.

Baker, David, ed. *Jane's Space Directory: 2001–2002*. Coulsdon, UK: Jane's Information Group, 2001.

Berger, Carl. *History of the 1st Missile Division*. Vandenberg AFB, CA: Strategic Air Command, 1960.

Berger, Carl, and Warren S. Howard. *History of the 1st Strategic Aerospace Division and Vandenberg Air Force Base, 1957–1961*. Vandenberg AFB, CA: Headquarters, 1st Strategic Aerospace Division, 1962.

Bulfinch, Thomas. *Mythology*. New York: Dell, 1959.

Burgess, Colin, and Chris Dubbs. *Animals in Space: From Research Rockets to the Space Shuttle*. Chichester, UK: Springer-Praxis, 2007.

Del Papa, Michael. *From Snark to Peacekeeper: A Pictorial History of Strategic Air Command Missiles*. Offutt AFB, NE: Office of the Historian, Strategic Air Command, 1990.

Gibson, James N. *Nuclear Weapons of the United States: An Illustrated History*. Atglen, PA: Schiffer, 1996.

Goldberg, Alfred, ed. *History of the Strategic Arms Competition, 1945–1972: Part II*. Washington, DC: Office of the Secretary of Defense, 1981.

Hagopian, Martin. *From Tanks to Missiles: Vandenberg Air Force Base*. Vandenberg AFB, CA: 20th Air Force History Office, 1993.

———. *From Tanks to Missiles: Vandenberg Air Force Base and the 30th Space Wing from Camp Cooke to the Present*. Vandenberg AFB, CA: 30th Space Wing History Office, 1995.

Haines, Gerald K. *Critical to US Security: The Development of the GAMBIT and HEXAGON Satellite Reconnaissance Systems*. Chantilly, VA: National Reconnaissance Office, 1997, www.nro.gov/foia/declass/GAMHEX/GAMBIT%20and%20HEXAGON%20Histories/2.PDF.

Heefner, Gretchen. *The Missile Next Door: The Minuteman in the American Heartland*. Cambridge, MA: Harvard University Press, 2012.

Heppenheimer, T. A. *Facing the Heat Barrier: A History of Hypersonics*. Washington. DC: National Aeronautics and Space Administration, 2007.

Jacobs, Horace, and Eunice Engelke Whitney. *Missile and Space Projects Guide 1962*. New York: Plenum, 1962.

Launius, Roger D., and Dennis R. Jenkins. *Coming Home: Reentry and Recovery from Space*. Washington, DC: Government Printing Office, 2012.

Launius, Roger D., and Dennis R. Jenkins, eds. *To Reach the High Frontier: A History of US Launch Vehicles*. Lexington: University of Kentucky Press, 2015.

Lloyd, A. *Cold War Legacy: A Tribute to the Strategic Air Command: 1946–1992*. New York: Turner, 2000.

Lonnquest, John, and David Winkler. *To Defend and Deter: The Legacy of the United States Cold War Missile Program*. Washington, DC: Department of Defense, Legacy Resource Management Program, 1996.

McDonald, Robert A., and Sharon K. Moreno. *Raising the Periscope: GRAB and POPPY; America's Early ELINT Satellites*. Chantilly, VA: National Reconnaissance Office, Sep. 2005.

Narducci, Henry. *Strategic Air Command and the Alert Program: A Brief History*. Omaha, NE: Office of the Historian, Strategic Air Command, 1988.

Neal, Roy. *Ace in the Hole: The Story of the Minuteman Missile*. New York: Doubleday, 1962.

Neufeld, Jacob, George M. Watson Jr., and David Chenoweth, eds. *Technology and the Air Force: A Retrospective Assessment*. Washington, DC: Air Force History and Museums Program, 1997.

O'Leary, Beth, and P. J. Capelotti, eds. *Archaeology and Heritage of the Human Movement into Space*. Cham, Switzerland: Springer, 2015.

Page, Joseph T., II. *Space Launch Complex Ten: Vandenberg's Cold War National Monument*. Stroud, UK: History Press, 2016.

Palmer, Kevin. *Central Coast Continuum: From Ranchos to Rockets*. Santa Maria, CA: BTG, 1999.

Peebles, Curtis. *The CORONA Project: America's First Spy Satellites*. Annapolis, MD: Naval Institute Press, 1997.

Perry, Robert L. *History of Satellite Reconnaissance*. 7 vols. Chantilly, VA: National Reconnaissance Office, 1969–74.

———. Vol. I, *CORONA*. Chantilly, VA: National Reconnaissance Office, Oct. 1973, www.nro.gov/foia/docs/hosr/hosr-vol1.pdf.

———. Vol. IIA, *SAMOS*. Chantilly, VA: National Reconnaissance Office, Oct. 1973, www.nro.gov/foia/docs/hosr/hosr-vol2a.pdf.

———. Vol. IIB, *SAMOS E-5 and E-6*. Chantilly, VA: National Reconnaissance Office, Oct. 1973, www.nro.gov/foia/docs/hosr/hosr-vol2b.pdf.

———. Vol. IIIA, *GAMBIT*. Chantilly, VA: National Reconnaissance Office, Jan. 1974, www.nro.gov/foia/docs/hosr/hosr-vol3a.pdf.

———. Vol. IIIB, *HEXAGON*. Chantilly, VA: National Reconnaissance Office, Nov. 1973, www.nro.gov/foia/docs/hosr/hosr-vol3b.pdf.

———. Vol. IV, *NRO History* (draft). Chantilly, VA: National Reconnaissance Office, n.d., www.nro.gov/foia/docs/hosr/hosr-vol4.pdf.

———. Vol. V, *Management of the National Reconnaissance Program, 1960–1965*. Chantilly, VA: National Reconnaissance Office, Jan. 1969, www.nro.gov/foia/docs/hosr/hosr-vol5.pdf.

Polmar, Norman, and Robert S. Norris. *The U.S. Nuclear Arsenal: A History of Weapons and Delivery Systems since 1945*. Annapolis, MD: Naval Institute Press, 2009.

Ruffner, Kevin C., ed. *CORONA: America's First Satellite Program*. Washington, DC: CIA Center for the Study of Intelligence, 1995, www.cia.gov/library/center-for-the-study-of-intelligence/csi-publications/books-and-monographs/corona.pdf.

Sheehan, Neil. *A Fiery Peace in a Cold War: Bernard Schriever and the Ultimate Weapon*. New York: Random House, 2009.

Spires, David. *On Alert: An Operational History of the United States Air Force Intercontinental Ballistic Missile Program, 1945–2011*. Colorado Springs, CO: Air Force Space Command History Office, 2012.

Stumpf, David. *Titan II: A History of a Cold War Missile Program*. Fayetteville: University of Arkansas Press, 2000.

Walker, Chuck. *Atlas: The Ultimate Weapon*. Burlington, ON: Apogee Books, 2005.

Waltrop, David. *An Underwater Ice Station Zebra: Recovering a Secret Spy Capsule from 16,400 Feet below the Pacific Ocean.* Langley, VA: Central Intelligence Agency, 2012.

Webster, Julie L., Patrick Nowlan, and Martin Stupich. *Historic American Engineering Record: Documentation of Three Peacekeeper Facilities at Vandenberg Air Force Base.* Vandenberg AFB, CA: 30th Civil Engineering Squadron, 2004.

CHRONOLOGIES

Air Force Space Command. *Peacekeeper Missile Chronology: 1971–2005.* Colorado Springs, CO: Air Force Space Command Office of History, Dec. 2008.

Emme, Eugene M. *Aeronautics and Astronautics: An American Chronology of Science and Technology in the Exploration of Space. 1915–1960.* Washington, DC: National Aeronautics and Space Administration, 1961.

Hanner, Ray. *Chronology of the 392d Missile Training Squadron (THOR).* Vandenberg AFB, CA: Headquarters, 1st Strategic Aerospace Division, 1960.

———. *Chronology of the 576th Strategic Missile Squadron (Atlas-ICBM).* Vandenberg AFB, CA: Headquarters, 1st Strategic Aerospace Division, 1961.

Hunter, Peter. "All Thor-Delta Launches—Prime Payload, Chronological." 23 Jan. 2005.

Strategic Air Command Office of History. "SAC Missile Chronology, 1939–1988." N.d.

———. "Strategic Air Command Operations in the Cuban Crisis of 1962." *SAC Historical Study* 1, no. 90 (n.d.). Offutt AFB, NE: Strategic Air Command History Office.

DATABASES

Department of the Air Force. "eFOIA: Vandenberg Launch Summary." 3 Dec. 2015. www.foia.af.mil/shared/media/document/afd-100316-046.pdf

Hansen, Chuck. *Swords of Armageddon.* Vol. 7, *Artillery Shells, Missile Warheads, etc., Histories.* CD-ROM. San Jose, CA: Chuckelea, 2007.

30th Space Wing. "Vandenberg AFB Launch Summary: 1958–2017." Electronic edition. Vandenberg AFB, CA, 2017.

FACTSHEETS

Air Force Ballistic Missile Division. "Agena Fact Sheet, Release 59-64." NRO WS117L Collection, www.nro.gov/foia/declass/WS117L_Records/484.PDF.

———. "BOMARC-B Factsheet." Hill Air Force Base, UT, 2007, www.hill.af.mil/About-Us/Fact-Sheets/Display/Article/397255/bomarc-b.

Department of the Air Force. "Fact Sheet: Atlas Launch Vehicle." Current as of Jan. 1999. www.au.af.mil/au/awc/awcgate/smc-fs/atl2_fs.htm.

———. "30 Operations Group (AFSPC)." Air Force Historical Research Agency, 2008, www.afhra.af.mil/factsheets/factsheet.asp?id=11642.

———. "595 Space Group (AFSPC)." Air Force Historical Research Agency, 2008, www.afhra.af.mil/factsheets/factsheet.asp?id=10272.

———. "394 Maintenance Support Squadron." Air Force Historical Research Agency, 2008.

———. "576 Flight Test Squadron (AFGSC)." Air Force Historical Research Agency, 2008, www.afhra.af.mil/factsheets/factsheet.asp?id=12034.

———. "BGM-109G Ground Launched Cruise Missile Fact Sheet." 15 Oct. 2008, www.hill.af.mil/About-Us/Fact-Sheets/Display/Article/397188/bgm-109g-gryphon-ground-launched-cruise-missile.

———. "Fourteenth Air Force (Air Forces Strategic) (AFSPC)." Factsheet, Air Force Historical Research Agency, 2010, www.afhra.af.mil/factsheets/factsheet.asp?id=11030.

———. "Twentieth Air Force (Air Forces Strategic) (AFGSC)." Air Force Historical Research Agency, 2011, www.afhra.af.mil/factsheets/factsheet.asp?id=11036.

———. "532 Training Squadron (AETC)." Air Force Historical Research Agency, 2012, www.afhra.af.mil/factsheets/factsheet.asp?id=19893.

———. "Air Combat Command (USAF)." Air Force Historical Research Agency, 2012, www.afhra.af.mil/factsheets/factsheet.asp?id=10982.

———. "1 Air and Space Test Squadron (AFSPC)." Air Force Historical Research Agency, 2015, www.afhra.af.mil/factsheets/factsheet.asp?id=9703.

———. "4 Space Launch Squadron (AFSPC)." Air Force Historical Research Agency, 2015, www.afhra.af.mil/factsheets/factsheet.asp?id=11637.

———. "30 Space Wing (AFSPC)." Air Force Historical Research Agency, 2015, www.afhra.af.mil/factsheets/factsheet.asp?id=11643.

———. "392 Training Squadron (AETC)." Air Force Historical Research Agency, 2015, www.afhra.af.mil/factsheets/factsheet.asp?id=13359.

Department of Defense. "Fact File: C-141A/B Starlifter." Factsheet, Apr. 1993, www.dod.mil/pubs/foi/Reading_Room/Selected_Acquisition_Reports/454.pdf.

———. "Fact File: U.S. Strategic Command (STRATCOM)." Factsheet, Apr. 1993, www.dod.mil/pubs/foi/Reading_Room/Selected_Acquisition_Reports/454.pdf.

———. "SAMOS II Fact Sheet." www.nro.gov/foia/declass/WS117L_Records/662.PDF.

Donohue, Joseph. "Minuteman Notes of Interest." Vandenberg AFB, CA: 1st Strategic Aerospace Division History Office.

Lockheed Martin Space Systems Company. "Titan II Space Launch Vehicle." Jun. 2000.

National Museum of the United States Air Force. "Emergency Rocket Communications System." 27 May 2015, www.nationalmuseum.af.mil/Visit/MuseumExhibits/FactSheets/Display/tabid/509/Article/196330/emergency-rocket-communications-system.aspx.

———. "SV-5D PRIME Lifting Body." 22 May 2015, www.nationalmuseum.af.mil/Visit/MuseumExhibits/FactSheets/Display/tabid/509/Article/195893/sv-5d-prime-lifting-body.aspx.

National Reconnaissance Office. "QUILL Fact Sheet." N.d., www.nro.gov/foia/declass/QUILL/34.%20QUILL%20Fact%20Sheet.pdf.

Smithsonian Air and Space Museum. "Nike-Cajun Sounding Rocket." N.d., https://airandspace.si.edu/collection-objects/rocket-booster-nike-nike-cajun-sounding-rocket.

United Launch Alliance. "Atlas V: Maximum Flexibility and Reliability." N.d., www.ulalaunch.com/products_atlasv.aspx.

———. "Atlas V/DMSP F-19 Mission Overview." Vandenberg AFB, CA, 2014, www.ulalaunch.com/uploads/docs/Mission_Booklets/AV/av_dmsp19_mob.pdf.

JOURNALS

Baucom, Donald R. "The Rise and Fall of Brilliant Pebbles." *Journal of Social, Political, and Economic Studies* 29, no. 2 (Summer 2004): 143–90.

Berglund, Michael, and Jennifer Luce. "United Launch Alliance—Establishing Heavy Lift Capability on the West Coast." Paper presented at the 61st International Astronautical Congress, Prague, 2010, www.ulalaunch.com/uploads/docs/Published_Papers/Evolution/West_Coast_Delta_IV_HLV.pdf.

Johnson, Ray, and Edmardo Tomei. "Launch Readiness Verification on the Evolved Expendable Launch Vehicle Program." *High Frontier Journal* 3, no. 1 (Nov. 2006): 16–20, www.dtic.mil/dtic/tr/fulltext/u2/a521420.pdf.

Kalogeris, John. "Atlas E/F Launch Vehicle Research and Development Capabilities." Paper presented at SAE International, 1 Feb. 1966, http://papers.sae.org/660444/.

McDonald, Robert A., and Patrick Widlake. "Looking Closer and Looking Broader: Gambit and Hexagon—the Peak of Film-Return Space Reconnaissance After Corona." *National Reconnaissance Journal of the Discipline and Practice* 2012-U1 (Jan. 2012): 39–74, www.nro.gov/history/csnr/articles/docs/journal-03.pdf.

Meyers, J. F. "The McDonnell Douglas Delta." International Astronautical Federation, IAF-94-V.1.518, Oct. 1994.

MEMORANDA

Director of Defense Research and Engineering. "Additional ATLAS/AGENA Launch Facility." 1960. NRO Staff Records Collection, www.nro.gov/foia/declass/NROStaffRecords/18.PDF.

Haines, Gerald. "Dr. Hans Mark Interviewed by Gerald Haines." Chantilly, VA: Center for the Study of National Reconnaissance, 12 Mar. 1997, www.nro.gov/foia/docs/Hans%20Mark.PDF.

Heck, Joseph. "Availability of SM 65A Missiles for WS-117L." WS-107A-1 Program Office, 2 Aug. 1956, www.nro.gov/foia/declass/WS117L_Records/109.PDF.

King, William. "Analysis of Gambit (110) Project." Air Force Office of Special Projects, NRO GAMBIT Collection, www.nro.gov/foia/declass/GAMHEX/GAMBIT/1.PDF.

Martin, John. "Summary Analysis of Program 206 (GAMBIT)." Chantilly, VA: National Reconnaissance Office, NRO GAMBIT Collection, www.nro.gov/foia/declass/GAMHEX/GAMBIT/2.PDF.

National Reconnaissance Office. "National Reconnaissance Program's Planned Use of the Space Shuttle." 11 Mar. 1981, www.nro.gov/foia/docs/F13-0119_NRP_Use_of_Space_Shuttle.pdf.

———. "NRO Brochure." N.d., www.nro.gov/about/nro/NRObrochure.pdf.

National Security Decision Directive 8. *Space Transportation System.* 13 Nov. 1981, http://marshall.wpengine.com/wp-content/uploads/2013/09/NSDD-8-Space-Transportation-System-13-Nov-1981.pdf.

MONOGRAPHS

Bradburn, David D., John O. Copley, and Raymond B. Potts. *The SIGINT Satellite Story.* Chantilly, VA: National Reconnaissance Office, 1994, www.nro.gov/foia/declass/sigint/SIGINT_Satellite_Story.PDF.

Hall, R. Cargill. *Missile Defense Alarm: The Genesis of Space-Based Infrared Early Warning.* Chantilly, VA: National Reconnaissance Office, 1988, www.nro.gov/foia/docs/foia-mda.pdf.

———. *SAMOS to the Moon: The Clandestine Transfer of Reconnaissance Technology between Federal Agencies.* Chantilly, VA: National Reconnaissance Office, 2001, www.nro.gov/foia/docs/foia-samos.pdf.

———. *A History of the Military Polar Orbiting Meteorological Satellite Program.* Chantilly, VA: National Reconnaissance Office, Sep. 2001, www.nro.gov/foia/docs/foia-polar-orbiting.pdf.

Jenkins, Dennis, Tony Landis, and Jay Miller. *American X-vehicles: An Inventory—X-1 to X-50.* Monographs in Aerospace History 31. SP-2003-4531. Washington, DC: National Aeronautics and Space Administration, Office of External Relations, Jun. 2003, http://history.nasa.gov/monograph31.pdf.

National Reconnaissance Office. *History of the Poppy Satellite System*. Chantilly, VA: NRO Office of History, 1978, www.nro.gov/foia/docs/History%20of%20Poppy. PDF.

———. *Hexagon (KH-9) Mapping Camera Program and Evolution*. NRO Hexagon Collection. Chantilly. VA: National Reconnaissance Office, 2012, www.nro.gov/foia/declass/mapping1.pdf.

———. *NRO Review and Redaction Guide, Version 2.0*. Chantilly, VA: National Reconnaissance Office, 2012, www.nro.gov/foia/docs/NRO_RRG_v2_2012ed.pdf.

Oder, Frederic, James Fitzpatrick, and Paul Worthman. *The GAMBIT Story*. Chantilly, VA: National Reconnaissance Office, Aug. 1988, www.nro.gov/history/csnr/gambhex/GAMBIT%20and%20HEXAGON%20Histories/6.PDF.

———. *The HEXAGON Story*. Chantilly, VA: National Reconnaissance Office, Nov. 1988, www.nro.gov/history/csnr/gambhex/GAMBIT%20and%20HEXAGON%20Histories/7.PDF.

———. *The CORONA Story*. Chantilly, VA: National Reconnaissance Office, Dec. 1988, www.nro.gov/foia/docs/foia-corona-story.pdf.

PRESS RELEASES

National Reconnaissance Office. "NRO Satellite Successfully Launched." 20 Dec. 1996, www.nro.gov/news/press/1996/1996-09.pdf.

REPORTS

Air Force Cambridge Research Laboratories. *Geophysical Explorations in Aerospace during 1961*. Bedford, MA: Air Force Cambridge Research Laboratories, Hanscom Field, 1961, www.dtic.mil/dtic/tr/fulltext/u2/273758.pdf.

———. *History and Progress of AFCRL: January 1961–June 1962*. Bedford, MA: Air Force Cambridge Research Laboratories, Hanscom Field, 1962, www.dtic.mil/dtic/tr/fulltext/u2/291685.pdf.

Air Force Special Weapons Center. *Users Guide to Payload Planning for the SLV-1B Space Probe*. Jan. 1963, www.dtic.mil/get-tr-doc/pdf?AD=AD0402767.

Air University. *AU-18: Space Primer*. Maxwell AFB, AL: Air University, n.d., http://space.au.af.mil/au-18-2009/au-18_chap20.pdf.

———. *Space Handbook*. Maxwell AFB. AL: Air University, Jan. 1985.

Alford, George. *Fabrication of Twenty-Two Sounding Rocket Vehicle Systems*. Thiokol Chemical Corporation, Sep. 1972, www.dtic.mil/dtic/tr/fulltext/u2/753089.pdf.

American Rocket Company. "Embedded Pressurization System for Hybrid Rocket Motor." US Grant US5119627A, 1989.

"Annex A: SAMOS." www.nro.gov/foia/declass/NROStaffRecords/892.PDF.

Battles, Lee, and James Plummer. *The DISCOVERER Program*. Inglewood. CA: Air Force Space Systems Division, n.d., www.nro.gov/foia/declass/WS117L_Records/198.PDF.

Bendix Corporation. *Orientation Handbook: Emergency Rocket Communications System (ERCS)*." Bendix Corporation, 30 Sep. 1976, http://coldwar-c4i.net/ERCS/39645477-Emergency-Rocket-Communications-System-Orientation-Handbook.pdf.

Boeing Aerospace Company. *ABRES/Minuteman System Handbook for Payload Designers*. Mar. 1973.

Clapp, William. *Space Fundamentals for the Warfighter*. Maxwell AFB, AL: Air Command and Staff College, 23 May 1994, www.dtic.mil/dtic/tr/fulltext/u2/a279703.pdf.

Corliss, William. *NASA Sounding Rockets, 1958–1968*. Washington, DC: National Aeronautics and Space Administration, 1971, http://history.nasa.gov/SP-4401/sp4401.htm.

Dembrow, Daniel. *Flight Performance of FW-4D Solid-Propellant Rocket Motor on Delta 50 (AIMP-E)*." Washington, DC: National Aeronautics and Space Administration, Mar. 1969, https://ntrs.nasa.gov/search.jsp?R=19690011514.

Department of the Air Force. *Cooke AFB Welcome Packet*. 1957.

———. *SAMOS Satellite Reconnaissance System*." 18 Mar. 1960, www.nro.gov/foia/declass/WS117L_Records/720.PDF.

———. *Thor: A Study of a Great Weapon System*. Los Angeles AFB, CA: Office of History, 1972.

———. *Strategic Air Command Weapon Systems Acquisition, 1964–1979*. 28 Apr. 1980.

———. *Environmental Assessment: Titan IV / Solid Rocket Motor Upgrade Program*. Los Angeles AFB, CA: Headquarters, Space Systems Division, Feb. 1990, www.nro.gov/foia/declass/Archive/15-09.PDF.

———. *History of the Air Force Capsule Return Program (Draft)*. N.d., www.dtic.mil/dtic/tr/fulltext/u2/a248695.pdf.

Department of the Air Force, Space Systems Division. *Standardization of Agena B: A Presentation of the Case for Standardization Including Contractual Aspects*. NRO WS117L Collection, www.nro.gov/foia/declass/WS117L_Records/797.PDF.

Department of Defense. *Exoatmospheric Re-entry Vehicle Interception System (ERIS)*. Washington, DC: Strategic Defense Initiative Organization, Aug. 1987, www.dod.mil/pubs/foi/Reading_Room/Homeland_Defense/390.pdf.

Department of Defense Inspector General. *Brilliant Pebbles Program (Project No. 3AS-0077)*. Arlington, VA: Department of Defense, 1994, www.dodig.mil/Audit/Audit2/94-084.pdf.

Dick, Steven J., ed. *Historical Studies in the Societal Impact of Spaceflight*. Washington. DC: NASA, 2015, www.nasa.gov/sites/default/files/atoms/files/historical-studies-societal-impact-spaceflight-ebook_tagged.pdf.

1st Strategic Aerospace Division. *Peacekeeper Rail Garrison Facts Book*. Vandenberg AFB, CA: 1STRAD/TOXD.

Fragola, Joseph R., Lewie Booth, and Yu Shen. *Current Launch Vehicle Reliability Practive [sic] and Data Base Assessment*. Vol. 1, *Executive Summary and Report Body*. New York: SAIC, Jun. 1989, www.dtic.mil/dtic/tr/fulltext/u2/a213600.pdf.

General Dynamics. *Atlas—Free World's First ICBM*. Aug. 1963, http://atlasbases.homestead.com/Searchable_PDF_Files/Atlas_Brochure_1963.pdf.

———. *Atlas E/F Boosters and ABRES—a Criteria for Payload Designers*. Ft. Belvoir, VA: Defense Technical Information Center, 1967, www.dtic.mil/dtic/tr/fulltext/u2/824972.pdf.

———. *Atlas Mission Planners Guide*. San Diego, CA: General Dynamics Commercial Launch Services, Apr. 1992, www.dtic.mil/dtic/tr/fulltext/u2/a258845.pdf.

Hallion, Richard P., ed. *The Hypersonic Revolution: Eight Case Studies in the History of Hypersonic Technology*. Vol. 2, *From Scramjet to the National Aero-space Plane (1964–1986)*. Wright-Patterson AFB, OH: Aeronautical Systems Division, 1987, www.dtic.mil/cgi-bin/GetTRDoc?Location=U2&doc=GetTRDoc.pdf&AD=ADA302634.

Hicks, John W. *Flight Testing of Airbreathing Hypersonic Vehicles*. NASA Technical Memorandum 4524. Oct. 1993.

Institute of Defense Analyses. *STRAT-X: Volume 16, Reaction—USSR Strategy*. Arlington, VA: Research and Engineering Support Division, Aug. 1967.

Iram, Donald G. *A Transportable VLF/LF Repeater Terminal—a Design Study*. Rome Air Development Center In-House Report RADC-TR-86-86 (Griffiss AFB, NY: Rome Air Development Center, Jul. 1986), www.dtic.mil/dtic/tr/fulltext/u2/a171780.pdf.

Jet Propulsion Laboratory. *JASON-3 Mission Summary*. N.d., http://sealevel.jpl.nasa.gov/missions/jason3/.

Kamm, J. M. *Final Report for Blue Scout Junior Flight 02*. Air Force Special Weapons Center Technical Report AFSWC TDR-62-24 (Kirtland AFB, NM: Air Force Special Weapons Center, Mar. 1962), www.dtic.mil/dtic/tr/fulltext/u2/274086.pdf.

Krause, Merrick. "Attack Operations for Missile Defense." Occasional Paper 28, Center for Strategy and Technology. Maxwell AFB, AL: Air War College, May 2002, www.dtic.mil/dtic/tr/fulltext/u2/a464558.pdf.

Lewis Research Center. *Thrust Augmented Thor-Agena Performance for the Orbiting Geophysical Observatory OGO-IV Mission*." Technical memorandum. Cleveland, OH: NASA Lewis Research Center, Dec. 1969, https://ntrs.nasa.gov/archive/nasa/casi.ntrs.nasa.gov/19700003428.pdf.

Lockheed Missiles and Space Division. *The Agena Satellite: What It Has Done . . . What It Can Do*. Sunnyvale, CA: Lockheed Aircraft Corporation, 1 Jul. 1960, www.nro.gov/foia/declass/WS117L_Records/987.PDF.

Los Alamos Scientific Laboratory. *A 'Quick Look' at the Technical Results of STARFISH PRIME*. Los Alamos Scientific Laboratory, 1962, www.dtic.mil/dtic/tr/fulltext/u2/a955411.pdf.

National Aeronautics and Space Administration. *Fourth Semiannual Report to Congress: April 1. 1960 through September 30. 1960*. Washington, DC: National Aeronautics and Space Administration, 1960.

National Park Service. *Historical American Engineering Record: Space Launch Complex 3*. San Francisco: US Department of Interior, 1993.

National Reconnaissance Office. *National Reconnaissance Almanac*. Jan. 2011, www.dtic.mil/dtic/tr/fulltext/u2/a595020.pdf.

———. *AFTRACK (1960–1965)*. N.d., www.nro.gov/foia/declass/aftrack/53.pdf.

———. "QUILL Declassification Guidance." www.nro.gov/foia/declass/QUILL/33.%20QUILL%20Declassification%20Guidelines.pdf.

Office of the Deputy Under Secretary for Research and Engineering (Strategic and Space Systems). *ICBM Basing Options: A Summary of Major Studies to Define a Survivable Basing Concept for ICBMs*. Washington, DC: US Department of Defense, Dec. 1980, www.dtic.mil/docs/citations/ADA956443.

Office of History. *Thor: A Study of a Great Weapon System*. Los Angeles AFB, CA: Office of History, 1972.

Orbital ATK. *Pegasus User's Guide*. 2015, www.orbitalatk.com/flight-systems/space-launch-vehicles/pegasus/docs/Pegasus_UsersGuide.pdf.

Penman, George. *History of Air Materiel Command Test Site Office, United States Air Force, Vandenberg Air Force Base, California 1 July 1959–31 December 1959*. US Air Force, 1960, www.nro.gov/foia/declass/WS117L_Records/278.PDF.

Piper, Robert. *History of Titan III: 1961–1963*. Air Force Systems Command Publications Series 64-22-1. Los Angeles AFB, CA: Space Systems Division.

Rockefeller, Alfred, Jr. *History of Thor, 1955–1959*. Los Angeles: Air Force Ballistic Missile Division, 1960.

Space Department. *Artificial Earth Satellites Designed and Fabricated by the Johns Hopkins University Applied Physics Laboratory*. Baltimore: Johns Hopkins University, Jul. 1978, www.dtic.mil/dtic/tr/fulltext/u2/a066299.pdf.

Space Exploration Technologies. *Falcon 9 Launch Vehicle Payload User's Guide*. 21 Oct. 2015, www.spacex.com/sites/spacex/files/falcon_9_users_guide_rev_2.0.pdf.

———. "Falcon Heavy." www.spacex.com/falcon-heavy.

Space and Missile Systems Organization. *Agena Flight History, Volume One*. Los Angeles AFB, CA: Air Force Systems Command, Jun. 1969, www.nro.gov/foia/declass/WS117L_Records/287.PDF.

SRI International. *Strategic Systems Test Support Study (SSTSS): Final Report Volume II, Supporting Analyses*. Menlo Park, CA: SRI International, Nov. 1981, www.dod.mil/pubs/foi/Reading_Room/MDA/113.pdf.

———. *Strategic Systems Test Support Study (SSTSS): Final Report Volume III, Appendices*. Menlo Park, CA: SRI International, Nov. 1981, www.dod.mil/pubs/foi/Reading_Room/MDA/114.pdf.

Sturdevant, Rick W. "NAVSTAR, the Global Positioning System: A Sampling of Its Military, Civil, and Commercial Impact." In *Societal Impact of Spaceflight*. Edited by Steven J. Dick and Roger D. Launius, 331–51. Washington, DC: NASA, 2007, http://history.nasa.gov/sp4801-chapter17.pdf.

30th Space Wing. *Launch Facility 05: LF-05's Role in the Development of the ICBM Program*. Vandenberg AFB, CA: 30th Civil Engineering Squadron, n.d.

TRW Systems. *Minuteman Weapon System History and Description*. Jul. 2001, www.nukestrat.com/us/afn/Minuteman.pdf.

Western Space and Missile Center. *WSMC Annual History, 1989–1990*. Air Force Systems Command, 1990.

TECHNICAL ORDERS

Boeing Corporation. Technical Order 21M-LGM30G-1-1: Minuteman Weapon System Description. Seattle, WA: Boeing Aerospace, 1973.

Boeing Corporation. Technical Order 21M-LGM30G-1-22: Minuteman Weapon System Operations. Seattle, WA: Boeing Aerospace, 1973.

Boeing Corporation. Technical Order 21M-LGM30G-2-1-7: Organizational Maintenance Control, Minuteman Weapon System. Seattle, WA: Boeing Aerospace, 1994.

Douglas Aircraft Company. Technical Order 21-SM75-01, Missile and Equipment: SM-75 Weapon System, 1958.

WEBSITES

The Bunker. "Greenham Common Bunker: Secure through the Years; A Brief History, 1944–Present." N.d., www.thebunker.net/app/uploads/2015/05/Newbury-History.pdf.

Canadian Space Agency. "CASSIOPE: Observing Space Weather with a Hybrid Satellite." www.asc-csa.gc.ca/eng/satellites/cassiope.asp.

Cleary, Mark C. "The Cape: Military Space Operations, 1971–1992." 45th Space Wing History Office, Jan. 1994, http://afspacemuseum.org/library/histories/TheCape.pdf.

Department of the Air Force. "Colonel Regis Baldauff Official Air Force Biography." http://afcea-la.org/sites/afcea-la.org/files/gpsmc/mc/mc7/shared-files/Baldauff%20Bio%202011.pdf

Koopman, George. "Getting into the Launching Business: The AMROC Story." https://forum.nasaspaceflight.com.

Krebs, Gunter. "GemStar 1/VITASat 1." Gunter's Space Page. http://space.skyrocket.de/doc_sdat/gemstar-1.htm.

Kyle, Ed. "Thor Burner." *Space Launch Report*, 27 Feb. 2011, www.spacelaunchreport.com/thorh6.html.

McDowell, Jonathan. "Jonathan's Space Report No. 533 2004 Aug 27." 27 Aug. 2004, www.spaceref.com/news/viewsr.html?pid=13797.

National Aeronautics and Space Administration. "SP-4402." Origin of NASA Names. Jun. 1975, http://history.nasa.gov/SP-4402/ch1.htm.

National Park Service. "Emergency Action Messages." Minuteman Missile National Historic Site, www.nps.gov/mimi/learn/historyculture/emergency-action-messages.htm.

National Reconnaissance Office. "CORONA System Information." www.nro.gov/history/csnr/corona/sysinfo.html.

Nuclear Information Project. "U.S. Changes Name of Nuclear War Plan." 15 Sep. 2006, www.nukestrat.com/us/stratcom/siopname.htm.

Nuclear Weapon Archive. "Gallery of U.S. Nuclear Tests." N.d., http://nuclearweaponarchive.org/Usa/Tests/.

Parsch, Andreas. "Directory of U.S. Military Rockets and Missiles." www.designation-systems.net/dusrm/app4/index.html.

Public Broadcasting System. "The Gulf War." *Frontline*, 6 Jan. 1996, www.pbs.org/wgbh/pages/frontline/gulf/.

Wade, Mark. "Aerobee 170." Astronautix, www.astronautix.com/a/aerobee170.html.

———. "AMROC." Astronautix, www.astronautix.com/a/amroc.html.

———. "Atlas H." Astronautix, www.astronautix.com/lvs/atlas.html.

———. "Dac Roc." Astronautix, www.astronautix.com/d/dacroc.html.

———. *Encyclopedia Astronautica*. www.astronautix.com/u/utetomahawk.html.

———. "Seagull." Astronautix, www.astronautix.com/s/seagull.html.

———. "Terrier / Asp IV." Astronautix, www.astronautix.com/t/terrieraspiv.html.

———. "Ute Tomahawk." Astronautix, www.astronautix.com/u/utetomahawk.html.

Wells, Helen T., Susan H. Whiteley, and Carrie E. Karegeannes. *Origins of NASA Names*. Washington, DC: National Aeronautics and Space Administration, 1976, http://history.nasa.gov/SP-4402/ch5.htm.

White, J. Terry. "Thor Burner II Finale." *Seattle Post Intelligencer*, 4 Jun. 2012, http://blog.seattlepi.com/americanaerospace/2012/06/04/thor-burner-ii-finale/.

Notes

CHAPTER 1:

1 Quicksilver, "Entering Vandenberg Air Force Base," *Earth First! Journal* 23, no. 5 (Jul.–Aug. 2003): 20.

2 Carl Totemeier, "Gardening; Marigolds: America's Beautiful Native," *New York Times*, 31 May 1987, accessed 15 Oct. 2016, www.nytimes.com/1987/05/31/nyregion/gardening-marigolds-america-s-beautiful-native-by-carl-totemeier.html.

3 Carl Berger, *History of the 1st Missile Division* (Vandenberg AFB, CA: Strategic Air Command, 1960), 2.

4 Carl Berger and Warren S. Howard, *History of the 1st Strategic Aerospace Division, 1957–1961* (Vandenberg AFB, CA: Headquarters, 1st Strategic Aerospace Division, 1962), 2.

5 Associated Press, "Management Had Agreed to Let Board Act," *AP Archives*, 21 Oct. 1941.

6 Averam Bender, "From Tanks to Missiles: Camp Cooke / Cooke Air Force Base, 1941–1958," *Arizona and the West* 9 (Autumn 1967): 219–42.

7 Associated Press, "Guardsmen Get Ready for Speed-Up Duties," *AP Archives*, 3 Aug. 1950.

8 Associated Press, "'Scared Down to My Toes' Says GI from A-Bomb Area," *AP Archives*, 2 Nov. 1951.

9 Associated Press, "Oil Forces Army to Put Camp on Inactive Status," *AP Archives*, 8 Nov. 1952.

10 Associated Press, "Rocket Range Is Maximum Security Area," *AP Archives*, 14 Nov. 1958.

11 United Press International, "Camp Cooke May Become Missile Site," *UPI Archives*, 2 Jan. 1958.

12 Darrell Garwood, "2 More Year-End Roundups on What to Expect in 1959," *UPI Archives*, 18 Dec. 1958.

13 United Press International, "Missile Testing Center Commissioned by Navy," *UPI Archives*, 10 May 1958.

14 Berger and Howard, *History of the 1st Strategic Aerospace Division and Vandenberg Air Force Base 1957–1961*, 14.

15 Associated Press, "AF Building Ballistic Missile Base," *AP Archives*, 10 May 1957.

16 Associated Press, "Air Force Announces New Ballistic Division," *AP Archives*, 13 Sep. 1957.

17 Associated Press, "Work Underway on First Ballistic Missile Center," *AP Archives*, 13 May 1957.

18 Associated Press, "Air Force Starts Construction on First Strategic Rocket Base," *AP Archives*, 10 May 1957.

19 Department of the Air Force, "Cooke AFB Welcome Packet," n.d.

20 "AFMDC Role Not Changed by 'Shifts,'" *Alamogordo Daily News* (Alamogordo, NM), 8 Dec. 1957.

21 Associated Press, "Air Force Confirms Anti-missile Missile Now on Drawing Boards," *AP Archives*, 30 Nov. 1957.

22 Associated Press, "Rocket Range Is Maximum Security Area," *AP Archives*, 14 Nov. 1958.

23 Associated Press, "Camp Cooke Gets Name Change," *Alamogordo Daily News* (Alamogordo, NM), 6 Oct. 1958.

24 Bonnie Henry, "Famous Airman's Son Had Own Remarkable Air Force Career," *Arizona Daily Star* (Tucson, AZ), 1 Oct. 2007.

25 Associated Press, "Combat Ready Unit Fires Giant Rocket," *AP Archives*, 17 Dec. 1958.

26 United Press International, "Moon Shot Set on West Coast," *UP Archives*, 28 Oct. 1958.

27 Associated Press, "IRBMs May Be Used Awhile Yet," *AP Archives*, 16 Nov. 1958.

28 Douglas Diltz, "Missiles-Men Are Married at Vandenberg," *St. Petersburg Times* (St. Petersburg, FL), 1 Mar. 1963.

29 Associated Press, "Secret Satellite Launched by AF," *Toledo Blade* (Toledo, OH), 18 Sep. 1962.

30 Associated Press, "Satellite Attempt Fails," *Lawrence Journal-World* (Lawrence, KS), 22 Jan. 1965.

31 Associated Press, "Across the Nation," *Reading Eagle* (Reading, PA), 19 Oct. 1963. The Vela Hotel satellites were launched from Cape Canaveral and placed into an orbit one-third of the way to the moon.

32 Chicago Tribune Press Service, "Pacific Missile Range Goes from Navy to Air Force," *Chicago Tribune*, 21 Nov. 1963.

33 Associated Press, "Pacific Missile Range Established," *AP Archives*, Jan. 30, 1958.

34 United Press International, "Air Force Plans Manned Space Lab by '70," *UPI Archives*, 12 Jun. 1966.

35 Martin Hagopian, "From Tanks to Missiles: Vandenberg Air Force Base" (monograph, 14th Air Force History Office, 1995), 10.

36 Department of the Air Force, "30 Space Wing (AFSPC)" (Factsheet, *Air Force Historical Research Agency*, 2015), www.afhra.af.mil/factsheets/factsheet.asp?id=11643.

37 Department of the Air Force, "30 Operations Group (AFSPC)" (Factsheet, *Air Force Historical Research Agency*, 2008), www.afhra.af.mil/factsheets/factsheet.asp?id=11642.

38 Department of the Air Force, "Twentieth Air Force (Air Forces Strategic) (AFGSC)" (Factsheet, *Air Force Historical Research Agency*, 2011), www.afhra.af.mil/factsheets/factsheet.asp?id=11036.

39 Department of the Air Force, "Air Combat Command (USAF)" (Factsheet, *Air Force Historical Research Agency*, 2012), www.afhra.af.mil/factsheets/factsheet.asp?id=10982.

40 Department of the Air Force, "Fourteenth Air Force (Air Forces Strategic) (AFSPC)" (Factsheet, *Air Force Historical Research Agency*, 2010), www.afhra.af.mil/factsheets/factsheet.asp?id=11030.

41 Department of the Air Force, "4 Space Launch Squadron (AFSPC)," (Factsheet, *Air Force Historical Research* Agency, 2015), www.afhra.af.mil/factsheets/factsheet.asp?id=11637.

42 Department of the Air Force, "Colonel Regis Baldauff Official Air Force Biography," last modified 2011, http://afcea-la.org/sites/afcea-la.org/files/gpsmc/mc/mc7/shared-files/Baldauff%20Bio%202011.pdf.

43 Department of the Air Force, "1 Air and Space Test Squadron (AFSPC)" (Factsheet, *Air Force Historical Research Agency*, 2015), www.afhra.af.mil/factsheets/factsheet.asp?id=9703.

44 Department of the Air Force. "eFOIA: Vandenberg Launch Summary," last modified December 3, 2015, www.foia.af.mil/shared/media/document/afd-100316-046.pdf.

45 Associated Press, "Missile Launch Provides a Spectacular Light Show," *AP Archive*, 20 Sep. 2002.

46 "Force Improvement Program Gives Airmen Direct Line to Air Force Leaders." *Targeted News Service*, 7 Feb. 2014.

47 Department of the Air Force, "576 Flight Test Squadron" (Factsheet, *Air Force Global Strike Command*, 2015), www.afgsc.af.mil/Library/FactSheets/Display/tabid/2655/Article/629069/576th-flight-test-squadron.aspx.

48 "Bomber Crew Reunites," *Lewiston Daily Sun* (Lewiston, ME), 14 Jul. 1987.

49 Department of the Air Force, "576 Flight Test Squadron" (Factsheet, *Air Force Global Strike Command*, 2015), www.afgsc.af.mil/Library/FactSheets/Display/tabid/2655/Article/629069/576th-flight-test-squadron.aspx.

50 Ibid.

CHAPTER 2:

1 Charles Petit, "Rockets for the Rest of Us," *Air & Space*, 1 Mar. 1998, 52–59, accessed 10 Aug. 2016, http://infoweb.newsbank.com/resources/doc/nb/news/13E65205DE5B54F0?p=NewsBank.

2 *New York Times*, "Company Introduces New Rocket Engine," *Times-News* (Hendersonville, NC), 21 Feb. 1993.

3 J. E. Ferrell, "Little Rocket Company Set to Compete," *The Telegraph* (Nashua, NH), 27 Jan. 1987.

4 Associated Press, "U.S. Rocket Makers Frustrated by Red Tape," *AP Archives*, 16 Sep. 1987.

5 Mark Wade, "AMROC," *Encyclopedia Astronautica*, 2016, www.astronautix.com/a/amroc.html.

6 United Press International, "Private Rocket Readied for Launch," *UP Archive*, 25 Aug. 1989.

7 Associated Press, "Major Space Role for State Envisioned," *AP Archive*, 5 Oct. 1990.

8 Associated Press, "Getting into Orbit on the Cheap," *Los Angeles Times*, 8 May 1989, http://articles.latimes.com/1989-05-08/business/fi-2600_1_amroc-president-george-koopman-smaller-payloads-rocket-engine.

9 Western Space and Missile Center, "WSMC Annual History 1989–1990" (annual history, *Air Force Systems Command*, 1990).

10 David Brooks, "Launch Failure Haunts AMROC," *The Telegraph* (Nashua, NH), 5 Nov. 1989.

11 "Business Friday: Failed Launch," *Milwaukee Journal* (Milwaukee, WI), 6 Oct. 1989.

12 Michael Dornheim, "AMROC Retains Key Personnel despite Cutbacks after Pad Fire," *Aviation Week and Space Technology*, 131, no. 18 (30 Oct. 1989): 20.

13 "AMROC Rocket in Launch Position," *Aviation Week and Space Technology*, 4 Sep. 1989, 32.

14 Associated Press, "Obituaries: George A. Koopman," *Santa Fe New Mexican* (Santa Fe, NM), 21 Jul. 1989.

15 Dornheim, "AMROC Retains Key Personnel despite Cutbacks after Pad Fire," 20.

16 Koopman, George, "Getting into the Launching Business: The AMROC Story," https://forum.nasaspaceflight.com.

17 American Rocket Company, "Embedded Pressurization System for Hybrid Rocket Motor," US Grant US5119627A, 1989.

18 Brad Stone, "Pushing That Frontier," *Newsweek*, 21 Nov. 2003, accessed 10 Aug. 2016, http://infoweb.newsbank.com/resources/doc/nb/news/10041677C5738487?p=NewsBank.

19 30th Space Wing, "Vandenberg AFB Launch Summary: 1958–2017" (electronic edition, Vandenberg AFB, CA, 2017).

20 William Corliss, *NASA Sounding Rockets, 1958–1968* (Washington, DC: National Aeronautics and Space Administration, 1971), http://history.nasa.gov/SP-4401/sp4401.htm.

21 Associated Press, "Rockets to Test Space Radiation," *AP Archive*, 19 May 1960.

22 Thomas Bulfinch, *Mythology* (New York: Dell, 1959), 108.

23 Helen T. Wells, Susan H. Whiteley, and Carrie E. Karegeannes, *Origins of NASA Names* (Washington, DC: National Aeronautics and Space Administration, 1976), http://history.nasa.gov/SP-4402/ch5.htm.

24 Corliss, *NASA Sounding Rockets, 1958–1968*, http://history.nasa.gov/SP-4401/sp4401.htm.

25 Ibid.

26 Eugene M. Emme, comp., *Aeronautics and Astronautics: An American Chronology of Science and Technology in the Exploration of Space, 1915–1960* (Washington, DC: National Aeronautics and Space Administration, 1961), 118–35.

27 Associated Press, "Pacific Test to Study High Radiation Belt," *AP Archive*, 16 Sep. 1960.

28 National Aeronautics and Space Administration, *Fourth Semiannual Report to Congress: April 1, 1960 through September 30, 1960* (Washington, DC: National Aeronautics and Space Administration, 1960).

29 Colin Burgess, *Animals in Space: From Research Rockets to the Space Shuttle* (Chichester, UK: Springer-Praxis, 2007), 274.

30 "Second BIOS Launching Fails," *Aviation Week and Space Technology*, 27 Nov. 1961, 29.

31 Associated Press, "Studying the Earth's Pulse," *AP Archive*, 20 Apr. 1986.

32 30th Space Wing, "Vandenberg AFB Launch Summary: 1958–2017."

33 Los Alamos Scientific Laboratory, *A "Quick Look" at the Technical Results of STARFISH PRIME* (Los Alamos Scientific Laboratory, 1962), www.dtic.mil/dtic/tr/fulltext/u2/a955411.pdf.

34 Associated Press, "Rocket Probes Radiation Belt," *AP Archives*, 12 Feb. 1963.

35 Corliss, *NASA Sounding Rockets, 1958–1968*, http://history.nasa.gov/SP-4401/sp4401.htm.

36 30th Space Wing, "Vandenberg AFB Launch Summary: 1958–2017."

37 Ibid.

38 John Whitehead, "ASTRID Rocket Flight Test," *Energy and Technology Review* (Livermore: University of California, Lawrence Livermore National Laboratory, 1994), https://str.llnl.gov/etr/pdfs/07_94.2.pdf.

39 Department of Defense Inspector General, *Brilliant Pebbles Program (Project No. 3AS-0077)* (Arlington, VA: Department of Defense, 1994), www.dodig.mil/Audit/Audit2/94-084.pdf.

40 William Broad, "What's Next for 'Star Wars'? 'Brilliant Pebbles,'" *New York Times*, 25 Apr. 1989, www.nytimes.com/1989/04/25/science/what-s-next-for-star-war-brilliant-pebbles.html.

41 Whitehead, "ASTRID Rocket Flight Test," https://str.llnl.gov/etr/pdfs/07_94.2.pdf.

42 30th Space Wing, "Vandenberg AFB Launch Summary: 1958–2017."

43 Donald R. Baucom, "The Rise and Fall of Brilliant Pebbles," *Journal of Social, Political, and Economic Studies* 29, no. 2 (Summer 2004): 184.

44 30th Space Wing, "Vandenberg AFB Launch Summary: 1958–2017."

45 Corliss, *NASA Sounding Rockets, 1958–1968*, http://history.nasa.gov/SP-4401/sp4401.htm.

46 Ibid..

47 Air Force Cambridge Research Laboratories, *Geophysical Explorations in Aerospace during 1961* (Bedford, MA: Air Force Cambridge Research Laboratories, Hanscom Field, 1961), www.dtic.mil/dtic/tr/fulltext/u2/273758.pdf.

48 Aviation Week, "U.S. Research Rockets," *Aviation Week and Space Technology*, 16 Mar. 1964, 200.

49 Air Force Cambridge Research Laboratories, *Geophysical Explorations in Aerospace during 1961*, www.dtic.mil/dtic/tr/fulltext/u2/273758.pdf, 170.

50 Aviation Week, "Project Cambridge Flash Flares Photographed over Pacific Ocean," *Aviation Week and Space Technology*, 18 Dec. 1961, 29.

51 Associated Press, "Rocket Shot for Flares in Space," *AP Archives*, 8 Dec. 1961.

52 Air Force Cambridge Research Laboratories, *History and Progress of AFCRL: January 1961–June 1962* (Hanscom Field, 1962), www.dtic.mil/dtic/tr/fulltext/u2/291685.pdf.

53 Air Force Cambridge Research Laboratories, *Geophysical Explorations in Aerospace During 1961*, (Bedford, MA: Air Force Cambridge Research Laboratories, Hanscom Field, 1961), www.dtic.mil/dtic/tr/fulltext/u2/273758.pdf.

54 Los Alamos Scientific Laboratory, *A "Quick Look" at the Technical Results of STARFISH PRIME*, www.dtic.mil/dtic/tr/fulltext/u2/a955411.pdf, 9.

55 30th Space Wing, "Vandenberg AFB Launch Summary: 1958–2017."

56 Jeffrey M. Lenorovitz, "Lockheed Develops Low-End Launch Vehicle," *Aviation Week and Space Technology*, 10 May 1993, 29.

57 Michael Dornheim, "Lockheed Must Prove LLV Reliability by June," *Aviation Week and Space Technology*, 21 Aug. 1995, 18.

58 Michael Dornheim, "Lockheed Completes LLV Mockup Stacking," *Aviation Week and Space Technology*, 1 Aug. 1994, 69.

59 Bruce D. Berkowitz, "The Nine Lives of Slick Six: Vandenberg's Space Launch Complex 6," *Air & Space*, 1 Mar. 1997, 68–73, accessed 25 Aug. 2016, http://infoweb.newsbank.com/resources/doc/nb/news/13E65206FB8C5AB0?p=NewsBank.

60 Gunter Krebs, "GemStar 1/VITASat 1," *Gunter's Space Page*, http://space.skyrocket.de/doc_sdat/gemstar-1.htm.

61 Ironically, then-Captain Boltz would later return to Vandenberg as commander of the Joint Space Operations Center, and later as the commander of the 30th Space Wing.

62 Michael Dornheim, "Lockheed Must Prove LLV Reliability by June," 20.

63 Michael Dornheim, "Vectoring, IMU Destroyed LLV-1," *Aviation Week and Space Technology*, 18 Dec. 1995, 96.

64 "LMLV Readies for Return," *Aviation Week and Space Technology*, 7 Apr. 1997, 42.

65 Michael Dornheim, "LMLV-1 Gives Good Delivery to Orbit," *Aviation Week and Space Technology*, 1 Sep. 1997, 28.

66 30th Space Wing, "Vandenberg AFB Launch Summary: 1958–2017."

67 Joseph Anselmo, "Bigger Satellites Drive Plans for New Atlas, Athena Launchers," *Aviation Week and Space Technology*, 13 Apr. 1998, 34.

68 Bruce D. Berkowitz, "The Nine Lives of Slick Six: Vandenberg's Space Launch Complex 6."

69 Michael Mecham, "Faulty Athena Shroud Ruins Ikonos 1 Launch," *Aviation Week and Space Technology*, 3 May 1999, 45.

70 Joseph Anselmo, "OrbImage and Spot Link Up; Ikonos Readied for Launch," *Aviation Week and Space Technology*, 20 Sep. 1999, 42.

71 Michael Mecham, "Ikonos Launch to Open New Earth-Imaging Era," *Aviation Week and Space Technology*, 4 Oct. 1999, 41.

72 Michael Berglund and Jennifer Luce, "United Launch Alliance —Establishing Heavy Lift Capability on the West Coast" (paper, 61st International Astronautical Congress, Prague, 2010), www.ulalaunch.com/uploads/docs/Published_Papers/Evolution/West_Coast_Delta_IV_HLV.pdf.

73 Janene Scully, "Firms Team to Revive Athena Rocket," *Lompoc Record*, 26 Mar. 2010, http://lompocrecord.com/news/local/military/article_aa462caa-3897-11df-b796-001cc4c002e0.html.

74 30th Space Wing, "Vandenberg AFB Launch Summary: 1958–2017."

75 John Lonnquest and David Winkler. *To Defend and Deter: The Legacy of the United States Cold War Missile Program* (Champaign, IL: US Army Construction Engineering Research Laboratories, Nov. 1996), 211.

76 30th Space Wing, "Vandenberg AFB Launch Summary: 1958–2017."

77 General Dynamics Astronautics, *Atlas—Free World's First ICBM* (pamphlet, Aug. 1963), http://atlasbases.homestead.com/Searchable_PDF_Files/Atlas_Brochure_1963.pdf.

78 National Aeronautics and Space Administration, "SP-4402," Origin of NASA Names, Jun. 1975, http://history.nasa.gov/SP-4402/ch1.htm

79 "Ballistic Missile Chronology," *Aviation Week and Space Technology*, 6 Aug. 1956, 105.

80 Joseph Heck, "Availability of SM 65A Missiles for WS-117L" (memo, WS-107A-1 Program Office, 2 Aug. 1956), www.nro.gov/foia/declass/WS117L_Records/109.PDF.

81 Richard Sweeney, "Atlas Generate Fabrication Advances," *Aviation Week and Space Technology*, 4 Jan. 1960, 38–49.

82 "Convair-Astronautics Fabricates Atlas Pressurized Fuel Tankage," *Aviation Week and Space Technology*, 25 May 1959: 112–113.

83 Richard Sweeney, "Atlas Generate Fabrication Advances," 45.

84 "Convair Will Use Four Atlas Bases," *Aviation Week and Space Technology*, 19 Nov. 1956, 34–35.

85 Lonnquest and Winkler, *To Defend and Deter*, 211.

86 "Guidance Changes Made on Atlas, Titan," *Aviation Week and Space Technology*, 28 Jul. 1958, 22–23.

87 Chuck Hansen, *Swords of Armageddon*, vol. 7, *Artillery Shells, Missile Warheads, etc., Histories*, CD-ROM (San Jose, CA: Chuckelea, 2007), 218–219.

88 Karen Weitz, 576G/OSTF.

89 George Penman, *History of Air Materiel Command Test Site Office Vandenberg Air Force Base, California 1 July 1959–31 December 1959* (document, US Air Force, 1960), www.nro.gov/foia/declass/WS117L_Records/278.PDF.

90 "SAC Cuts ICBM Crews, Maintenance," *Aviation Week and Space Technology*, 20 Jun. 1960, 110.

91 Ray Hanner, *Chronology of the 576th Strategic Missile Squadron (Atlas-ICBM)* (Vandenberg AFB, CA: 1st Strategic Aerospace Division, 15 Dec. 1961), 14.

92 30th Space Wing, "Vandenberg AFB Launch Summary: 1958–2017."

93 "All-SAC Crew Fires Initial Atlas ICBM," *Aviation Week and Space Technology*, 14 Sep. 1959, 32.

94 "Service Use Modifies Missile Concepts," *Aviation Week and Space Technology*, 13 Mar. 1961, 125.

95 "SAC Shapes Missile Force for Survival," *Aviation Week and Space Technology*, 20 Jun. 1960, 104–109.

96 "Vandenberg Coordinates Ballistic Effort," *Aviation Week and Space Technology*, 25 Sep. 1961, 183.

97 "SAC Fires Atlas ICBM from Horizontal Pad," *Aviation Week and Space Technology*, 9 May 1960, 84.

98 "Project GOLDEN RAM," *Aviation Week and Space Technology*, 19 Dec. 1960, 25.

99 "GOLDEN RAM Produces Successful Atlas Shot," *Aviation Week and Space Technology*, 26 Dec. 1960, 24.

100 "Vandenberg Coordinates Ballistic Effort," *Aviation Week and Space Technology*, 25 Sep. 1961, 183.

101 "USAF Had 13 Straight Atlas Failures," *Aviation Week and Space Technology*, 20 Apr. 1964, 27.

102 "Atlas-D Phase-Out," *Aviation Week and Space Technology*, 21 Sep. 1964, 25.

103 "Nike Zeus Intercepts Atlas Re-entry Body," *Aviation Week and Space Technology*, 17 Dec. 1962, 34.

104 "Department of Defense Restricts Nike Zeus Testing Information," *Aviation Week and Space Technology*, 5 Feb. 1962, 32.

105 Barry Miller, "Studies of Penetration Aids Broadening," *Aviation Week and Space Technology*, 20 Jan. 1964, 72.

106 "Advanced Missile Re-entry Flight Tests Planned," *Aviation Week and Space Technology*, 10 Dec. 1962, 27.

107 "Golden Ram Payoff," *Aviation Week and Space Technology*, 12 Mar. 1962, 137–38.

108 30th Space Wing, "Vandenberg AFB Launch Summary: 1958–2017."

109 Lonnquest and Winkler, *To Defend and Deter*, 212, www.dtic.mil/dtic/tr/fulltext/u2/a337549.pdf, 212.

110 "Atlas ICBM Geared to Total Development," *Aviation Week and Space Technology*, 25 Sep. 1961, 147.

111 "Atlas Coffin Firing Fails," *Aviation Week and Space Technology*, 12 Jun. 1961, 35.

112 "Atlas E Fails," *Aviation Week and Space Technology*, 3 Jul. 1961, 26.

113 "Atlas E Flight Test Program Reviewed," *Aviation Week and Space Technology*, 10 Jul. 1961, 24.

114 "Atlas ICBM Geared to Total Deployment," *Aviation Week and Space Technology*, 25 Sep. 1961, 143.

115 Chuck Walker, *Atlas: The Ultimate Weapon* (Burlington, ON: Apogee Books, 2005), 154.

116 "SAC Shapes Missile Force for Survival," *Aviation Week and Space Technology*, 20 Jun. 1960, 104–109.

117 Jacob Neufeld, George M. Watson Jr., and David Chenoweth, eds., *Technology and the Air Force: A Retrospective Assessment* (Washington, DC: Air Force History and Museums Program, 1997), 121.

118 Ibid., 113.

119 General Dynamics, *Atlas E/F Boosters and ABRES—a Criteria for Payload Designers* (Ft. Belvoir, VA: Defense Technical Information Center, 1967), 5, www.dtic.mil/dtic/tr/fulltext/u2/824972.pdf.

120 30th Space Wing, "Vandenberg AFB Launch Summary: 1958–2017."

121 Neufeld, Watson, and Chenoweth, *Technology and the Air Force: A Retrospective Assessment*, 121.

122 John Kalogeris, "Atlas E/F Launch Vehicle Research and Development Capabilities," Paper, SAE International, 1 Feb. 1966, http://papers.sae.org/660444/.

123 Barry Miller, "Studies of Penetration Aids Broadening," *Aviation Week and Space Technology*, 20 Jan. 1964, 72–73.

124 General Dynamics, *Atlas E/F Boosters and ABRES—a Criteria for Payload Designers*, 5, www.dtic.mil/dtic/tr/fulltext/u2/824972.pdf.

125 30th Space Wing, "Vandenberg AFB Launch Summary: 1958–2017."

126 United States Air Force, "Factsheet: Atlas Launch Vehicle," www.au.af.mil/au/awc/awcgate/smc-fs/atl2_fs.htm, current as of Jan. 1999.

127 J. W. Powell and G. R. Richards, "The Atlas E/F Launch Vehicle—an Unsung Workhorse," *Journal of the British Interplanetary Society* 44 (May 1991): 229–40, www.atlasmissilesilo.com/Documents/Operational/AZ-D-O-999-99-ZZ-00005_Atlas_E_F_LaunchVehicle_UnsungWorkhorse.pdf.

128 Neufeld, Watson, and Chenoweth, *Technology and the Air Force: A Retrospective Assessment*, 121.

129 Powell and Richards, "The Atlas E/F Launch Vehicle—an Unsung Workhorse," 229, www.atlasmissilesilo.com/Documents/Operational/AZ-D-O-999-99-ZZ-00005_Atlas_E_F_LaunchVehicle_UnsungWorkhorse.pdf.

130 National Park Service, *Historical American Engineering Record: Space Launch Complex 3*, San Francisco: Department of Interior, 1993, 21.

131 Rick Sturdevant, "NAVSTAR, the Global Positioning System: A Sampling of Its Military, Civil, and Commercial Impact," in *Societal Impact of Spaceflight*, ed. Steven J. Dick and Roger D. Launius, 331–51 (Washington, DC: NASA, 2007), 331, http://history.nasa.gov/sp4801-chapter17.pdf.

132 Steven J. Dick, ed. *Historical Studies in the Societal Impact of Spaceflight* (Washington, DC: NASA, 2015), 473, www.nasa.gov/sites/default/files/atoms/files/historical-studies-societal-impact-spaceflight-ebook_tagged.pdf.

133 Ibid., 474.

134 Powell and Richards, "The Atlas E/F Launch Vehicle—an Unsung Workhorse," 236, www.atlasmissilesilo.com/Documents/Operational/AZ-D-O-999-99-ZZ-00005_Atlas_E_F_LaunchVehicle_UnsungWorkhorse.pdf.

135 United Launch Alliance, "Atlas V/DMSP F-19 Mission Overview," Vandenberg AFB, CA, 2014, www.ulalaunch.com/uploads/docs/Mission_Booklets/AV/av_dmsp19_mob.pdf.

136 30th Space Wing, "Vandenberg AFB Launch Summary: 1958–2017."

137 United States Air Force, "Factsheet: Atlas Launch Vehicle," www.au.af.mil/au/awc/awcgate/smc-fs/atl2_fs.htm, current as of Jan. 1999.

138 Mark Wade, "Atlas H," *Encyclopedia Astronautica*, www.astronautix.com/lvs/atlas.htm.

139 National Park Service, *Historical American Engineering Record: Space Launch Complex 3*, 45.

140 Mark Wade, "Atlas H," *Encyclopedia Astronautica*, www.astronautix.com/lvs/atlas.htm.

141 National Park Service, *Historical American Engineering Record: Space Launch Complex 3*, 128.

142 Edward H. Kolcum, "Defense Dept. to Retain Expendable Launchers as Backup to Shuttle," *Aviation Week and Space Technology*, 18 Mar. 1985, 115.

143 Joseph R. Fragola, Lewie Booth, and Yu Shen, *Current Launch Vehicle Reliability Practive [sic] and Data Base Assessment*, vol. 1, *Executive Summary and Report Body* (New York: SAIC, Jun. 1989), 162, www.dtic.mil/dtic/tr/fulltext/u2/a213600.pdf.

144 30th Space Wing, "Vandenberg AFB Launch Summary: 1958–2017."

145 United States Air Force, "Factsheet: Atlas Launch Vehicle," www.au.af.mil/au/awc/awcgate/smc-fs/atl2_fs.htm, current as of January 1999.

146 General Dynamics, *Atlas Mission Planners Guide* (San Diego, CA: General Dynamics Commercial Launch Services, Apr. 1992), www.dtic.mil/dtic/tr/fulltext/u2/a258845.pdf.

147 Ibid.

148 Ray Johnson and Edmardo Tomei, "Launch Readiness Verification on the Evolved Expendable Launch Vehicle Program," *High Frontier Journal* 3, no. 1 (Nov. 2006): 17, www.dtic.mil/dtic/tr/fulltext/u2/a521420.pdf.

149 Michael Mecham, "Terra Launch Puts EOS Program on Track," *Aviation Week and Space Technology*, 1 Jan. 2000, 38.

150 National Reconnaissance Office, *National Reconnaissance Almanac*, Jan. 2011, 52, www.dtic.mil/dtic/tr/fulltext/u2/a595020.pdf.

151 "World News Roundup," *Aviation Week and Space Technology*, 20 Aug. 2001, 20.

152 Michael Mecham, "New Pad Signals Shift for NRO," *Aviation Week and Space Technology*, 10 Jan. 2000, 31.

153 Craig Covault, "Launch Surge Begins for Secret NRO Missions," *Aviation Week and Space Technology*, 10 Sep. 2001, 43.

154 National Reconnaissance Office, *National Reconnaissance Almanac*, 52, www.dtic.mil/dtic/tr/fulltext/u2/a595020.pdf.

155 30th Space Wing, "Vandenberg AFB Launch Summary: 1958–2017."

156 United Space Alliance, "Atlas V: Maximum Flexibility and Reliability," n.d., www.ulalaunch.com/products_atlasv.aspx.

157 Ibid.

158 Aviation Week, "Atlas V Debuts at Vandenberg," *Aviation Week and Space Technology*, 17 Mar. 2008, 22.

159 30th Space Wing, "Vandenberg AFB Launch Summary: 1958–2017."

160 Space and Missile Systems Organization, *Agena Flight History, Volume One* (Los Angeles AFB, CA: Air Force Systems Command, June 1969), ix.

161 Wells, Whiteley, and Karegeannes, *Origins of NASA Names*, SP-4402, http://history.nasa.gov/SP-4402/ch1.htm.

162 Burritt was thought to have coined the name from alpha and gena ("the knee") because he had located the star near the "right foreleg" of the constellation.

163 Air Force Ballistic Missile Division, "Agena Fact Sheet, Release 59-64," NRO WS117L Collection, www.nro.gov/foia/declass/WS117L_Records/484.PDF.

164 Space and Missile Systems Organization, *Agena Flight History, Volume One*, 1–2.

165 Ullage motors provide acceleration to move the liquid propellants for the main engine to the bottom of their tanks. This keeps the fuel nearest the flow-piping pathway to be fed into the main engine.

166 Irving Stone, "U.S. Schedules Additional SAMOS Launches," *Aviation Week and Space Technology*, 17 Oct. 1960, 28–29.

167 Director of Defense Research and Engineering, "Additional ATLAS/AGENA Launch Facility," memorandum, 1960, NRO Staff Records Collection, www.nro.gov/foia/declass/NROStaffRecords/18.PDF.

168 Department of Defense, "SAMOS II Fact Sheet," n.d., 1, www.nro.gov/foia/declass/WS117L_Records/662.PDF.

169 United States Air Force, *SAMOS Satellite Reconnaissance System*, presentation, 18 Mar. 1960, 6, www.nro.gov/foia/declass/WS117L_Records/720.PDF.

170 R. Cargill Hall, *SAMOS to the Moon: The Clandestine Transfer of Reconnaissance Technology between Federal Agencies* (Chantilly, VA: National Reconnaissance Office, 2001), 1–2.

171 30th Space Wing, "Vandenberg AFB Launch Summary: 1958–2017."

172 Space and Missile Systems Organization, *Agena Flight History, Volume One*, ix.

173 Department of the Air Force, Space Systems Division, *Standardization of Agena B: A Presentation of the Case for Standardization Including Contractual Aspects*, NRO WS117L Collection, p. 5, www.nro.gov/foia/declass/WS117L_Records/797.PDF.

174 Lockheed Missiles and Space Division, *The Agena Satellite: What It Has Done . . . What It Can Do* (Sunnyvale, CA: Lockheed Aircraft Corporation, 1 Jul. 1960), www.nro.gov/foia/declass/WS117L_Records/987.PDF.

175 "Annex A: SAMOS," n.d., www.nro.gov/foia/declass/NROStaffRecords/892.PDF.

176 30th Space Wing, "Vandenberg AFB Launch Summary: 1958–2017."

177 Space and Missile Systems Organization, *Agena Flight History, Volume One*, ix.

178 Ibid.

179 John Martin, "Summary Analysis of Program 206 (GAMBIT)," memorandum (Chantilly, VA: National Reconnaissance Office, 13, NRO GAMBIT Collection, www.nro.gov/foia/declass/GAMHEX/GAMBIT/2.PDF, 13).

180 Robert A. McDonald and Patrick Widlake, "Looking Closer and Looking Broader: Gambit and Hexagon—the Peak of Film-Return Space Reconnaissance after Corona," *National Reconnaissance Journal of the Discipline and Practice*

2012-U1 (Jan. 2012): 15–19, www.nro.gov/history/csnr/articles/docs/journal-03. pdf.

181 R. Cargill Hall, *Missile Defense Alarm: The Genesis of Space-Based Infrared Early Warning* (Chantilly, VA: National Reconnaissance Office, 1988), 2, www.nro. gov/foia/docs/foia-mda.pdf.

182 Ibid., 30.

183 Ibid., 32.

184 Powell and Richards, "The Atlas E/F Launch Vehicle—an Unsung Workhorse," 234–35, www.atlasmissilesilo.com/Documents/Operational/AZ-D-O-999-99-ZZ-00005_Atlas_E_F_LaunchVehicle_UnsungWorkhorse.pdf.

185 30th Space Wing, "Vandenberg AFB Launch Summary: 1958–2017."

186 Powell and Richards, "The Atlas E/F Launch Vehicle—an Unsung Workhorse," 232, www.atlasmissilesilo.com/Documents/Operational/AZ-D-O-999-99-ZZ-00005_Atlas_E_F_LaunchVehicle_UnsungWorkhorse.pdf.

187 "First Atlas / Burner 2 Launch Fails," *Aviation Week and Space Technology*, 26 Aug. 1968, 22

188 30th Space Wing, "Vandenberg AFB Launch Summary: 1958–2017."

189 Dennis Jenkins, Tony Landis, and Jay Miller, *American X-vehicles: An Inventory—X-1 to X-50*, Monographs in Aerospace History 31 (Washington, DC: National Aeronautics and Space Administration, Office of External Relations, Jun. 2003), SP-2003-4531, http://history.nasa.gov/monograph31.pdf.

190 John W. Hicks, *Flight Testing of Airbreathing Hypersonic Vehicles*, NASA Technical Memorandum 4524, Oct. 1993, 2–3.

191 Roger D. Launius and Dennis R. Jenkins, *Coming Home: Reentry and Recovery from Space* (Washington, DC: Government Printing Office, 2012), 141.

192 National Museum of the United States Air Force, "SV-5D PRIME Lifting Body," 22 May 2015, www.nationalmuseum.af.mil/Visit/MuseumExhibits/FactSheets/Display/tabid/509/Article/195893/sv-5d-prime-lifting-body.aspx.

193 30th Space Wing, "Vandenberg AFB Launch Summary: 1958–2017."

194 Andreas Parsch, "Bristol of Canada *Black Brant*," Directory of U.S. Military Rockets and Missiles, appendix 4: Undesignated Vehicles, www.designation-systems.net/dusrm/app4/blackbrant.html.

195 30th Space Wing, "Vandenberg AFB Launch Summary: 1958–2017."

196 Lonnquest and Winkler, *To Defend and Deter*, 30.

197 Richard McMullen, *History of Air Defense Weapons*, 7.

198 Ibid., 9.

199 Merrick Krause, *Attack Operations For Missile Defense*: 11.

200 Christopher Bright, *Continental Air Defense in the Eisenhower Era*: 8.

201 Lonnquest and Winkler, *To Defend and Deter*, 59.

202 "Improved Bomarc Offers Greater U.S. Protection," *Albuquerque Tribune*, 21 Nov. 1958: 37.

203 Lonnquest and Winkler, *To Defend and Deter*, 198.

204 30th Space Wing History Office. *Vandenberg Air Force Base Launch Summary: 1958–2017*." Electronic edition, 2017.

205 Hill Air Force Base, "BOMARC-B Factsheet," 2007.

206 Lonnquest, *To Defend and Deter*, 200.

207 Ibid., 202.

208 30th Space Wing, "Vandenberg AFB Launch Summary: 1958–2017."

209 Ibid.

210 T. A. Heppenheimer, "Scramjets Pass Their Peak," in *Facing the Heat Barrier: A History of Hypersonics* (Washington, DC: National Aeronautics and Space Administration, 2007), 199.

211 Richard Hallion, "The Hypersonic Revolution: Eight Case Studies in the History of Hypersonic Technology," in *The Hypersonic Revolution: Eight Case Studies in the History of Hypersonic Technology*, vol. 2, *From Scramjet to the National Aero-space Plane (1964–1986)*, ed. Richard P. Hallion (Wright-Patterson AFB, OH: Aeronautical Systems Division, 1987), vi–xvi.

212 Ibid.

213 Jonathan McDowell, "Jonathan's Space Report No. 533 2004 Aug 27," 27 Aug. 27, 2004, www.spaceref.com/news/viewsr.html?pid=13797.

214 30th Space Wing, "Vandenberg AFB Launch Summary: 1958–2017."

215 Andreas Parsch, "Appendix 4: Undesignated Vehicles," Directory of U.S. Military Rockets and Missiles, www.designation-systems.net/dusrm/app4/index.html.

216 30th Space Wing, "Vandenberg AFB Launch Summary: 1958–2017."

217 Mark Wade, "Dac Roc," *Encyclopedia Astronautica*, www.astronautix.com/d/dacroc.html.

218 30th Space Wing, "Vandenberg AFB Launch Summary: 1958–2017."

219 "Rocket Probe Nuclear Blasts," *Aviation Week and Space Technology*, 10 Aug. 1959, 29.

220 Aviation Week, "U.S. Research Rockets," *Aviation Week and Space Technology*, 16 Mar. 1964, 200.

221 Nuclear Weapon Archive.org, "Gallery of U.S. Nuclear Tests," n.d., http://nuclearweaponarchive.org/Usa/Tests/.

222 30th Space Wing, "Vandenberg AFB Launch Summary: 1958–2017."

223 Air University, *Space Handbook* (Maxwell AFB, AL: Air University, Jan. 1985), 6–3.

224 Wells, Whiteley, and Karegeannes, *Origins of NASA Names*, SP-4402, http://history.nasa.gov/SP-4402/ch1.htm.

225 J. F. Meyers, "The McDonnell Douglas Delta," International Astronautical Federation, IAF-94-V.1.518, Oct. 1994, 3.

226 Peter Hunter, "All Thor-Delta Launches—Prime Payload, Chronological," 23 Jan. 2005.

227 30th Space Wing, "Vandenberg AFB Launch Summary: 1958–2017."

228 Tim Furniss, "The Thirteenth Delta," *Flight International*, 7 Jan. 1989, 35.

229 National Security Decision Directive 8. "Space Transportation System," 13 Nov. 1981, http://marshall.wpengine.com/wp-content/uploads/2013/09/NSDD-8-Space-Transportation-System-13-Nov-1981.pdf.

230 Tim Furniss, "The Thirteenth Delta," *Flight International*, January 7, 1989, 36.

231 Justin Ray, "What to Do with the Final Delta 2 Rocket?," *Spaceflight Now*, 8 Apr. 2015, https://spaceflightnow.com/2015/04/08/what-to-do-with-the-final-delta-2-rocket/.

232 30th Space Wing, "Vandenberg AFB Launch Summary: 1958–2017."

233 Ibid.

234 Space Exploration Technologies, "Falcon 9," n.d., www.spacex.com/falcon9.

235 Space Exploration Technologies, *Falcon 9 Launch Vehicle Payload User's Guide*, 21 Oct. 2015, www.spacex.com/sites/spacex/files/falcon_9_users_guide_rev_2.0.pdf.

236 Space Exploration Technologies, "Falcon Heavy," n.d., www.spacex.com/falcon-heavy.

237 Space Exploration Technologies, *Falcon 9 Launch Vehicle Payload User's Guide*, 44, www.spacex.com/sites/spacex/files/falcon_9_users_guide_rev_2.0.pdf.

238 Publication cutoff date was 31 Dec. 2016.

239 Canadian Space Agency, "CASSIOPE: Observing Space Weather with a Hybrid Satellite," n.d., www.asc-csa.gc.ca/eng/satellites/cassiope.asp.

240 Jet Propulsion Laboratory, *JASON-3 Mission Summary*, n.d., http://sealevel.jpl.nasa.gov/missions/jason3/.

241 Jackie Wattles and Robert McLean, "SpaceX Rocket Explodes after Landing," 18 Jan. 2016, CNN, http://money.cnn.com/2016/01/17/technology/spacex-launch/.

242 30th Space Wing, "Vandenberg AFB Launch Summary: 1958–2017." Electronic edition, 2017.

243 United States Air Force, "BGM-109G Ground Launched Cruise Missile Fact Sheet," 15 Oct. 2008, www.hill.af.mil/About-Us/Fact-Sheets/Display/Article/397188/bgm-109g-gryphon-ground-launched-cruise-missile.

244 The Bunker, "Greenham Common Bunker: Secure through the Years; A Brief History 1944–Present," n.d., www.thebunker.net/app/uploads/2015/05/Newbury-History.pdf.

245 30th Space Wing, "Vandenberg AFB Launch Summary: 1958–2017." (electronic edition, Vandenberg AFB, California, 2016).

246 30th Space Wing, "Vandenberg AFB Launch Summary: 1958 – 2017"

247 Andreas Parsch, "Rocket Power Inc. *Phoenix*," Directory of U.S. Military Rockets and Missiles, appendix 4: Undesignated Vehicles, www.designation-systems.net/dusrm/app4/phoenix.html.

248 30th Space Wing, "Vandenberg AFB Launch Summary: 1958–2017."

249 "The World," *Aviation Week and Space Technology*, 21 Feb. 2011, 14.

250 Michael Dornheim, "ITT to Invest $31 Million in California Spaceport," *Aviation Week and Space Technology*, 5 Dec. 1994, 20.

251 "World News Roundup," *Aviation Week and Space Technology*, 31 Jan. 2000, 23.

252 Frank Morring Jr., "In Orbit: Indefinite Delay," *Aviation Week and Space Technology*, 12 Oct. 2009, 16.

253 "Minotaur IV Launches SBSS," *Aviation Week and Space Technology*, 4 Oct. 2010, 16.

254 Michael Dornheim, "Rendezvous Trials," *Aviation Week and Space Technology*, 18 Apr. 2005, 35–36.

255 "The World: Space," *Aviation Week and Space Technology*, 3 Mar. 2014, 12.

256 30th Space Wing, "Vandenberg AFB Launch Summary: 1958–2017."

257 Boeing Corporation, Technical Order 21M-LGM30G-1-1: Minuteman Weapon System Description (Seattle, WA: Boeing Aerospace, 1973).

258 Neal, Roy. *Ace in the Hole: Story of the Minuteman Missile* (New York: Doubleday, 1962).

259 The SIOP nomenclature fell out of usage during the Bush administration. It was renamed on 8 February 2003 to OPLAN 8044, fitting nicely within USSTRATCOM's "Family of Plans"; www.nukestrat.com/us/stratcom/siopname.htm.

260 The Minuteman ICBM was originally designated SM-80. The current designation was introduced by the Department of Defense in 1963 to standardize naming conventions across all the military services: (L) Silo Launched; (G) Surface Attack; (M) Missile.

261 Initial Weapons System Training (IWST).

262 Patsy Robertson, "394 Maintenance Support Squadron Fact Sheet," last modified 3 Sep. 2008.

263 Patsy Robertson, "392 Training Squadron Fact Sheet," last modified 16 Mar. 2015, www.afhra.af.mil/factsheets/factsheet.asp?id=13359.

264 Picariello, Erica. "Historic Training Squadrons Merge, Missions Continue at Vandenberg," *30th Space Wing Public Affairs*, 13 Jul. 2013, www.vandenberg.af.mil/news/story.asp?id=123309905.

265 30th Space Wing, "Vandenberg AFB Launch Summary: 1958–2017."

266 LF-10, LF-21, and LF-23 through LF-26.

267 LCF-DO (Delta Oscar), EO (Echo Oscar), and CO (Charlie Oscar).

268 TRW Systems, *Minuteman Weapon System History and Description*, briefing, July 2001, 11.

269 Ibid., 1.

270 Office of the Deputy Under Secretary for Research and Engineering (Strategic and Space Systems), *ICBM Basing Options: A Summary of Major Studies to Define a Survivable Basing Concept for ICBMS* (Washington, DC: US

Department of Defense, Dec. 1980), 11, www.dtic.mil/docs/citations/ADA956443.

271 "Minuteman 3 Launch," *Aviation Week and Space Technology*, 30 Jun. 1969, 25.

272 "Minuteman 3 Deployment Slated," *Aviation Week and Space Technology*, 16 Mar. 1970, 23.

273 Strategic Air Command Office of History, "Strategic Air Command Operations in the Cuban Crisis of 1962," *SAC Historical Study* 1, no. 90 (n.d.): vii; Offutt AFB, NE: Strategic Air Command Office of History.

274 Ibid., 63.

275 Ibid., 65.

276 Joseph Donohue, "Minuteman Notes of Interest," factsheet (Vandenberg AFB, CA: 1st Strategic Aerospace Division History Office, n.d.), 3.

277 Strategic Air Command Office of History, "Strategic Air Command Operations in the Cuban Crisis of 1962," 72.

278 Ibid., 68.

279 30th Space Wing, "Vandenberg AFB Launch Summary: 1958–2017."

280 Goldberg, Alfred, ed., *History of the Strategic Arms Competition, 1945–1972: Part II* (Washington, DC: Office of the Secretary of Defense, 1981), 572.

281 Ibid.

282 Ibid., 559.

283 Ibid., 545.

284 TRW Systems, *Minuteman Weapon System History and Description*, 38.

285 Bendix Corporation, *Orientation Handbook: Emergency Rocket Communications System (ERCS)*, technical report (Bendix Corporation, 30 Sep. 1976), http://coldwar-c4i.net/ERCS/39645477-Emergency-Rocket-Communications-System-Orientation-Handbook.pdf.

286 National Museum of the United States Air Force, "Emergency Rocket Communications System," factsheet, 27 May 2015, www.nationalmuseum.af.mil/Visit/MuseumExhibits/FactSheets/Display/tabid/509/Article/196330/emergency-rocket-communications-system.aspx.

287 SRI International, *Strategic Systems Test Support Study (SSTSS): Final Report Volume III, Appendices* (Menlo Park, CA: SRI International, Nov. 1981), 13.

288 Institute of Defense Analyses, *STRAT-X: Volume 16, Reaction—USSR Strategy* (Arlington, VA: Research and Engineering Support Division, Aug. 1967).

289 William Burr, "The STRAT-X Report and Its Impact," *Unredacted: The National Security Archive Blog*, 6 Jan. 2010, https://nsarchive.wordpress.com/2010/01/06/the-strat-x-report-and-its-impact/.

290 TRW Systems, *Minuteman Weapon System History and Description*, 33.

291 SRI International, *Strategic Systems Test Support Study (SSTSS): Final Report Volume II, Supporting Analyses*, Nov. 1981, 14.

292 Boeing Aerospace Company, *ABRES/Minuteman System Handbook for Payload Designers*, Handbook, March 1973.

293 SRI International, *Strategic Systems Test Support Study (SSTSS): Final Report Volume II, Supporting Analyses* (Menlo Park, CA: SRI International, Nov. 1981), 36.

294 Associated Press, "Missile Test Succeeds," *Pittsburgh Post-Gazette* (Pittsburgh, PA), 29 Jan. 1987.

295 In 1970, the Air Force redesignated its testing efforts. OT became OT Phase I, while FOT became OT Phase II.

296 SRI International, *Strategic Systems Test Support Study (SSTSS): Final Report Volume III, Appendices*, 40.

297 Department of Defense, *Exoatmospheric Re-entry Vehicle Interception System (ERIS)* (Washington, DC: Strategic Defense Initiative Organization, Aug. 1987), 14.

298 Department of Defense, "Fact File: U.S. Strategic Command (STRATCOM)," factsheet, Apr. 1993.

299 United States Strategic Command, "USSTRATCOM Mission Statement," Feb. 2017, www.stratcom.mil/About/Mission.

300 Department of Defense, *Exoatmospheric Re-entry Vehicle Interception System (ERIS)*, 8–9.

301 Strategic Air Command Office of History, "SAC Missile Chronology, 1939–1988," 23.

302 30th Space Wing, "Vandenberg AFB Launch Summary: 1958–2017."

303 Ibid.

304 Ibid.

305 Ibid.

306 William Corliss, *NASA Sounding Rockets, 1958–1968*, http://history.nasa.gov/SP-4401/sp4401.htm.

307 Mark Wade, "Aerobee 170," Astronautix, www.astronautix.com/a/aerobee170.html.

308 30th Space Wing, "Vandenberg AFB Launch Summary: 1958–2017."

309 "New Rocket Research Vehicles Detailed," *Aviation Week and Space Technology*, 3 Dec. 1956, 27.

310 30th Space Wing, "Vandenberg AFB Launch Summary: 1958–2017."

311 Smithsonian Air and Space Museum, "Nike-Cajun Sounding Rocket," factsheet, n.d., https://airandspace.si.edu/collection-objects/rocket-booster-nike-nike-cajun-sounding-rocket.

312 30th Space Wing, "Vandenberg AFB Launch Summary: 1958–2017."

313 Ibid.

314 Horace Jacobs and Eunice Engelke Whitney, *Missile and Space Projects Guide 1962* (New York: Plenum, 1962), 209.

315 30th Space Wing, "Vandenberg AFB Launch Summary: 1958–2017."

316 "Leading U.S., International Research Rockets," *Aviation Week and Space Technology*, 13 Mar. 1972, 110.

317 30th Space Wing, "Vandenberg AFB Launch Summary: 1958–2017."

318 SRI International, *Strategic Systems Test Support Study (SSTSS): Final Report Volume II, Supporting Analyses*, 189.

319 Air Force Space Command, *Peacekeeper Missile Chronology: 1971–2005* (Colorado Springs, CO: Air Force Space Command Office of History, Dec. 2008), 147.

320 1st Strategic Aerospace Division, *Peacekeeper Rail Garrison Facts Book*, handbook, (Vandenberg AFB, CA: 1STRAD/TOXD, n.d.), 41.

321 30th Space Wing, *Launch Facility 05: LF-05's Role in the Development of the ICBM Program*, trifold (Vandenberg AFB, CA: 30th Civil Engineering Squadron, n.d.).

322 Air Force Space Command, *Peacekeeper Missile Chronology: 1971–2005*.

323 30th Space Wing, "Vandenberg AFB Launch Summary: 1958–2017."

324 Orbital ATK, *Pegasus User's Guide*, 2015, 3, www.orbitalatk.com/flight-systems/space-launch-vehicles/pegasus/docs/Pegasus_UsersGuide.pdf.

325 Air University, *AU-18: Space Primer* (Maxwell AFB, AL: Air University, n.d.), 262, http://space.au.af.mil/au-18-2009/au-18_chap20.pdf.

326 30th Space Wing, "Vandenberg AFB Launch Summary: 1958–2017."

327 Air Force Special Weapons Center, *Users Guide to Payload Planning for the SLV-1B Space Probe*, Jan. 1963, www.dtic.mil/get-tr-doc/pdf?AD=AD0402767.

328 J. M. Kamm Jr., *Final Report for Blue Scout Junior Flight 02*, Air Force Special Weapons Center Technical Report AFSWC TDR-62-24 (Kirtland AFB, NM: Air Force Special Weapons Center, Mar. 1962), www.dtic.mil/dtic/tr/fulltext/u2/274086.pdf.

329 Donald G. Iram, *A Transportable VLF/LF Repeater Terminal—a Design Study*, Rome Air Development Center In-House Report RADC-TR-86-86 (Griffiss AFB, NY: Rome Air Development Center, Jul. 1986), www.dtic.mil/dtic/tr/fulltext/u2/a171780.pdf.

330 National Park Service, "Emergency Action Messages," Minuteman Missile National Historic Site, www.nps.gov/mimi/learn/historyculture/emergency-action-messages.htm.

331 Department of the Air Force, *Strategic Air Command Weapon Systems Acquisition 1964–1979*, 28 Apr. 1980.

332 30th Space Wing, "Vandenberg AFB Launch Summary: 1958–2017."

333 National Aeronautics and Space Administration, "SP-4402," Origin of NASA Names, http://history.nasa.gov/SP-4402/ch1.htm.

334 William Clapp, *Space Fundamentals for the Warfighter* (Maxwell AFB, AL: Air Command and Staff College, 23 May 1994), www.dtic.mil/dtic/tr/fulltext/u2/a279703.pdf: 18.

335 Robert A. McDonald and Sharon K. Moreno, *Raising the Periscope: GRAB and POPPY; America's Early ELINT Satellites* (Chantilly, VA: National Reconnaissance Office, Sep. 2005), 18, www.nro.gov/history/csnr/programs/docs/prog-hist-03.pdf.

336 National Reconnaissance Office, *History of Poppy* (Chantilly, VA: NRO Office of History), www.nro.gov/foia/docs/History%20of%20Poppy.PDF: A1-7.

337 David Arnold, *Spying from Space* (College Station: Texas A&M University Press, 2005), 104–108.

338 Joseph T. Page II, *Space Launch Complex Ten: Vandenberg's Cold War National Monument* (Stroud, UK: History Press, 2016), 105.

339 Beth O'Leary and P. J. Capelotti, eds., *Archaeology and Heritage of the Human Movement into Space* (Cham, Switzerland: Springer, 2015), 103.

340 30th Space Wing, "Vandenberg AFB Launch Summary: 1958–2017."

341 Public Broadcasting System, "The Gulf War," *Frontline*, 6 Jan. 1996, www.pbs.org/wgbh/pages/frontline/gulf/.

342 Stacee Bako, "Team Vandenberg Launches Scud Missile on Data-Seeking Mission," *Space & Missile Times*, 22 Nov. 2002, www.techexpo.com/WWW/opto-knowledge/Mssile-Defense.pdf.

343 "Israelis Monitor VAFB Launch," *Santa Barbara News-Press*, 26 Nov. 2002, www.techexpo.com/WWW/opto-knowledge/Mssile-Defense.pdf.

344 Ed Souza, "A Scud Missile Blasts Off from Vandenberg Air Force Base Early Monday Morning . . . ," *Santa Maria Times* (Santa Maria, CA), 26 Nov. 2002, http://santamariatimes.com/a-scud-missile-blasts-off-from-vandenberg-air-force-base/article_a3af8d34-790a-5e55-ae43-3ea175b5d587.html

345 30th Space Wing, "Vandenberg AFB Launch Summary: 1958–2017."

346 Mark Wade, "Seagull," Astronautix, www.astronautix.com/s/seagull.html.

347 30th Space Wing, "Vandenberg AFB Launch Summary: 1958–2017."

348 Air Force Space Command, *Peacekeeper Missile Chronology: 1971–2005*, 115.

349 Associated Press, "Midgetman Test Flight Cut Short," *Milwaukee Journal* (Milwaukee, WI), 12 May 1989.

350 30th Space Wing, "Vandenberg AFB Launch Summary: 1958–2017."

351 Lewis Research Center, *Thrust Augmented Thor-Agena Performance for the Orbiting Geophysical Observatory OGO-IV Mission*, technical memorandum (Cleveland, OH: NASA Lewis Research Center, Dec. 1969), 5, https://ntrs.nasa.gov/archive/nasa/casi.ntrs.nasa.gov/19700003428.pdf.

352 Robert Perry, *History of Satellite Reconnaissance*, vol. 1, *CORONA* (Chantilly, VA: National Reconnaissance Office, Oct. 1973), xv.

353 Curtis Peebles, *The CORONA Project* (Annapolis, MD: Naval Institute Press, 1995), 156–157.

354 Frederic Oder, James Fitzpatrick, and Paul Worthman, *The CORONA Story*, NRO CAL Collection (Chantilly, VA: National Reconnaissance Office, NRO CAL Collection, Dec. 1988), 96.

355 Robert Perry, *History of Satellite Reconnaissance*, vol. 1, *CORONA*, xii.

356 Ibid., 157.

357 McDonald and Moreno, *Raising the Periscope: GRAB and POPPY*, 18, www.nro.gov/history/csnr/programs/docs/prog-hist-03.pdf.

358 National Reconnaissance Office, "QUILL Declassification Guidance," n.d., 3, www.nro.gov/foia/declass/QUILL/33.%20QUILL%20Declassification%20Guidelines.pdf.

359 National Reconnaissance Office, "QUILL Fact Sheet," n.d., www.nro.gov/foia/declass/QUILL/34.%20QUILL%20Fact%20Sheet.pdf.

360 30th Space Wing, "Vandenberg AFB Launch Summary: 1958–2017."

361 "Tech Update: Blastoff from the Middle of Nowhere," *Popular Mechanics* 170, no. 7 (Jul. 1993): 17.

362 Stephen Clark, "Taurus Rocket on the Market with New Name, Upgrades," *Spaceflight Now*, 24 Feb. 2014, http://spaceflightnow.com/news/n1402/24minotaurc/.

363 Air University, *AU-18: Space Primer* (Maxwell AFB, AL: Air University, n.d.), http://space.au.af.mil/au-18-2009/au-18_chap20.pdf: 264.

364 Stephen Clark, "Taurus Rocket on the Market with New Name, Upgrades," http://spaceflightnow.com/news/n1402/24minotaurc/.

365 "The World: Space," *Aviation Week and Space Technology*, 3 Mar. 2014, 12.

366 30th Space Wing, "Vandenberg AFB Launch Summary: 1958–2017."

367 Mark Wade, "Terrier / Asp IV," Astronautix, www.astronautix.com/lvs/teraspiv.htm.

368 30th Space Wing, "Vandenberg AFB Launch Summary: 1958–2017."

369 Rockefeller, Alfred, Jr., *History of Thor, 1955–1959* (Los Angeles: Air Force Ballistic Missile Division, 1960), chapter 1.

370 G. R. Richards and J. W. Powell, "Waste Not—the Use of Ex-RAF Thor Vehicles," *Journal of the British Interplanetary Society* 50 (1977): 1.

371 Office of History. *Thor: A Study of a Great Weapon System* (Los Angeles AFB, CA: Office of History, 1972), 863.

372 Neil Sheehan, *A Fiery Peace in a Cold War: Bernard Schriever and the Ultimate Weapon* (New York: Random House, 2009), 318.

373 Douglas Aircraft Company, Technical Order 21-SM75-01, Missile and Equipment: SM-75 Weapon System, 1958, 1–2.

374 Ibid., 1–1.

375 Berger and Howard, *History of the 1st Strategic Aerospace Division and Vandenberg Air Force Base 1957–1961*, 5.

376 Ray Hanner, *Chronology of the 392d Missile Training Squadron (THOR)* (Vandenberg AFB, CA: Headquarters, 1st Strategic Aerospace Division, 1960), 2.

377 U.S. Army Engineer Research and Development Center, SLC-10 HAER, 35.

378 Hanner, *Chronology of the 392d Missile Training Squadron (THOR)*, 19.

379 Strategic Air Command, "SAC Missile Chronology, 1939–1988," 23.

380 Ibid., 34.

381 30th Space Wing, "Vandenberg AFB Launch Summary: 1958–2017."

382 Jos Heyman, "Douglas SLV-2 *Thor* / Boeing (McDonnell Douglas) SB-3 *Delta*," Directory of U.S. Military Rockets and Missiles, appendix 3: Space Vehicles, www.designation-systems.net/dusrm/app3/b-3.html.

383 Federation of American Scientists, "The Cape: Chapter One Footnotes," http://fas.org/spp/military/program/cape/Cape1fn.htm.

384 "U.S. Rocket Motors," *Aviation Week and Space Technology*, 16 Mar. 1964, 197.

385 Space Department, *Artificial Earth Satellites Designed and Fabricated by the Johns Hopkins University Applied Physics Laboratory* (Baltimore: Johns Hopkins University, Jul. 1978), 7, www.dtic.mil/dtic/tr/fulltext/u2/a066299.pdf.

386 Ibid., 67.

387 "Launch Vehicles," *Aviation Week and Space Technology*, 13 Jan. 1997, 124.

388 30th Space Wing, "Vandenberg AFB Launch Summary: 1958–2017."

389 NASA, "SP-4402," Origins of NASA Names, 1http://history.nasa.gov/SP-4402/ch1.htm.

390 Burritt was thought to have coined the name from alpha and gena ("the knee") because he had located the star near the "right foreleg" of the constellation.

391 Air Force Ballistic Missile Division, "Agena Fact Sheet, Release 59-64," NRO WS117L Collection, www.nro.gov/foia/declass/WS117L_Records/484.PDF.

392 Space and Missile Systems Organization, *Agena Flight History, Volume One*, 1–2.

393 Ullage motors provide acceleration to move the liquid propellants for the main engine to the bottom of their tanks. This keeps the fuel nearest the flow-piping pathway to be fed into the main engine.

394 Lee Battles and James Plummer, *The DISCOVERER Program*, briefing (Inglewood, CA: Air Force Space Systems Division, n.d.), www.nro.gov/foia/declass/WS117L_Records/198.PDF.

395 National Reconnaissance Office, "CORONA System Information," www.nro.gov/history/csnr/corona/sysinfo.html.

396 Department of the Air Force, *History of the Air Force Capsule Return Program (Draft)*, n.d., www.dtic.mil/dtic/tr/fulltext/u2/a248695.pdf.

397 Oder, Fitzpatrick, and Worthman, *The CORONA Story*, 48.

398 Kenneth E. Greer, "CORONA," *Studies in Intelligence* S17 (Spring 1973): 1–37.

399 National Reconnaissance Office, *NRO Review and Redaction Guide, Version 2.0* (Chantilly, VA: National Reconnaissance Office, 2012), www.nro.gov/foia/docs/NRO_RRG_v2_2012ed.pdf.

400 National Reconnaissance Office, *AFTRACK (1960–1965)*, presentation, n.d., www.nro.gov/foia/declass/aftrack/53.pdf.

401 David D. Bradburn, John O. Copley, and Raymond B. Potts, *The SIGINT Satellite Story* (Chantilly, VA: National Reconnaissance Office, 1994), www.nro.gov/foia/declass/sigint/SIGINT_Satellite_Story.PDF.

402 30th Space Wing, "Vandenberg AFB Launch Summary: 1958–2017."

403 Department of the Air Force, Space Systems Division, *Standardization of Agena B: A Presentation of the Case for Standardization Including Contractual Aspects*, 5, www.nro.gov/foia/declass/WS117L_Records/797.PDF.

404 Lockheed Missiles and Space Division, *The Agena Satellite: What It Has Done . . . What It Can Do*, www.nro.gov/foia/declass/WS117L_Records/987.PDF.

405 30th Space Wing, "Vandenberg AFB Launch Summary: 1958–2017."

406 Space and Missile Systems Organization, *Agena Flight History, Volume One*, ix.

407 Ibid.

408 McDonald and Moreno, *Raising the Periscope: GRAB and POPPY*, 10–11, www.nro.gov/history/csnr/programs/docs/prog-hist-03.pdf.

409 Associated Press, "Across the Nation," *Reading Eagle* (Reading, PA), 3 Sep. 1965.

410 30th Space Wing, "Vandenberg AFB Launch Summary: 1958–2017."

411 Aviation Week, "U.S. Research Rockets," *Aviation Week and Space Technology*, 16 Mar. 1964, 200.

412 Ed Kyle, "Thor Burner," *Space Launch Report*, 27 Feb. 2011, www.spacelaunchreport.com/thorh6.html.

413 National Reconnaissance Office, *Hexagon (KH-9) Mapping Camera Program and Evolution*, NRO Hexagon Collection (Chantilly, VA: National Reconnaissance Office, 2012), 104, www.nro.gov/foia/declass/mapping1.pdf.

414 "Industry Observer," *Aviation Week and Space Technology*, 1 Mar. 1965, 13.

415 R. Cargill Hall, *A History of the Military Polar Orbiting Meteorological Satellite Program* (Chantilly, VA: National Reconnaissance Office, Sep. 2001), 40, www.nro.gov/foia/docs/foia-polar-orbiting.pdf.

416 Ibid., 108.

417 30th Space Wing, "Vandenberg AFB Launch Summary: 1958–2017."

418 Aviation Week, "U.S. Research Rockets," *Aviation Week and Space Technology*, 16 Mar. 1964, 200.

419 Kyle, "Thor Burner," www.spacelaunchreport.com/thorh6.html.

420 Powell and Richards, "The Atlas E/F Launch Vehicle—an Unsung Workhorse," 232, www.atlasmissilesilo.com/Documents/Operational/AZ-D-O-999-99-ZZ-00005_Atlas_E_F_LaunchVehicle_UnsungWorkhorse.pdf.

421 J. Terry White, "Thor Burner II Finale," *Seattle Post Intelligencer*, 4 Jun. 2012, http://blog.seattlepi.com/americanaerospace/2012/06/04/thor-burner-ii-finale/.

422 30th Space Wing, "Vandenberg AFB Launch Summary: 1958–2017."

423 Daniel Dembrow, *Flight Performance of FW-4D Solid-Propellant Rocket Motor on Third-Stage of Delta 50 Launch Vehicle* (Washington, DC: National Aeronautics and Space Administration, Mar. 1969), https://ntrs.nasa.gov/search.jsp?R=19690011514.

424 National Aeronautics and Space Administration, "SP-4402," Origin of NASA Names, http://history.nasa.gov/SP-4402/ch1.htm.

425 30th Space Wing, "Vandenberg AFB Launch Summary: 1958–2017."

426 Space and Missile Systems Organization, *Agena Flight History, Volume One*, ix.

427 Kevin C. Ruffner, ed., *CORONA: America's First Satellite Program* (Washington, DC: CIA Center for the Study of Intelligence, 1995), www.cia.gov/library/center-for-the-study-of-intelligence/csi-publications/books-and-monographs/corona.pdf: 39.

428 30th Space Wing, "Vandenberg AFB Launch Summary: 1958–2017."

429 Roger D. Launius and Dennis R. Jenkins, eds., *To Reach the High Frontier: A History of US Launch Vehicles* (Lexington: University of Kentucky Press, Jan. 2015), 150.

430 Lonnquest and Winkler, *To Defend and Deter*, 231, www.dtic.mil/dtic/tr/fulltext/u2/a337549.pdf.

431 Michael Del Papa, *From Snark to Peacekeeper: A Pictorial History of Strategic Air Command Missiles* (Offutt AFB, NE: Office of the Historian, Strategic Air Command, 1990), 15.

432 Ibid., 231.

433 Associated Press, "Experts Study Ruins of Titan," *Eugene Register-Guard* (Eugene, OR), 5 Dec. 1960.

434 Goldberg, *History of the Strategic Arms Competition, 1945–1972: Part II*, 576.

435 30th Space Wing, "Vandenberg AFB Launch Summary: 1958–2017."

436 Ibid.

437 Lockheed Martin Space Systems Company, "Titan II Space Launch Vehicle," factsheet, Jun. 2000.

438 David Stumpf, *Titan II: A History of a Cold War Missile Program* (Fayetteville: University of Arkansas Press, 2000):.

439 David Baker, ed., *Jane's Space Directory: 2001–2002* (Coulsdon, UK: Jane's Information Group, 2001), 267.

440 30th Space Wing, "Vandenberg AFB Launch Summary: 1958–2017."

441 Space and Missile Systems Organization, *Agena Flight History, Volume One*, ix.

442 Martin, "Summary Analysis of Program 206 (GAMBIT)," 13, www.nro.gov/foia/declass/GAMHEX/GAMBIT/2.PDF.

443 Frederic Oder, James Fitzpatrick, and Paul Worthman, *The GAMBIT Story*, NRO GAMBIT Collection (Chantilly, VA: National Reconnaissance Office, Aug. 1988), 60–61, www.nro.gov/foia/declass/GAMHEX/GAMBIT%20and%20HEXAGON%20Histories/6.PDF.

444 Ibid., 58.

445 William King, "Analysis of Gambit (110) Project," memorandum, Air Force Office of Special Projects, NRO GAMBIT Collection, p. 3, www.nro.gov/foia/declass/GAMHEX/GAMBIT/1.PDF.

446 30th Space Wing, "Vandenberg AFB Launch Summary: 1958–2017."

447 "Titan 3D Award," *Aviation Week and Space Technology*, 4 Dec. 1967, 105.

448 Robert F. Piper, *History of Titan III: 1961–1963*, Air Force Systems Command Publications Series 64-22-1 (Los Angeles AFB, CA: Space Systems Division).

449 Ibid.

450 Robert Perry, *History of Satellite Reconnaissance*, vol. IIIB, *HEXAGON* (Chantilly, VA: National Reconnaissance Office, Nov. 1973), 49, www.nro.gov/foia/declass/GAMHEX/GAMBIT%20and%20HEXAGON%20Histories/5.PDF.

451 Gerald K. Haines, *Critical to US Security: The Development of the GAMBIT and HEXAGON Satellite Reconnaissance Systems* (Chantilly, VA: National Reconnaissance Office, 1997), 87, www.nro.gov/foia/declass/GAMHEX/GAMBIT%20and%20HEXAGON%20Histories/2.PDF.

452 30th Space Wing, "Vandenberg AFB Launch Summary: 1958–2017."

453 Gerald K. Haines, *Critical to US Security: The Development of the GAMBIT and HEXAGON Satellite Reconnaissance Systems*, 88, www.nro.gov/foia/declass/GAMHEX/GAMBIT%20and%20HEXAGON%20Histories/2.PDF.

454 30th Space Wing, "Vandenberg AFB Launch Summary: 1958–2017."

455 National Reconnaissance Office, "NRO Brochure," n.d., p. 11, www.nro.gov/about/nro/NRObrochure.pdf.

456 30th Space Wing, "Vandenberg AFB Launch Summary: 1958–2017."

457 National Reconnaissance Office, "NRO Brochure," 11, www.nro.gov/about/nro/NRObrochure.pdf.

458 "Titan 3D Award," *Aviation Week and Space Technology*, 4 Dec. 1967, 105.

459 *USAF Mishap Report Index Tab: Part One—Facts* (Vandenberg AFB, CA, 1986), www.thespacereview.com/archive/1268.pdf.

460 National Security Decision Directive 8. "Space Transportation System," http://marshall.wpengine.com/wp-content/uploads/2013/09/NSDD-8-Space-Transportation-System-13-Nov-1981.pdf.

461 Gerald Haines, "Dr. Hans Mark Interviewed by Gerald Haines" (Chantilly, VA; Center for the Study of National Reconnaissance, 12 Mar. 12, 1997), p. 16, www.nro.gov/foia/docs/Hans%20Mark.PDF.

462 National Reconnaissance Office, "National Reconnaissance Program's Planned Use of the Space Shuttle," memorandum, 11 Mar. 1981, p. 2, www.nro.gov/foia/docs/F13-0119_NRP_Use_of_Space_Shuttle.pdf.

463 Dwayne A. Day, "Death of a Monster," *Space Review*, 15 Dec. 2008, www.thespacereview.com/article/1268/1.

464 United Press International, "Rocket's Explosion Deals U.S. a Blow," *Mohave Daily Miner* (Kingman, AZ), 20 Apr. 1986.

465 Department of the Air Force, *Environmental Assessment: Titan IV / Solid Rocket Motor Upgrade Program* (Los Angeles AFS, CA: Headquarters, Space Systems Division, Feb. 1990), F-1, www.nro.gov/foia/declass/Archive/15-09.PDF.

466 30th Space Wing, "Vandenberg AFB Launch Summary: 1958–2017."

467 Department of the Air Force, *Environmental Assessment: Titan IV / Solid Rocket Motor Upgrade Program*, F-2, www.nro.gov/foia/declass/Archive/15-09.PDF.

468 Mark C. Cleary, "The Cape: Military Space Operations, 1971–1992," 45th Space Wing History Office, Jan. 1994, p. 27, http://afspacemuseum.org/library/histories/TheCape.pdf.

469 National Reconnaissance Office, "NRO Satellite Successfully Launched," 20 Dec. 1996, www.nro.gov/news/press/1996/1996-09.pdf.

470 30th Space Wing, "Vandenberg AFB Launch Summary: 1958–2017."

471 "U.S. Rocket Motors," *Aviation Week and Space Technology*, 13 Mar. 1972, 138–39.

472 George Alford, *Fabrication of Twenty-Two Sounding Rocket Vehicle Systems*, Thiokol Chemical Corporation, Sep. 1972, p. 11, www.dtic.mil/dtic/tr/fulltext/u2/753089.pdf.

473 Mark Wade, "Ute Tomahawk," Astronautix, www.astronautix.com/u/utetomahawk.html.

474 30th Space Wing, "Vandenberg AFB Launch Summary: 1958–2017."

CHAPTER 3:

1 The remaining years (2014–2016) were not available before the publication cutoff of 31 Dec. 2016.

GLOSSARY:

1 30th Space Wing, "Vandenberg AFB Launch Summary: 1958–2017."

About the Author

JOSEPH T. PAGE II considers White Sands Missile Range, New Mexico—location of the first atomic bomb test—his home. He is no stranger to rockets and missiles flying (and exploding) overhead. Page was a member of the United States Air Force, being assigned to various space and missile assignments. Granted a unique opportunity to live at Vandenberg Air Force Base in California's Central Coast, Page joined forces with the Vandenberg Space and Missile Technology Center to help record the history of the base. He lives in Albuquerque, New Mexico.